INTER-WORLD MESSAGES

Timeless Teachings from the Seventh Plane

Winifred Willard

INTER-WORLD MESSAGES
Timeless Teachings from the Seventh Plane
by Winifred Willard

This edition is comprised of three books:
From the Seventh Plane (1946), Ariel Press, Chicago, IL
Seeing the Invisible (1950), J. F. Rowney Press, Santa Barbara, CA
Peace That Is Power (1957), J. F. Rowney Press, Santa Barbara, CA
Compilation copyright © Square Circles Publishing

Cover and interior: Syrp & Co.
Cover image globe: 123RF © OlegDudko

SQUARE CIRCLES PUBLISHING
www.SquareCirclesPublishing.com
www.LifeOnOtherWorlds.com

eISBN: 978-1-7344621-0-4
Print ISBN: 978-1-7344621-1-1

Contents

Foreword by Ethel Hueston ix

FROM THE SEVENTH PLANE 1
   PROLOGUE TO PART ONE 3
   BACKGROUNDS 5
      A Door Opens 6
      The Theme Changes 11
      I Have Another Personal Word 17
      He Speaks of the Future 18
   PROLOGUE TO PART TWO 19
   FIRST MESSAGES 21
      Patience Illuminated 27
      Life on the Counsellor's Planes 28
      Youth and War and God 31
      Glories of the Spirit World 34
      No Death! 36
      Speaking of Love 41
      Another Facet of the Jewel 49
      One Exuberant Leap 51
      The Blind Will See Anew 57
      Of Giving in Marriage 59
      Healing the Body 62
      The Free Will Gift 65
      The Practice of Prayer 68
      Utter Silence of Communion 69
      Heaven is so Practical a Place 72
      An Entrance Credential 73
      The Fine, White Line 75
      Of Course We Remember 77
      Service to Service Men 82
      Inter-World Communication 84
      Carriers of God-Consciousness 88
      Facts of Service 90
      Where Nothing is Lost 92
      His Personal Promotion 94
      Escort of Guardian Angels 98

Progression of the Spirit Planes.. 102
When the House is Vacated 106
Flame-Like Faith 109
Both Sides of the Veil.. 112
Where Young and Old Mature 116
Continuing Chance... 118
PROLOGUE TO PART THREE... 121
FURTHER MESSAGES 123
Crux of the World Muddle 123
When the Transition Comes.. 131
When the Door of the Spirit is Closed 142
The Essence of Timelessness... 146
Methods of Communicating 148
The Features of our Countenances 150
"As We Forgive".. 153
The Paradox in Sacrifice.. 157
There is Glory in the Transition 160
A Sweeping Pictures 163
Frustration or Fulfillment 165
Love's Major Message.. 169
Missions to Earth 173
The White Line... 179
Experiencing These Messages... 181
Steady Growing 183
Deep Roots.. 186
The Garment of Flesh 188
Both Sides of Pride... 192
The Direction of Your Eyes 196
Our Father... 198
Comforts of Companionship.. 201
When the Physical Presence Passes 205
The Power of Praise... 212
Gleaming Gold 215
Great Destroyer 219
The Way for Nations and Men... 224
This Sunny Side of Life 229
When Brush Fires Blaze 232
Blest With Humility... 235
Adjusting to the New Life 239

SEEKING THE INVISIBLE 245
FOREWORD 247
THE MESSAGES 251
- The Voice 251
- How It Is on the Sunny Side 253
- Unspeakable Peace 255
- Our World and Your World 257
- Compensation 260
- Experiencing God 261
- The Open Door 263
- Balanced Rations 265
- Guerdon 267
- Electrical Impulse 269
- Tests and Standards 271
- Deep Places 273
- Antennae of the Spirit 275
- For Them Beyond the Veil 277
- Light 279
- Booked for Passage 280
- Things that Abide 281
- Steady Reins 283
- Growing Pains 284
- The Other Side 286
- Liberation from the Flesh 287
- Seeing Him 289
- Aflame with Power 290
- Short Word 292
- Solidarity of Power 292
- The Holy Seventh 294
- Supreme Fact 297
- Dynamics of Praise 298
- "Be Ye Therefore Perfect" 300
- Potent Prescription 301
- Two Worlds 303
- Sanctuary of the Soul 305
- The Power House 306
- Rank and Poisonous Weeds 308
- Spiritual Therapeutics 309
- For Your Remembrance 312
- Nothing Short 313
- Divine Gift 315

Blow Ups	317
Never a God of Loss	318
The Power Line	319
Without Beginning or End	321
Sufficiency	323
"According To"	324
Lines of Communication	326
Seed Thoughts	328
The Law of Growth	330
Which Way the Atom?	332
Readiness	333
Deep Rootage	335
Understanding	336
Errors of Devotion	338
Sure Source	339
"Why?" Has an Answer	341

PEACE THAT IS POWER ... 343

FOREWORD	345
THE MESSAGES	349
These Things We Teach	349
Tremendous Tests	352
How Light We Are	353
God Manifest	354
In Days Ahead	355
No Light	356
Free!	357
On Top of the Load	358
Crests and Troughs	359
Your Patterns for Living	360
It Is Not Escape	361
Nothing Just Happens	362
Your Protection	363
Sufficiency	364
Won't You Try It?	365
Powers of Praise	366
Glimpses of Glory	367
The Master's Way	369

No Resentments	370
Some One Prays	371
There Is No Death	373
The Rule of Life	374
Abounding Life	375
Race Tracks and Furrows	376
Subtle Business	377
Life Here and There	378
Where It Finds You	379
True Love	380
Cosmic Unit	382
When Days Are Dark and Difficult	383
Great Glory	384
The Size of Your Cup	385
The Answer Depends on Your Choosing	386
Taking Time	387
When the Bell Rings	388
The Joy of This Purpose	389
Meeting a Glorious Condition	391
Earth's Greatest Gift	392
When Earth's Way Is Hard	393
Magic of Forgiveness	394
The Way of the Flower	396
The Compassion of Christ	396
The Kettle Boils Over	398
God-Power	399
Harvest	400
Pin-Pricks	401
Light	402
School	403
The Workable Way	404
Trying to Look Beyond Today	405
His Protecting Presence	406
Why Pray?	407
Your Thought	408
Two Halves	409
Without Haste or Hurry	410
Tailspins	411
Fog	412
Smug	413
Reincarnation	415

Readying	416
Rough Going	417
Released Power	418
The Journey Across	419
Further Glimpses	421
The New Age	422
Unexpecteds	423
A Spiritual Synthetic	425
God's Truth	426
The Splendor of Service	427
Highest and Most Holy	428
The Score Board	429
Clearer Concepts	430
God!	432
A Grace Divine	433
Soul	434
Concerning Results	436
God's Way of Working	437
The Cup of Life	438
The Lord Christ Draws Near	439

FOREWORD
by Ethel Hueston

*F*ROM THE SEVENTH PLANE is fascinating reading. Emphasizing the earth and spirit worlds and their interdependence one upon the other, it is a book of practical and inspiring lessons.

No mystical trappings are involved. There is no suggestion of supernatural phenomena. They are frank, straightforward lessons from one who has always been a student and a teacher.

I am a writer. Most of my thirty-odd books are novels in the lighter vein. I am a grandmother. Nothing of the mystical or supernatural is in my background or personality.

The Counsellor of these pages was the President of my college. Winifred Willard is my dear friend. I know intimately all those mentioned in this book except the "receiving station" of the earlier messages.

I read the original manuscript as Doctor Willard recorded it on the typewriter word for word as it came to her fingertips. I read it again in finished form, then in galleys. There were deletions for brevity. Personal messages to the close group of friends were deleted as not pertinent to the general theme. But no blue-penciling was done on it.

A surprising effect of our first reading of these messages aloud together, was that unconsciously we discontinued using the past tense in speaking of the Counsellor. Since there is no death, there can be no past tense in life, in friendship, or in love.

I was surprised that the Counsellor was able to make earth contact so soon after is transition and delighted that he retains the familiar and loved characteristics of his life here—his naive surprise at the suddenness and ease of his passing which he had dreaded; his frequent reference to "classes," "lessons," "teachers," showing the same ardour there as here for education; his slightest word of censure or reproof followed as always with quick, warm words of praise. Service was the keynote of his earth life. So it is not surprising that the work assigned him there is in continuing service.

Even those skeptical of the form of these communications must be impressed by the dignity, the naturalness, the sanity of the lessons. The virtues which he recommends for earth dwellers in preparation for "higher classes" there, are sometimes surprising but always reasonable and inspiring.

His frequent reiteration that "There is no death," entirely banishes the dreaded sting of it and denies the grave all trace of victory. Instead the final earth adventure is portrayed as a pleasant journey into a pleasant land, not far away, where there are exciting new lessons to be learned and thrilling new jobs to be undertaken, without hardships and rich in joy.

As an antidote to the timid fear of transiton and to the emotional pangs of parting, I heartily prescribe this book.

ETHEL HUESTON[1]

---

[1] Ethel Hueston (1887-1971) was a popular author who published over 50 novels between 1915 and the 1950s. The daughter of a Methodist minister, she was a graduate of Iowa Wesleyan College. She was listed in the 1950-51 edition of *Who's Who* in America. This Foreword is taken from the inside dust jacket of the original hardcover book.

FROM THE SEVENTH PLANE

To him
Who for many years was my senior associate and my partner;
Who sought to make life significant in terms of eternal values;
Who loved life passionately and clung to it eagerly;
Who faced the future without fear and met it with superb faith;
Who welcomed truth in every realm and trusted Him who
is all truth.

PROLOGUE TO PART ONE

THE COUNSELLOR and I were associated for many years. Our responsibilities interlocked until it was difficult to say where the line of demarcation was.

Because of limited vision, he had need of some one as eyes for him. I was the one available. Through the years, he trusted me with many responsibilities. Thus it seems natural for him to trust these messages to me.

Soon after his passing, they began to come from the Inner Planes in ways which I shall explain as clearly as I can. They came so simply from the other side of life, without trappings of any sort and without apparent atmosphere of mystery. Though, of course, it is one vast mystery!

A little Scotch woman was the "receiving station" for the messages in Part One. These came within six months, usually mornings.

Most of the time she and I were alone. She sat, fully conscious, beside my east window. Twice a third person was present. Once there were four of us. But the presence of others depleted her strength to such extent that it was necessity to limit these hours to her and me.

I sat close at her hand, but not touching her. The first day I asked if it would disturb her if I put on paper what came through the ether waves. "I think you should," she replied quietly. And so I wrote word for word, record which I have kept with meticulous care.

As The Counsellor's words became audible to her inner ears, she repeated them. At times the reception was excellent and her delivery rapid. Then it was leisurely. When vibrations were especially strong and the theme masterly, her voice was fairly masculine, cords of her neck standing out and her delivery propulsive, as his always was on the platform when he was on the earth plane.

When incoming messages blurred as with static and vibrations became confused, we sat in quiet relaxation until the contact strengthened and the words came clearly again.

If, as sometimes happened, a word or sentence was difficult to understand, The Counsellor repeated patiently until there was no doubt of our having it as he said it. He never left us in doubt of his exact meaning.

The occult had never been acceptable to The Counsellor's beliefs. My rearing had been conventionally orthodox. The messages herein seem, therefore, the more amazing in their revelations of his spiritual progress on the Inner Planes.

In the following chapters, I shall report the strange way of my meeting the "receiving station" and give the messages word for word, as they came through the ethers, from him whom I knew well on the earth plane.

I attempt no explanation of techniques; nor of the strange power which was in active operation. Of the authenticity and veracity of the messages there is no doubt in the minds of those who were close to these experiences.

WINIFRED WILLARD
Washington, D.C.
July, 1943

BACKGROUNDS

THE COUNSELLOR is the dominant figure of this book. Proud of being a Buckeye, he was loyal to his last day on earth, to his native Noble County. He headed high. Mathematics and science were his fortes, mental arithmetic, his hobby.

I have heard him tell many a board of trustees that their figures were wrong. Always they admitted it—finally! His mind was clock-like in its exactness. The distance was "forty six and nine tenths miles;" the hour, "nineteen and a quarter minutes past seven"! I annoyed him with my careless saying that it was about six weeks since this or that happened. Always he came back at me with the exact time, to the fraction of a day.

He chose law as his profession. Later, he turned from it to the church as a career and a conviction. His spiritual vision was unerring, despite long years when his physical eyes were blinded. During those years, he did the most brilliant work of his life.

The 1933 bank moratorium was financial tragedy to him. Squaring his shoulders, lips tight and white, voice hoarse with strain, he said across the desk to me, "We are many thousands of dollars worse off than nothing this morning!" He paused a tense moment. Then, "But we must find the way through. And we shall." Through the darkness of financial disaster, while he was in Washington, he went often to stand before the great bronze of John Paul Jones. Reverently raising his hat, winter or summer, to the Father of the American Navy, he always reminded himself and me that we "haven't begun to fight yet!"

He had eleven academic degrees and appeared at length for many years in Who's Who in America. The keys of Phi Beta Kappa and Pi Gamma Mu were scholarly satisfactions to him.

While he was of earth, he did not believe in the possibility of communication between the two worlds. For he says in this book how surprised he was to learn that one could speak from that side of life to this.

Often he said there were possibilities of magnitude for the human mind to explore in regions called occult and he hoped to see the day when search for this knowledge would be accepted in the dignity of scientific service.

His diction was unique. When he used long words, it was because they expressed his meaning better than short words. The language in these messages and the literary style are completely his. They have not been edited.

A relative whom he dearly loved, brilliant lawyer and president of a great university, heard some of these messages read. Repeatedly he interrupted to exclaim, "I can just hear Uncle John say that! Nobody else would say it that way."

The lilt of a phrase gave him the keen pleasure a musician finds in rich chords. The day air mail was first flown commercially, the significance of it impressed him mystically. He handed me a letter and said, "We'll send this sky-ward!"

Four of us went with him one day to the Washington Air Port. He was to fly the continent, Atlantic to Pacific. Like a gallant soldier, he strode ahead to his plane. His head was high. It was his first flight. The light in his eyes revealed new wings to his spirit unfolding. He was headed into great adventure. After that, when he must go, he wanted to fly. Happily he has his wings!

He often surprised us by the vehemence with which he would say, "I hate death!" So it is with peculiar satisfaction that this record demonstrates through his own messages that there is no death!

We call him The Counsellor. Of his many titles, this was the one he loved best.

A DOOR OPENS

On a mid-April afternoon in 1942, my telephone rang. A friend spoke, woman of international reputation—Elizabeth. She told me of a traveler she had met that day in Washington. This traveler had come to Washington and faced finding rooms in this war-time Capital. Inwardly guided, she stopped in the suburbs to ask directions; following them, she drove across the city to the National Woman's Party Club House, not far from the Supreme Court building.

Walking through its corridors, she was introduced to Elizabeth. As far as they knew, they had nothing in common. But they were drawn together by an invisible force which they did not seek to deny. Chatting in the club library, she told Elizabeth that she had always had the gift of communication with Spirit Realms, as a "receiving station." As they stood talking, the traveler said to Elizabeth, "You have recently lost a dear friend. He is here now!" Elizabeth confirmed the friendship and spoke aloud the name of The Counsellor.

The Scotch lady said to Elizabeth, "He wants you to know how much he enjoyed the long talks he had with you and how he admired your quality of patience." Because of my long association with him, Elizabeth asked whether there was a message for me. Instantly, the "receiving station" who had no previous knowledge of us, answered to the point of exact experience: "He says to tell her that he was distressed at leaving things so incomplete; he begs her only to have faith, more faith than ever, and to know that all is working out for her good." One more word came through for me: "I greatly admired her quality of loyalty."

A week later, Elizabeth called me again. In another chat the little Scotch lady told her, "Your friend has come again and wishes to identify himself by saying that he was very fond of cheese!" We laughed. His appetite for cheese was insatiable, mostly the plain, mouse-trap variety. He had cheese every morning for breakfast, always topped off his dinner with it and frequently had a big snack of Longhorn or other kind at midnight, if he couldn't sleep.

This cheese evidential thrilled us. It made us so certain that he retains his unique characteristics and his active remembrance of life on the earth plane.

Elizabeth suggested that the two of them come to my apartment for a spot of luncheon, say Tuesday, to see what might develop. "Of course we may get nothing," she cautioned.

Tuesday came. My guests arrived. I was not sure how to act for never before had I any contact with a person of occult powers.

This whole matter of which I was a bit afraid, was making its way with me slowly. I had been prejudiced by my ignorance. But I did have an open mind!

Though we were hoping to contact psychic realms that day, we were yet in the physical.

So I went to the kitchen for finishing touches to the luncheon.

"Would you come here a moment?" she called.

Fork in hand, I came into my living room. The Scotch lady whom we call Tim said at once, "The Counsellor is telling me that not many men wore capes. But he did. It was an Inverness with a large velvet collar, fastened at the neck with a very large hook and eye and when the weather was cold, he wrapped his hands in the cape to keep them warm." Elizabeth and I looked at each other incredulously. We had seen him wear it many times, exactly as he described it to Tim. He loved wearing it and always had a good laugh when people said, "Good morning, Father!" He was so striking a figure in this cape that people turned to look after him as he passed.

He asked Tim to tell me to keep it as long as I live.

"For," said he, "it helps to build a bridge through the ethers."

That afternoon wonderful evidentials came. The Counsellor told Tim, "I was met by the surgeon whom I loved as my own son." Years before, he had taken a nephew into his home, to give him a liberal education. Medical college followed and the nephew became a distinguished surgeon of Minneapolis. Several years ahead of The Counsellor, he preceded him to the world beyond our sight. Who shall doubt but that he met and greeted his Uncle John?

Later that afternoon, along the ether waves, this came, "Life over here is so much more marvelous than anything I had ever imagined." Something prompted me to say that I wished to know about the process of cremation as it applied to him, that being his insistent desire for many years. Instantly this word came, "The disposition of the garment of flesh is inconsequential. The growth of the soul is all that matters."

"I am so much more alive than when I was on the earth plane," he told us. I asked Tim whether she supposed he could see again. Like a flash came, "I see as clearly as a youth of twenty!"

Having tried for years to be eyes to him, that word thrilled me. How wonderful that he could see again! He said too, that he was much surprised when he found he had made the Great Transition.

In early May

Personal issues were pressing when Tim came to listen with me for such messages as might come from the Inner Planes. With no lapse of time, The Counsellor began to explain to her about one who was making demands on me. Through the years, there were two words he always used when he wished me to stop thinking along negative lines; always the same two words. Through Tim he spoke those two words to me that morning—"Dismiss it!"

If I had needed further convincing that it was he from whom these messages were coming, his "Dismiss it!" would have effaced my doubt. "I will help to alleviate the spirit of the one who is disturbing you." Then again the dynamic "Dismiss it!"

"From the other side of life, I will sweep away obstacles that are oppressing you. I am better able to work for your benefit than when I was held back by physical limitations. I am in power to touch the Divine for your help."

He revealed experiences, sensations and emotions which he had not understood while he was on the earth plane and which closely preceded his passing that mid-February night of 1942. "I had a sense of spiritual sight," he said. "I knew you would not have accepted it. So I did not tell you. For a month before I passed, there was a gradual withdrawal of my soul from earth matters. I was not sure what it meant. The moment my soul left the body, the freedom was marvelous."

Tim's voice was strong as she expressed the vibrancy of his words repeated several times, "There is no death!"

June 5

Tim and I were attuned for whatever would come from The Counsellor. Promptly came his words, "I am proud at having accomplished connection between this side of life and my friend on the earth plane. Communication between us is no more marvelous to you than the knowledge was to me, though I followed the religious path while I was on the earth plane.

"The many years we worked together cemented a bond that not death itself could break! A new door of self expression is open to you; a new avenue of service! The wonderful truths of religion are no barrier to my direct communication with you the immediate future.

"I wish to express my deep gratitude for your constant and faithful care over that protracted period. I am again possessed of all the faculties that are necessary for me to continue my work through you, my friend.

"I will communicate with you quite frequently in the near future. The inspiration that will permeate your brain will be a direct contact with my own soul powers which the Divine conferred upon me.

"The work ordained for me while I was still on the earth plane, I shall continue from this higher Plane of Consciousness. With renewed vigor I take up this spiritual work at my Master's command.

"Fear not! All will be made plain to you. Your future welfare is our concern from this side of life. You have a definite mission to perform. I ask of you who always were so ready to help in every way regarding my welfare while I was still residing on the earth plane, to go forward with confidence, knowing that God works in many mysterious ways."

Later in early June

Tim was with me. None too comfortably she said, "I see you as in an iron ring. It encompasses you and your affairs completely. Apparently you cannot move in any direction at present."

Immediately she heard The Counsellor say, "But it will be broken—that iron ring!" A pause, then he spoke again, "These matters will be taken care of. You are to relax and leave them to the Higher Powers. I myself am putting things in motion that will unwind your difficulties."

Sensing my special need for guidance, he added, "We do not wish you to become tense. It is a barrier to help from the Inner Planes. Remember that the Heavenly Powers are much stronger than earth powers!"

A late bedtime in June

I was alone. Suddenly I was conscious of invisible activity. The heavy, humid air stirred. There was no breeze. The curtains hung limp. The activity continued.

Then what seemed like a feather passed across my head, over my cheek, down my left arm and hand to the finger tips.

The Counsellor's voice came clearly to my inner ears, the first time he had spoken directly to me, save for speaking my name.

His manner was commanding. He spoke with sternness and said, "Why don't you take what I give you?"

The invisible activity continued. Then, "—has stopped persecuting you." The familiar voice spoke again. But the tension was gone. His message had reached me. He seemed relieved as he said in a visity tone, "School is out for tonight. And I must go!"

The invisible stirring ceased. Again I was alone.

The last day of June

The Counsellor knew it might be easy for doubt to spring up in our minds about the source of these messages, especially with me who was a novice in these things. So he gave frequent evidentials of homely, personal significance.

Today he remarked through Tim that his feet caused him much trouble through most of his earth life. "This is just to bolster your faith," he added. One day doing a broad jump at the country school, he injured both feet. From then on, they were distress and discomfort to him. No evidential could have been more convincing. "One grows spiritually through suffering," he said that day. "It is the opening road to spiritual consciousness."

A few days prior, a letter had reached me from a dear mutual friend. It brought a gracious offer of help. "The offer in her letter," said The Counsellor, "was my opened door. Her consciousness was awakened to help you. You must accept it, for it is her way of helping her own soul's progress. You will help her if you accept. If you turn it down, you put a stumbling block in her spiritual path." A moment later he added, "When she leaves the physical plane, she will be on a higher spiritual level for having done this."

THE THEME CHANGES

The Counsellor launched at once into a discussion of world problems: "Mankind has come to the cross roads. The choice between the spiritual and the material is obvious.

"People turn often to their churches, asking for bread and are given a stone!

"Because of their sufferings, they question whether there is a God and whether the God they have been taught to pray to, is still within reach. The great destruction on the earth plane ushers in a new religion. Men demand more truth of the Bible. They have been spiritually blind. I do not say this in condemnation. For spiritual vision in the superior material world is apt to become definitely beclouded.

"My mission is to prove that God's miracles can be performed in this day and age. The day has arrived when the Veil called death, will be rent asunder.

"My own appointed mission is to contact you, my friend, in this manner, so that these established truths may be given out in printed form. This will be to you the most soul-satisfying of any endeavor in a literary manner which you have ever attained.

"We go forth with renewed vigor. We work still in harness together, but our work is now on a more glorious basis. The contact between the spiritual and the physical will be strengthened as time goes on. My earnest desire is to be a forerunner through this contact, with the new Universal Church!

"Encompassed with minds and knowledge from those who have passed the Veil many years ago, I stand comforted and enthusiastic in connection with the mission that lies ahead of me. The faithful pen that worded so many of my thoughts while I was on the earth plane, will work even more rapidly in the future with this wonderful message to mankind—There is no death!

"From henceforth men will communicate with their beloveds who have passed over the border into richer, fuller life. The word that emphasizes this new life is service to others who are groping vainly in the physical body with material burdens too heavy to bear.

"This wonderful truth will come to them with the brilliance of the rising sun. Their dark mantles of depression, fear of want, poverty, suffering and disease, will fall away before the glorious radiance of the true way of soul progression, when once they realize that all which is required is absolute faith, as a child would have in its mother.

"If that faith they once portray in their earthly problems, the Divine Intelligence working through and from these Higher Spheres, will take care of every situation with which they are confronted.

"The Divine asks so little. Yet men in their extremities turn cold shoulders to the solutions of life's major and minor problems."

Changing from world needs to my small perplexities, The Counsellor's voice came, "Your practical, material way will be taken care of in an unusual manner. Our ways are often taken care of in unusual fashion. The same sort of help—spiritual instruments in material bodies—will be sent for your help. Please do not let it trouble you. Your path of life is all planned out. All you have to do is to trust in the Lord, call on your spiritual friend and you shall be comforted.

"Many new friends will seek you out. Do not bother about material things. You will be carried through.

"I am so pleased to have rent the Veil once more. Lay aside the problem. We will take care of the issue. All I ask is faith."

He turned again to the theme which he had been discussing, "A certain sadness comes over my spirit at the thought that so little of the continuity of life is taught in the orthodox religion.

"In the near future, worshippers in every religion will be blest with knowledge of the continuity of life. Then the spiritual fervor of the soul of mankind will transcend the limitations of the physical world.

"Where there is a link binding souls together on the earth plane, that link although it be apparently broken when one enters the door of a newer and fuller life, is only forged the stronger.

"I have better opportunity of helping you now that my spirit is no longer encompassed in a frail physical structure. Remember that I shall be near you in any doubtful or difficult moment. God bless you! I have to leave for the present. Conditions do not permit of further conversation at this period."

Mid-July

Almost as soon as Tim came this Sunday morning, The Counsellor gave us another evidential saying that "he always wore his watch chain across the front of his vest." Then he launched into the theme of the morning.

"Now as to time! On this side of life, time passes quicker. It is as though everything goes forward at a more rapid rate. We manifest on a quicker rate of vibration and we have to step down—or so it seems—to reach the level and rate of vibration on the physical sphere.

"This is why we think of time in terms of relativity. Your brilliant scientists generally understand the contact with this fifth dimensional plane but cannot as yet accept the theory of the resurrection taking place the moment the mortal sheds the physical body. My instructors from the Seventh Plane have taught me many wonders. I realize now why my physical eyes were withdrawn in their mortal sight while I was resident on the earth plane. It was that my spiritual sight might become more clearly defined very shortly after the Transition called death.

"It was well. All is well that is ordained from this side of life, because the pattern of man's life is eternal. Destiny is a matter of the soul. As we unfold in character and divinity, time and all which it brings is but relative.

"The glorious future stands out. It is the goal that counts; not the material goal so many seek while in the physical vehicle. Their eyes are blinded to the truths of reality. It is they who are dead. For their eyes see not. The material passes away. It is swift. It is here today. It is gone tomorrow. The true riches are those which do not rust nor corrupt.

"The materialist struck down in the prime of his earthly life is entirely lost when he reaches these Shores of Eternal Life. His gold crumbles to dust before his eyes. It is what he himself has brought over, that counts; not what he has attained with self-satisfaction in his spiritual blindness.

"In making the Transition from the physical to the spiritual, he is like a child that is lost, groping blindly in the darkness with which he has encompassed himself. Such people have shut the door to their own spiritual development.

"They think occasionally of the life beyond. If they live to advanced age, such thoughts cross their minds more frequently. Then they decide to play the role of philanthropist, endeavoring to use gold or its equivalent to advance their souls' growth. This is entirely wrong. It is what a man has built within himself that makes him a candidate for these Higher Spheres.

"A man's worldly wealth is but a loan to him, put into his mortal hands, to see to what use it will be put, either to retard or to help his true self. It is a great test for any man. For the greater the worldly success, the more is expected of that man. If he binds himself with selfishness, arrogance and disregard of the less fortunate, he breaks the trust."

The Counsellor began to speak of the help that is given to those newly come to the Ether Planes.

"If you could only realize what it means to the countless numbers who arrive on these Shores, some not even knowing they have left their earthly garments! A reassuring sentence is like a rope thrown to a man when he is drowning. It is a marvelous life saver!

"They immediately question, 'Where are we?' 'Whence came all these strange faces?' 'Where can we find faces dear to us in former years?'

"I will try to give you a picture of what sometimes occurs. A man will have lost an arm; in some instances his sight. He will say, 'I have lost my right arm.' Our reply from instructors must be, 'Your right arm is there; nothing is lost.' You see one clothes himself by thoughts on these Inner Planes.

"We see the most radiant forms, wonderful manifestations of eternal life, eyes and features that portray the depths of the soul. One is known for what he really is when he enters the spiritual life!

"Many who fell in the last war eagerly greet the sons of their former friends. It is marvelous to see these greetings. The young aviator, shall I say, who crosses to this side of life in the twinkling of an eye, is wonderfully comforted to find his own father's best friend awaiting him.

"Would it seem strange if I tell you that plans for peace are being formulated in these Eternal Realms? Men's minds are trained from the higher side of life, to be ready when the conflict is ended. Their souls are prepared for this greatest of all missions to mankind—a just and lasting peace.

"These men may not be world leaders. Some of them are serving in obscure positions. But it is the spirit glowing through the physical form that counts. There must be a inundation built whereon the peoples of earth can live in security from fear and want. It may seem utopian to think that it can be put into concrete form. But we here are privileged to see what is going to take place.

"The slums of large cities will be eliminated, because through suffering, major minds still in the physical, will endeavor to correct many glaring discrepancies of the past. For how can men's souls grow when even the body is not sufficiently nourished? These victims of men's colossal selfishness are about to be released from their imprisonment.

"There will not be failures from children being placed in the wrong trade or profession. When man is allowed to use his inherent qualifications to the best advantage, we shall have human society contributing to better citizenship.

"You will be surprised to learn that many will be taught to contact the Inner Planes directly for first-hand information in connection with what earth people call 'wonderful inventions.' Those who are specifically magnetized will be the recipients of the plans for these inventions.

"We in our day, you, my friend, and I in particular, saw many wonderful inventions in operation which we had never before visualized. These marvelous contributions to the welfare of mankind are in the future to be advanced to no uncertain degree.

"In twenty of your earth years, transportation facilities will become outstanding. Methods of this particular time will be obsolete. No doubt it will seem strange to you when I say that I have seen a design fully formed, for a miniature set of wings. These can be firmly attached with a small mechanism to an individual's shoulders and man will propel himself through the air. He himself will be the air plane.

"I shall try to give you a description of this seemingly impossible contraption. One steps into a harness. Tiny wires connect with the battery. Power is released by pressing a button in the switch, on the chest. There is also a device for propelling oneself in the direction in which one wishes to travel.

"All this may seem strange. But fifty years ago, would it not have seemed strange had someone told me that I could hear beautiful music emanating, shall I say, from a box-like affair? The radio was a wonderful invention. But beside what the future holds, that marvelous gift to humanity will seem comparatively small.

"I have digressed from what I originally intended to speak about. The stress of the present period was uppermost in my mind. I am sure you must have wondered what happens to the soldier when he so hurriedly leaves the physical world. I beg of you to give comfort to any parent you may meet who has had such a loss. It is disturbing when they realize how their dear ones are grieving at the loss of the physical form. The voices they looked eagerly forward to hearing again, can still be recognized if they will accept the truths of eternal life!

"At first, emphasize, 'There is no death!' Their dear ones have only entered into a wider field and a more glorious existence. It gives me much pleasure to know that you will endeavor to clarify people's minds in connection with Crossing the Bar.

"You will come to feel that it is a particular mission which you desire to perform. In the elucidation of these facts, you will help your own soul's growth. You will feel as time goes on, that you become nearer the spiritual than the material side of life. This will give you comfort and assurance.

"Reach out and touch the Infinite! In so doing, life will take on a much deeper and wider concept. In sharing these blessed truths with others, you yourself will grow in God's wisdom and much will accrue from the different steps which spiritually you will take."

Later that afternoon

"You who still reside on the earth plane are stepping into a new era. The spiritual will prevail over the material in men's consciousness. This suffering that is taking place in so many sections of the globe is prelude to the new era. The selfishness that has prevailed in the consciousness of a major portion of humanity, will finally be eradicated.

"The tearing-down process extends over a large area. The innocent, as always, suffer with the guilty. My friend, do not doubt. There is a marvelous plan behind this seemingly senseless destruction. As one suffers, the soul grows. It reaches out when all earthly help fails, reaches into the Beyond, into the limitless expanse of the Divine.

"A new vision will be presented to the minds of Waders in different countries. They who have seen buildings, treasures of art, evidences of culture accumulated through the centuries, swept away in the twinkling of an eye, will realize the futility of earthly aspirations and accumulations.

"They are asking why at the present time, these terrible catastrophes are taking place. The souls of men are being quickened. They begin to see a true meaning of this conflict. Forces of light and darkness are at close grips with each other. The wonderful golden light of spirituality will prevail and men will be taught the lesson of God's will and plan.

"Does it not say in the Bible, 'Am I my brother's keeper?' This, along with the Golden Rule is the concrete foundation of men's religious attitude of the future.

"My heart is filled with love and compassion for those who have suffered. Those who have made the greatest contribution to alleviation of suffering, have envisioned the Torch of Freedom that glimmers at present, but that will break into a glorious flame

"This handful of whom I just spoke, are already aware of the continuity of life. They can immediately make the contact necessary for putting workable plans into operation for care of the destitute, the bereft, in these different countries.

"You remember the parable of the loaves and fishes, the food that was brought forth and multiplied. This miracle will again happen. The faith of the few is necessary for the well being of the whole. There will be avenues seemingly miraculous appear for nourishment, so these poor creatures may be temporarily sustained until they can be properly cared for.

"The ones who are spared have a mission to perform. It is all part of the great plan. Through the suffering of the physical, spiritual enlightenment takes place."

I HAVE ANOTHER PERSONAL WORD

On a day when my thoughts were far removed from matters of these messages, I became conscious of that strange, invisible activity which several times preceded my hearing The Counsellor's voice. Clearly there were "presences plain in the place." He spoke my name.

Then again. Then, "Get your pad." In a few seconds, "Don't get discouraged; all will be well." Aloud I said, "Don't let me mistake anything." To which came, "Do you doubt me?"

Again his voice spoke, "Times and seasons are not in your hands. They are for us to decide." Still speaking, he said, "God bless you—and He will." Eight or ten seconds later, he followed with, "I'm not through! Guard yourself against the defeat—" (I was not certain whether he said "of" or "or.") But I did not speak.

As clearly as could be, came, "I said 'of.' Guard yourself against the defeat of discouragement. All that comes is from the Inner Planes. Take it that way."

HE SPEAKS OF THE FUTURE

"Henceforth deeper, more significant truths will radiate from these revealing communications beyond ordinary human concepts. They will build ever. stronger the indestructible tie that only temporarily changed in outward appearance.

"Changes occur but these changes do not close the doors of communication. You will receive many impressions from me, knowing that it is I who have spoken to you, lifting up the flagging spirit when the physical is exhausted. The strong cord of communication will not be broken. It is only lowered for a while. This flowing of personal experience will continue. Adjustments will be made but you will find your inner consciousness more receptive to the spiritual transmission of messages helpful to your human problems. This is not the end. It is but the beginning. Remember that the path we tread is now illumined with celestial emanations ever precluding dense physical limitations.

"There are many who will question and be keenly analytical of the accuracy and veracity of these vibratory messages based upon the unseen.

"Those who accept unquestioningly the evidences of these messages from the other side of life, are they who have broken through the encasement of their material propensities and the crystallization of their former, rigid orthodox concepts.

"To others who will undoubtedly cast aside lightly these vibrant, living truths, I would say, 'Be tolerant in your attitude; mentally reserving judgment; recognizing as justifiable this elucidation of factors which connect different spheres of the human consciousness that never dies!"

PROLOGUE TO PART TWO

TIM LEFT Washington in mid-autumn of 1942. The etheric messages which for months had been coming through her, seemed therefore at a standstill. They were not ready for publication. There seemed nothing I could do to make them ready. So I waited!

Two years later, lunching with a friend at New York, she surprised me by relating her experiences of many years with extra-sensory matters. She talked. I listened. She spoke of a woman in Washington through whom many people are helped.

When I was again in Washington, I asked to see her, not giving my name nor any information concerning me. Nor did she seek to find out who I am nor what my interests are. She bought me from the ethers many significant things.

A fortnight later, on September 1, I was strangely restless and went again to see her, not knowing what prompted my going. Almost immediately she told me, "There is a manuscript which is incomplete. The one from whom it came wishes it completed directly through you."

I showed plainly that I did not see how that could be done. Her quick reply was that I had no right to say such things; that I must go home; sit down at my machine; put my hands on the keyboard and promise to take whatever came!

"Whatever," she stressed, "may not at first make connected sense. But you must write it. If only abcdefg come, write them. You will thus establish the contact that is destined for you."

I waved it off. The night was hot. I was tired. I did something else. On successive nights the same, with underlying sense of irritation at this which I did not want to undertake.

September 8 was humid and hot. When evening came, I sat by my window, reading. No one was in my apartment but me. Had not been for several weeks.

Suddenly, by a power I did not understand and could not explain, I was lifted from my chair, pushed vigorously across my living room floor and put down at the typewriter. How it happened, I do not know.

I ran some paper into the machine, put my hands on the keyboard and said aloud, "Well, here I am!" "And here am I," said he.

In less than a dozen seconds, it began to come, without one irrelevant word, just as you read it on these pages, as clear and distinct to my inner ears as spoken words could be.

When the first message was completed and the voice of The Counsellor had ceased, my apartment seemed alive with spiritual presences. I was deeply conscious of them for hours, in great degree of power.

As the messages continued to come, I wondered why the presences did not come again. Except twice, when they did. The Counsellor tells why. Each night for more than four months, save when I was prevented by earth responsibilities, the messages came. These which appear in this volume are part of the whole, selected with care, and verbatim.

It was difficult to learn to be a channel and to prevent one conscious mental process of my own from intruding. Often I became drowsy and many evenings when the Spirit Planes had tuned out, I could not recall much that had come. The drowsier I was, the more easily the words seemed to come!

Given to me from the Inner Planes, I send them forth in faith and loyalty.

WINIFRED WILLARD
Washington, D. C.
February 19, 1945

FIRST MESSAGES

FROM THIS place on, The Counsellor spoke directly through me as I sat at the typewriter, taking his messages verbatim and not knowing from word to word where they were leading.

September 8

Whatsoever your hands find to do, do with your will, with body, mind and spirit. For thus shall you accomplish that which is divinely ordained for you to do in this world.

It is not what you want, but what the Inner Planes decree for you. Thus do, my friend, and don't quibble. Don't fear. Just go ahead. The way will open, the means become apparent and all be well.

This is your work. It will open as you proceed. You are not to doubt; nor hesitate; nor be afraid. Infinite mind is greater than human. Death gives way to life. Here is your open door. I will speak to you whenever you lend me your hands and your mind through which I may work.

There is much to do. Earth people are needy. Your power us considerable. Mine is more on these Inner Planes of higher satisfaction. Just trust your hands to me. I will not lead you astray. Your might will increase as you become familiar with the channel of service. Give yourself up to it and know that I am guiding you aright.

There are many who do not know the way to go. They fear death. They fear life more. It is yours to shed the light of God's love through these writings which will come from me in the days ahead.

Pay no attention to whether others like them. You are not being guided according to human standards but in harmony with the ways of the spirit world. Again I say to you that this is the best thing that ever happened to you. Your horizons are being extended, your faith strengthened and the ways of your service amplified beyond anything that you have ever dreamed.

The material side is being taken care of. You have nothing to fear in that way. The spiritual is the thing for which many are hungry. I am in power through you to lead them to Waters and to the Bread of Life. Keep your hands free and your mind open. Do not try to anticipate my thoughts. They will flow more freely without help from the earth side. be receptive and patient and keep on knowing that good is destined to come out of all this. I know whereof I speak.

The other side of life is more radiant than you can dream at present. There is such glory here as the world does not imagine.

Your aloneness has been the preparation for your carrying this comfort to the many who think that death ends all. It is only the beginning of life transcendent. You must be obedient and faithful as you always were when I was with you in the flesh. I am with you in ways of greater power now than ever. I have been assigned to work with you to the end of preparing many who do not yet understand the ways of God with man. You do not. But you are learning. You have much to learn; much to overcome; much to acquire; much to give.

Through you I shall give my messages to people of earth who need them and can interpret them helpfully. Do not be discouraged if sometimes this comes slowly. It will come surely. For this I have been prepared since I came over here. The way for you has been hard. But it has been the way of your spiritual development. And isn't that worth all it can cost?

For this service you are not dependent upon any one of earth. You will feel my presence and know my power as you sit at your machine, receptive to the spirit world. As we work together again, all of this will come easier and you will have no sense of tense anxiety. You will know you are being guided and that all is well. Do not fear that you are being misled.

This is all for tonight. God bless you! And I bless you! This is a glorious highway we shall travel together. Good night!

September 9

Whatever comes is for your good. Take it that way. And be grateful. Have no fear lest you may not hear my message. I shall see that you do hear. From out these vast reaches of Eternity will come wisdom which man is yearning to know about those things which have been inscrutable mysteries.

Mankind is wielding enormous power for good in this dire world conflict, power that will transmit itself into righteousness when the day of din is over. You are a little anxious tonight lest I do not come to speak to you. Be not anxious nor afraid. This is ordained from the highest and nothing can stop it except your reluctance to offer me your hands and mind through which I may work.

You have wondered why it was to you so long a time in which I did not speak to you in any deliverance such as had come through in those earlier days. It was that you might ripen in the knowledge which you had acquired of my enduring personality and undiminished powers to transmit to earth something of the glory that is the spirit world. Nothing of earth can compare with it.

Our days here are very busy with the multiplied millions who are coming from battle to these peaceful shores of immortality. They come in bewilderment, seldom in pain, but always wondering what has happened to them. They find it difficult to conceive that they are dead. For they are so alive! They are so light! All the old heaviness is gone. Radiations of light and love entirely surround them, healing the wounds of war and beginning to build them up into permanent stature as children of the Kingdom. You are not to be afraid that I will not stay and finish a message when once I have begun it with you. Tenseness complicates the issue and I ask you to relax and be free and easy. I stand beside you as I give you these messages.

Oh, my friend, learn to depend wholly upon the Infinite for everything you need! There is nothing that His goodness and glory cannot accomplish for you, even to taking away your loneliness. With the passing of time you will sense my help more keenly than in the past. That is part of the order of growth. And you are growing.

Over here we all grow. Life is not static with us. Always there is more to learn and more to do in carrying out the Divine purpose among people of earth who are becoming more and more aware of the power of the spiritual. I am leading you to greater heights of interpretative power than you would have thought possible.

You belong more to us here than to your small circle on the earth plane. Turn more and more often to the spiritual side of life, my friend. It has the enduring quality that counts, that cannot pass away. Temporary values are gone with the speed of thought. But the things of God abide and meet every emergency which can come to the human heart.

Remember that you are not alone. Cohorts of beauty and spirit radiance hover about you often and their vibrations change the tenor of your thoughts to higher levels when the physical would tend to be depressed.

God's plans for His children are more marvelous than can be comprehended by mortal mind. Over here on these higher planes where we are not cumbered about with the weight of the physical, we see and know so much more than is given to earth people. It is of these things that I wish to speak through you. You will be the medium of great power to comfort and help those whose burdens are heavy. I shall empower you with words from on high and you will always know that the words you speak are with authority. Remember; I am guiding you into all truth. And all is well.

You are not to feel responsible for words which I shall speak. They will come through in ways which are right and when you read them, you will see how right they are. Don't think for a moment but that I have been under instruction here. We are taught on rigid schedules and our every power of concentration is given to the lessons which we are assigned. None of it is drudgery. It is all compassed about with love. Light shines on our spirits and learning our lessons is sheer joy. Always it is this way over here, where we go from one level of service to a higher, reflecting the glory that is God. The power of the Divine is round about us all the while.

Don't ever again let anybody with whom you have influence think of death as darkness and cold, as the end of all. Death is the opening door to such development of personality, such increase of understanding, such radiance of concept of God's plan for humankind, as before my Transition, I could not have comprehended. Take that from me with the confidence you always reposed in my every earth word.

Death is light and life and glory and beauty and service. It is life relieved of its weight of suffering an limitation; life raised to the nth degree of intelligence and always reaching out toward higher levels of Infinite glory. It is the order of the universe. I beg of you to do all in your power to keep people from fear of it.

It is not a dark river; nor a time of great fear. It is the coming Home to the Father's House, to those who are happy to welcome you, to activities that call forth one's best effort in all the new and increasing power that comes when one lays aside the garment of flesh for the immortal coverings.

Death? No! I used to say that I hated death. I spoke with the limitation of the human. It was great deliverance from the frail body of unusual limitations to the freedom that I cannot explain but which characterizes these realms. How gladly you will sense it all when you come over here! And you will not fear, for you will know more than many do, of the glory that awaits your coming.

I used to think that the trappings of death as we observed them in the physical, were significant. They mean less than nothing for all of life that counts is the spirit. Nothing can matter much which is purely material. But it does matter whether our spirits are centered in God and whether we are concerned in helping to bring about the fulfillment of His eternal purposes. This is a theme too vast to discuss now. Later, perhaps.

We are at the beginning of an unusual experience for which we both have been prepared and for which we shall be equal. You will see from day to day the enlarging scope of it. And you will thrill to your part in it. I am off now for the night. God bless and keep you and guide your feet in paths of pleasantness. This is no inconsiderable service which you will be rendering. I am so eager for the significance of it to grip you! But now, good night!

September 10

God bless you, my friend! I was waiting for you to be ready.

God is the one hope of this world in the present maze and in all the future when mighty changes will be taking place. Do not be misled into thinking that the minds of men alone can chart the course of life in the peace-time world.

Life is governed from these Spirit Planes and in harmony with the laws of the Divine. He who transgresses the law, must pay the penalty. Always it is so. Watch that you do not fail in understanding the significance of this which is fundamental in God's plan. Sometimes contact with the earth plane is confused, because your vibrations do not synchronize with ours. But always it does clear and my words will come through to you.

Many people wonder how it can be that I have been able to communicate with you. They think that such communication is impossible. I say to you that it is often done by those spirits that are in tune and that in the future it will more often be the channel through which God's will and purposes will be made known to mankind. Do not hesitate to let your faith in such communications be made known, for in so doing, you will strengthen others who are in doubt.

If I can come through in ways like this, you ask why others who may wish to have the same experience, do not succeed. The reason is manifold. They may not have the spiritual power or their desires may be grounded in selfish ambition instead of in unselfish desire to serve the Kingdom of God.

For you must know that in the invisible realms are spirits who do not seek the goodness of God nor reflect the white purity of His life. When they strive for earth contact, their motive is selfish and their goal is disconnected from human good.

Some who would like to speak to their dear ones on the earth plane have not yet acquired the knowledge or skill that makes possible these cosmic communications. Technically, it is a matter of electrical vibration and of regulating this in harmony with Infinite wisdom.

You would be surprised if you knew how many and what wonderful inter-world lines of communication are in operation these days. The line of demarcation between your world and mine is very faint. It grows fainter as time passes and you become more familiar with and less afraid of the mysteries which I shall reveal unto you.

Do not try to think ahead with me. Just listen and make very sure that whatever comes clearly is for your good and for the help of others.

Life over here is ordered after a definite pattern. Each one who comes brings just what he has built into his life during the earth years, be it little or much. The one so rich in things of earth may be pathetically destitute of qualities of goodness that characterize life on these Spirit Planes. He does not see why his wealth does not stand him in good stead. It is because his wealth was wholly material. And no man may carry the material over to these spiritual realms. Guard that well and look to it that material successes do not loom too large. They are no more to be depended upon than any will o' the wisp. Do not put your trust in them. As long as you remain in the physical, you must have that with which to meet the needs of the earth life. But do not set your heart upon any of that which is as transient as the on-sweeping wind.

You remember how often we used to talk of your dear ones. I have seen them all—your father, your mother, your sister. The little brother I have not yet met. It would comfort you to know how constantly they watch over you and with what joy they see your growth in things of the spirit. When you come to join us here, your welcome will be royal. Every obstacle that has been surmounted, every fear that has been dispelled, every antagonism conquered, gives you that much wider an entrance into these eternal realms. Do not doubt, my friend. You are building each day that which you will need when you join us here. Even the little things of daily life and the spirit in which you meet and vanquish them, tell in the total of your enduring achievements.

Nothing that is good, is little. Only that which can stand the test of the white light of God's truth, is good. Here the true record stands and shows us for just what we are. The poor of earth are often very rich in the values of Eternity.

PATIENCE ILLUMINATED

Patience is a quality not always easy to manifest. But it weaves into the fabric of the eternal pattern and is one standard by which over here, one's growth is determined. Yes, my friend, you will need patience in receiving and recording these messages. Just as in radio, there are many lines of radiation electrically, but I am in power to overcome and to carry these talks through you to those of earth who need and will use them.

Patience even with little things and little minds characterized our Lord during His life on earth. As you pass through the years, you will see increasingly how sublime a quality patience is.

It is not negative. It is positive, compounded of loyalty and love and willingness to serve in whatever ways and places the Divine decrees. Peace grows with patience and determines much of the texture of life and living.

When I was so recently with you on the earth plane, my quality of patience often did me no credit. Over here, I have learned what a mighty force it is and how far forward it sets one on the spiritual path.

Cultivate patience, Divine, Infinite patience, with petty details and insignificant issues, and you will acquire a Godlike quality of character which will stand you in good stead while you are in the physical and after you have made the Great Transition and joined us here.

I had not thought to speak of this tonight. But it enters into the composite of Truth which has as many facets as there are grains of sand on the shores of all the seas. Truth cannot be limited. It bursts all bounds when it is restricted, just as new wine in old bottles. Truth cannot be limited to any group or sect or creed. It is infinitely free to all who seek it with open heart.

Because so many men have sought to confine Truth to their puny wishes, it has been misinterpreted and misunderstood. But Truth is its own strength and stands forth in pristine beauty, however men have sought to warp its values.

Truth, evaluated after Divine and eternal standards, is mankind's stronghold. It will never lead him astray; never disappoint him; never fail him when he seeks it with his whole heart. As a measuring rod, Truth can be depended upon to solve many perplexing problems. Keep close company with Truth. And you will be laying up for yourself much treasure on these Eternal Planes.

And now a personal word! Do not be disturbed when occasionally my words come more slowly. It takes some of this patience of which I was just speaking for us to become accustomed to this manner of communicating. But fear not! All is working out and you shall see many wonders as you come closer to the heart of the spirit world.

God's love be over you; His peace flood your heart; the way of His working be increasingly clear to you! Through it all, know how grateful I am that I am privileged to take up anew these messages directly with you. Radiations are thus much stronger, much clearer, and by that much, more convincing. Good night and may God bless and keep you!

LIFE ON THE COUNSELLOR'S PLANES

September 11

I want to make more clear some things that have bewildered the minds of men. Here on these Ether Planes, time as you know it does not exist. There is no day nor night. We need no rest for we have left behind us on the earth plane all the gross weight of the body. And we have become ministering spirits.

This is something which mortal minds do not easily understand. Men have had such misconception of that which, is called death. Some think it is eternal sleep. Some think it is purgatory. We used to hear much about hell fire and brimstone, yes and the lake that burned with eternal fire in punishment of those who had not accepted God and Jesus Christ Whom He had sent.

Since I came over here, I have learned better. God does not punish. He is not a cruel God. He would draw all men unto Him. But in coming, they must follow the law which governs cause and effect. To the evil doer, the law is fearsome. You remember how it says in the Bible that the righteous are as bold as a lion but the wicked flee when no man pursueth. From these High Planes, we see that law in constant operation. It cannot be otherwise since Divine laws are never abrogated. Fear them not, for they are founded in love that is Infinite and in wisdom that transcends all human concept. Law is love just turned the other way round. It meets every human need and will carry civilization through to safe harbor when men learn that their own wisdom is foolishness compared to God-wisdom. Slow indeed are they to learn!

Here there is no desire to evade but always to fulfill; always to go with the law of love and growth in the things of the spirit. There are no cross purposes here. We are at unison one with another and our one ambition is to know more of the ways of God. As His might unfolds before us and His eternal purposes clarify before our eager eyes, we are moved to such adoration as the hearts of the human cannot conceive!

The greatness of the Creator, the Infinity of His Wisdom grow upon us here where the atmosphere is alive with His glory. Let no one tell you that coming over here is a thing to shun or to dread. It is like stepping out of murky mist and fog and darkness into the glory of the knowledge of Jesus Christ.

The day I came so suddenly, I could not imagine that I had laid aside the body which had been the abode of my spirit these many years. I had never wanted to die. Always I had shunned it, though I was not lacking in faith while I was with you on the earth. It came so quickly, in a twinkling. And here I was on the Far Shore, the old, broken body left behind and my spirit robed immortal! For a while it was difficult to adjust to the new order. My thoughts travelled quickly to the earth plane. My heart grieved at some of the things you were called upon to endure. It was divinely ordered that Tim should come to you and that through her, help would reach you from these Inner Planes.

How surprised you were and how incredulous at the messages which first came through! You wondered whether it could be true that they were coming from me whom you knew so well in earth activities. So I gave you my personal statements to strengthen your faith and assure you that it was I speaking, different only in that I was no longer held back by the body. Otherwise, the same as you knew me so many years. I beg you to believe just that.

Here we communicate by the power of thought and we have nothing to hide from anyone else. We are purified by the love of God and we grow from one stage of development to the next higher, until we shall come into the full stature of likeness with Him! The teaching of the orthodox church as I look back upon it, seems iron-clad and lacking in qualities of Godlikeness which would draw men to the church and through it, to God and His service. I do not say this in a spirit of cavil. But because I have come closer to the essence of all Truth and all Love.

From these exalted Planes, I would that I might breathe into the heart of the church more of the spirit of the Christ and show them who minister how relatively unimportant and insignificant is much upon which great stress is laid. The church is endangered by over-load of superficials and by desire to shine in the eyes of men.

If only upon their Altars there burned the Flame that cannot be extinguished! If only from their pulpits came just the simple, sweet things of Truth which endures for all Eternity! If only it were the voice of the prophet knowing himself the representative of God and burning to carry His message!

The church is not destined as a social agency. It should stand only for those things which speak of God and His enduring power to save. Oh, my friend, such a church could have averted this world holocaust had it not been bound about with things essentially of the earth.

A great day is coming soon when its Altars will glow with live coals of Messianic power and purpose; when its corridors will ring with the unchanging story of the God-head and His unfailing purposes for this universe of His creating. When that day comes, there will be no question of people willing to serve. Their hearts will impel them to live and to serve in true radiance of Christian discipleship. Then shall there be a mighty turning from the husks of life to that which satisfies. And Love shall pervade the entire world. Then shall the lion lie down with the lamb. And then shall earth know war no more!

War comes when love is not; comes from greed for such power as is a broken reed; when the material has overshadowed the spiritual and when for the most part God has become relegated to the back seat.

But the throne of the Eternal is of the endlessness of time, without beginning or end. The toys of mankind, their ambitions and aspirations, are like a puff of wind that vanishes in an instant of earth time.

It will be a glad day for earth when this change comes. More and more men are coming to look for essentials in their spiritual life, things to which they can pin their faith. Slowly in many parts of earth, groups are gathering with whom the Word of Truth abides and upon whom the Spirit of Truth rests. These groups are like light houses to which men look who are all but shipwrecked on the shoals of materiality and who need to re-chart their courses in life by the Star of Bethlehem.

It is all so clear to us over here. We wonder why you of earth see it so dimly, which thing I say in absence of any spirit of criticism; only in grief at what so many hungry people are needing and wanting on which to feed their souls, when all the time it is within them where the Infinite dwells!

The technique of this team work between you and me is proving easier than you had thought. Your hands and mind are wholly subservient to my wishes. You will have your reward through knowing you have done your part in a great piece of Christian and cosmic service, straight from the Inner Planes to the hearts of mankind. Let that knowledge rest upon you as a benediction and abide with you as a blessing.

It is great joy to me here, as I know it is to you there, that we go forward together again as partners in a great Christian adventure. We shall make glorious headway. As I fulfill my mission over here, you are growing in the richness of the spirit. That pays a better dividend in eternal values than any other thing in life. Thank you for your hands tonight and for your mind through which these words have come from the Inner Planes. I am off now to serve in the far quarters of earth where men are suffering and where they need the help we can give them. It is blessed service. Good night!

YOUTH AND WAR AND GOD

September 12

I would talk with you now about the soldier and his coming to these fields of light out of all kinds of sore struggle and bitter conflict. Many of them are mere boys, untutored and not understanding the issues that underlie this dire conflict. They should have been the mainstay of the future generation except for the rampaging of the god of war, loose throughout the world now for years.

This global issue is about to be terminated and these young soldiers will return to the ways of peace which latterly they have all but forgotten. The transition will be difficult for them. They have been accustomed to obey. And when no longer are there orders, these youth will flounder. They will be like ships without rudders. Some of them, many of them, will ground upon the sandbars of sensual and material decay. Their pattern of life has been despoiled and few there be who know how to re-draft a map of human behavior that will be adequate and satisfying. The leadership of the nations falls far short of the high planes of understanding and of spiritual concept that should be the foundation of all such plans.

God alone is wisdom sufficient for this mighty re-vamping of civilization's pattern. Unless He is taken into the councils of war and peace, futility awaits. And the world faces a peace debacle of gigantic proportions. Seldom do those in the seats of the mighty realize their utter impotence. Only when in humility and earnestness they ask for wisdom from the Fount of all, are they guided in far-flung ways of righteousness.

That is more an issue today than materials of peace and war. This of which I have been speaking is ultimate in the final setting up of a new civilization out of what is largely a wreckage of the old.

Youth is the greatest loser. Snatched into conflict before it was prepared for understanding, it returns bewildered, to try to pick up the threads of living, only to find that it does not know how to weave. This is the most awful price of war. Beside it, material costs shrink to nothingness.

Many of these youth found a new sense of God as they flew the highways of the air or ploughed their way through unbelievable jungles or unflinchingly faced down-pouring torrents of enemy steel. To most of these, God had been merely a name, empty name at that. But when all else seemed against them, somehow there appeared to their needy hearts a sure knowledge that God was equal to whatever they needed.

He knew the highways of the blue empyrean when the pilot's compass was gone. He showed them lanes through the watery deep. He was food and drink to them and the one influence that held their minds calm, their courage steady.

He was so close to them they felt they could reach out and touch His hands; so close that their whispered words reached His ears; so near and so dear that they wondered how they had ever lived without Him.

This God whom they found through long, torturous nights when danger lurked on every hand and there seemed no way through, is not a denominational God. His love reaches beyond the utmost bounds of man's thoughts and includes any color, any creed, any human.

Here on these Celestial Planes there is no distinction. All are the creation of Infinite Mind. All are the children of His love. If only the church and the world will see and follow that in the days ahead when there must be so much reorganization, it will be great gain for the Kingdom of the Highest.

Then the God who became real to millions in the heat of world conflict, will have readier access to their lives when they return to living that is devoid of such physical danger when it is easier to think the human is sufficient.

How strange a concept men have that we who have passed the Veil, have no missions to perform and no lessons to learn! We go everywhere under orders from our instructors, assigned to minister to any who need us.

As they pass the boundary between the human and the spiritual, their faces often glow with surprise and joy at what they see and begin to experience. The experience called death is really a promotion card which entitles us to go up higher, to share greater joys and to learn deeper, richer lessons of eternal purposes and plans.

I would I could impress this upon the hearts of humankind. Most of them think of death as the Dark Valley, symbol of irretrievable loss and sadness. It is as far from the truth as high noon is unlike the darkness of moonless midnight. It is the climax of the human cycle, the end of one phase of existence and the beginning of a better. Please feel that part of your service is to help establish this brighter, truer acceptance of the transition from one plane to the other and of the joy which it represents.

Your way ahead is clear. Your path is bright. Have no fear of any threatening cloud. When disturbance appears, turn your heart toward the Infinite. Just know that in Him dwells all good, all joy, all peace and satisfaction. Know too, that all you can ever need—and more—is ready and waiting for your help. Real achievement awaits you. It will open before you in ways that will surprise you, and bring comfort to your heart. Take what offers itself and know that it comes from the Inner Planes.

Again let me tell you that your welfare is our concern and all your needs will always be met. This is part payment for the loyalty of your spirit and for the unflinching quality of your service through long years when you sacrificed yourself to do for me at my need. Other influences crowd in upon me at this time and I bid you goodnight and God speed. You are under our constant watch care. And no harm will befall you!

GLORIES OF THE SPIRIT WORLD

September 13

Tonight the vibrations are crisscrossing. But the channel will clear and my voice come through to your inner ears. Did you ever know the Inner Planes of Spiritual Power to fail when once they begin a mission to hearts of the human? That is part of the joy of service over here on this side of life. Always we are in power to carry through when once we have begun!

It was hard for you, following Tim's departure, to feel that your source of contact with me was closed for you. But do you not remember that I said through her that the line of communication would not break and that the door would not close?

The messages which preceded these were all for which you had faith at that time. You had to learn little by little and your faith reach out to absolute assurance that each message originated with me.

Thus there were many personal references that were tonics for your faith and revealers that communication between these two realms is feasible. Just two and a half years ago, as you of earth reckon time. But you were so new in the realm of the occult that you had to begin with the simplest of lessons.

In the period intervening, I too, have learned much and now am privileged to share through these daily missions to you, some of the glory that permeates the higher reaches of spirit existence.

Colors abounding here are beyond compare. They are like nothing to which I might liken them for your earth understanding. Shades and harmonies of coloring on every hand are like a great, swelling symphony. How I wish I might describe it to you! It is as lavish as all other forms of beauty with which the Master Designer has glorified His universe.

Your scientists sometimes in their limited wisdom declare that if there were a heaven, its locations and dimensions would ere this have been discovered among the starry systems. They fail to appreciate that things which are unseen are eternal and that nowhere in God's Word is it said that the Kingdom of Heaven is a material or physical location.

It is wholly spiritual and thus may not be seen with physical eyes nor measured by the dimensions of physical science.

The Spiritual Planes are the realest things in the universe, peopled by those who have come up through tribulation, who know only the desire to come closer to the heart of the Infinite and to reflect His love in such service as they are assigned to render.

The color radiance of which I spoke is only one manifestation of spirit glory. We here have such magnificence of verdure, plants and trees and flowers, as the earth does not conceive. Each leaf, each bud and flower, seems bursting with perfection of beauty. I have seen so many varieties here in this rarefied atmosphere, of which earth planes have no knowledge.

How can mankind dwell in thought on the tomb and the dankness of the grave?

There is music too, with harmonies so marvelous that the imitations of the human could not endure them; tuned to such lofty vibrations as only ears of the spirit can catch. No wonder the angel songs on Christmas Eve continue to echo through the hearts of men! They are manifestations through harmony of sound, of the glory that is God! When you come to hear the angelic choruses sing His praise, you will know what it means to worship and adore!

When I was with you in the human and through the period of my physical blindness, it meant much to me to lift up my voice in song. Always my spirit soared as I sang until often I was able to forget the limitations of the human and to imagine that I was having a foretaste of the radiance which now I enjoy without limitation. Those simple songs of God and His goodness were carriers on which my soul surmounted its human bounds and leaped Godward where always it found rest and peace and comfort from the perplexities that filled the days.

Music comes most easily to express the glory of God and affords an outlet of worship for the aspiring spirit. How I can sing now with all my being overflowing in adoration to Him Who loved me and brought me through the years of earth life to this place of greater development!

Tune the ears of spirit to listen for melodies coming through the ethers, melodies that are not of the earth. You can learn to attune your hearing until your life can be transformed by even occasional snatches of celestial song.

How I wish I might open all this to those who think that life is drab and dreary! There is no drabness to those who are attuned to spiritual levels, even though they must make their ways through the routines of earth life and negotiate the affairs of living against odds.

It is all a question of whether the heart is centered on things of earth which so often disappoint; or whether it seeks that which is of the spirit which never disappoints! The downward pull is strong. But the resources of Almighty God are beneath and roundabout everyone who seeks to reach higher planes of life and understanding.

My instructors from the Seventh Plane tell me that never since the earth was created out of the void, has there been such chaos among people on the earth plane as now. Why? Because men have loaded life with temporary, transient and foolish ambitions for power which they do not know how to use; for sensual display and luxury which enervate and never bring satisfaction or growth.

Thus the seeds of things which men have sowed have grown and choked the flowers of spirituality. The power they have sought has turned in upon them. These things of the earth have wrought sad havoc with the children of men. Not until the people of earth turn in sincere humility to God and ask for His will and His way to be revealed, will a new and enduring order of justice develop among the nations.

Intellect alone cannot accomplish this. Leaders think brains alone can chart the new order of life. Brains wrought much of the downfall of the governments of earth. For the brains were not centered in the will of God. The law works unfailingly and "As you sow, so shall you also reap."

The glad day will come when men will see the folly of trying to build without taking God into their plans. It comes sooner than many think. It is the one hope of a civilization that can stand against the onslaughts of greed for place and power. Of this I shall speak at another time.

I leave you now with my blessing. I give you God's blessing and may His sweet peace rest upon you and abide. Tomorrow night in terms of your earth time, I shall speak of other matters of great moment. And now, good night!

NO DEATH!

September 14

I greet you tonight from these Far Shores. They are not so far, either, for we make the journey in a breath, in the twinkling of an eye.

It is not from life to death but from life to more life, as one moves from one level of achievement to the next higher.

By earth thought, the passing has been made a time of great sadness, draped around with thoughts of gloom. Every physical aspect of death has been magnified and intensified with the negative, until it is no wonder that those who lose loved ones, allow themselves to be overborne with grief.

If loved ones were taking any other kind of journey into lands of beauty and glory, how we would rejoice! How much more when they slip the bonds of earth limitation and find themselves free to expand, to see and to serve in ways beyond the scope of earth. Everything is to gain by their coming!

But the glorious significance of it has been all but swallowed up.

It is only a shadow that passes like a watch in the night. Then shines the light that knows no darkness; the day that never is swallowed up by night! Why cannot earth teachers feel and believe this? Why does not the church hold this aspect of physical death convincingly before the minds and hearts of its followers? The reason is because so few who should be speaking with the thunder tones of the prophet see much more clearly than the multitude. The day must come and it is coming when they who minister will themselves have been on the Mountain of Transfiguration. They will have seen beyond the earthly to glory such as has been revealed only on the heights. They will have been baptized into sorrow and learned through it that life has no beginning nor ending and that laying aside the physical, means using that which is never subject to decay nor to the ravages of age.

It is so glorious a transformation that hearts should rejoice at the promotion. False teachings of eternal punishment and all that has been attached to it, with the fear that is part of the dread of death, are largely responsible for this misinterpretation of the Divine Master's plan.

Never lose opportunity to throw light upon the joy of the Transition and to show that life in this other Realm where I now am, is a place of growth where we move from one level to a higher as we learn our lessons of God's will and plan and as we become equal to service to His needy children wherever, they be on the earth plane.

We go on wings of light to such human darkness as is hard to comprehend. We seek always to alleviate pain and suffering and distress of every kind. We do not go always as spirits from this Realm but often in physical form, to offer the succor that is needed. All of this is under the careful planning and instruction from those who have been many aeons in this Celestial World and have come close to the power of the Godhead. Their wisdom is drawn from the never-failing Source of all wisdom and becomes dynamic through contact with All-Power.

Thus miracles are worked everywhere. Men say that this and that happen. These things of great wonder do not happen, as earth people use that term. Marvelous things come to pass through the miracle-working power of the Creator.

Do you remember that early in the messages I said to you that my mission is to prove to earth people that miracles can and do appear now, as in the days when the Son of God walked the highways of His beloved Palestine? It is worth all the discipline that the human can endure and that the grace of the Infinite can impart, to be counted worthy of such service!

Are we recognized in our relations to this other realm? What matters that? All that matters is to serve in the name and the might of Him Whom we adore.

You have many times been visited by us in your earth home when you did not know that we were with you. Sometimes I have come alone. Some of these times you will see me with your physical eyes. But that is less significant than for you to realize how the sudden uplifting of your spirit, the quick relief from great weariness, the surprising surge and sense of spiritual contact reach you in time of your need and do for you what human presence could not do. You must keep open heart and receptive spirit so as never to fail of royal welcome to these visitors from the Realms of Light!

In the earth sense, you are so alone, so deprived of human companionship, that you have been the object of our special consideration. Many times we have sent you help the spiritual origin of which you have not surmised. And under the ordeal of earthly aloneness, you have turned to higher things and have grown in values that never fall below par. This is the best investment you can ever make!

Tonight I would speak further of matters that are of real import. It is hard to get the right perspective on life when Sometimes we feel too close to its problems. But unless we see a picture in true perspective, it is out of focus, blurred and befogged. (Patience a moment until the contact clears!) You are manifesting the same quality of cooperation now with these messages as you always did when we served together on the earth plane. Always your dependability held true.

Such a series as this one can come only on direction of those wiser than I and more empowered with the wisdom of the Infinite. Under their guidance, these doors are opened and as much is given as will answer a certain purpose.

If any of your earth circle take exception to any portion of this which comes, pay no heed. For as you are the earth channel offering your hands and your mind, I also am the channel through which wisdom of the ages is made available for earth acceptance.

It is marvelous to be a part of the sweep of such cosmic forces; to work directly with the Spiritual Realms instead of being bound down to the dimensions of earth tasks!

You should grow through this experience until never would there be any tendency to impatience or to lowering the standards of excellence to which the children of the Highest may attain.

I do not say this critically. But I am so eager for you to prove the adequacy of the spiritual in every detail of your living! For I know some things that are ahead for you in which you will render marvelous service.

Stretch up through the details of the days! Grow with every passing hour! Absorb every gem of wisdom which is imparted to you! Make it yours in the warp and woof of your being! And be ready to transmit it to those who are very hungry in their spiritual natures.

There are those who will question you and be incredulous about this contact and these messages. If they are sincerely seeking light and truth, you will be in position to give them what their hearts desire. If their minds are barred against any except traditional ideas, keep your treasures of knowledge and wisdom from the other side of life until they can be more wisely used.

Always there are doubters who seem not to wish to learn. Our Lord met them in His earth days. You will. Have no dread, no fear that you have failed, no resentment against them, no concern except to be used in right ways when the time is ripe.

I wish I could tell you more of the ways of life over here. But as I could not have comprehended it while I was yet in the physical, so you cannot comprehend it while you are of the earth. But rest assured that it transcends anything of which the mind of man has conceived. It makes all the suffering and losses, all the sacrifices and the service which earth people experience, look so little in exchange for so great a reward.

It is light and peace and joy and glory and power and wisdom. It is freedom from the littlenesses of the human. It is momentum toward the Divine and constant incentive to reach upward. It is heavenly harmony and beauty and strength and all those things which are part of God and come from God.

Have I made it at all clear and plain to you? It is wonderful beyond the power of earth words to express. But you will be seeing for yourself when the day comes that your work there is done and you come up higher to work on in these Celestial Realms.

I go now to serve in joy and gladness. My eyes see perfectly and I behold marvelous things of which no man may yet be told. Good night. And God bless you!

September 15

It is just one week tonight, according to your understanding of time, since these messages began to come to you. We have covered much ground and many things have been revealed unto you. Much more will be revealed. You are the channel for receiving and for giving out to those who otherwise would lack this knowledge.

Ways of which you do not dream, will open to you. The demand will be great and the reward commensurate. So, steady, my friend, and be not weary as night after night you listen with the ears of your spirit for these words from the Unseen World.

If this starts a little slowly tonight, it will nevertheless be worth listening for. The days and nights of your earth time see such slaughter as cannot be expressed or imagined. Into the midst of it we go as ministering angels. We help some of the boys to go painlessly out of their wounded bodies and to get their first start on the other side where all is so new to them.

Again here on the earth side, we mitigate suffering in ways that are spiritual. We offer them the Water of Life, carry messages of love to their dear ones and in every way do all that can be done to make their passing comfortable.

Sometimes they are afraid to die. But not often. They have been so many months in the atmosphere of physical death that they shrink less from it than would have been the case in normal times.

But when the soldier himself knows or suspects that his own time has come, he craves a tender hand to minister unto him and a soft voice to tell him that he is going into more radiant life than he has ever known. He can't quite believe it.

For he has been taught so differently.

But when these boys land safely on the Far Shore, their broken bodies left behind with all the attendant weight and weariness, they almost leap with rapture and wonder what has happened. It can't be that they are dead, they say. They see the beauty, sense the harmonies of music and of the spiritual atmosphere, they feel so different, they see members of their families waiting here to welcome them and their faces glow with delight.

Coming from the fox holes, the jungles, the deep-sea rafts, the crashing planes, the awful heat of battle, the shores of the Heavenly Land are beyond their comprehension; almost beyond their powers to believe! Sometimes they have been so terribly wounded that it takes them a little time to gain strength enough to become active in the spirit world. But from the first they are helped and healed by the enveloping mantles of love and service in which they find themselves. It is beyond anything they had ever thought of heaven!

Those who have been spiritually retarded on the earth plane, begin just where they left off, learning those lessons which life seeks to teach us; lessons of truth and tolerance; of justice and patience and goodness; of God and His service. Many of these who come over both at this time and through the ages, find they must begin their spiritual schooling as it were, with the primer, learning slowly and surely the things of enduring values. As they progress, they go to higher levels where they learn ever more of the will of the Highest and of the glory in which that will is manifest.

A cloud comes over their spirits sometimes when they become conscious of the grieving of their dear ones of earth and of the gloom in which they enwrap their lives. Those newly arrived on these shores find their happy satisfactions decreased by this negative attitude of mind and heart. If only you can help people to see death as promotion and as the open door, as entrance into ineffable glory, and to see the selfishness of lessening these joys for them who have gone on a little ahead, you will do great service. Gradually earth minds will comprehend that earth is but the preparation for these higher reaches of living and learning and serving.

SPEAKING OF LOVE

Love, you read in God's Holy Word, is the fulfilling of the law. To understand what love is, is to understand what God is. Even those who have been in these Celestial Realms for uncounted ages, cannot comprehend the depth and height and breadth of the love of God which manifests in such Infinite care as He provides for the least of His creatures. Love is the essence of the heart of God. It is at the center and is the center of His plans and purposes for the universe of His creating.

The earth significance of "Love" is so far afield from the richness of its meaning here on the Spiritual Planes, that there seems little kinship, except that from the mighty fountain of Divine love flow the small streams that trickle down through human hearts where sometimes the paths of life are barren, fertilizing the mind and the soul.

These little trickles carry impulses that are born of the Divine and make possible rich harvests of beautiful living that otherwise could not mature.

Every little or great manifestation of Divine love, is the voice of God seeking expression, drawing the souls of His children closer to Him and uniting them more firmly in the bonds of His life.

How can life be sordid if it is centered in such vastness of unending love? How can it be despairing? Or gloomy? Or unworthy? As God is love, so love in its worthiest is God. And makes all the difference as you strive to make the most of living out your appointed span upon earth.

Do not be afraid to share the love of your heart with those with whom you come into contact. It will enrich the quality of your life and give fresh impulse of courage and power to those whose paths cross yours. God would have no one stingy or withholding of love. It holds within itself the ultimate riches of the spirit of God and is the seed from which grows the best of life's fruitage.

As you give love, love comes back to you. It multiplies as you use it. It increases as you share it. The more you use, the more you have. Such is God's ordering of His greatest gift to mankind—such love as only an Infinite Father could give to His children. Love costs! It cost Him! But what dividends it pays in coin of the Eternal Realms!

Many there be of earth whose lives are deprived of love that satisfies. Their souls are as barren as fields in which no refreshing rain ever falls. Their hearts are parched and their spirits are like the dust of the highway lacking all the richness of soil which is ready to bear good harvests.

When into such lives you can pour some of the wealth of love that has been bestowed upon you, you are doing God's service and carrying out His will both for yourself and for the ones whose hearts you are refreshing.

It is no light thing to be the carrier of love to lives that need it; no mean service to shed abroad in weary souls such love as God counts worthy of Himself! True love knows no sordidness, no selfishness. It has no part in the low or the unworthy. It is the highest quality of the heart of God—and given into the keeping of humans with which to build lives meet for Eternal Realms.

In this atmosphere of God-love, we live and serve wherever we are needed. The feeling of love is the conscious knowledge of all who come to these Spirit Planes. And on this love we feed our souls, as humans feed their bodies on bread. It is meat and drink to us. It is the solvent of all earth's problems. When nations and governments are founded on that love which is of God and take His spirit of love into their affairs, then will come the lessening of suspicions between nations and peoples.

When love is allowed its mighty way in governing the peoples, laws will be fair and just. Human life will reach its highest evaluation. Powers of humankind will rise to their greatest and civilizations will have a stability hitherto never dreamed.

Without love, nations are building upon sand. Foundations thus laid, do not abide. The love which God gives makes foundations as firm as granite from the hills.

When will men cease their futile seeking for that which cannot satisfy and pass by the mightiest influence earth has ever known, the greatest power the heavenly hosts know as through the ages they sing of that love from the heart of the Father which can heal all wounds of earth and end all conflict between mankind and his organized civilization!

I know not, since I made the great Transition, what it is to be weary. My spirit is tireless and I look forward to the endlessness of living where limitations are not and where the impulse is constantly toward the highest which God has provided for all whose earth cycles have been completed.

God bless you as you make your way through days that often are difficult. You are sowing well and faithfully. You will reap in proportion to your sowing.

September 16

I would speak to you tonight of matters momentous to the spiritual life. Emotion does no harm, provided it is controlled. Emotion of the spirit is a tonic which tones up the spirit from dead levels of mediocrity. Here on these Inner Planes of life and growth, we are not afraid to sing and to revel in glorious abandon to God's love and power.

While we were on the earth plane, most of us were constrained by convention and customs and we pared down our religious emotions until they were as thin as paper and about as vital. We were afraid of what others might think! Thus we lost the dynamic for our lives that wholesome emotion, rightly directed, would have given us.

When the heart sings for joy in the goodness and greatness of the Creator, it is good for it to sing with vigor and holy enthusiasm.

Here, unhampered by the body, we rejoice and shout for joy throughout all these Spirit Planes. We wonder how it can be sometimes that you of the earth life do not hear us and wish to join in the celestial anthems!

Let your heart sing! It will drive away much gloom, much sadness, foreboding and anxiety over the affairs of living. Let your heart sing; and lift up your voice too, in paeans of praise and love and gratitude to the Father of us all! If people of earth sang more in this lofty way, influences of despair and distress would lose most of their power. There is vast therapeutic power for body and spirit in songs that well forth in unrestrained streams of praise for God's goodness and love and plans and provisions for the welfare of His children.

While I was on the earth plane, I conformed outwardly to customs of restrained emotion in my spiritual expressions. By that I was the loser. I allowed the warmth of religious fervor to lessen and temperatures of religious zeal to lower. But here I may let myself speak out in full ardor and sing with full-throated zeal to the glory of the Three in One, the Mighty God, the Everlasting Father.

I would that you take heed of the power of right emotion keeping your spirit life tuned to high pitch and in harmony, with the need of the soul for exultation, lest the light within become darkness!

If only I might have learned during my earth stay more of the essentials which I am learning here, I could have made more rapid progress on these Planes of Power. It is such joy to learn here where there is so little hindrance to our efforts and where minds are free to concentrate on the deep things of eternal wisdom which are part of the infinity of growth. The more one learns and the faster one grows, the more illimitable seem the heights beyond to which we constantly reach out.

In all phases of life save the spiritual, earth people do not fear to give emotion free sway. I beg of you to study, to see how much good will come to you by giving freer rein to the exuberance of feelings which comes when the spirit is abandoned to the will of God. The Divine One never leads us into undesirable excesses. So fear not! And now the theme changes.

Each time I come to this change of theme, there is apparent fear in your mind lest the stream of thought dwindle or run dry! At the best, it would be impossible to compass more than a bird's-eye view of the whole great field of life in these upper reaches of experience where we are clothed in the fadeless robes of immortality and where every thought is attuned to the perfection of standard that is in the very God. I want to talk tonight about the battle fields of earth and some manifestations of spiritual light and power there where unnumbered men are battling for supremacy of earthly power.

You must know that on both sides of those battle lines, no matter where they form in whatever part of earth or with nations of whatever racial stock, there are men whose motives are pure and whose beliefs would pass for righteousness, in the presence of our Lord.

We who go on wings of light to minister to human suffering and to spiritual darkness, know no distinction between races or battle arrays. Our mission is to serve wherever there is need of that courage and confidence which God alone can impart. And so on one side and then on the other, we go into the thick of the struggle, invisible often; sometimes in physical form; but always armored by the protecting mantle of His grace.

I have been with the soldiers of both sides as they dropped out of the skies to uncertain landings on the surface of the earth. Some have not made the landing with earth life intact. And as they have felt the sweep of celestial currents drawing them from earth, it has been my inexpressible joy to speak peace and comfort to their frightened minds and to assure them that the landings on the heavenly shores would be beyond anything of joy and gladness which they could dream.

Where tumult of fear had raged within their hearts, there has come a peace that only God's power could bestow.

I have ridden the tossing waves of ocean with men in their tiny rafts and have seen the savage terror which gripped their minds at prospect of no water or no food, smooth away; dread become calmness; fear die out as they recognized the presence of the spiritual and felt its power where nothing of earth could be mainstay or comfort or solution of their problems.

I have seen men who never took the name of God on their lips except in profane ways, become as little children and say together the sweet and simple words of Jesus when He walked the earth. I have seen them pray who never before had acknowledged the name of God in prayer. And I have seen their faces glow with calm assurance that the Christ who walked the waters of the angry sea was their protection and their Comrade in dire distress. From the lips of such men I have heard devoutly spoken many an "Amen" when one of their comrades in distress had voiced a simple prayer for the things of sustenance and of power for their spirits, that they might endure to the end of their ordeal.

I have stood beside the cots on which the wounded lay and have felt the change from fright to calm acceptance that came over them when God's power to help was offered them and His presence interpreted to them.

Their readiness to accept these offerings of spiritual succor has been great joy to me and the missions on which I have been permitted to go in my Master's name have been glory beyond my power to express.

It seems to me that everything I seek to relate to you in this talk, is superlative. But that is because language is so impotent to convey the glories about which I am speaking. You remember from our earth days together, that I was not given to extremes of expression and so you will know that it is only the glory beyond earth words to express, that makes many matters difficult to convey intelligently to you.

When this dire conflict is ended, will come the mighty struggle for reorganization of life in the countries of the whole world. In this struggle for readjustment, the things of spiritual permanence and wisdom must be as yeast to leaven what otherwise would be a soggy mass of materialistic dogma.

More than perhaps you think, the "other world" will have power when the pattern is being re-formed from which civilization will begin almost anew to build a just and lasting peace for all nations and races of men. Only where the yeast of the spirit is present, will results be good and worthy of the bitterness of the struggle.

And now once more, a personal word to you! Your spirit has been wonderfully gripped by all of this, as I knew it would be. By your devotion to all which it represents, you will have great values to people to whom these talks in printed form will go.

There is so much more ahead that I bid you give heed to rest and relaxation. You will be guarded as you sleep and when you wake, you will come afresh to be the channel of this cosmic service to people of earth.

September 17

As we take up the theme of the evening, I ask you especially to have no fear of its content or its vitality. In all of this I am prompted and supported by my instructors who are close to the heart of God through the service of the ages. Even they, you see, have work to do!

You call them "Masters." But as in God's Holy Word, they are also they who serve. As new comers arrive constantly, those long here are put in charge of the ones who need instruction in every detail of life over here. For it is very different and except for these instructors, many would be lost in the maze of newness, bewildered and frustrated. It is part of the Infinite plan for these to be guided, instructed, companioned, and shown beginnings of the way of life over here. The gratitude which shines in their faces, is wonderful to behold.

Those whose lives have been lived on lofty principles of rightness and who have endeavored to follow the ways of righteousness, easily fit into the new order. They begin to grow in understanding and love, their spirits opening like buds that blossom into the perfection for which they were made.

These whose spirits are attune, add their own rays of beauty and glory to the already Infinite beauty that makes up our landscape here. They enrich the heavenly harmonies that swell through the unobstructed spaces of eternal realms.

Their hearts turn earthward often, in longing to share with those whom they have left behind, something of the life they have entered. When they see their beloveds shrouded in gloom and enveloped in sadness, these new ones among the heavenly beings are saddened. They crave earth contacts for the sake of entreating their dear ones to rejoice and not to weep; to wear garments of praise and to lay aside the spirit of heaviness.

Seldom do the very newly come succeed in making the earth contact for reasons which I have told you earlier in these discourses. When they do, they often find their families so steeped in traditional thinking as to be unable to believe that the voice which has spoken is truly the voice of the one who has gone. They fear to involve themselves in something which they fear is bespoiled with chicanery. And so they turn away and close the door in the face of the one who would open their eyes and cheer their hearts. It is sad indeed.

The church has lost one of its mightiest opportunities in refusing to acknowledge and use this avenue of approach to one of the vastest mysteries of Infinite Mind, leaving it to those who frequently are unprincipled and who use it largely for personal gain.

Slowly the eyes of spiritual leaders within the church are being opened and they are beginning to see how faint is the line between the two worlds and how possible is the power of communication between those over here and those yet on the earth.

When the church throws off its shackles of fear and accepts the leadings of the great spiritual masters from this side of life, who will teach and reveal in harmony with God's will, then the church will add a mighty power for good to its instrumentality.

What of those who come hither, whose earth lives have been lived on low planes of morality; whose instincts do not readily yield to purity and love; who have lied and stolen; been indifferent to the rights of others; intolerant and self-seeking and have cared not for the things of Eternal wisdom and Divine love? What of these?

At first they resent the goodness and purity of these heavenly spheres. They have brought with them nothing which enables them to understand and be willing to begin the new life on new planes. Many of them have come from earth of much material influence. They have been rich and powerful and with enormous sway over others on the earth plane. They have given no thought to the Transition which they knew had to come, except to shudder and to turn their thoughts away from it . They thought by so doing, they could prolong earth life and stall off the day when the body would no longer obey their demands and they be required to lay it down, outworn and useless. These, oh! so many of them, have lived either wicked lives or lives indifferent to the things of God and have brought over nothing from all their accumulations, that can help them in beginning the new way. They are bewildered and at first resent the futility of their earth possessions and power.

The king, crowned in pomp and living in magnificence, wonders when he finds his crown turned to dust and his pomp of no value. For only what men bring here of goodness and truth and unselfishness and desire to serve and know God, empowers them for understanding and aligning themselves with the growth and development which make life here so glorious.

Those who bring only materialistic equipment when they come, must learn to undo the wrongs of their earth lives and learn one by one the lessons which on earth they refused to learn. Only as they do this can they advance and come to higher planes.

The fact of their being surrounded from the first with the manifestation of Divine Love, burns into their very consciousness. But does not God's Word say that Jesus died for the ungodly as for the godly, and that He came to call sinners as well as the righteous to repentance? These souls have much to un-learn before they can begin in humility and earnest desire to atone for all which they have done and which they have left undone.

Such misconception of all this has ridden the church through the centuries that I am impelled to speak of it at length. When I was on the earth plane, my concept of these matters was not in unison with orthodox teachings, but much of this which I have given you was beyond my knowledge.

Not until I came over to this side of life did the Divine Plan unfold itself and give me complete satisfaction. Always while I was of earth, my soul was in rebellion at what I believed was incorrect interpretation of God's will and plan. I may not go farther on this theme at this time. It has vastness of Infinity within itself.

ANOTHER FACET OF THE JEWEL

And now I want to speak about the quality of tolerance as it needs to manifest among you who walk the ways of earth a while longer. It is a Divine quality, hard to learn and hard to live. It is of the essence of the Christ spirit and in its most complete fulfillment is akin to the God nature.

Tolerance admits that others who differ from you may be as nearly right as you—or more nearly right. That is hard to accept by those many who think sincerely that their ways are bound to be right. Not so!

Where tolerance abides, is never dissension nor strife. It is a form of unselfishness, of willingness to accede to ways and convictions of others who are sincere and true in their beliefs. Had tolerance held sway in the high councils of those countries where this war holocaust began to blaze and to burn away the rights of man, there could have been no war. There would have been no vast armaments, no murderous assaults upon innocent peoples, no greedy assumption of rights and titles to governments that owed their allegiance elsewhere.

If tolerance, which is another facet of the jewel of Divine love, had held sway, mankind would have gone on in orderly ways of peaceful life through the ages. And peace on earth would have come long since. I speak not alone of this global devastation through which the world has been weltering for years; but of the warring madness which often has broken out upon the surface of man's life, because the spirit of tolerance has not prevailed in human councils and in the hearts of men.

When human vision is clearer and men see the rightness of consideration for others and the fairness of crediting others with wisdom and desire for the right, wars and all human strife will fade into nothingness.

In daily life, in little things which are not little, this same Divine quality of tolerance is entitled to sway in human hearts. For small dissensions grow quickly to large; spirit is prone to clash against spirit; and motives are easily misunderstood, making for turmoil where peace should sit in quietness in human hearts. The work of the world is done well only when peace reigns within; when tolerance holds power over the activities of living.

No man is truly great who has not learned to exemplify the beautiful grace of tolerance in his inner thoughts and his outer living. It is like oil which lubricates wherever friction makes wheels grate and belts bind. It goes to the center of the issue and relieves the tension. In every phase of your earth life, I commend faithful and persistent cultivation of that tolerance that always smoothes and never ruffles the spirit.

And now this has been a long message. I beg of you not to be disturbed because the spirit communications which began to come to you so soon after I passed from earth life and which now have been renewed in this series, are of a different quality and context from those which others receive. Nothing is loftier than these messages which I am privileged to transmit through you from the heart of Infinite wisdom. Just rest on that! And may the peace of God abide with you! This is great business we are doing in this way. Rewards will be enduring!

ONE EXUBERANT LEAP

September 18

Thank you for being ready for these messages from the other world. Always there are some who doubt. But there are more who look earnestly for the light. It is to these latter that I speak directly through you.

You will remember from your earlier experiences with Tim that I spoke of those who will disbelieve these truths from the other side of life. Their motives are honest. But they are firmly grounded in materialistic interests. They will believe only when reason and sight approve and confirm.

Here on the Inner Planes is life of a kind which cannot be pictured by your earth cameras nor described with earth words. It is irradiated with the luminous quality of spirit and can be understood only by the qualities of spirit. While it might appear that spirit is evanescent and intangible from the earth point of view, too fragile for placing confidence in it, let me say at the outset of this discourse that spirit is stronger than bands of steel, stronger than any influence of earth. It is mightier than all earth forces combined. And most unusual results transpire when hearts turn to spirit and ask its help.

Faith is called into play when help is asked of spirit. And faith is that without which mighty things cannot be accomplished, even here in the realm of the Inner Planes. Faith looks Godward and though it cannot see the desired end, it knows that in God is all power and all knowledge.

When faith is partner of the human, all things are possible. As faith comes into the heart, fear goes out. I wish you could know the marvelous quality of faith that we witness here, that transforms and glorifies and is of the very Godhead.

When I came over to this side of life, I sent you word frequently that you were to have faith and more faith, and that things would work out for good. Faith is not easy to use because it is the evidence of what is not seen. Therein is its greatest strength that it calls out power to take God at His word, to know where one cannot see and to believe where one cannot know! Faith is partner of love and these two work the mightiest miracles of which earth knows.

Taking me at my word, you turned the eyes of your spirit upward and began to develop a quality of faith that enabled you to pass through deep waters with poise and quietness, to place utter dependence in the power of the Divine to carry you through whatever the difficulty. Day after day you carried that faith in your heart which made you know that the issues of your life would be good and that you would not be left comfortless.

Faith is a catalytic agent and grows nourished by itself. There is no limit to heights to which it can go. It is a beautiful experience to place faith in a God Whose word was never known to fail and Who plans only good for His children.

There are those over here whom I have seen in utter radiance and who came through trials of earth that were severe and testing. But their hearts were united in bonds of unbreakable faith to Him Whose promises underwrote this faith. Here their luminous presence continues to lean upon faith that has no limitations and that can go always deeper into the holy things of God with Whom there is no limitation. The heaven which we experience is witness to the working power of this faith, the enduring, satisfying power that fails not.

On the earth plane, people make it hard to have faith. They want first to see. And when one sees, faith no longer holds sway. Faith is the simplest, most natural thing in the world, if only earth people would take it as it is. And if only they would take God as He is! The little child does not hesitate to place implicit confidence in its father's strong arms and its mother's tender love. No other thought enters the child mind. Though storms rage, the child feels perfectly secure if father's arms are about it and if mother's smile lightens the darkness. That is faith; the faith that knows, that faces and moves mountains of difficulty.

It is all that the Divine asks in return for Infinite guidance and power. There is nothing simpler than faith when it is given right of way. But to the materialistic mind, it is foolishness which men say does not square with the practical type which must see and measure before it can accept.

The practical mind is often utterly honest. And by the hard way, it may arrive at the same result to which faith came with one exuberant leap, trusting the promises of the Almighty. I wish I might illustrate to you how wonderfully and simply faith operates and how beautifully it brings results!

Witnesses are here who testify to how light loads of earth became when faith took hold and held tight to the promises of God that did not fail. Faith is like floating on the surface of the water when specific gravity keeps the body from going under. There one floats in perfect confidence that the water will hold the body. And there is no danger.

Sometimes on your earth plane, faith is confused with struggle and is hindered by it. Faith is the simplest, the quietest, the most effective experience of the human heart. It is not compounded of struggle nor turbulence. It just takes God at His word and brings results.

I am telling you of faith in this detail tonight because there is such need for it in the life of the world and so little understanding of its power. Like love, the more one uses, the more one has! I beseech you to make it increasingly the mainstay of your life. Lean upon it in every moment of uncertainty and at every time of anxious concern. Trust your problems to it—and fear not! You have been wonderfully carried through times of stress. Mightier experiences are ahead for you in which you will learn more and more of the power of the spirit as exemplified through faith.

The mind that will not trust anything save materialistic substances will find little to comfort him at many a critical place in life from which he might have been saved, if he had sensed the tremendous strength that is faith.

Here on these Planes our hearts rejoice constantly as we learn and in turn try to teach others what we are learning of the ways of God with man.

Shall we turn now to another line of thought? You have craved to know whether we here on these Planes know those whom we knew and loved on earth. I remember how we used to discuss it while I was yet with you in the physical. Can there be any doubt of it after all I have told you of my own experiences?

I came with great suddenness and was much surprised when I knew that I was out of the body. The experience which for years I had dreaded, had proved so light that it was over and done with before I realized it. And here I was in the spirit world surrounded with many whom I recognized at once and whom it rejoiced me to meet again. The luminous quality of their faces, the radiance of their presence, the utter spirituality of them, yet withal the same friendliness which I had known on the earth plane, caused me to marvel.

Earth people bother so much over the fear lest one loses his individuality when he comes to these Higher Planes. Of course he does not! He has simply stepped up higher, laid aside the outworn body, robed in garments of immortality and exchanged the physical for the spiritual.

But he does not forget that which was his earth life. He only begins to learn the lessons which he did not learn and moves on into higher realms of existence and service which were not revealed to him while he was on earth.

You are often tempted to long for your time to come when you may become part of the life over here. Your time is not yet. You have much to do on earth. And you will be loyal to it. Until one has lived earth life to the full of service in all loyalty to every responsibility, one should not wish to be released from its tasks. For in each task, there is richness of growth that the soul needs and good that is to be accomplished, however simple the task.

Rewards over here are not for the ones whom earth called great. They are for them who lived in love, worked their way through difficulties and by faith transformed living into a victorious experience akin to God's likeness.

You would be surprised to know what beauty of life is here revealed through these spiritual qualities of which I have been speaking with you tonight—the power of faith and the strength of the spirit, so closely interwoven that they are one.

To see these who have reached such heights of spiritual power is to feel one's own heart expand with Infinite longing for growth and always more growth in the knowledge of God and His ways.

Nothing else matters. All else is superficial. Only that endures. In it are all joy and perfection and satisfaction both here and on the earth plane which is merely a training school for the soul.

Sometimes you are sorely tried by experiences through which the work of your days takes you. Often you seem to be standing alone. But you are not alone.

You are being guided every step of your way and not a day but that you are under the constant companionship of those from the Inner Planes who are teaching you and preparing you for greater work. God's blessing be upon you! I have great joy in giving this message tonight to your willing hands through the channel of your open mind. Good night! And God keep you, as He will!

September 19

Blue prints are made here for plans to be consummated on the earth plane along lines that are for the good of mankind. These are of such varied sorts that it would be impossible to describe them to you.

They cover a vast number of earth needs and many of them are projected far into the future.

People think of the spirit world as wholly separated from the practicality of earth experiences. But I say to you that the two are closely interlinked, with many interests in common.

The sublimated intellectual powers of many who have crossed the Bar to these higher reaches of experience, are devoted to designing in minute detail many mechanical appliances and scientific devices with which earth people are to be blest after the devastation of this era has passed. Many of these are so far in advance of what thoughts of men have yet conceived that only we here on these Inner Planes know anything of them.

As the time matures when certain of them will be helpful for earth people, designs and plans are transmitted to earth minds. Then men say they have invented these appliances! In a sense, yes! But the impulse, the idea, the concept were formed on the Spirit Plane, then given to earth minds to be available in physical terms and for physical needs.

Is all of this amazing to you? Does it surprise you that from Spirit Planes come these things for mankind's daily needs? It should not surprise you. It is part of Infinite goodness and wisdom and is the explanation of many a new invention, as men speak of it, in the material world.

You see we who have passed within the Veil come nearer the source of all wisdom and learn without the handicap of the body and its limitations. So we learn more easily and quickly. We travel with the speed of thought, unhampered by the clumsy weight of the physical. Thus it is reasonable that minds purified and spiritualized can achieve many things and pass them on in virtually finished, blue print form, for the help and comfort of earth people.

Much of the rapid progress in uses of light on the earth plane, was made here where light is so glorious, softly diffused, always enough, never too much, beautifully shaded in ways earth does not know.

Your instrumentalities of music are many of them designed here and patterned after those which give us the matchless strains of celestial harmony. Does not all of this show you ways in which the two spheres are linked closely?

While I was part of earth life, my major professional interest and concern were for the education of our youth that they might learn to live and serve largely and well. Here we also have our systems of education. We study and learn and apply what we learn in service to any who need and to whom we are sent. It seems very different from ways of learning on the earth plane, for here it is impregnated with leaping desire to know. There is no compulsion, but always eagerness which has no bounds.

We know that the faster we learn, the more service to those in need will be trusted to us and the finer our opportunities in the spirit of our Lord for showing forth His love and goodness.

Our systems of learning are carefully organized. For you see, we are as much as ever distinct entities, with our own individualities, our own gifts and talents, as when we were of the earth life. Some of us can do one thing better than others. And we are steadily assigned to study along lines where we can produce better results in the whole vast plan and purpose of the Divine for His universe.

The wonder of it never ceases. The limitlessness of these purposes cannot be comprehended. Only as we occasionally get larger glimpses of the glory of it, does the majesty of the Creator's work stand forth in overpowering splendor.

There are no words of earth language equal to expressing that which I seek to share with you. Therefore I am vague when I would be explicit. But I want you and others of earth who are open-minded about things of the Spirit Spheres, to know that this is a realm of constant study and preparation for larger service, revealing new ways to adapt Infinite laws to human uses and needs.

It is the most inspiring atmosphere which the mind can conceive. You with your earth limitations, cannot conceive it. Seeing that I never attempted to deceive you while I was in the earthly form, you will believe me when I say that the wonders of life, love and all the mysteries of creation thrill me more the longer I serve on this exalted Sphere of Spirit Existence.

It would be easy for you to become dissatisfied to stay there and struggle to live within relatively small dimensions, if you were able to see in clear outline how glorious it is to live here and what sweep of spiritual experience there is for us.

Because it is divinely ordained for the human species to live on the earth plane until they are ready to come up higher, most of this overpowering glory is concealed from you until you have mastered your earth lessons, met and conquered your earth temptations and made fully ready for life here. Otherwise you could not endure it to play your part in the human drama until the curtain of earth experience was rung down and you were freed to larger and more wonderful roles in the heavenly world.

All is so marvelously ordained that we thrill at the provisions which the Creator has made for His children, through which they come to their full stature as children of the Spiritual Kingdom.

The more faithful you are there to your work and your life, the greater glory will be yours when you come home to join us here! Isn't that worth striving for? And waiting for? Not one single thing about the traditional heaven is verified on these planes here, except the manifestation of the love and glory of God. Mankind in his search for Truth, has misinterpreted much and he has been unwilling to accept anything save that which comes with the aura of tradition.

The day of the opening of his eyes is coming closer when many things will be revealed in proportion to his willingness to learn and his eagerness to serve with his new knowledge. That will be a good, glad day.

And now another theme before I leave you for the night! Do not be concerned when people show indifference at things spiritual. Always it has been so. Many are embarrassed to show interest in matters which relate to the unseen. Not always does that indicate lack of interest, though sometimes it does. Just bide your time and know that always one or another portal will open through which you may pass in speaking the right word or in rendering acceptable service to your Lord for His hungry, thirsty children.

THE BLIND WILL SEE ANEW

You are hearing much of Braille these days and its usefulness to those whose eyes are withheld from earth vision. Uncounted thousands are returning in little short of desperation. On the battle fields of the world, they gave the sight of their eyes in the effort to save civilization from influences seeking to destroy every good thing.

As they return to an orderly civilian life, they are at desperate odds to know what to do with their minds; unable to read, to work as formerly, unable to be independent as they used to be! He who opens the door of reading through the human finger tips, is doing God's service!

There is coming soon, a better way of mechanical reading. Plans for it are here on this Plane, worked out and ready when the time is ripe, for transmission to earth uses. Thereby men deprived of physical vision may read and all but see in ways easier to provide and simpler to manipulate by the ones whose eyes were offered on the Altar of Freedom.

From the many years when my vision was darkened and my world was limited to what the other senses could impart, I know what these mechanical systems can mean to the sightless.

Words of great power will be vividly brought before their minds and their spirits will be heartened. Their hearts will be cheered and they will many a time give thanks to the good God for the provision whereby their minds and souls could be nourished though the curtain of physical blindness had fallen before their bodily eyes.

From experience of those hard years of which you know so well, I can say with profound gratitude that through those years I was able to reach more closely into the heart of the Father, to see more of the wisdom of His ways with men, and to see with spiritual vision some of the mysteries of Divine wisdom which might have been denied me, had I been blest with normal, human vision.

When I came over here, it was indeed wonderful to have the Veil removed and see anew with the freshness and clarity of youth the marvels He has prepared for them who love Him.

And now good night, with all my blessing and with deep appreciation of the loyalty with which you give yourself to these important messages coming at this time for a very specific purpose which will be revealed to you at the right time. In this, as in other things, you will trust me explicitly. This is great service on which we are embarked.

September 20

We both are ready for another in the series of significant talks from the brighter side of life, where never the sun sets, never clouds lower, never hearts are broken; the side of life where always the inhabitants desire God's will above any other thing and where His Holy Will is shown to be the acme of all that is good. How I wish I might reveal to you more fully the manifold ways in which this side of life is so satisfying and never disappoints, however much those of earth have anticipated it prior to coming hither.

Only a small part of the spiritual realms may be opened to you while you are of earth. You could not endure it otherwise. God's will in this is supremely best, as in all other things. But it is desirable to impart to you and through you to others, some of the life that prevails in these sacred precincts where all is activity and growth and service and love and worship.

There is no night here. That you learned many years ago from Holy Writ. What does it mean? That being in the spirit, minus the weight and weariness of the flesh, there is no need for the recuperation which you of earth must have. How great the relief was when I came over here, I cannot express.

Others have the same experience, even men who come from their physical prime, from the heat of the struggle for earthly power. They speak often of the lightness and sense of freedom which now is theirs and of their ability to go with the swiftness of thought to uttermost parts of earth.

But they do not go aimlessly. They, as everyone else who comes here, are first instructed in primary knowledge, things they must needs know to render their best service, even when they are new in this spirit life.

Everything in these Realms is organized. Instructors give us our lessons according to our stage of development. And as we are able, we are sent where we are most needed to represent the love and power of God. It is mighty service, worthy the archangels, yet given to people who have won their triumphs and finished their courses in earth discipline.

Can you comprehend what it means when I tell you that here there is no jealousy? No one of the countless millions who have come up higher and whose robes have been washed, is jealous of any other or of the progress the other makes. It puts life here on an entirely new basis. When one makes rapid progress, every other one rejoices with such hearty eagerness as can scarcely be imagined on earth planes. None of the old, bitter envy or jealousy remains. There is no room at all in these Eternal Fields for qualities that are unworthy the children of the Kingdom.

I would not take time to discourse on the folly of jealousy. It bespeaks its own weaknesses and has no place in the hearts of any who seek high things of the spirit. Rather I would direct your thinking now to other things of which you cannot know except in such ways as this.

OF GIVING IN MARRIAGE

One of the great stumbling blocks in earth-thought of this heavenly world stems from the Scripture which says there is here no marriage nor giving in marriage. Do you not see that this is the acme of Divine wisdom? Each one who comes to these realms comes bringing his own spiritual equipment. No one enters on the credentials of anyone else. Families are not necessarily together as on the earth plane, though often we meet those who were bound by family ties in the flesh. The surging of the physical is left behind when one crosses the narrow line which separates the two planes. What remains is eternal and immortal, the spirit, with which there is no kinship in the flesh.

We meet and mingle here in the unity of the spirit, with perfect understanding, yet without the divisiveness that separates family units on earth. There is no loneliness here; no longing that goes unsatisfied. We are all one in the bonds of the spirit and we seek in our mutual aspirations to reach the highest in spiritual development of which we can be capable.

Thus the family divisions which are necessary and highly potent for earth civilization, are not a part of the Divine economy and do not prevail here. Do not misunderstand. Your father and mother and sister whom you loved so devotedly and whose passing over made so empty a place in your life, watch over you, help you, love you and feel great rejoicing as they see you growing in ways of spiritual power. When you come, they will welcome you, as shall I. But the family idea is lacking. It just does not exist. And while to one in the flesh this may seem forbidding, to those who have reached these Planes of great insight and closeness to Infinite love and wisdom, it is natural, satisfying and just as it should be. You see, we here do not doubt and question and fear. We see the majesty and glory of the Divine order and know that anything else or less, would leave something lacking.

If only the church would seek light on these moot points and share the light and the knowledge that are available through channels such as this, then instruct its adherents who stumble and falter through failure to understand these things, how great progress the church would make! When people of earth wander in mental darkness, fear is bred and doubt comes into the heart to abide where only faith should be.

Though there is no marriage bond in the Eternal Realms, neither is there any lack whatsoever in spiritual bonds and in raptures which completely satisfy. It is the order of the Creator in His wisdom. This does not mean that we have forgotten those whom we loved on the earth level or ceased to love them. Far from it! Beyond this I may not go at this time.

Another line of thought I wish to bring you now to challenge your spirit and comfort your heart. There are many who wish to know more of this channel of communication and its functioning. The motivating quality of their desire would be partly curiosity, which is rife on the earth plane; partly an intelligent wish to prove whether it seems reasonable to communicate with the Unseen World and partly a longing to find out whether for themselves any message would come through the ethers. These messages to you are for your unselfish using when the right time comes and the right way has been revealed to you. They will reach far and wide and find many earnest seekers for the true light which will shine through these words on the printed page.

Even then, there will be doubters. There will be those who scoff. But many there will be who are eager for the light and who will sense the truth, the genuineness of conviction in these words. In their spirits the soil is right for sowing the seed of truth in the belief that we can communicate with the Unseen as naturally as we talk with those whom we meet in the flesh. As you sit night after night at your machine, you are as conscious of me and of the veracity of these words as if I stood in the flesh beside you. Is it not true?

Study to learn more of the gateways to the Spiritual Realms, that you may make contacts of great spiritual power for solutions of your every problem and earth perplexity. There has been tapped for you in this way, such a vein of riches as perhaps you do not even yet comprehend.

Do not talk of these things if you sense that hard quality of mind which represents determined opposition that is not open-minded and refuses to see in this anything of significance. No good will come from effort to interest such. Beyond this word of advice, you need no guidance along lines related to how to use the riches that are contained within these messages.

In speaking of them in this way, I have no pride nor vain glory. For I am only the privileged instrument of those who have progressed spiritually much farther than I and who teach me what is to be said. This is that only such things may be given as will have most potentiality in helping human hearts which are hard beset at this devastating time. How grateful I am that this service is permitted to me and that you were chosen again to work with me, as so many years we worked together on the earth sphere.

You wonder how you are to use all of this. You are not to wonder to the end of weariness or of doubt in the ultimate success of the whole plan. You are to take it on faith that knows the way will open and the manner of your doing be made plain. Isn't that enough for you? Faith, you remember, rests on that which is unseen. Therein is its vast power and its Infinite value. Nothing can take the place of it for the aspiring life.

Feed your soul on the Divine daily and know that no earth successes or recognitions can compare with satisfactions that come from the Ether Planes of spirit life. All else passes. This abides. It is true riches. And now I give you my blessing of peace and rest and joy and power. God be with you as you rest and as you rise to the duties of another earth day!

HEALING THE BODY

September 21

We come tonight to the discussion of a most important matter to you who are yet of the earth life. The air is filled with static and it is not easy to make the contact. But have no fear! I will come through with the message which is destined for this evening.

I want to talk with you about healing the body through spiritual faith in prayer and the power of God. As you well know, no other theme in the Scriptures has more attention than healings, called miraculous, by the power of Jesus Christ during His earthly ministry.

Often you asked me why the church pays small attention to this form of Christian service to which Our Lord gave so much of His earth time. Reasons are varied. The church must get its messages across through the ministry of human personalities who often differ in talents and in conviction; also in interpretation of what is God's teaching.

Healing the body through spiritual agencies, the spoken word, the prayer of faith, the laying on of hands, is one of the places down the centuries, where the church abandoned the great opportunity which it had exercised. It laid aside the healing of sick bodies as no special part of its ministry.

Always there have been some who adhered to the doctrine and the practice of healing by faith in God. They have been rewarded with many victories of bodies renewed and hearts strengthened. Much has been made of this holy power in ways perhaps not entirely ethical, from the standard of the Highest. But none of that concerns us.

While the Nazarene was about His mission, travelling the highways and byways of that hill country, He gave special heed to those who needed His healing touch. He made many whole and as He gave new strength to their bodies, He made clear that their sins were forgiven them. In some cases, He spoke only of forgiving their sins, as He imparted wholeness to their disease-ridden bodies.

This He did to draw their minds to Him as the spiritual Teacher and to teach them that their bodies were sick because their souls were out of harmony with the Divine. It is true today. Mankind is enormously concerned to have its physical ills healed but not always willing to seek first the Kingdom of God, the order in which the Divine places the process.

The body for the sake of the body, was not the Master's concern but that it might be the opening wedge for His spirit to enter and galvanize the entire personality into radiant spiritual power.

To us here and to some who seek earnestly while on earth to know the truth, this science of spiritual healing is not mysterious. It takes cognizance of the omnipotence of God and His omnipresence, and leads through physical needs and release from weakness, directly to spiritual strength and experience. There is no more reason why the ills of the physical should not have the healing touch of the Master than why earth-men should lack any other good thing which He stands ready to offer.

It is the human that offers resistance, the human that questions and doubts and fears lest Omnipotence cannot touch the sick body into perfect health. Against that wall of resistance, the Divine will never impose its power. Only as earth people seek physical wholeness through the acceptance of Omnipotent and Omnipresent desire to heal both body and soul, does the miracle occur.

It is not correct to speak of this as a miracle. For it is in accord with the law of truth which knows that God is Spirit and that man is essentially Spirit. When man reaches out in faith and earnest wish to be made whole, his spirit leaps to meet the life of God-Spirit and he can no more fail to be healed of earth ills than the law can fail of functioning.

If this seems strange to you coming from me who did not pay heed to spiritual healing while on the earth plane, just know that when one comes up higher to these Planes of clearer vision, he sees vast array of Truth from which his eyes had been holden while he functioned as man on earth, Truth which now that the eyes of his spirit are open to fuller understanding, comes with radiant impact. It makes him wonder how he could ever question the manifest truth which would have meant so much to his physical comfort while on earth.

I marvel at myself. But I saw it then from limited viewpoints. I only acknowledged partial interest in the power of the Divine to galvanize the body into perfect health upon a spiritual basis. But so it is. And it is open to any who will.

We here see it manifest often as we travel hither and yon upon our special missions to suffering humanity.

With the speaking of our Lord's promise to come and heal, we see diseased bodies come clean and pure, eyes light with renewed vision and power come to useless organs. It is all a matter of the faith that accepts Omnipotence and lets go of human limitations. There is no other form of spiritual service in which our Master was more appealing than as the Healing Christ who went about doing good. For always men's bodies have been as lode-stones of sickness and weakness and incapacity for vision or for hearing. It is because they do not see farther into the will and nature of the Divine Who came to heal and to help all who accept what He promises. So you see, in the last analysis it is the human who accepts or rejects.

And now, I would discuss another phase of life in which you are interested and through which you can have values as you grow in stature as a child of God.

The physical aspects of death, the disposition of the body, the habiliments of death, the gloom of the grave, the aloneness of those who are left, all contribute to the dread of people as they face the inevitable transition from one plane of life to the next.

They think to ease it by display of things which are temporary and fleeting when the end of earth life has come; and to use all possible physical science to prevent the return of the body to earth constituency. None of this has value. It reaches only the outer surface of the situation. The return of the body to the dust from which it came is natural order. Nothing prevents it.

The body is never anything except the housing of the soul. When the housing is outworn, it is laid aside as of no further use. Then the spirit which lives eternally, leaves its no-longer-useful-home and goes to a better dwelling.

Why place such heavy stress upon that which is wholly material and which is destined by all laws of nature and God to be abandoned when the spirit, the God-like part, is released from narrow limits of inadequate housing to limitless glory? Isn't there room in the human heart to rejoice unselfishly at the great good and glory into which the loved one has gone?

Yes, I know the heart aches at physical loss. Mine did. Yours does. That is natural. But even then, the eyes of the soul may look upward and see the other side of it, knowing that the beloved who has gone, is not gone at all but is just out of sight. Human eyes no longer behold. But the human heart knows it is not death but is life higher and more beautiful, no longer subject to death. You will render real service from time to time as you help people to accept this viewpoint.

You will be wiser never to think of those who have passed from earth vision as "dead." Think of them only as having passed from earth contact to higher planes, as living more gloriously than ever and no longer limited to a body of frailty. Your courage in thus thinking and speaking to others, will help remove much of the unnatural gloom and the false concept of physical aspects of death.

If only you of earth could catch one glimpse of the radiance and beauty and stimulus of life over here, of the Godlikeness that pervades the landscape, of the ideas of service and unselfishness, of the desires of those who come hither to carry far and wide the knowledge and love of God and thus ease the load of living for so many, you would wonder at the lamentations which surround physical death. It is the opening door to everything which is Divinely good and beautiful. More than that I may not say.

And now I thank you again for your patience tonight when conditions have not been easy for the transmission of this message. May the sweet peace of God rest upon you and abide through the hours of this night as you rest. I shall be about my Master's business in other ways of which you shall hear later. This is all for tonight.

THE FREE WILL GIFT

September 22

The day in which you are living is most complex. Highways of the human wind and interwind until it is difficult for mankind to know which to follow. That many lose their ways, is not strange. Only God can direct in safety through this hazardous time.

When men ignore Him and trust their own devices, they lose the points of their spiritual compasses and know not which road to go.

As they wander, they fear. As they fear, they become panicky. In panic they act unwisely. The result is almost total loss of power which they might have harnessed to Infinite potency and have won through, their compasses pointing true, their hearts calm with spiritual poise, the glory of God's leadership shining in their faces.

This brings me specifically to one thing I want to talk about with you. If God can do that for mankind, why doesn't He do it? Why doesn't He take control of man's life at all times, regardless of anything else? Why doesn't He tell the human how to go and what to do from day to day? Why doesn't He thus avert so many tragedies and prevent so much wreckage?

It would seem on first thought that the argument is right. Countless men have asked the questions and resented what they called the indifference of God to human suffering. They ask by the millions, why God did not prevent this terrible holocaust. Why did God permit this nation or that, to go wrong; these people to mire themselves in the mud of beastliness? Why does God permit epidemics to go rampant through communities? Why does He take ones so dearly loved? Why does He not sit at the helm and guide all peoples everywhere to safe port on the other side of life?

The answer is simple in its fundamentals. In His Infinite wisdom and power, God could do all these things. But instead He has given man the right of free will, to make his own choices, to be good and do right, or to be evil and go wrong.

He has given nations the same right to their choices. If a nation determines to lower the moral standards and luxuriate in crime and sensuality, that nation is free to do just that. If it prefers to have government of the people, it may. If it elects autocracy and concentration of power, it may follow that path to the logical end. If it becomes a warring nation, lusting on human blood and reaching out in aggrandizement toward ever more power, that nation may go as far as its resources permit.

God never takes the reins and makes the human follow where He drives. Infinitely higher is His gift to mankind, the gift of free will. With the gift, He places upon nations and individuals the responsibility of exercising this freedom of will and of choice and then taking the consequences of choice. It could not be otherwise.

If nations or local governments permit conditions which breed disease, those nations must pay the price of the working of the law. If nations or men forget their highest selves and live on lower levels than are clean and pure and God-like, they may! For they are free agents. But they reap what they sow. The law thus laid down, is never abrogated. The nation which wars for selfish ends and through greed of selfish power, will perish by the sword and be its own undoing.

God does not send war; nor pestilence; nor tragedy; nor sickness; nor any other hard thing. But He has put into the hands of the children of men the freedom of will that enables them to direct their choices and thus to reap their own harvests of goodness and righteousness and peace and joy—or the reverse.

God's law is no respecter of persons. It knows no difference between high estate and low. It is an impersonal law which is one of God's greatest gifts to humankind. It makes it possible for the human to hold himself in pride and with conscious greatness as he makes his way through the world, knowing that he is not slave or servant of any, not even of God; but that he is permitted the glorious right to choose for himself.

How this gift of free will does dignify life! It should make us humbly proud and grateful to the Father that He has trusted us, His children, with this great instrument by which we may make life truly magnificent!

Does this mean, people will ask, that the individual upon whom trouble descends like a blighting cloud, has done some wrong and is being punished by an angry God? Could it mean that? No! It does not mean that. But the law does not operate with each individual as an isolated case, independent of the group with which he lives and works. It meshes into the community, the nation, the world in which each one finds himself. If an engineer is careless and wreckage follows, with human life lost, those whose lives are forfeited on earth are victims of that carelessness. Just so in war and elsewhere when man is associated in groups.

This law of the universe could not isolate each individual and deal with him through the years as a separate entity. For God put mankind into families. They organized themselves into communities and neighborhoods. Nations that have been serfs to the dictates of some ruler have never risen to the stature that men have who are free to choose their comings and goings, their ways and desires in life. Thus we can see that the Creator's gift to mankind of being free agencies, is beyond earthly compassing.

And never fear! What man earns in the Spirit Realms, he receives. What he sows, he reaps. The generous heart of the Infinite Father never gives sparingly but pressed down and running over with good gifts is His largess to those who seek His Holy will. You will be rendering needed service when you try to clarify the mental confusion of many who fail to see how God can be excused for letting the world welter in blood and reel in suffering through the centuries, especially in this latest orgy of death and ruin. Whenever you can, do make it clear as we see it so easily from these Ether Planes, that it is the outworking of man's choosing and not of God's will that the earth has turned red with shed blood because there are those who know no limits of greed for wicked power.

Please understand that not one of these gigantic themes is more than touched upon in this series of talks. Each of them is big with Infinite dimensions and ramified possibilities. It is my privilege to discuss each of them sufficiently to give you of earth clearer understanding of the Divine will and plan, and to open your eyes to more of the magnitude and wonders of these Inner Planes where so much is being set up for later use on earth.

THE PRACTICE OF PRAYER

You will remember how often we used to talk about prayer and its power in human life. I was given to prayer while I was on the earth plane. It was the mainstay of my spirit. I thought I knew something of what it meant to pray and get results. I did to a degree. But prayer as I knew it and as most earth people know it, even those who lean the most upon it, is as different as day is from night, compared with prayer as we here know and practice it.

On the earth plane, much prayer seeks to enlighten the Deity and then ask favors of Him. So little earth prayer is praise and thanksgiving. To just that degree is it earth bound and futile. As I see it now in perspective related to my own life, I did not gain more than a small proportion of the strength and growth for my needs that I should have done, because I did not know how to pray.

Prayer to avail, should lift us out of ourselves toward God, worshipping Him with our whole hearts, acknowledging His power for every need, committing our every problem to Him, laying aside every problem when once we have committed it, trusting in Him and His word until we grow into a unity of spirit with the Divine that can claim whatever we need and know that it is ours!

Prayer may be the greatest joy in life. It is communion with the loving Father. On these Planes, it is the warp and woof of our existence. We live in the atmosphere of prayer and praise and from it we grow in those qualities that are closely related to the Divine.

I beg you to cultivate the power of believing prayer. It will solve more problems, give you greater satisfaction, lift you to higher planes, sweeten your life and empower you to greater service than any other influence which can come to you during your residence on earth.

In its sweetest essence, prayer is communion. It need not be uttered aloud. It reaches into the deepest places of the human heart and touches there the very mainsprings of life. It roots out bitterness and implants graces of the spirit; takes away the sting of sorrow and gives courage for the living of the days. It removes earthly narrowness of concept and substitutes heavenly wisdom.

Prayer is to our souls what air is to human lungs. As earth people cannot breathe without air, so spirit derives nourishment from the communion of prayer, from the raptures which come with praise and thanksgiving in humility and love and devotion.

Practice prayer while you are on earth. It will build you up more strongly than any other influence. It will equip you with much you will need when you come over here. Prayer uttered in faith reaches the heart of God and brings the richest rewards which can be desired. Make prayer a large part of your conscious life as you work and rest. And you will be more than ever blest. Thank you for taking this message under handicaps of inconvenience. Good night and God's blessings be upon you!

UTTER SILENCE OF COMMUNION

September 25

The interruptions which come cannot be avoided in your earth life and you are not to be disturbed at them. Take them in calmness and with knowledge that such interruption carries its own lessons of patience and poise.

Shall we discuss now some matters which enter into understanding life as a whole, both on your earth plane and here on these higher spheres? I want to talk with you about the necessity of communion between your spirit and God Who is spirit. In our human limitations we think of God as a person with the attributes of a person. That is well in part, for it gives the human concept of love and power and such qualities as draw us close to the heart of God. But it is well as we remember that in essence God is not a person but is Almighty and Divine Spirit. He is the One from Whom came all that is or ever will be; all law, all order, all beauty, all provision for mankind's welfare, all plans for governing the nations and for ordering the universe. He, Spirit, is all. From Him comes everything that enables us to live and serve.

We may not rightly limit this Infinite Spirit to the outline and attributes of a person, except as it helps our consciousness to closer feeling of contact with Him, the mighty Principle.

Don't let this make you shy away on the theory that Principle is cold and abstract and formless and has no pulling power for the lives and hearts of men. It is much vaster a concept of the Source of all things when we let our minds soar to the thoughts of His Allness and know that He far transcends any possibility of being limited to the terms of human thought in the person of any man.

God is all law. He is all love, all that man can ever need or desire. If He were limited to the form and powers of man, He could not be what He is. And the hearts of the human would suffer with hunger for what He is and gives. This is a troublesome question to earth minds. Many stumble over it and refuse in their ignorance to think it through as far as the mind of man can think through such gigantic and Infinite issues.

I am talking with you about this briefly because I want you to know and to share it with them whom you reach and influence, that spirit does not have human form. It is above all that. Spirit combines all human desires and needs, all ambitions and powers and raises them to the nth degree of possibility.

He is both Giver and Gift. He is the Word which was in the beginning of all things. Can such concept be cold or unsatisfying? It is too vast for earth to understand. But earth minds can accept it even though understanding be delayed for the wisdom that will come through the centuries. To accept by the powers of faith where we do not understand, is real progress. To limit acceptance to what we can understand, is to lose the best and to try to be satisfied with less than our capacity.

Never try to curb your outsweep of mind to a lesser orbit than it is reaching out to compass! Never be satisfied with less than the all which is open to you, if you seek and aspire in earnestness!

For you are made to inherit the earth, patterned after that which shall have dominion, entitled to share in the Infinite goodness and greatness which God the Father can bestow upon you.

So think of God with the full stretching of your mind to the widest circle of all greatness and goodness of which mind is capable. And know that by whatever name you call Him, He is the Beginning and the End, the All; know too, that He created the earth and men upon the earth that they might inherit and exercise dominion, develop in soul stature as they grow in intellectual power, and in very truth, be His children.

Such God is Spirit, Principle, All that is or is to be. And they who worship Him, must worship Him in spirit and in truth.

When you worship Him in the silent places of your heart, just accept this as you accept the Father-concept and know that God, Spirit; God the Father; God the Creator is your God and that there is no need which He cannot meet, provided the asking and seeking are in faith and confidence and trust.

Often we get bogged down in our thoughts and go along in our routines instead of reaching out in conscious effort to compass every possible bit of God-life which limitations of the flesh can comprehend and use.

You will be surprised how the capacity of your heart and your mind will be enlarged when you set such standards for your living and for your spiritual feeling.

As in everything else, exercise develops. Stretching the muscles of your spirit will enlarge your capacity for faith and vision and service in ways and to degrees of which now you can scarcely conceive. Try it! Never again will you be willing to go back to former levels of static spiritual life. What I say to you, I say to all. The God-Spirit cannot be comprehended by any mortal. But any mortal can comprehend much more of Him by conscious outreach of desire, than man or woman dreams.

Communion with this Spirit God is the sweetest, most satisfying experience the heart can know. I speak from experience while I was yet of earth. And I speak from the far greater experience of my spirit since I came from the flesh into the Realms of Spirit where one breathes the very air of worship.

Communion is quiet. It is deep. It is personal. It is the outreaching of the finite with its unsatisfied longings to the Infinite in Whom dwells all the fullness of the Godhead.

Communion is not asking for things. It is like resting in unspeakable comfort and joy in the arms of one's dearest beloved, just resting, sharing the very life, needing not to speak to communicate, needing only to be together in understanding and confidence, knowing that what one has, is available to the other.

Communion is contact of spirit human with Spirit Divine, asking only that the wisdom, peace and high consciousness of the Divine be imparted to the earth person which needs such power.

Real communion changes life as no other thing can do. It takes away the superficial, the unworthy and the temporary, giving in exchange consciousness of power for every need and sure knowledge of the presence of God in the heart every moment of the day and the night.

Communion is utter silence when the human merges with the Divine and values of life are changed, standards altered and God fills the heart to overflowing. I beg of you not to fail of learning the glory of daily communing. Nothing else can substitute for it. Without this deep heart experience, life fails of its highest.

HEAVEN IS SO PRACTICAL A PLACE

This land which people speak of as being above the stars, really is right with the people of the world, as we come and go and serve those who need. Those who have gone are closer than your nearest earth associates. So you see we aren't gone at all, except from the flesh and from sight. We see your struggles, know what you are thinking, appreciate your enlarging viewpoints and always are present to help you and others of the world citizenry, at need.

Heaven is such a practical place. Our activities mesh in with earth plans, only a little ahead. We are privileged to foresee farther than earth residents and because of that, we work on faster schedule. The things which will arise for settlement at the peace table are foreseen here among us and spirits of men are being guided definitely from these Planes, that their earthly wisdom may be tempered with Infinite wisdom and their knowledge be increased by what the Inner Planes give them from sources at the Fountain of all knowledge.

There is more earnest desire than you might suppose among those charged with preliminary responsibility for postwar settlements, to know the Truth and to be guided by Unseen Forces. This is the result of the suffering that almost every heart of the world has endured. And it is part of the determination not again to permit the drenching of blood to flow over the mountains and plains of this world, but this time to bring about a peace that shall be just and righteous and lasting.

They who are unseen will be present with the groups who will debate and discuss and decide terms of present and permanent settlement. These unseen forces will be empowered by the Lord of the Universe to reveal many things of rightness to those at the table. As the struggle draws to an end, there will begin to come over the face of earth a consciousness of new power, of closeness of unseen forces which can be called upon to help in divers ways, as peoples and nations seek to lay the foundations of a better civilization.

These messages will be great help to those who are spiritually prepared for them, showing the vitality of relation between the worlds of the seen and the unseen. This will hearten many who feel that their loads are heavy. The closer you personally can come to intimate knowledge of the life which these talks from the other side of life portray, the greater influence you can have.

It is no impractical thing which we from these Ether Planes ask of you. It is at the heart of where people think and wonder and live.

You will find the way to do all of this to make these talks available to the many needing them.

God's blessings be now upon you.

Have no fear. And do not doubt. All is right.

AN ENTRANCE CREDENTIAL

September 27

These messages come to you from the High Planes of Life, carrying wisdom and knowledge which earth minds do not have, save as it is imparted from the Inner Planes.

Again I say to you that these are given through you, that you may give them out for nourishment of hungry hearts and thirsty souls. Nothing that is earthly can satisfy. Only that which is of the Divine goes to the deep places of experience and gives peace and joy and satisfaction. Hence I speak to you these days on weighty matters of the eternal verities.

Turn now, if you will, to consider with me ways in which the man or woman of earth may make more abundant entrance into the life and love of the Spiritual Planes when earthly career is ended. No material successes will count then. No earthly honors will avail. Stocks and bonds in impressive amounts are less than nothing.

Only spiritual stature is considered; those qualities which have been developed in life and service on the earth plane.

Unselfishness rates high as an entrance requirement to these Realms; that quality which on earth has led man or woman to forget personal preferment for the sake of doing for some other one. It is the way the Master trod. He asked nothing for Himself and gave all that He might ease the sorrows of heavy hearts; lift the burdens of suffering from diseased bodies; open blinded eyes to earth beauty and to the glory of goodness; unstop deaf ears to words of life and purpose and teach the ways of God with man. He never had a thought of Himself. And earth people are adjured to follow Him in thought and example and action!

It is tremendous responsibility to set out upon the road of unselfish living. It involves eyes single to other people's good; ambitions devoid of self-centered purpose; turning the heart and mind outward toward others instead of dwelling upon self. Many there be in ages past and present, who travel that road. And they find it blessed, filled with peace and inner rewards. Always the joy that comes from this quality of living exceeds highest expectations. It is the pattern which we here follow and which we seek to make our own in very truth.

Unselfishness has no partnership with greed for wealth or power, two things the love of which has done more to wreck civilizations of earth than all other influences together. If the unselfishness of which I speak with you this afternoon prevailed among nations of earth, there would be complete transformation of ideals and goals. Earth would then come nearer the standards of the Spiritual Planes than is possible while greed for one's own or one's nation's selfish power stands at the controls.

In the reorganization of world comity following the war, nation by nation must come to consider in a perfectly detached spirit, the good of the whole world and the good of each nation, especially the minority nations which have suffered such dire losses of life and goods and territory, with equal fairness.

When these goods have been considered and included in the general aim of the world reorganization, then it is proper and fitting that fairness toward one's own nation should be expected and achieved. But first, there must be that unselfish concept toward others, nations or men, which is part of the unselfishness of which I speak this afternoon.

It is one of the supreme qualities of the Christ-like life. The word has been bandied about in light ways, so that it seems to lack some of the luster which Divine qualities are supposed to have. But let not that superficiality disturb you or any. There is Infinite luster and glory in the living of unselfishness, in putting others first; in building up a reserve of Christ-like character through following where He led out among the needy; where sorrow has taken its abode; where guidance is called for; where things of the spirit count for more than things of earth. That is unselfishness!

To bring that record of living when one comes to these Planes of Glory, will mean foundations of strength on which to build yet higher structures of the soul. Let no one despise the essence of unselfishness or think of it as weak or negative. It is the very epitome of courage and Godlikeness. It is the life the Master lived when His feet trod the highways of the Holy Land and when He paid the penalty of unselfishness on the Cross of Calvary.

Think of unselfish living as filled with the glory of God, however humble the services which one renders on the earth plane; as direct preparation for the home-going to the Father's House when one's work is done on this plane of the physical and the doors to more abundant life are opened.

What a credential it is to offer that one has lived with thoughts uppermost of doing for others what they needed and could not do for themselves! I know of no more Divine quality which the human is asked to exemplify than this of unselfishness which has no ulterior motive and asks only the joy of serving! Many such stand among the saints, apostles, prophets, martyrs. See to it that no selfish aim ever lodges within your heart or finds place in your way of living!

THE FINE, WHITE LINE

September 28

It has been hard for you to accept the run of interruptions of late. But such come all through life on earth and the way in which you can accept them, is measure of your spiritual growth. It amounts to this, that wishing to hear these messages, it would be easy for you to resent the affairs that come occasionally to prevent. When you have reached the stage of development where you know that whatever comes is right, you will register real achievement.

Now for tonight! Shall we begin with a matter of much importance not commonly discussed? Here on our Planes, we know more of the significance of truth than is known by those living according to earth standards. Truth and truth-telling! The two are a master-team when they are employed together.

It would appear to be so simple always to tell the truth as one makes his way through the days of earth living. Not so! Often it is a difficult issue, with much involved. We here learn how like a bright white light is the clean, pure truth spoken in fearlessness and for purposes of honor and integrity. Such light reflects in rays and ways that enhance the cause for which the true word is spoken. As you know and as I remember so well, there is often that shading off from the bright, clear light of absolute truth into murky fog of partial truth; partial deception. On our Planes, this looks to us very disheartening, as we see any child of God forgetting himself so far as to mix the issues. Never does such policy profit the one who uses it.

In high places where one has right to expect utter integrity, there is this shading by a word or phrase from strict lines of what is truth. To veer seems desirable because it appears to gain some point. Often it does win the point and seem to make gains for the one who uses that double standard. But remember that on this plane of spiritual life, everyone is known not by what he says but by exactly what he is. He is clothed by his thoughts and it is impossible to deceive or conceal by so much as a hair's breadth what is true and good and what is spurious.

It is worth much while on earth to learn what real truth is worth, how beyond compare its values are and how simple and clean it enables one to keep his slate of earth life. Truth carries no complications with it. Veering off from it involves one in difficulty at once that binds the mind and heart and leaves one all but helpless.

There is such radiation of light emanating from the free telling of what is true, even though it concerns simple, daily affairs. It lifts one high and places him though unconsciously, in an aura of brilliance which to spirit intelligence is significant, however dull of understanding the mind of earth may be toward it.

When you and others of earth come home to these Inner Planes, you will bring with you such merit, such substantial evidence of character founded on strong pillars of truth in every dealing in life, as will start you well forward in the life and growth which you will experience here.

Let no one disparage the fine line which distinguishes the purity of utter truth from the jagged line which indicates half truth or less than half. That never pays, however old-fashioned this may sound to sophisticated ears. But heed my words! The sophisticated life of earth provides very little equipment for these eternal shores, very little that endures and little that is of use over here.

Strange to talk with you about truth and truth-telling! But you will share these words with some who need to consider the fine shades of meaning herein expressed and to come to new understanding of the vast dignity and beauty which stand forth in undisguised lines of absolute truth! Truth is so vast an issue. It goes so deep into the heart of the Creator's laws and plans that only one small segment at a time may we consider together.

I have chosen to talk with you tonight about the homely values of knowing the truth and adhering to it in whatever the issue is. These homely qualities will surprise you some glad day when you see them in the light of spirit where no fog obscures!

OF COURSE WE REMEMBER

September 28

It is hard for you to believe fully when I start on some new line of which you have not the slightest inkling, that I am leading where you will wish to follow.

Ways of life over here are very different from earth ways. That is to be expected and could not be otherwise. We do not weary nor hunger nor thirst. For we have left blessedly behind us the bodies which helped us during the years of physical existence. But the disposition of that out-worn garment is of no consequence. We make so much too much of that on earth. It is so unimportant. The soul is all important. Sometimes we do not learn these lessons until we have come up higher where the light of spirit enables us to see without difficulty and to distinguish what is transient from what endures.

But though we neither hunger nor thirst nor need the relaxation of rest, we retain all of our mental and spiritual powers intensified a thousand fold from what they were on earth. Where we learned haltingly in the flesh, we learn and grasp and understand with a strange new eagerness over here. And we remember earth life, its problems, and its lessons. Memory here is very keen.

There has been much discussion among earth peoples whether those who have passed out of sight remember those they loved so dearly. Why of course we remember! Then, asks someone, how can those on the Inner Planes be happy when they see the misery and suffering rampant on this material plane, the loneliness and heartbreaks which their dear ones endure? How can they be happy or enjoy the life of spirit existence?

We do remember vividly. Some things we remember with sorrow, as we recall ways in which we might have built more wisely on spirit lines; things we might have done that would have made us more useful; lives we might have lived closer to the ideals and standards of our Lord. Yes, we remember all of that. But we see, it from a different angle up here, where the beginning is visible and the end, at the same time. We see through the softening light of eternal understanding. It makes such difference when we get the right perspective on happenings and on motives. Here we have that privilege.

Of course we remember those whom we have known and loved on earth. Would it be like God to give us such power to love and be loved, then after a few short years, take away all power to remember those beloveds, the while we live on for the ages of eternity? That does not sound like God, does it? And it isn't!

The sweetness of greeting here many whom we have known on earth, seeing them free from all handicaps of the flesh, all lines of weariness gone, all anxiety passed away, all sense of struggle obliterated, and only that left which was richest in their spiritual lives, which had been acquired by devoted lives after the pattern of the Sermon on the Mount, transfigured into beauty and radiance which earth minds cannot conceive, is more than I can express to you.

Can you not imagine something of what it is? When we see the grief of earth, we are not unhappy over it, for we see beyond it to the way it will be resolved in the order of living and overcoming, until the ones who grieve come across the Shining River to these Fields of Asphodel where all is joy and growth and service and love and adoration. Often the ones most newly come to these Planes, are overcome as they realize the tears and mourning of them they so recently left. They try to reach them to beseech them to dry their tears. Then they grow to better heights and see the tears of earth gradually replaced with courage and strength to endure to the end. Seeing the end from the beginning as we here are enabled to do, makes such blessed difference. It gives perspective and power to see things in right proportion and with values never distorted. Herein you have the answer to the oft-repeated question of earth.

How anyone who knows the goodness of God can imagine that He would require our forgetting the features, the characteristics, the loyal hearts, the dear loves when by the order of physical law we lay aside the flesh and come to the spirit world, has always been something I could not understand. Now I know why I could not understand it. Because it is not true! We remember; we recognize; we look forward to the coming of those we especially loved; we welcome them to adjust to the new order of existence and we rejoice in their manifest growth in this exhilarating atmosphere of rapt devotion to God and His Kingdom.

I beg you never to admit into your thinking or your feeling the slightest doubt of the welcome you will receive when you come, welcome by the many who have known and loved you on earth. And do not doubt, as I think you have not doubted, that those who have come over here, are as recognizable as they were on the earth plane, save for the spiritualized countenance which is part of the growth toward which we strive.

Part of the wonder of this realm is that we meet, thrill to see dear friends, then go on about the missions to which we are assigned. There is never any clinging in selfish desire to possess, which characterizes so much of the personal experience of earth.

Wherever we are, whatever is given us to do, it all is satisfying. It leaves no void of unhappiness or unfulfilled longing. There is no sense of lack or loneliness.

It is all so marvelous, so perfect, with nothing left out, no jarring tone of incompleteness anywhere. There is no Sabbath here. Of course not! Every day is a holy day. Every day is worship and service. Every day we adore and seek to come nearer to perfect stature of God-men.

The longer I am here, the more I marvel at the heights and depths of Infinite wisdom and power and glory of which my mortal mind never dreamed. I could not compass such thoughts as here we learn slowly to think after Him.

No Sabbath? No, for there is no time, no day nor night as you of earth know these divisions of time. It is all such perfection of existence as would disqualify any one of earth who had even a glimpse of it while still in the body.

There is so much to look forward to when your work in the body is done! So never have a moment's dread of the Transition nor of leaving the life which you are living in all loyalty. For you are coming to what is so much more beautiful that the two are simply incomparable. Remember how the Scriptures tell us that "Eye hath not seen nor ear heard neither have entered into the hearts of men to conceive the things which God hath prepared for them that love Him." Please believe me as you always did while I was on earth, those words are very truth of very truth. You will someday prove them for yourself as I have proved them for myself; as uncounted millions through the ages have proved for themselves.

Some day the church will begin to learn to interpret much of this which is not now accepted, or is set aside as belonging to the occult. That term is cumbered with opprobrium in many quarters and hence discredited. This is wrong and the time comes when this will be rectified. The world of the physically unseen, is the real world. It is only the other side of life, as real as and infinitely more beautiful than earth. Again speaking of the church, it has failed sadly in not making clear the continuity of life. That phrase should be sung into the hearts of mankind until no one again could think of a separating line called death. It is all one life. There is no death. It is but a passing from one side to the other and more blessed side of life. Continuous! Never-ending! Radiant! And fulfilling every longing which the human heart has experienced.

The minds of men have been dull. They have not seen the truth, or seeing it, have feared to set forth their new beliefs against traditional faith. All of this will someday be overcome. And death will have lost much of its sting.

September 29

In three weeks of your time, you have compassed much knowledge from beyond the Veil. Your spirit is enriched and you are stronger in faith of what the meaning of life is on the earth plane and some of the mysteries from beyond. It is well. But it is not the end. I have much yet to say to you that will be for the good of mankind both now and on the Higher Planes.

For here, we progress as children do at school. They learn one set of lessons. Then they pass to higher grades. So it is with us here in the invisible world. Invisible? Only to the physical eyes. But what matters that? The eyes of spirit are much keener and the things of spirit are much better worth learning. Lessons of spirit life and growth are worth learning at whatever cost.

In the short time I have been on this Higher Plane, it has been my joy to see many who have been here for centuries, whose spirits have grown to such glorious stature as to be all but God-like. Their personalities are radiant like the bright shining of the sun. Their garments glitter with brilliance and beauty beyond earth textures to illustrate. Their countenances are like the morning. Oft times they are our teachers, masters in those lessons which we need to learn.

As I have told you before, there is no drudgery in our tasks, be they of whatever sort. All are taken care of in the atmosphere of holy and divine love, motivated by desire to serve the Kingdom of God and the children of the King.

How glorious to see how glad everyone is at every sign of progress which any of us makes! It was not so on the earth plane, where qualities of living and serving do not always do credit to the human. That is past now, part of the luggage which we were privileged to leave behind, having grown beyond it.

Don't you see how much glory there is in death? How it has so many aspects of release instead of loss? O my friend, if you could convince people of the right way to view this experience which mankind calls death, you would be rendering real service. There is much else you are expected to do while you remain in the flesh. This though, you will accept as a major joy and responsibility.

I wish to inject here some things of a different nature. They may seem incongruous in relation to those things of which I have been speaking through you. Particularly I want to discuss that too-rare quality of self control among residents of earth. Like a flash the occasion comes when as it were, control levers fail to function. The quick word, the hasty judgment, the unworthy flashback, the flashing retort, are released by word of mouth. Does any good ever come of it? Injustice of accusation, false reports, all tend to exhibitions that are not what they should be, in the light of what Divine Spirit decrees.

To keep the control always functioning properly, is evidence of distinct growth in measurements of the spiritual side of life. These latter weeks you have several times been tried in ways that were exceedingly difficult. You were in position to make a telling retort each time.

But you did not! From our vantage point of clearer vision, we see how every such experience of earth is the means of soul growth, than which nothing is more to be desired. It all equips you with what you will need when your time comes to accomplish the Great Transition.

Does self control seem trite and little as a theme from our world to yours? It would not if you saw as we see and could know in what high places the spirit power to control the words of the mouth and the actions of the body, is all but lacking. No truer word was ever given through Holy Writ than that which says that "Grievous words stir up anger." Where anger is stirred or resentment, there is the breeding place of experiences which are out of harmony with Divine will and out of accord with His reign of love and peace and joy.

The hot and hasty words which come so frequently, reveal that lack of inward poise which bespeaks broken connections with the Source of all power, all poise, all control, all peace. Cultivate self control while you live and work with those who sometimes have not cultivated it. If you have it under any and all conditions, you will be a living example to them who do not possess this quality of spirit. It is worth all it can cost in spirit power.

Under the tensions of world conflict, people of earth excuse themselves because of conditions in which they live and work. By so doing, they but increase the tensions, loosen the controls and subject themselves to more severe strains than could possibly afflict them if they were masters of their own emotions. If only you of earth could see how plainly all of this stands out to us on these Inner Planes, the importance of it would be enhanced to earth minds.

SERVICE TO SERVICE MEN

You have been eager to know more about those who are coming to our shores in such vast numbers as result of this global conflict. I would that you could be with me on some of my missions of service that you might see and know for yourself. Knowing, you could never again doubt the reality and significance of the Christian faith. I do not mean that you as a person doubt it. For you do not. But many there be who do doubt it, to the impoverishment of their earth life.

When there is special service to be rendered wherein any of us from the Inner Planes can help, we are instructed and assigned to specific duty which it is ours to render within the careful instructions of our masters. Such varied conditions confront us in war zones and in peace areas, that always we must be qualified for the right help by word or deed. There may be those of earth who tell you that in armed service men care not for things of spirit life and sustenance. It is not true. Millions of soldiers who in peace times might have thought they were sufficient unto themselves, quickly reach their limitations when death surrounds them, death in a thousand different and often terrifying forms. Then theories these men may have held, quickly desert them and hearts cry out to the God of Whom they sang and read when they were children. Some of them have paid no heed to Him since then. But in times like these, they somehow know He will not fail them.

I have seen men struck down in roaring battle, fires raging all about, physical torment racking their frames. But on their faces, all suddenly there comes a smile, a look of radiance, a whispered prayer to the God of all mankind, a relaxing of all sense of strain as they appear to rest back in the arms of Infinite Love. Often the last whispered word on their lips is of Him. They will hum some tune familiar in childhood, some song of Jesus' love, as spirits leave the broken bodies and they take their flight to the other world.

Endurance which comes with consciousness of the presence of the Holy One and courage to bear whatever the suffering, is witness beyond doubt, of the power of spirit in any time of trouble. Out of this awful conflict has come such quickening of men's hearts to the need for the Infinite Presence in adjusting to the business of earth, as should hearten mankind for the problems of the years ahead.

These men on battle fronts learn the power and beauty of God the hardest ways and under the most trying conditions of which life is capable. If in the brighter years of the future, that line of communication between the human heart and the heart of God could be kept open and in instant repair, never again need civilizations of earth be blasted to nothingness and the ground be saturated with blood of war's victims.

But again it will come if men turn to their own devices and follow where the enticing finger of lust for power beckons them. Only as God is at the helm of this post-war world, as His wisdom is asked and His guidance followed, as His love motivates the lives of people and His plans are permitted to come to fruition, can the price of this devastation be justified.

It is strange that men do not see clearly how the only way of safety and of peace which abides, is parallel with God's way! For His way is founded on Infinite wisdom, builded on Infinite love and offered to men for their greatest good.

But I deflected a while back and I wish to return to speaking further about what we see and experience at scenes of conflict. Never have I seen the Water of Life offered to any suffering, frightened, dying man, fail to bring him a conscious and apparent joy and sense of blessing. It is to them better far than water for their parched tongues, though often we take that to them, too. But that Water for their thirsty spirits is life indeed to them. Many a time I have met them again on the Spirit Planes to hear their expressions of gratitude for what it meant to them in their earth crises. What blessed service this is!

In no place or time have I seen men reject the comfort of offered spiritual help, thus proving the eternal quality of that to which they turn when trouble lays its heavy hand upon them. But from it, they too lightly turn away when they feel adequate to handling the problems of life alone.

Often before bodily life ceases, on the lips of these men will be formed the name of some dearly beloved and it is wonderful to see the light which flashes through suffering and the physical pallor of approaching death, when love again speaks to them, the love of dearly treasured ones of earth and the love of the Comforter into Whose tender care they commit their spirits amid such incongruous surroundings.

But there is where we see other marvels. Surroundings mean nothing in the face of fundamentals. The altar on which the body and blood of the Risen Lord are served in Holy Communion may be a rough board. But the Divine Lord presides at that communion in sweetness of present power to help, which many an altar arrayed in earth's richest gorgeousness, never experiences. The trappings mean nothing. The spirit means everything. The material is as dust. The spirit is life eternal and peace and joy. And now good night to you. My richest blessings be upon you!

INTER-WORLD COMMUNICATION

September 30

You will not be disturbed if this message comes through more slowly tonight because there is static in the air and contacts are not easy to make and keep. Nevertheless, it will come, for there is much to say. Just relax and be unconcerned, knowing that the issues are not with you but with these Ether Planes.

So much confusion has resulted among people of earth with relation to earth contact that I desire to speak more at length concerning it. No word of Scripture indicates the impossibility of such communication. The world mind has apparently taken it for granted that the grave seals all powers of communion between the two worlds. Not so! Human lips are closed forever when the body is laid aside. But the lips were only the exterior instrument of communication. Other ways are available and the contact, world with world, person with person, is made in perfect order and to rich purpose of service to humankind. The church having failed to put its approval upon authentic types of such communion, has deprived earth people of vast comfort and of much knowledge of spirit realms about which they should and might know. In my earth life, I had no contact with what you call the occult. I questioned it, for I was reared traditionally. And though I broke away in my independence of thinking and my search for truth, I still had no special interest in such powers of communion.

All that I had heard of it was connected with methods and personalities that were more or less questionable ethically. It was enormous surprise, after I made the Great Transition, to find that such channels were open as did permit the spirit world to communicate with the earth world. It was no stranger to you when you became convinced of the fact of such contacts than it was to me. You were hesitant to accept it, lest you be mistaken and deceived. I took care that you were taught carefully and not too rapidly for your faith to mature.

Gradually from the first, you showed such eagerness to know and to be willing to learn, that much was opened to you through Tim which usually comes more slowly to the novice.

Your earth scientists are coming to know at last that all is energy, electric vibration in one and another form. Earth vibrates to a much slower rate than these Planes and the process of synchronizing the two is sometimes difficult to learn. There is no desire on the part of those who have lived in this glorious atmosphere for centuries and aeons, and who are our instructors, to prevent lines of communication between the two worlds.

But in addition to there being a sending end, there must be a receiving end to the line of communication. Those who get their messages through, not only must be instructed until they know the method and until the messages they would send are true and right, but there must also be those to receive and hear, if the contact is to be complete.

Often the failure is at the earth end. This I do not say critically but only to indicate the reluctance of orthodox-minded men to change their views on such subjects. They have not known that such communion was possible and feasible, because the church has frowned on the occult and the atmosphere in which much of this experimentation was made, was guided not by desire to serve God and His Kingdom but for personal and questionable purposes. Thus conservatively-minded people have been afraid of all such investigation and have chosen to brand all such as fraud. It is not fraud. It is genuine and is one of the lines of startling development in the coming eras.

The church concedes that after death, mankind lives on in some mysterious place called heaven. If living, why is communication not possible? No reasonable answer in the negative has ever been made to that question. Indeed there is no such answer.

Men say that if it were possible to talk between the worlds, the Bible would have made it plain. That is specious. The Bible did not make claim of revealing all that man needed and was entitled to know but only main doctrines by which God made known His ways unto man and by which man might guide aright his way through the years of earth life until he would come to these higher spheres of learning and living.

Man was not told inspirationally about the vibrations whereby radio became a possibility and one of the greatest of modern blessings. Man followed the laws of nature as gradually he learned them. And radio was one of the results. Man is following more and more the laws of inter-world communication and increasingly benefits are accruing from knowledge that enriches the minds and hearts of men. Rest assured, my friend, that as you speak with people about this type of contact, you are speaking on a topic of the greatest interest because there is nothing for which the inquiring mind of man seeks more eagerly than for knowledge of the spirit world.

This is natural. Everyone has seen dear ones go to the land beyond physical sight. Everyone knows that the time of his own departure from earth is uncertain. And he wants to know about it, where it is, what it is, what it is like, what those do who have already reached it and as much as possible what he can expect from it when he too arrives at this destination. All perfectly natural.

The wide divergence in the teachings of different churches is largely responsible for the confusion in earth minds; responsible too, for the fear which results from the confusion engendered by differing interpretations of the church. When followers of Our Lord come together and take Him at His simple word, earth will be freed of much spiritual unrest.

The mere fact of physical death does not make a sinner into a saint. It does not change his moral or spiritual quality in the slightest. When he comes to these Realms, he is just as he was on the earth plane save that he has left the hampering weight of the body behind him and has come to where every surrounding is impregnated with the life and love of Almighty God and where every association is spiritual in its impact. He thus is so surrounded and encompassed with the spirit of God's love and life and service that his recently released spirit begins to grow in the grace that is God and to learn what the spirit world has to teach him.

This teaching and learning process goes on forever, because there is no possibility of ever compassing the ultimate of Divine wisdom or power or purpose or plan. However long, aeons after aeons, one is on the Spirit Planes, always there is more to learn and more to love and to worship, with always more service to render in the name of the Father, The Son and the Holy Spirit the Comforter.

It is everlasting delight in increasing outreach of activity through which we are doing for others that which helps to open the eyes of their spirits to vaster reaches of God's omnipotence.

If only you and others could learn and actually believe that there is no need of your lives which cannot be fully met by the Infinite One, met in ways that thoroughly satisfy, earth would come nearer heaven in rapid strides.

But you go on carrying your loads, wondering how this shall be met, what you can do to relieve that situation, how you can overcome the negative factors, when if only you would open yourselves entirely to Divine guidance to do and to live exactly after that guidance, you would find your problems solved and your difficulties overcome. You are learning. But you have much to overcome of spiritual inertia and of doubt lest if you do not work it out yourself, it won't be done right! The human is weak. His knowledge is limited; his powers restricted. His vision is within a small area. The Infinite has no limitations. All you can ever need or desire is with Him. I beg you take Him at His word and really try His way of life.

The joyousness of life here on the Inner Planes, is one of the outstanding qualities, one of the great inspirations. Sheer joy fills our lives every minute, no matter what our lessons may be, or our tasks. Joy flows out in worship and spiritual communion, in our association with others, joy that we have been counted worthy to lay aside the weights that cumbered us about on earth and come to these better opportunities of growth and development.

Earth is so sorrowful. Hearts of people are burdened. Faces are lined with anxiety. When we come here and find release from all with which we were familiar in these ways of earth, it seems almost incredible. But it is blessedly true. And so I am telling you at length some of these phases of life up here that you may the more wholeheartedly continue your preparation against the time when your earth tasks will be completed and you come home.

After the many years when your earth home has been lonely, the joy of companionship and of association with your loved ones will be beyond anything which you now anticipate. We see it all the time on every hand, as groups are reunited, after earth separation. It is good to see and to share; good too, for you to know about ahead of time.

And now a change of theme! I want you to know that you are not being left alone to work out the special problems which confront you these days. You are being guided from these Planes and your way is being opened.

The blessing of the Comforter be yours. I give you my blessing. We are learning to work together with greater ease in this special task of privilege. For tonight I leave you!

CARRIERS OF GOD-CONSCIOUSNESS

October 1

And now at the close of your Sabbath Day I greet you gladly. We have covered much ground since the series began. From it will radiate influences that will tell through all the ages. Whatever influences the minds and lives of mankind, knows no termination. The familiar illustration of the pebble in the pool explains what I mean. These matters, though, are of such significance that the illustration seems a little puny. You understand. And that is sufficient.

Would you like to hear tonight of another phase of our life and service? Different people react differently to the same situation. And in those reactions lies the key to their characters and their individualities, often to their abilities and their ambitions.

On our side of the River of Life we see and are conscious of futilities with which you of the earth plane are faced. We are in power to set influences in motion that start help to you in ways beyond your knowing. To you of the earth, it often appears to be a chain of circumstances which results in various kinds of assistance which you need.

Circumstances, yes. But not in any way, chance. Rather, by the operation of help from these Super Planes where help, inspiration, guidance were guaranteed you that proved to be exactly what you needed in particular instances. Always know that the Spiritual Realm is working with you when you ask it. Know, too, that such help never wearies and never becomes discouraged. Knowing that, isn't it reasonable that you should not become discouraged, however puzzling your path seems at times?

The rituals, the observances, the sacraments of the church, are all fraught with much sanctity in earth worship. They differ, one church and another, reaching out toward the same end by varying routes. In observing these various celebrations, men find much comfort to their souls, for in them, they find a consciousness of God within themselves. The rituals, the forms, the ceremonies, mean nothing of themselves except as they are carriers of God consciousness. Whatever raises the consciousness from earth levels toward God and the Divine, is worth more than it could cost. Through these sacraments, the life and passion of our Lord are exemplified in ways that portray them vividly to the minds of men.

As you eat the Bread and drink the Wine of Holy Communion, you draw nearer the heart of the Father than otherwise you could. It illustrates and makes vivid to human minds all for which the sacrament stands. As you remember, communion with bread and wine was instituted by our Lord while He was yet on earth and is an example of the way men should observe it.

Do not mistake the outer observance of any of these churchly sacraments and rituals, for the heart of them, which always is God, Wisdom, Love, Power, Presence! Unless they mean these to you, they are relatively futile and are only a show. Here on the Plane of the Spirit, we do not need the symbols nor the rituals. For we have the essence of the Godhead, the presence of the Spirit in ways and degrees which the human does not know. Our worship is of the Spirit and needs no formal nor exterior manifestation. At first it was strange to me so long accustomed to the ways of earth. But quickly I accepted the deeper significance of it, to the great joy of my spirit.

I knew you would be sincerely interested in this difference between your worship and ours. Have you not noticed how differently people feel about the sanctities of life? To some, these are stumbling blocks while to others, they are helps. Whatever is of assistance to a person earnestly striving to live the Godly life, should always be cultivated and encouraged. That tends to tolerance and its essential quality in the good life, as humans live it.

FACTS OF SERVICE

I would like to talk with you now about service. Yes, I repeat the word, Service, for I thought you did not understand it at first. So much that passes for it is twaddle, accomplishing nothing, not even giving real pleasure. The word service has been bandied about as other words have been until they appear almost threadbare in the human vocabulary. That cannot be helped. But the actual facts of service, are tremendous in their scope. They cover countless acts of kindness and goodness, unselfishly prompted from the Higher Planes and carried out by willing hearts of men and women who wish as far as possible, to emulate their Lord in doing good.

Where service is rendered without any ulterior motive of selfishness or show off or applause, but to express the spirit of our Lord to those in need, it is of the loftiest and is so accounted and rewarded.

This is the background, the motivation of all our activity here on these Planes. It is this which sends us to uttermost parts of earth to people of all sorts and all needs. They do not recognize us when we go garbed in human form. But somehow the motive carries, the help is given, their hearts are lightened and our mission is accomplished.

More often we go as invisibles, just as so often we come to you when your need for comfort is great. Then we speak to the heart alone, guide and influence in ways that are better than riches. For always our service is the outworking of Divine mind and purpose, than which nothing is better on earth or in heaven.

Skeptical people say they do not believe in ministering spirits, do not believe in any help from Spirit Planes. Generally such talk is bravado. But we are as ready and willing to serve such minds as any other kind. And often we see faces light with consciousness of relief which has come to them from somewhere, they do not know where.

We see signs that hearts have been lightened, they do not know why. But we know that we have been privileged to give them such help from the inexhaustible riches of Spirit as alone could relieve their gloom and depression. It is joy which some day you will share!

You ask how it is that we can come and go throughout the universe faster than on the wings of the wind. Many have wondered about that. I did when I was on the earth with all the limitations which oppressed me. But here we travel without weight or hindrance of any kind, as fast as thought can go. So you see distance is no barrier. To those in the body this utter lightness is inconceivable. Absence of all weariness which used to oppress the flesh, is more than can be understood. Do not be concerned about that. It is not necessary for you to understand. Just take my word for it, for you know I would not lead you astray.

To us here, your earth methods seem very clumsy, marvelous though the winging through the air has become. But soon you will be flying without wings. Does that sound fantastic? It is not. It is part of the blueprint which awaits only the needs of earth to be transmitted to human minds and by them worked out in terms of human practicality, every detail of which was first blueprinted here on these Inner Planes. I may not explain more in detail just now how many of these new devices are to be accommodated to earth needs. But as you read of their being achieved for earth use, you will know in your deep heart that it is another great gift from these Inner Planes to people of earth.

Much is ahead in these ways in the days following the war. Some of it will increase the trend toward materialism which was so rampant before the war. But it will work out beyond that into ways of genuine service to humanity. Planes without wings are just one of the new surprises for which none of you of earth will be quite prepared. But they are coming, through the goodness of the Creator.

I congratulate you upon the growth you are making in ways of spiritual stamina and power. Formerly you were easily downed. Now you turn your thoughts upward on the instant, seeking help from the only Source of real strength; seeking vision when your way is obscured; seeking comfort when you need companionship; seeking illumination when you do not know which way to go nor where to turn. As this becomes easier for you and as you find greater returns from it, you will be serving most helpfully when you point others to the way that lifted you when you were low. That too, is real service! I go now. Infinite blessings be upon you always.

October 2

Tonight I shall talk more briefly because you are weary from a hard day. What wonder it will be to you when you are through with your earth course and come to where there is no need for rest! But that is not yet! Until that day comes, your strength will be as your day.

The theme I want to discuss tonight is closely related to earth life and hence of interest to all earth people. You wonder what it is, having no clue to what is in my mind. But fear not! All is planned from the beginning in regular order and comes to you in that way.

On earth often the one point of greatest power is self—what each one can get for himself. It motivates most enterprises and many individual lives. Self-centeredness turns in for self alone and does not think of what one can do for others. That is not the life that grows. Self is stunting, defeating in the largest sense. It holds out hands to grasp for self. There is vast difference between holding out hands to grasp and holding out hands to give in generosity or to help someone who needs. The one who wants always to get, does not see how that of itself defeats him. The large life which wishes always to give, finds more and more coming to him which never would come if his hands were reached for getting. It is the same thing which our Lord meant when He said, "He that would be greatest among you, let him be the servant of all." But on earth sometimes our vision is limited and these simple things of life do not always appear in their true significance.

WHERE NOTHING IS LOST

October 3

I thank you for being ready tonight to continue the message. Your load has been heavy of late. But it will be lighter now and you have been brought through a difficult situation. The Inner Planes helped you from the moment you asked for help until your problem was solved. It is always so when the earth mind is willing to leave guidance and direction to the Spirit Planes—and really trust!

We were talking last night about the difference between grasping and giving. Here where we now live who have left the fleshly bodies behind us, there is no desire to grasp, no spirit of wanting anything for self. All is wishing to give every possible service to anybody anywhere who has need of any kind. It is wonderful what a difference there is between the two attitudes of mind and heart.

Everything over here is on quick vibrations, on electrical impulse. Everything is filled with life and glory and beauty. There are no divisions of purpose, no sense of disagreement or of vain strife. All is harmony. So it is no wonder that when men from the strife of battle come so quickly to the peace and joy of these abodes, they cannot quite comprehend it at once. Is it wonder that the contrast is hard for them to understand? Quickly many of them adjust to this new regime, learn the methods of earth contact or devote themselves to helping countless others who come and must have help in getting accustomed to the new world and its ways.

It is thrilling to see the ones here longer help the ones newly come, and the joy and pride in being able to do for others what was done for them when they came. When they find that the Heavenly Home is a place of constant work and growth and aspiring effort, their faces glow at the prospect. It is constant challenge animated by all the spiritual powers of peace and joy and satisfaction.

When those come who on earth planes have had special gifts and talents, let no one think that those gifts and talents are lost on the Spirit Planes. They are not. They are capitalized much more completely than if it were the earth level where so much is lost motion and lost effort. Here nothing is lost; nothing is wasted. Every talent, every gift is used and the use gives great joy.

It is a radiant world here. Clouds never lower before us, neither does the sun shine too brightly. Can you of earth picture that? Of course you cannot. But I ask you to believe it and to multiply it a thousand fold and to know even then that it is beyond your farthest calculations.

Don't ever let anyone, if you can prevent it, think or speak of death in terms of gloom and depression and loss and dark and cold and the end. Death is none of these things. It is the open door to a world of light and warmth of association, of effort that never is futile, of lessons which lift us to steady pitch of concentration and which in learning put us forward in the scale of spiritual progress.

God bless you and keep you and prosper you. Good night!

HIS PERSONAL PROMOTION

October 5

I want to talk to you tonight about the way in which physical death affects the one who is leaving the body and taking on the new garment of spirituality. It comes differently, slowly or painfully or suddenly as it came to me. There was no pain, no mental expectation of the immediate passing except that for many days my entire nature had been undergoing a process of separation from things of this world. I did not know what it meant. I did know that some far-reaching change was coming. My physical organism was letting go of the things of the body though I was continuing to conform to the daily routine of life. My spirit was reaching out in new ways toward greater satisfaction than earth could afford.

As I sensed the gradual break-down of the bodily cells, I knew it could only tend to one thing, the thing from which I had always shrunk. For I had hated physical death. But strangely and graciously, as I approached it, that shrinking disappeared. I felt reluctant to leave the things of earth with much incomplete and some things chaotic. Despite that reluctance, my mind and spirit were so manifestly loosening their hold on earth things that I could only accept the inevitable. The adjustment between the two worlds was made with such relative ease that there was no shock and I found my spiritual body almost before I realized that I had left my physical body. What sense of lightness grew in me, what power, what feeling of completeness instead of the frailty that had held me back and hampered me so long! How clearly I could see the glories from which my eyes had been holden so long! It seemed to me I could not see enough to make up for the years of my restricted vision.

How radiantly the whole wonderful plan of God the Father burst upon my inner sight as I saw and knew for the first time, how the plan for the eternities of all mankind was to function. It is such a blessed dispensation! So filled with mercy and wisdom and love and grace and Infinite glory! So vastly different from the narrow confines of what the world calls the orthodox plan for saints and sinners!

I have told you in the early days of my first elementary messages to you how I was met and welcomed by him who had been very close to me through the ties of blood and mutual congeniality. How blessed it was to see him again, not sick and suffering and shrunken, as the last few times I saw him on the earth plane, showing in his body the ravages of awful disease. Not that at all! But with an elasticity of presence, a joyfulness of countenance, a confidence of bearing that told me at once how wonderfully he was adapted to his new order in which he had been living only a few short years, as you count earth time. Nothing could have given me greater satisfaction or sense of well-being in that time of transition than to be met by him. To be introduced to the life over here by him whom I knew so intimately on earth and loved so dearly, made my path indeed easy.

Since then I have seen and communed with many whom I had known when we were earthbound. Always such meeting is fraught with joy and gladness and the spirit is filled with consciousness of growth in the things that are worthwhile. All the superficialities are disposed of. The temporary earth weaknesses are gone. The jealousies and petty qualities of soul that sometimes obscured the real worth of the earth person had vanished and only the Divine remained. What a difference it makes! In them! In me! How blessed it is and no earth words can express the tidal wave of thanksgiving that swept over my spirit as I realized it the way it is, not the way I had dreaded it all the long years.

What matters it how the body is disposed of? It has done its work, accomplished its purpose and like any other outworn tool should be laid aside for one better adapted to change and growth. The body which has housed the immortal spirit for more or less years, should be put away with respect and dignity. But the attention which is paid to details, at so great expense and at such cost of heartbreak and emotional straining as is often indulged in, is all wrong!

It hampers the soul in its adaptation to its new environment because it is difficult for the one newly leaving the bonds of earth to be held back by the unwillingness of earth's dear ones to release him and let him go.

Sometimes the spirit of the one being released from earth bonds is unable to go free for too long after the body has ceased to be the abode of the spirit, all because of a mistaken sense of love and devotion on the part of earth friends and family.

How much deeper devotion is manifest when all the restraining bonds can be loosened by earth loved ones and the one who is being promoted left free to go upward to life that is not hampered nor hindered by the limitations of the body! How slowly we learn while we are on earth. It is not strange. For then we see with the vision of the finite and hearts shrink from the feeling of earth loss and uncertainty of what the future holds for the one who is going and for those who are left to struggle with conditions of earth.

You have been through this experience so often of losing your dear ones and you have done it valiantly, though with deep sense of loneliness for their beloved presence again. Each time you have experienced it, you have come nearer the reality of understanding that "There is no death!" It is just around the corner, out of sight awhile. Never out of mind or thought or love.

What of those who leave their earth houses out of terrible suffering and under conditions of much uncertainty concerning their readiness to accept the spiritual side of living? No two such experiences are alike, even as no two people on earth experience the same round of living. To some of these the pains of separating from the body are severe. I knew nothing of this in my own case. I laid me down for the night. And lo! my spirit had triumphed over the body. And I was being welcomed by those who awaited my coming with joy and gladness. I tell you this for your satisfaction. And I tell you further, that when you come to join us you will have royal welcome to make up to you in some degree for the aloneness of the path along which you have travelled these years.

However difficult and strained the transition is for some, for reasons of bodily function, always there does come the freedom from earth restraints and the beginnings of true spiritual development. It is greater joy than words of mine can convey to you. I wish I could make you see it from this view point. Your heart would thrill with joy and you would know how wonderfully worthwhile it is to study to be ready for making this change from the body to Spiritual Realms. It comes to everyone. It is promotion and development. It is not loss! Not ever loss! Talents which old or young of earth possessed, work which they were equipped in special degree to do on earth, personalities that were particularly gracious and acceptable for difficult situations, all are utilized here in ways of so much larger service than earth could ever afford, that we who see the end from the beginning rejoice when we see the one who is freed from restrictions coming up here to employ his talents, his powers, his personality in ways of so much vaster usefulness than earth could ever afford.

Do tell anyone of earth when you have opportunity, anyone who grieves at loss of some highly gifted dear one whose talents and gifts and equipment seem to earthly vision to be lost, do tell such an one how much vaster is the field in which these very gifts are employed in the sweet reaches of eternity. Here, there are no restrictions, no limitations, no weariness of the body, no unfulfilled desires. Here everything is ready for the largest and best uses to which all one's best can be put. It is really wonderful—weak and impotent though words of earth may be for expression.

There will open to you many avenues for such service to those who do not understand and who have never had satisfaction through the teachings of the church with its earthbound interpretations of these spiritual matters. I do not say this in criticism. For when I was of the church militant, I shared some of the narrow views. I knew no better. But I did have my doubts, which were evidence of the vitality of my faith. Thus perhaps it became easier for me to adapt to new standards of thought and interpretation which prevail on these Spirit Planes.

I think the church as such, will not wake up and throw off its intellectual and spiritual shackles until it undergoes a tremendous change within and without, discarding much that is traditionally sacred but without any valid sanctity; until it opens itself to a Divinely-given program. Too much—so much too much—of the church program, is earth-born. It offers toys when it should offer the Bread and Water of Life. Hearts that seem the most self-sufficient, are all but perishing for that which spiritually satisfies. And the church gives toys of rituals, of social programs, or physical activity or discussion groups—anything except that for which the heart is perishing.

Not willfully does the church fall short. It is that its sights have been set too low; too near; that its heart-beat has been attuned to superficials instead of to the essence of the God-life and God-ordained purposes and wisdom.

When the time comes that men are willing to lay aside that which is ordained of man and accept what is ordained of God, live and work and achieve for God alone and in His Name, then will come such fruition in the realms of spirit growth and power and satisfaction and peace and joy as earth never before has known.

But such change must be God-inspired; not man-planned and set up as a formal program to be carried through on set schedules. Does this sound strange for me to say? You see my entire outlook is changed for the richer and the better.

What a fine talk this has been tonight! Feed on it in your soul, my friend, and share it with those who need. There will be more when next you are ready. And now I bless you and I thank you for your ready willingness to cooperate not alone with me but with the whole plan of the Inner Planes. Bless you!

ESCORT OF GUARDIAN ANGELS

October 8

Welcome, my friend! You are fulfilling a close schedule these days. On this your Sabbath, I rejoice that you have time and desire to join me again in this line of inter-world communication. You long to hear my voice as in the olden days. You wonder why you do not hear it. You say some people have the privilege of hearing the earth voice. Even so, this is better for the present and you accept it as a step toward further communion which will come in the future.

I ask you not to be disturbed at the crisscrossing of earth influences in your daily life, at the quirks of jealousy and temperament, at the one-sidedness of many views which are presented to you—not at any of the things which worry and weary you as you carry your responsible load. Be not concerned. Just move calmly, quietly, evenly through the days. Do all you can. Leave undone what is not within the scope of your time and strength and know that you are guided as you work.

Your mind leaps ahead so often to things you want to do, to people you wish to contact; and you see no time for doing them. I beg you to take moment at a time, do all which each moment makes possible, plan as you see the way opening. Do not go beyond that nor let anything get control of your nerve poise. Now perhaps you are ready for a talk on other lines.

On earth you have so many divisions of the church. What you call religion is split into so many segments, large and small. As time passes, these draw closer together, with few exceptions. They are seeing more nearly eye to eye, and coming to know that the separation is almost wholly a matter of things which are superficial—not of things which are eternal. It is good that they draw closer. The union will continue by degrees as men come to see that questions of earth organization and policy are negligible in the last analysis. Nothing really counts except that which centers the heart upon God and His love and His will.

The earth heart longs for joy and pleasure and peace and happiness. It looks everywhere for them except the one place where they are to be found! The human thinks that someday when the sweets of earth have been enjoyed to the full and the desire for pleasure has been sated, he will turn to "religion" and begin to think about God and religion and heaven. Then of course the heart fails of satisfaction. Peace and joy do not come. Pleasure falls short. Nothing seems left. How strangely the human heart follows its own devices which often are twisted and perverted to less than the best!

There just isn't any experience half as rich, as sweet, as beautiful, as satisfying as the close knowledge of God and His will. Here we see it everywhere. On the countenances of the young, of those who lived longer on earth, in the individualities of the uncounted who compose these Inner Planes! It is joy and peace and rapture in living and serving and worshipping Him who made us and provided for our every good.

It is a marvelous dispensation, this one of earth and the Ether Planes! Most people think of them as widely separated. But they are closer than breathing. Guardian angels are around and about you all the while, around and about others of the earth life, guiding, guarding, helping, inspiring at every turn! Here and there a comparative few are conscious of their presence and their help. You are now! But you didn't use to be! You would have doubted it and been as skeptical as the majority are now. The difference lies in your having learned through the messages which it has been my high privilege to bring through to you.

Earth people in their limited knowledge of this guiding, guarding, inspiring presence around them from the Invisible, say they've had an idea; or they've just worked out a plan, or something which they needed for an emergency just came to them, they have no idea from where! Rarely do they suspect that these ideas which they needed, all were the gifts of the Presences which work with them from the Invisible and who know the thing needed at just the right moment!

You start from your home some morning in a moment of haste. Before you have closed your door, there comes vividly before you the suggestion that a certain thing which you will need acutely in your day's responsibilities, has been left behind. You say you just happened to remember it. So you turn back and recover that without which you would have been hampered in your day's work. Did it just happen that it was brought to your attention? By no means! You and all are living surrounded by the glorified presences of guardian angels whose privilege it is to help you in every way.

Is it not wonderful? Does it not dignify living? Does it not show you that earth and the Higher Planes are inseparably associated? And are you not warmed in your spirit and comforted in this sure knowledge that you are never left to your own devices? But that always you are surrounded in practical and unfailing ways by the goodness of the Infinite Father? Could anything be more wonderful for you and for all, as you make your way through earth life, than to know that not a single moment are you left to travel alone, to find your own way, but that always the Father has provided you an escort of angels to surround you, to guide and guard you and help in every way which you will accept? Live this to the very full, my friend. And it will profit you much!

Many there be who will say that this is very strange in light of those who meet disaster, accident, trouble and the tragedies of earth. Where are their guardian hosts? Why is trouble permitted to come to them? Why does sickness torment them, if there are these Presences from the Inner Planes to help and protect them?

You remember a few evenings back that we talked together along somewhat this line, with a slightly different approach; and it was then said that man has as great gift from the All-Father wonderful power of choice. That power of choice has been crusted over with theological terms and debatings for centuries under the general heading of "Free Will."

If you and all others will break away these crustings of debate and know that it means nothing at all except the Infinite love and goodness of the Father who allows each of His children to choose for himself what he will do and which way he will go, you will make great spiritual strides.

There is the answer. Guardian spirits often urge and seek to influence the human away from the path that heads certainly into trouble or sickness or disaster. You hear people say that they "had a hunch" they ought not do such and such a thing. But they couldn't see why they shouldn't. So they went on into some dark abyss. No ministering spirits can go beyond the power of human choice which is inviolately the gift of God to man.

When man will not listen and heed, he takes the consequences. And it does not militate in any way against the fact that no human is ever left without such guidance and protection and inspiration as he needs. It remains with him alone to accept or reject it and the logical consequences which accompany it. That is clear, isn't it?

I used to pride myself while I was on earth, on seeing clearly with my physical eyes until the veil was dropped before them. I said many times, speaking of vision in the dark that I had "night eyes." When this physical vision was no longer mine, the eyes of my spirit began to see more clearly and I was grateful that I could understand better and interpret more wisely the issues of earth and many mysteries of the other side of life.

But when I was thought worthy of coming to these Realms of radiant service and life abundant, the scale of measurement was altered. The earth measuring rod is on a different basis from that which we use up here. Naturally so. You of earth must be concerned with many temporary and transient things which enter into living your physical lives, things which pass away like morning mist but are necessary while they last. So your human measuring rods need to be different from ours which do not take into consideration these human needs.

I wish I had power to enable you to see something of what it is to live here on these Exalted Planes of Spirit life! Mercifully your eyes of body and spirit are holden in their vision, for yet there is work for your doing where you are. And the two sets of measurement must not be confused, lest you be hampered.

All of this I say to try to show you that as we see with eyes of the spirit and estimate all things with the measurements of the spirit, the whole problem of the universe is different. Little things no longer have power to torment or to harass. We see as someday you will see—in the large. That clarifies everything and gives freshness of tone and quality to every phase of life and service.

We here are very eager for you to learn to evaluate that which is eternally valuable from what has only passing merit and to choose only and always the former. It will contribute enormously to your equipment, to the equipment of everyone who will learn these lessons which you will need to know as you come nearer the beautiful shores of immortal life. I've said it before. I say it again, for it cannot be said often enough, that these shores are not gloomy and forbidding and treacherous and to be dreaded. They are hospitable shores where those who have filled their allotted spans make their happy landings, finding to their inexpressible joy that here is music which only angelic choirs can make. Here is beauty beyond earth words to describe or earth minds to conceive. Here is radiance of color which the earth artist has never achieved on his palette of paints. Here is atmosphere of joy and gladness and worship and love and life everlasting.

Would such life be approached across a dark river filled with dangerous rapids or on a shore where landing was inhospitable? Of course not! That is not God's way. I tell you these things again to impress upon you and others that this is very truth and that it may go deep into your hearts, alleviating forever the false concepts with which your heart has been burdened.

God bless you now, strengthen and empower you to meet every need. I shall be with you whenever you need and I shall come when your mind and hands are free for service.

PROGRESSION OF THE SPIRIT PLANES

October 10

Your altered attitude of mind brings much to you that formerly was not attracted to you. Thus that law works which most people do not understand. You are beginning to understand it as it says, "To him that hath shall be given and from him that hath not shall be taken even that which he hath."

It sounds cryptic as one first thinks of it. But it is sound at the core, hence sound all through. To the one who has love in his heart, more love comes because more love is attracted, capillary-like. From the one who has no love in his heart, is taken what small token of love he may have had, there being nothing to attract it to him.

To him who has talent, one, two, three talents or more, shall come added talents by virtue of the use of such as he has. And they are bound to bring other talents in whatever line these are exercised. You see how the law works as inevitably as the coming of day after night.

You are not to be doubtful when you do not understand the working of any law in the Spiritual Realms. Just watch for the evidence of how surely it works. And you will see that it is as clear-cut in cause and effect as morning and sun rise. That is one wonderful thing to realize in these Realms. There is no inconsistency of action, no crossing of purposes, no failure to bring desired results when the natural cause is set in motion. It makes a marvelous demonstration of the surety of Divine wisdom and Divine law.

In the earth world, the word law is harsh and fearsome. It engenders the idea of penalty and punishment and suffering for wrongs committed. In this Spirit World, it connotes rather the smooth, frictionless working of the Divine will and plan, the bringing of good where good is established, the enriching of mind and soul where harmonies of the law are observed.

We no longer think of penalties and punishments. We have grown beyond them to larger understanding of the will of the Father for all of His children to know and to share His law of love and good and joy and peace. These are the peaceable fruits of His Kingdom and are for all who will take them into the heart and measure every experience of spirit by them. These fruits of the spirit are not for those who wish only to get for themselves and who follow the selfish earth law of acquisitiveness.

Here on these Planes we learn that the way to get, is to give. The more we give, the more we get. You too, on the earth plane are slowly learning that. It is a radiant provision of Infinite wisdom and goodness and transforms the spirit of earth living when it is followed. It too is law, beneficent and great and good. It is another facet of the law of which I spoke a while back this evening.

One sees such marvelous manifestations of it here on these Spirit Planes. The transformations which it brings in character-forming are amazing. For here even as on earth, characters are continually in process of developing. As I have said to you often, life here is one steady growth. As we grow, our spiritual characters strengthen and enrich and glorify in ways that enable us to serve in ever larger scope of value.

You know thoroughly well how impossible it is for any one of earth to stand still. That is out of harmony with laws of growth. Either one goes ahead or he goes backward. So it is here. Nothing is static. It is in every spiritual way one increasing glory of growth and service in all of which every one participates in proportion as his spirit has matured and his powers of spirit have developed.

I want you to think all of this over very carefully and frequently. It is so contrary to the concept which earth people as a whole have of life on this side. It seems to most earth minds incredible and all but impossible. They think of those who have made the Great Transition as being motionless and finished, as losers in the great panorama of life.

On the contrary, we who have come to this side of life, the multiplied millions who through the ages have been completing their earth courses and coming up to these higher Planes of experience, change and grow and expand in knowledge and understanding, in wisdom and power, in love and beauty of spirit, as the seed of earth becomes the tiny shoot, then the leaf, the bud, and finally the full blossom.

The figure of your earth speech is just one illustration of what I am at liberty to use to try to make clear to you and all who read this, something of the order of progression which prevails on this Spirit Plane.

Hold this truth very close to your heart. Dwell on it until it becomes incorporated into the warp and woof of your consciousness. It will stimulate your own spiritual development.

It will show you incentive beyond anything else by which your spirit can measure its increasing stature. As you look back over your earth years, you will be amazed and profoundly grateful to see the change which has come over your spirit. You use new measuring rods by which to estimate life and its values. Your point of view is different and your vision is no longer clouded with dense fogs of materialistic desire and ambition. It gives us here great joy to follow you in these evidences of the outreach of your spirit.

You have come to this place wherein you stand today, the hard way of learning through loss and apparent defeat and loneliness and all but despair. But as you have travelled this earth highway, you have never given up and always you have kept an out-reaching desire for light and understanding and for the power to get at the center of the law of spiritual growth.

You have not yet reached that place. But you are progressing with such rapidity as is consistent with substantial growth. Some days look dark to you. Such days come to all on the earth level. That too, is part of the up-working of the spirit. Too much sunshine is never conducive to strength of growth. There must be rain and clouds and darkness in which the fiber of the soul may strengthen, as the roots grow and spread through earth soil.

There is never any failure here to achieve that for which one sets forth in the conquest of the spirit. Always he is helped and brought in due process of experience to the culmination for which he is best adapted. Marvelous it is to see how this works out in every case. For there is no failure of Infinite plans and law on these Planes. There is not the down-pull of, shall we say, the earth law of gravitation against which you have to work while you are on earth.

That too, contributes the quality of strength and hardiness which your body needs and which your spirit must have. Don't you see how it all dovetails together as one marvelous design of the Creator, beyond finite mind to comprehend, yet working steadily, daily to help each soul in his earth struggle, and when later he has been promoted to higher levels of progression?

This of which I am talking with you tonight is one of the mighty themes with which we work and of which we study and learn here in these Spheres, as you must do in the more restricted ways which earth allows. But it all synchronizes into one perfect whole when the right time and way come together. And you will see that not one effort is wasted, not one struggle fails to advance you, not one lesson does not carry you toward your desired haven of spiritual prowess.

When you reach an earth goal, you set a new one, higher and finer and farther. So it is here. Always we see higher reaches for our spirits to attain, deeper and richer and vaster. Always to new summits we strive, just as you do. Our momentum is greater and our strength is more adequate because we have completed our earth courses and been called up higher. But it is the same law of progress and rewards and goals which you follow and which I followed as best I could when I was of the earth family.

It is all so vast, so perfect, so completely one great whole, that I yearn to reveal it to you more entirely than I am able to do, or than would be good for you. As always, one grows in orderly process—not in leaps and bounds. But believe it; hold it in your heart; live up to it in your every day experiences and problems and you will see how it works to your every possible advantage of growth and stability of spirit.

And now I would digress from the theme of the evening to chat with you along another line. Today you achieved a goal of long desire in your earth relations. It will be worth much to you in the years ahead, as you give and receive through channels of service and fellowship and reciprocity of interest and friendship.

This new relationship is eminently fitting and we of the Inner Planes have been instrumental in bringing it to its culmination. There will be much for you to receive that will bring joy and gladness into your life. And there will be much for you to give to others who need the qualities, the knowledge and the gifts which you have. I am indeed glad for you. I have watched you as this new aspect of your life has been developing and have been able to help through the power of suggestion and influence, as I helped you often soon after my piping to these Planes.

Take this new affiliation for all it is worth. Make the most of it. Give yourself to it in every possible way. Adapt yourself to it. Love it and from it will flow streams of love to your heart. Go ahead in your way of growth spiritually. Let nothing hold you back. Let nothing discourage you or make you restless. Just know that all things do work together for good to them who love God. All is working together for your good, even as I said to you soon after I left the body of frailty. Your road has been rough and uncertain and narrow and winding. But it leads steadily higher and you are making good grades now. Grow as you climb. Serve in the true spirit of self sacrifice. And some glad day you will find that you are on the parapets of the World of the Spirit where all is peace and joy and rapture in worship and service. God bless you! I bless you. This has been a wonderful talk!

WHEN THE HOUSE IS VACATED

October 13

I want to talk with you now about other sides of this problem of living as it is related to our side of life. For the two are one in reality. That which makes the greatest heartache is the body. It is that which has represented the one so dearly beloved. That is the part which has been so familiar and so beloved. But as you know so well, it is only the housing. Perhaps I should say it is only the scaffolding for the permanent structure of life which is the spirit.

But when the body—the part which you and all have loved and cared for so tenderly—has come to the termination of its usefulness and life passes from it, the wrench to the human heart is terrific. The body comes to seem to be all. Changes which come to the body as soon as life has passed from it, give death most of its terrors. These changes are so strange and the whole picture is so utterly different that it seems more than frail human courage can stand.

But the body was not intended for more than transient usefulness on earth. It was not built for permanency of housing to the spirit. The elements entering into the body are transient. Soon or late these elements are no longer adequate for protection of the spirit. Then indeed the spirit should no longer be held within the earthly casement and thus be limited in its outreach and its possibilities of growth.

Then either by natural order or by what men call accident, the time of separation comes when the flesh lets go its hold upon the immortal spirit. The temporary, transient housing, the body, has done its work either in a few years or through the whole human span of years and there being nothing more for it to do, the Divine dispensation decrees for it to return to the dust from which it came. Why not? Its work is done. Its mission is ended. It is eminently fitting and right for it to return to its component earth elements, the spirit winging its glorious way to the endlessness of joy and peace and growth and service!

I wish to impress upon you and through you upon others, the mistake which is so often made by earth people of seeking to prevent the return of the physical body to its original dust. Science has not found any satisfactory or feasible way for protecting the body against the normal, natural decay which is due to set in the moment the spirit has passed from it. Why should the housing endure, the scaffolding if you please, when that which it has served no longer needs it? The sooner it returns to the dust, the better. Tendency to cling to the body has nothing good in it and hampers the spirit in its adjustments in the newer realms.

I hope you will take this message, this advice, seriously and do your best to further the belief in the wisdom of permitting the physical structure to resolve itself into its basic elements in the way which nature intended. Thus every best good is advantaged.

While I was among you of earth, I felt very strongly about methods of bodily disposition. To you I say now that the method of my choice is far the preferable from every view point, as I saw it with earth wisdom and as I see it now from this higher outlook and with clearer vision. Since there is no vital argument for or against any method, no moral argument in any event, it will always remain that people will follow their inclinations, those inclinations generally being the traditional method of disposition to which they have been accustomed. Seldom does one find the person who thinks clearly enough through such a problem to break away from custom and decide for himself what is to be done and to follow that decision to its conclusion.

When you can use your influence in such decisions as to the final disposition of the body, you will be rendering real service. I am grateful indeed for the choice I made many years before I left the earthly abode; grateful too, that I clung to my insistence of desire for that method when the day came for the release of my spirit. Oh, what freedom and joy and lightness I experienced the instant I was let loose from the shackles of the physical! I wish you could know what I am really trying to say!

If only these physical aspects of death were absent, much sorrow and unreconciledness to the flight of the spirit would be gone! For it is only the physical which passes away, having completed that for which it was made. Wherefore not rejoice for that fact?

The spirit instantly joins the great host of those similarly released from the bonds of earth and begins its larger, more radiant life. That which has no beginning and no ending, which is immortal and Divine, lives forever! It is this blessed truth upon which I base my statements made to you in these messages—"There is no death!"

When the great of earth who have lived and worked in high places, come to join the hosts of the Spirit World, their earth greatness carries no weight whatever. They are here exactly what their true spirit worth is. They are rated at just what they have brought with them of spirit worth, just what they have built within themselves during their earth years. Nothing else matters or counts. Their earth power or prestige or wealth is worth nothing at all. Their only wealth is the spirit values, the spirit qualities which they have built within their hearts and which qualify them for entrance into these Abodes of the Blest.

This is a sobering thought to those of earth who often lean unduly upon their material possessions, only to find when they come hither that they have crumbled as dust beneath their fingers. The truest test of the treasures one is amassing, is whether they will be of service in the life of the Spirit Planes or whether they are of the earth, earthy.

We see here many a look of amazement and shock when someone from the higher courts of earth comes here to these Planes and realizes that what he has brought with him is of no avail and has crumbled already as if it were dust of the earth. As indeed it is!

On the other hand come many, countless ones, from lives of lowly service, who have thought not of themselves nor their ease nor their pleasure and who find themselves very rich here with such treasures as do not rust nor crumble nor pass away. The joy on their faces as they realize what their lives of loyalty have done for their spirits, is transforming. And they have their rewards!

I wish so often that I might enable you to see the entire scope of life from this end of things so you might understand more easily what the significance of many things is. What is dark to you now, would be light and many things which are difficult to understand would be as crystal to your vision. But it will come, the day when you will see and know!

Loyalty is one of the greatest qualities in the human heart and when it is translated to these Higher Realms, is infinitely greater in its outreach. Stay by it in your life. Of course you will. It will repay you not only while you are upon earth, but later when your mortal has finished its tasks down there and you are ready to begin this loftier, more satisfying existence.

Loyalty is another word for or another aspect of love of the highest, in whatever realm is concerned. Love loyalty and practice it. Live it in every relation of your earth career and, you will be richly repaid both now and in the life to come. I speak of that which I see and know in many quarters.

God's richest blessings be upon you and upon that which you are doing in your earth work. Its outreach is greater than you think and it will continue to expand in values. I give you my blessing and shall be so glad to continue these talks. Good night!

FLAME-LIKE FAITH

October 14

It has been great joy and high privilege to prepare the "bones" of these discussions, then to complete as nearly as we are permitted to do for earth use, the arguments with their earth coverings of words and finally to transmit them through your mind and your hands. Rest assured that the influence of all this will be far-reaching, both for the earth world and for the preparation of minds and hearts of the human before they come to these Higher Realms, that they may be more ready to begin their growth in spirit life.

Tim's amazement at the quality of much that you read her, is indicative of the quality of life and thought on these Ether Planes where everything is geared to utter truth and in accord with the eternal purpose for which it is being prepared.

Does not all of this, my friend, intensify your feeling of lofty gratitude for the honor which is yours in being the channel through which these words flow from the upper levels of eternity? You have, throughout your earth life, chosen to serve. And that is one major reason why you were elected for this work. Every ounce of your strength and every hour of your time devoted to it, will be your great spiritual reward, in God's own good time and way!

Let not the fear that some will question the veracity and accuracy of these messages, or your dependability in putting them forth and in sponsoring them, hold you back one jot or one tittle. Always there is a spiritual price for such service. Our Lord in His earthly life, paid it. His followers have paid the price down the centuries. Of your part in receiving and transmitting these words from the Inner Planes, many will be critical and some will be sneering.

But did I not say to you early in this series, that you were to pay no heed whether others like what is contained in them? I say it again. I repeat further; that you are being guided in this not by earth standards but by standards of which the Inner Planes have full knowledge. Abide by them. Know that I shall not lead you astray. Let no anxious concern enter your heart. Trust! And go ahead! That way lies victorious service.

And now I would like to talk with you on another matter which is not remotely in your thinking. You wonder whither I am leading. But you no longer are fearful, as you were at the outset—great gain on your part, another exemplification of the high quality of faith necessary for every great spiritual adventure. If I could show you something of the rarity of faith, show it to you visually, you would see the most luminous and beautiful translucence of which your physical eyes are capable. Not only translucence but sheer radiance of white as clear as crystal, as pure as the driven snow, as eternal as God Himself! That would be the high quality of faith that does not waver nor ask proof in earth terms; faith that adventures ahead joyously, banking on the surety of the Eternal God—and never doubting! Such faith would move mountains, as the Holy Scriptures tell us. And as I told you soon after my passing into this glorified life, it is all the Divine asks of the children of earth—simple, child-like faith in every issue of life and work.

This quality of heart seems so simple to exemplify. It is simple. But it is the very peak of achievement when the human heart is able to reach out and step out in absolute faith on the promises which the Loving Father has given, and not waver; not hesitate; not doubt; just believe! Just trust!

There is no limit to the spiritual growth that comes to the heart which can so embody the great elements of faith that give those radiances of life and of experience of which I spoke a moment ago.

It is not necessary to urge upon the child the matter of having faith in its mother nor of trusting the strong arms of its father. The child could not do other than accept mother and father in complete and satisfying faith for everything it needs.

All who live on earth are children of the Father. His promises cover every need of life and of the human heart. In sorrow, they are comfort. In need, they are substance. In uncertainty, they point the unerring way. In suffering, they are strength. In anxiety, they are assurance. They are all that any human heart can ask for. Living by these promises is the sweetest, simplest, most satisfying experience of the heart. They solve every vexing problem!

Yet because the human cannot see faith with the physical eyes nor tell in advance how it is going to work out nor why it is the way it is, nor the fashion of its accomplishing the desired purposes, these simple carriers of God's assurances, His promises to humankind, are left unused, quoted often, rarely lived to the measure of their capacity. And to that extent are human hearts bereft of life's most exalted experiences and deprived of the richest rewards in soul growth that can come to the earth resident.

The greatest things in the world have been accomplished by faith. Without it, life is lacking a foundation. I speak commercially. All such transactions are carried forward on faith in the integrity of all concerned. Scientifically, faith is at the bottom of the greatest achievements. In the area of emotions, faith is to be depended upon and will bring great rewards. I beg you to remember that through faith in the Infinite, every need, every aspiration of your heart can be met!

It doesn't matter that you do not see how. If you could, there would be no need of faith. When the way is clear and the going easy, faith plays not so strong a part. But when the going is difficult and the road winding and shrouded in uncertainty, then magnificent faith plays such role as cannot be over-estimated. If only you of earth would reach out and take hold of faith and live by it; lean upon it; keep constant company with it; love it and know that the bonds of Almighty God are behind His promises and that they will not fail, there is simply nothing that could not be achieved!

In individual life and perplexities, in business affairs, in community and national and international problems, this clear, flame-like faith is the answer to the ills of civilization today. For faith represents God Himself Whose promises they are; Whose word is out to those who believe and accept what He offers. To those who do not accept what is offered, faith is a vacuity; a non-entity; a mere emptiness. And they are the losers of all life's best.

You wonder why I have elected to speak again tonight of this matter of faith. It is because from these Higher Spheres we see so clearly how the absence of faith is hampering the plans for reorganization of society and government and every form of civilization. Until it becomes a component part of the planning,—this child-like faith in the promises of God,—much that is being done is like the house that was builded upon the sand. When storms come and winds blow and beat upon it, there will be no foundations of strength beneath it. The storms will come and the winds will blow. The foundations are vitally necessary. And faith in the ways of the Almighty and in His words is the cornerstone of what will stand. Mark my word on this matter!

Here and there we see shining examples of the power of faith to achieve what seems utterly impossible. Nothing is impossible where God is. And He is everywhere! It is part of our business from these Ether Planes to influence human hearts to greater trust in that which never fails; to substitute that trust, that faith for the unreasoning fear and grief and lack of courage which are devouring many hearts and despoiling many lives.

Thus I speak earnestly to you this evening, commending you for the measure of faith which has grown up in your heart, urging you to unwavering confidence in the power of the Infinite to meet your every need, no matter what it is! Good night! God bless you and keep you and cause His face to shine upon you and give you peace!

BOTH SIDES OF THE VEIL

October 15

Does it matter how sidereal time synchronizes with time here on our Higher Planes? Not for any spiritual purpose and not for any victory in practical living which after all, are the two most vital matters for the human to consider. While you are on earth you govern your living by the time systems of earth. When we from the Ether Planes communicate with the earth plane, the adjustment of our time is accomplished with sidereal time, rates of vibration are harmonized and the lines of inter-world communication are open! Technicalities are not of interest to the earth masses and might not be comprehended by them easily.

Therefore since they are not essential to spiritual understanding, they are generally passed by and the matter is considered only when there is reason for it.

Tonight I want to talk with you on another theme which will be revealing to your spirit and to spirits of those others who will share the truths of these messages. How does it come about that many communications from the other world are open to question as to their genuineness; questionable often as to the integrity of those through whom they come? It comes about in these ways. Always there are those who seek to serve their own financial needs through playing on the credulity of people, especially when hearts are in grief and bowed with uncertainty of procedure, or aloneness, or who seek light on the way their feet should go. In these and many related conditions, the human seeks help wherever he believes he can find it.

From earliest times, there has been great curiosity of the human to know about those who have preceded them to the Spirit Realms. Put these two sets of circumstances together and you will understand why there grew up a body of people from time to time who, for compensation, alleged their contacts with Spirit Realms and claimed their ability to provide messages directly from our side of life.

From as far back in history as the Golden Calf—farther than that—the human has wished to see evidence of what he was worshipping or believing. This attribute of mind has led to the use of exterior devices through which many have believed that physical manifestations were conclusive proof that word was coming through from the other side of life.

Cruel deceptions have resulted. The spirit world has been prostituted through much that purported to communicate with these Realms which never left the lowest depths of earth! This type of thing has been profitable in terms of financial supply to those who trade on the desires of the human to penetrate the Veil, and almost destroyed faith on the part of careful, conscientious people in the power of inter-world communication. It is unfortunate that this is so. But it is.

People make their agreements each with the other, to the end that whichever goes first to the other side of life will get word back to earth planes, showing by the use of certain words or shibboleths, that the communication is genuine. Often such compact has been publicized widely and the world, always curious about such things, has watched to see whether the certain contact was made between the two realms of life. When failure has resulted, the spirit of skepticism is stronger grown and thoughtful people become convinced that inter-world communication is impossible and not ordained from God as within the Divine plan.

That always raises a barrier of lack of confidence in those who penetrate the Veil between the two worlds and who do bring the most authentic, the most genuine, the most inspiring words which the heart of man can conceive; bring such words straight from the heart of the Infinite, alive with His love and grace and goodness, to the end of earth lives transformed and faith immeasurably strengthened in all that is Godlike and good.

Often it is that the most purely spiritual of such contacts are accompanied by brilliance of illumination round about the one through whom the messages are coming or by a conscious sense of strange magnetizing of the person or the room where the messages are being received. But not always so. The Infinite is not limited to any one way. Neither is the spiritual subject to command from those of earth to the end that certain words or phrases be transmitted from higher to lower planes of existence.

The sure, unfailing test of the validity of spirit messages, of the integrity of all which purports to come through from those who have gone on ahead, is the effect that is left following the message. Where the spirit of the human is uplifted and inspired and strengthened and made more amenable to the will and love of the Divine Creator, it is sure evidence that there has been genuine contact with the forces of good on our side of life.

Such messages are healing to the body and cleansing to the spirit. There is no reason why there may not be frequent communication between these two realms, provided the desire is not one of self-seeking or self-aggrandizement or for the sake of earthly limelight.

Such marvelous contacts are being made in every part of the world by those who often need only the open mind and the aspiring heart and who know how to tune in with the vibrations along which these messages come.

But without such meshing of the two rates of vibration brought about by desire for what is good and serviceable, there is reason to question the validity of that which purports to come.

As I said to you before in this series, there are those spirits who have not completed the change from the evil of their natures, who have not come under the transforming power of the Divine and who do not desire the good, but always the evil, even as they did on earth. Of them my only word is, "By their fruits ye shall know them." These too, are eager for earth contact. Sometimes they accomplish it. But the results are evil and are to be avoided. The day will come when their spirits will be purified and their service be good and useful.

When I was of earth, it did not occur to me that such communication was permitted between the two worlds. It was rather of an order of thing to which I felt superior and I paid no heed to it. But I was not long here before I saw how in error I had been and realized that it is part of the Divine dispensation to provide this channel of communication along which help may flow, and comfort and wisdom and greater strength than earth can give.

Just at that time, Tim was brought to you and I began to prove to you the possibility and the genuineness of this earth-spirit contact. It has done more for you than any other influence in your experience. Even as I was ignorant of this open channel, likewise are many others who are as open-minded as I thought I was on earth.

Through this series, you will give them as much truth as will open their eyes, enlarge their spiritual understanding and enable them to see and believe the close participation of this life with that on the other side of the Veil. The church has always avoided this great channel of spiritual truth, fearing that deceit and trickery and the difficulty of regulating the vibrations of earth with those of Higher Realms, would bring the church into disrepute. Thus through fear, it has lost one of the great opportunities to serve and to bring comfort and light and power and understanding to the hearts of mankind in ways that would be compelling and beautiful. The church has lost this opportunity in just the way that it laid aside all responsibility for teaching the spiritual healing of the body. And the reason is that the mighty doctrines on which the church was built have had to be carried out and brought into manifestation by humankind, with all the weakness and littleness and lack of understanding of high things which too often characterize the human.

Pitifully often the doctrines which are so mighty and so God-ordained have been left to small minds to exemplify and to little men to bring into manifestation. Often the result has brought the church into greater disrepute than would have come by standing by the sure things of God and abiding in the strength of His Infinite plans. Even so, the church has made marvelous contribution to the world.

Avoid that which is spectacular in and of and for itself; that which is patently motivated for compensation or for publicity or to satisfy elements of curiosity or to play on the inherent credulity of the human heart.

All such—and you can tell them instantly—are definitely of the earth. As such they are to be avoided though they may not be grossly evil of themselves.

The beautifully spiritual, the true contact with these Inner Planes, is always characterized by the sense of the sanctity of the message, by the inner consciousness that knows that such words as come are genuine, that interprets the personal evidentials as comforting assurance of the validity of the sender. And it always leaves the heart stronger for life's battles, the spirit purified and the mind ready for greater wonders.

With this I leave you now, grateful that I have been privileged to clarify this difficult question through you, for the many who are in doubt and who do not know what to believe. I give you my unfailing blessing and the blessing of God the Father.

WHERE YOUNG AND OLD MATURE

October 16

It is good that the hour has come for continuing these talks with you. You need relaxation and the consciousness of the presence of the Divine upon your troubled mind. You must grow in spiritual stature until it will not trouble you when words are spoken that cut across the grain of something you have stated. Always that has been difficult for you. But you do grow in that way and some day you will be able to let such things roll off your consciousness with entire ease.

Tonight, a theme in which earth minds are always interested! Do those who have completed their work in the flesh remain at the ages at which they left the fleshly garment and took on the imperishable robes of immortality? Does the baby who passes over while yet an infant remain at that age of immaturity? The one of advanced years, does he remain what earth phraseology calls "an old man"? Does the half-grown boy or girl remain static at that point of earth age? In one way, what does it matter if the answer to these questions is one thing or another? Nothing, except that it will give comfort to that part of earth questioning in which abides an element of uncertainty and hence of fear. Thus the questions are desirable to answer without going into too much detail.

The babe who comes to these Fair Realms does not remain at that tender age; nor does the man of advanced age remain "an old man," nor youths at the point of development at which they journeyed across the River of Life. Each of these and of all groups coming hither, grows gradually to the point of his or her greatest power in intellect and spirit and power to serve. The baby matures in spirit stature and in powers of intellect and soul to the place of his best powers of development. From the old person drop away the years of frailty and he finds himself without signs and evidences of decrepitude but with alertness and ambition and all the things of which he was capable at his best on earth.

There is no one that stands still. Always there is progress, so that the original best of his powers of development is but the point of departure from which he, babe or man grown or woman skilled in earth leadership, begins a new and unending regime of progress in every way that is finest and best.

Can you imagine any point in life at which the Divine Creator has not anticipated the finest desires of the earth mind and planned so much more wisely and beneficently than could be conceived by humankind? It is never-ending source of amazement to us here who see the outworking of these plans as you who are still cumbered about with limitations of the human cannot possibly see.

Nothing here is left half-finished nor incomplete nor unsatisfying. Everything which is begun with the powers of the Spirit Planes, is carried through to radiant completion. And what is done, is done with no ragged edges, no loose ends nor with lack of satisfaction which attends enterprises of earth.

It is part of the supreme joy of existence and service on these Inner Planes of which I have so often spoken to you for your joy and for the comfort of those who will profit from these clear expositions of life and service on these Planes of Unending Life.

Does it sound egotistical for me to speak thus of what has come to you through me? It should not so sound. For I have told you before that as you are the channel through whom these words are given to people of earth, so the words that are given you from me are carefully prepared by those much wiser in the knowledge and Divinity of these Realms than I; prepared by them and shared with me; permitted to be given by me with the personal evidences out of experience while I was of earth and served with you, that you may know beyond shadow of doubt that they come from and through me.

That re-statement removes any charge of conceit that others might attach to my previous statement, I trust. For here cooperation reaches its highest peak of perfection. We work together. We learn from those who are our instructors and who from their ages of life in the Spirit World are able to interpret the will and wisdom and purposes of the Master:

There is no questioning except in the interest of clearer understanding; none that is tinged with doubt or misunderstanding or dissatisfaction. Neither is there selfish ambition to outstrip any other or to outshine. All of that seems too paltry even to remember from the years when we were residents of the earth plane. How blessed it is to leave them behind us and to go forward unshackled!

I commend all of this for your thinking and digesting intellectually; but principally for digesting with the powers of your spirit, that it may become entirely familiar to you and you be equipped to help others over what may be to them hurdles of mental darkness and uncertainty. That is the purpose of these messages entrusted to the human you!

Nothing more which I would say on the theme just presented, seems essential at this point. So we shall change to another line of thought which will have much interest to all of you. I want to talk about the justice of laws which prevails here and operates through the ages with the hosts that come from every clime and age to the Planes of Ether life.

CONTINUING CHANCE

For justice in the highest degree is at the center of the Creator's plans for His children. We were taught—you and I and millions of others—to believe that death ended our chance of the happiness of heaven. Anyone who passed from earth without consciousness of spiritual peace with God through Jesus Christ, was doomed forever to punishment and barred from the joys of spiritual reward.

Such is the teaching of the church, of almost every church on earth. I preached it while I was of earth. In lack of other knowledge except inward premonitions that the teaching was incorrect and out of harmony with God's will, there was no means of which I knew by which I could learn a better interpretation of the Divine will.

In my deepest heart, I never believed nor accepted that the loving Father would blast all hopes of eternal joy, if at time of physical death, the one passing upward was out of harmony with Him. It scored too large an element of loss in terms of the human potentiality. And loss is never in God's will.

When I was promoted to this life of the spirit, I learned to my intense joy and absolute satisfaction, that earth teachings were not correct, however orthodox they be called. For standards of what is or is not orthodox, are man-made and hence are susceptible to errors of the human mind!

When one comes through the gate of physical death to these Inner Planes, he is just as he was in spiritual stature when he left the earth house, no worse; no better. The fact of dying does nothing to him except relieve him of the fleshly body. If his heart is attuned to the love and the will of God through Jesus Christ while he is of the earth, he is able to start on higher levels of grace and service because of that which he brought with him from earth—things of faith and goodness and truth and loyalty to the Highest. These qualities of his spirit are the measure of him when he comes to us.

And from exactly where he was when he came, he begins his growth and understanding and service in these Realms. There is no camouflage; no pretense; no assuming that he is better than he is. The spirit atmosphere is not good for deception.

If the one who comes has lived on low levels of earth morality, of truth and goodness; if he has despised these and neglected the teachings and the spirit of the Son of God; if he has done dishonestly and lived unworthily, when he comes to the other side of life, he brings with him exactly the qualities which he developed while he was of earth. He is no different from what he was before death except that his physical body is left behind.

He must begin just where he was, often knowing nothing of the love and purity of God, caring nothing for them, seeking in no way to do His Infinite will. But justice that is Divine gives him his continuing chance to build up for himself those qualities of soul which ultimately will afford him the same joy and rapture in the life of the Spirit Divine that the one enjoys who was a saint of earth.

How long does such transformation require? Who can tell? Growth comes in varying degrees of rapidity, dependent upon the eagerness of the soul and the entirety of submission to the processes of growth. There is no more definite answer that can be given. Those who come hither with hate and malice and envy in their hearts, do not find it easy at first nor for a long while, to be surrounded with atmosphere of love. It is not acceptable to them. For their spirits are out of tune with vibrations of goodness and love. Therein abides their measure of punishment for failures of earth.

But nothing is impossible with God. And ultimately by the transforming power of Infinite love and goodness, these hearts are changed and as the ages pass, they by the justice that prevails throughout the Creator's domain, grow into likeness to Him Whom they come to love and serve. It rejoices me to talk this through with you and thus to give you the correct answer to these vexing questions that torment many earth minds. You have in your keeping much from these Inner Planes which will be new to the earth mind and it has been trusted to you for use. My blessings be upon you. God's grace grow in you and abound with His plenitude of joy and satisfaction. There is yet more for this series! Good bye for now.

PROLOGUE TO PART THREE

EACH PART of this book has different and dominant characteristics. In Part One, the messages began to come through the "Receiving Station," carrying their many personal and well-remembered evidentials. These were so manifestly designed to make us very sure of their origin; as also to make clearer the possibility and feasibility of Inter-World communication. Of this latter, I especially had to be certain. I was not skeptical. But I needed to be convinced beyond any shadow of questioning.

Part Two moves ahead directly through me who was at first a reluctant channel for receiving and recording these words of inspiration from the Inner Planes. The directness of delivery made possible in this way, became more powerful than when it was necessary for The Counsellor to speak through a third person. The messages rose to more profound levels of spiritual consciousness, revealing wisdom that every human needs. Each portion of all this centers in the vast mystery of the Unseen World and is animated by the purpose of the Spirit Planes to give earth people deeper and more satisfying insight of knowledge into the other side of life and its close relation to the earth side. There is even so, in Part Three, a definite stepping-up to higher interpretations of all that binds the two planes so closely together.

The themes presented in Part Three are utterly fundamental to the good life and appear to belong more closely together than by the mere fact of their chronological succession.

Often in the course of this book, The Counsellor speaks of his messages as "lessons." He takes up a theme, discusses it briefly and clearly, lays it aside, then later approaches it again, some of them several times, from another angle and goes more deeply into whatever phase of an issue he is discussing. The technique is that of the teacher with difficult lessons that need to be explained and repeated to his students until, step by careful step, the entire theme has been covered.

A significant aspect of the lessons contained in this book is their universality. Except for some personal references for the sake of effective illustration, each sentence from him seems as if spoken directly to the one who is reading it. This quality of universality has been attested repeatedly by those many with whom I have shared portions of these messages which came along the ether waves to take their places here.

WINIFRED WILLARD
Washington, D. C.
July 17, 1946

FURTHER MESSAGES

CRUX OF THE WORLD MUDDLE

October 18

The hour is again at hand and I rejoice. Your hours have been long and your work exacting. This will change for your good before long and you will have more freedom. Meanwhile, go on about your business and do not take it too seriously. A lighter touch will be better for you. Things will not go to smash if you do not get them done on the moment when you would like to. Learn that lesson! It is a good one.

Many problems are perplexing the world at this time. Some of them from human viewpoints, seem unsolvable. With human wisdom alone, they are. With Divine wisdom, the answers to the riddles will easily be found. There you have the crux of the world muddle. Man has tried to run things his way. And he has made a mess of it. It is too big a task for finite powers.

Only as man comes to see that he alone is inadequate to negotiate world re-organization and to make and keep world peace, will there be a turning to the way of the Spirit Divine for the power and the wisdom that will bring to pass what races of men need and must have.

Here on our Inner Planes we see so clearly the lines of demarcation in which is being blocked out the plan for immediate post-war adjustments. In places they show light, meaning that there is much that is hopeful in certain directions. In other parts the background is as black as night as we see and study it, meaning that the human elements of self seeking and greed for power so far over-rank the qualities of unselfishness and desire for human good, that it is as if a thunder cloud with its blackness were blotting out the sun of a summer day. Not in this way nor with this spirit can the new world order come about nor peace with justice abide among races of men.

You of earth say there has been so much suffering during this war, that men's hearts have been purified and civilization will be on new levels following the peace agreements. In a way and to an extent this is so. Suffering in some portions of the globe has been unbelievable.

But in your country, save for men with the colors, in others of the dominant nations in the same way, suffering has been at a minimum and hearts of many men qualified to lead, have been hardened by the acquisition of more gold than ever before they knew. Not only with gold but with the sweets of unusual power. This power and the gold they will not easily relinquish. All the vast hordes of enslaved men must be provided for, that they may come to their full stature of manhood and render their just account of life at its earthly close. Ramifications of problems enter from every direction and run hither and yon across the human pattern.

The human mind is not in existence which can grasp the problem in its entirety and find solutions to it that will rid earth people of the sorrows that compass them. It will be well for those in positions of power to remember that with the Almighty there is no great nor small and that He is no respecter of persons. Only to those who ask in loyalty of heart and commitment of purpose will He grant His wisdom and the strength of character to carry on and complete such revision of the civilization of the world as will justify in some degree the terrors of this global war.

Years will pass before final adjustments will be made and the last of the suffering be assuaged. In the interim the entire pattern of the life of the world will be re-made. Races of men will be transplanted to other portions of the globe, balances of racial power will be set up that will conform to new ideas which will be put in force and be radically different from former balances of national and commercial power. In both there are possibilities of good but almost over-balancing the potential good, is the danger of this dominant quality of supreme selfishness in human hearts. In no degree has it been eradicated. If this sounds to you like bringing religion into statesmanship, so be it! I am talking with you tonight on one of the most appalling themes of which your modern world knows and which it faces ill-prepared to find solutions that are true and righteous. Unless they do square with qualities of goodness and rightness, they will not abide and the equilibrium of life will again be despoiled, with worse despoliation of the things of civilization.

Religion or no, the word of Jehovah is true. His wisdom is supreme. His plans and specifications are Infinite in their scope and their truth and goodness are for all men.

Anything less good then these, less well-founded than on Him and His will, can endure only while favorable winds of earth life blow. But when storms of national disputes rise; when aggression mounts and attempts to ride against his neighbor nations; when power goes to some aspirant for world leadership and everything is grist for his mill, then the house ineffectively founded, the nation insecurely grounded other than on Omnipotent wisdom, will fall. And nothing can prevent it! Some of them of whom the world does not now think, are headed for a fall.

As in the ages gone, with Sodom and other ancient cities, the one redeeming factor is that there are those in whose hearts the love of the Father abides and who desire above all things to do His will. They are leaven to the human lump. The leaven grows and its effect is seen in many quarters. All that you can do to spread understanding of this among thinking people, will bear its own fruit.

This of which I have been speaking is of the essence of importance to human kind. There is nothing more important than to have this house of the human set up for endurance through the next epoch; so that minds and hearts of men may grow and expand and come to their best possible development in the climb Godward, leave the low levels on which much of the human race has been living and come closer to the full stature for which God Almighty destined His children.

We here see it so plainly. We watch the uneven, unequal struggle against powers that are strong and aggressive. On the other hand, we see the prayers of the righteous rising like incense, asking for guidance and for wisdom; for vision and courage to do always the Divine will.

This cloud of prayer-incense grows stronger all the while, as men realize little by little that human limitations must be supplemented by Divine almightiness, the smallness of the human concept be enlarged by vision of the entire plan of the eternities for all mankind. Only as we lose our own aims and plans, men and nations, can the good of all be safeguarded and the way of the world's going be girt with peace and joy and satisfaction.

Isn't such a goal worthy of sponsoring? And isn't it worth urging upon others? For this time and these pending solutions, the life of the world has come to this climax of the ages and of all the struggles of nations and men. The world is in the balance. One way or the other, it will begin to sway in the not distant future.

Still relating this talk to the question of adjustments, I wish you could take some things more lightly.

You see the materialistic side of life as meaning much less than formerly. You used to crave earthly success in larger measure than now. There is nothing wrong in that, other things being equal. But because of your special qualities of soul and mind, you have been elected to this particular work with the Inner Planes which will bring you deepest satisfaction as you go forward with it.

Accept it with abandon, with thanksgiving and joy. Forget that left to yourself you would have chosen some type of earth reward. This is greater. This is enduring. This is of the sort that is given to relatively few who are equipped to handle it. And I assure you it will bring you great joy.

It is not strange that the human heart is lonely and longs for human companionship. But it sometimes seems almost strange to us here where we are empowered to see with clearer vision and with greater sweep of horizon that the human heart does not learn more rapidly where to turn for what does satisfy and does not grow stale.

If I could, I would tear that old word "religion" to tatters and throw it on the discard. It is threadbare and forbidding and misleading. Instead I would substitute the peace and beauty and glory and joy and service of the All-loving Father Who never palls on the heart, never stales on any life, never grows commonplace with any one, never fails to do more than He promised, never stops short of completing whatever He sanctions in undertaking!

Him I would commend in substitute for the hackneyed word which turns many away from manifestations which have not commended themselves. That word has encrusted itself with much that is extraneous and irrelevant. Forget the word. It is merely a symbol. Accept the kernel of it, the rich heart of the Father, the essence of love and life and of all things good and pure and true.

I must draw this talk to a close now. Read it thoroughly. Let its meaning sink into your heart. Share it with others. The way will open before you, never fear, when you can use it to the advantage of many.

My blessing be upon you now as you rest during the night. And the rich, sweet blessing of the Father be upon you!

October 19

My theme tonight is a great one in which earth people are always interested but of which they have not been safely informed. Conditions of electrical vibration are not good just now. But the way will clear and the message come through, with your patient waiting. I have been very busy on the other side of the world where there is great need among the many thousands who are coming simultaneously to our side of life. The courage some of these men exemplify, far from their homes or loved ones, in climatic surroundings which are very trying, their bodies broken in such crucial ways, yet often their minds fairly alert, is very wonderful.

Just recently I have stood beside some of these whose breath was coming more and more slowly, whose physical eyes were failing of earth vision and as I have stood there, offering such ministry of comfort as was possible, I have heard each in his own way hum some dear familiar tune of God and His love. It is wonderful that in the hour of crisis, the spirit always soars to God! And always it finds just what it needs in the All-Father.

You remember how I was thrilled while I was among you of earth, at the passing of one whom I loved dearly, when I knew that hymns of God and love and grace were on his lips all the night before he passed over to these Realms of light and life. It was the same with these incidents of which I am now telling you. Nothing heals the soul in its crisis hours like the consciousness of God Who cannot, does not fail.

I have seen one and another of these men mortally wounded and moving out across the River of Life, reach up a hand or two hands, if there were two, and whisper, "God, go with me!" And such light has shone on the begrimed features as could come only from the Holy One of Israel. It is glorious service to minister to these in the varied ways at our command.

When they can talk, there is always some message of love and remembrance and courage they ask us to take back to their beloveds in the home lands, some word on which those who are left can live and find relief in their own spirits. The innate unselfishness which is thus manifested, is heartening. In the crucial moment, it is of someone else they think—not of themselves. And always it is of God!

Here we are learning as we minister far and wide, how trifling are the differences which separate the church of earth, those differences which through the centuries have brought strife and bloodshed and discord and discredit to the God of the church. To these men, such differences fall away and they see through to the essences of the love and forgiveness of the Father.

Here on these Ether Planes, there is no schism, no Protestant, no Catholic, no discord. All are one. And the superficialities that keep earth people apart, are wiped out and gone. How gracious it would be if they could be forgotten while the struggle of earth continues!

You will be surprised when I tell you that I have given the last rites on the battle fields to men of the Catholic faith—and I of the Protestant faith when I was on the earth plane! But what matters it? These men were facing their last hours. They wanted the consolation of the spirit made manifest to their hearts. They wanted the consciousness of the close presence of God with them. They craved the rites of their church. I was privileged to be present. My heart warmed to their need. It was to them that I was sent. As I used the words that were familiar to them and prayed for them and offered them the Bread and Water of Life the while their own life-fountains were ebbing, the relaxation of strain, the assurance which revealed itself in their faces, and in the atmosphere surrounding them, were very wonderful.

Over and again I watched them loose their last hold on the physical body and with a quiet sigh of peace and rest, float away to Spirit Realms beyond the carnage of earth.

Later I have met and communed with many of those whom I helped across the River. Their expressions of joy and surprise at the life on this side of the Veil were such as I wish earth people might hear! It would forever put an end to the selfishness of weeping and mourning and lamenting those who have slipped over to this side of life. It would do away forever with the idea of death as a separator. There is no death save only in the functions of the physical body which was intended for limited time use as a carrier for the spirit.

Life itself is endless, without beginning and without ending; one continuous growth and filled with joy of worship and service of the Almighty, Everliving God.

The errors of interpretation of this side of life which have been promulgated through ages of teaching, seem to me a crime to the spirits of mankind. The Ether Planes have been represented under the figure of speech as of golden streets and gates of pearl—all symbolic. But by too many interpreted literally! Of course this is a place where spirits rejoice and thrill paeans of praise to their Maker. But it is also a place where each has his lessons to learn, as I have told you before, and service to render to needy ones in whatsoever portions of earth they may be.

Such activity exists here where we never are tired or discouraged or dismayed or hungry or dissatisfied, as earth minds can scarcely conceive. We go and we come with the swiftness of thought, wherever we are sent by our instructors to do definite types of service. Some of us are best adapted to one type of service, some to another. And as we are most helpful, so we are sent to minister.

There are many things which may not be revealed to you of earth because they would be beyond your comprehension. They were beyond my understanding until I had slipped the weight of the body and come up higher to where the mind and spirit were freed to greater power of knowing and understanding the ways of God.

The longer one is here, the more he studies, the higher he moves in spirit power, the more marvelous it all becomes and the richer the reward for living at one's best on the earth plane. God's goodness and His love are Infinite.

To those who have suffered great agony on earth, the release and the peace and sense of well-being here are too good to seem true. Sometimes one has been weakened by long physical sickness and is weak at coming hither. But that soon passes and gradually strength comes that is beyond anything the earth mind can think.

It is with the hope that these messages will help, indeed the assurance from my instructors from the seventh plane that they will have large measure of comfort and help, that they are given to you for spreading widely among people of earth who crave to know something of this side of life. So often, because of false teaching, they are afraid to know, lest they be terrified. How blessed it is to take away from their minds all sense of dread and to release them to knowledge that the world beyond the physical is one of goodness and peace and joy and serving!

As good comes to you in increasing measure, I am grateful to see that you lean more and more to sharing it with others, some of whom are as perplexed as you were for long and weary years. Do not ever let your spirit become addicted to grasping and holding. Open your soul and your hands and share with others every good thing you have—

your supply and your spirit of hospitality and all such can be used for real good to yourself and to others.

Never does it pay to let the spirit of hoarding gain any hold upon one. You have never been in any slightest danger there, being inclined sometimes to forget yourself for the sake of the other person. Err on that side rather than on the side of greedy grasping and holding tightly for one's self alone.

The healing power of the Christ of God will permeate your body as you ask for it and accept it, for your strengthening. Do not question whether it will come to you. Know that it does come and that it washes away all weakness and sickness.

Take the healing touch, strength for weakness, as from Him Who is able to do and to be all things to you, whatever your need.

There is nothing the living, loving God cannot or will not do for you, when you ask in faith believing! And now our talk for the evening is over and I leave you for other service. God bless and heal and help you; keep you and guide and love you. Amen!

October 20

So much hinges on all of this being put out in printed form for the comfort of sorrowing hearts and the strengthening of doubtful spirits! Sheltered as you are, you cannot conceive the extent of the agony of the world these cruel days of suffering. Even those who seem in easy and affluent circumstances, are oft times at heart all but desperate for the inward comfort and consolation which these messages can give. Do not doubt, my friend. We here know the extent of the need. We know that these truths herein contained, are the essence of Divine truth that has power to heal the broken heart and comfort the stricken of earth.

Have you not noticed through this series that there is nothing save what is utterly basic? Is that other than carefully designed that every word may perform the mission whereto it is sent? As I have told you earlier, the content of each of these messages has been blue-printed by those with whom I study here on these Celestial Planes and who have joined to help me present all of this through you, to needy ones of earth.

Do not be insensible to the honor and the responsibility hereunto attached! I who knew you so well know that you are very sensitive to all of this. It is because of these factors that you make the excellent channel for this Divine truth.

WHEN THE TRANSITION COMES

I wish to talk with you again tonight about the transition which earth people call death and which is so close to human hearts these days of unimaginable destruction throughout the world. Many fail to understand—and it is not strange from the human viewpoint which I remember vividly—that when one from the earth plane comes over to this side of life, he is not "lost" to the service of earth.

His talents, be they what they may, are not lost to his generation. His education which may have been of the finest which earth can give, is not lost if all suddenly he is called to enter upon larger and finer service.

The young scientist equipped for what the earth calls great achievements, coming here to these Ether Planes, is not losing that magnificent intellectual equipment which he acquired at such study and cost. If only we here could make earth people understand that such an one, any one, who comes from the bondage of earth to the freedom of the Inner Planes, is promoted in joys of living and serving; in richness of understanding of all things fundamental; in opportunities to help and in possibilities of growth for his own spirit! Can such experiences be called "loss"?

Those who come are not the ones who cry out at loss which arrival at the other side of life entails. It is they who remain on the earth plane and face the necessary adjustment for living without the physical presence which often had been dearly beloved.

But true love has no place for selfishness. And is it not of the quality of selfishness to darken the spirit joy of the one just come to these High Planes by a grief that casts a shadow upon his heart? Is there not a measure of selfishness in wishing to retain the one who has been deemed worthy of greater spheres of service and more marvelous fields in which to develop his special talents? Is it not evidence of truly grand spirit stature to put in the background any sense of personal loneliness and rejoice in the promotion, the recognition, the opportunity, the joy that have been bestowed upon the loved one?

When such temporary separation as physical death comes, it always helps the ones who are left when they can be assured that the released spirit of their beloved often returns to the home which he had enjoyed. It is very truth and consoling truth. It helps assuage the sense of aloneness and gives a feeling of kindred fellowship with these Higher Planes whither their beloved has gone.

Many times on earth one hears a father or mother speak of being conscious of the presence of son or daughter or other dear one recently gone from earth. Then deprecatingly, they add that it probably isn't true but they "had such a strong feeling that son or daughter had been in the dear, familiar room where was the shrine of home."

Certainly it is true. The beloved presence without doubt has returned for a short visit, to bring comfort and consolation and if possible, to assuage the grief that is darkening his spirit radiance.

Please lose no opportunity to assure grieving friends or family that whenever the consciousness of the presence of loved ones from the other world, floods the heart, it is just as it seems and that smiles from them instead of tears, joy instead of lamentations, will add to the satisfaction as much as if they were on earth!

For certainly earth people by this time must know that we who are living and serving from Spirit Planes know and understand what is being experienced in the physical more clearly than when we were in the flesh. Please help us make this understood! To us here the whole plan of the universe, physical and spiritual, is transparent. We no longer see as through a glass darkly. Only residents of earth are restricted in their vision and those so newly come to the Spirit World that they have had no time for growth on these lines.

The clouds of grief that these days sometimes hang low like black fog, are almost fearful showing how much earth people have to learn of the relations that exist between the two worlds—especially that great lesson of the continuity of life.

So long men and women have accepted the separating quality of death with a finality that is entirely wrong. It is defeating in its reactions at both ends of the experience. For death is the merest matter of the physical body which has no more place in the permanent plan of the Creator than scaffolding has to the completed cathedral. It has place and responsibility for a while. Then it is taken away, its work done and the glory of the completed structure revealed.

Much better than many of earth, I understand how difficult some of these lessons are. For I was antagonistic toward the thought of physical death both for myself and for those whom I held dearest. But once having seen and learned how wrong my attitude was while on earth, I never cease striving to help others see the way of radiance and of correct understanding of this mystery.

For physical death is a mystery to the human. It is fundamentally part of the entire scheme of things, though earth people may not understand the reason for it. In every level of natural life, the entity comes, lives its life and passes on, be it earth worm or bird; root or stalk of corn or anything that crawls. Here. Its work done. Gone! Every flower, every blade of grass. Here. Its work done. Gone! Thus it is part of the plan for the human. He is not designed for permanence on earth. Here just long enough to do his work, he goes to his permanent abode.

There is the most marvelous unity throughout the whole plan of the Creator. No human mind can comprehend even half of it. Ages come and go yet there remain limitless reaches beyond the spirit comprehension of those on the Higher Planes. To wish for the human to remain on the earth plane for more than the human span of life, is to be willing for him to miss the greatness of the sweep of larger life and be shackled longer than he need be to a small scope of living and working and achieving.

It is not intended to have one jot of selfishness in it when the loving heart grieves for the return of the one who has gone. But in final analysis, it resolves itself into what I have paid. And it remains for you through these revelations to help change the attitude of as many earth people as the printed word can reach.

When the correct understanding of these things has been accepted, there can be no longer any wish for the dear one to be brought back to earth dimensions, were that possible. It would mean depriving him of those years of celestial joy to which he was entitled and for which he was ready. It is all so divinely arranged when one in calmness sees it in the way of spirit rightness.

Of course much of the desperation which attends physical death comes from fear of what the next world is and whether there is reunion; whether it is a place of blessedness or of torment; whether those there have left to them the earth powers of memory and whether they know the affairs of earth. The mis-teachings of so much earth doctrine are largely responsible for this. Large measure of responsibility attaches to those who interpret the teachings to human minds, instructing in that which they themselves neither know nor understand.

Material considerations enter in largely, to cause resentment at loss by death. The one who is left, wonders how to carry on; how to provide what is necessary for living; how to readjust the whole garment of the home or the business to make it fit the new situation. Often this is at the bottom of the desperate bitterness against physical death.

But you do not need to be told how marvelously even this works out to good where evil was feared; how fruition comes instead of defeat; how the mind and heart expand to meet the larger needs; how the outreach of the spirit is increased by virtue of the shifting of the base of the problem.

How often this is true! New talents are developed; new strength comes in place of weakness; new powers of mind and body grow into the life of the one who had thought the situation hopeless because death had come. It is not so. Death is often a rich fructifier of the soil of the human heart. Does it not sound strange for me to say a thing like that? It is true. I have learned it beyond a shadow of doubt, even as you yourself have learned it through your own experience.

Thus often what seemed utter desolation of hope and prospect and future prosperity, proves to come with healing in its wings, bringing fresh revelations of the goodness of the Father.

And now the evening talk draws to a close. It is blessed satisfaction to know that this much is now safely in your keeping. I give you my blessing, God's blessing also.

October 21

God bless you for being so loyal to this for which you were elected by the Highest. Though you do not quite see why this is your ordained path, you accept it even to the exclusion of earthly things which might give you earthly pleasure. You will have your reward.

Today I wish to talk to you about those who will accept the truths of these messages and those who will reject them. Do you remember that back in those days when your first receiving station was the channel through which my words reached you, I spoke briefly about this? I desire to go a little more deeply into it today.

For the most part people of earth are materialistically minded. They have been so taught by precept and example. Their concepts of the Spirit World have been so far afield that often the teachings have been rejected when at the same time there was desire for knowledge of the way of life that would satisfy. But they did not know where to turn to find it. So, accepting theoretically what the orthodox church teaches, they observed its teachings on the surface and fundamentally have been dissatisfied. I was myself, when I was on the earth plane.

Such people, hearing the truth as it is presented by the Inner Planes in these talks, will sense with their inmost hearts that this is the right teaching about death and life and the continuity of existence, about the service the ministering angels render and the other truth which is revealed in these talks.

They will accept it with joy and comfort to their spirits and be grateful for this which satisfies the deep places of their hearts. Each such earth person becomes the nucleus of a center of faith and through that nucleus the power of the word will spread to other hearts until vast numbers will know more of the truth of being than has been known before.

Those who reject the truth herein contained, will do no harm to the truth itself. They cannot. They are themselves the only losers, for they continue, like the Prodigal Son in the parable of our Lord, to live off the husks when the abundance of the Father's house was theirs for the taking.

Some of these will criticize you. They will call these truths by names that will hurt you and your feeling of integrity. They will hold them up as evidences of make-believe from your own mind. What matter? You will know their genuineness. Others will know. Our Lord was mocked, ridiculed and vilified. And is the servant greater than his Lord?

It is in ways like these that seeds of truth are planted. From the planting will come a harvest of increased faith. But here as everywhere, some seed falls on rocky soil and does not bring forth that which was intended. Pay no heed to this. It is the law of nature. And the law works, whether you like it or not. It brings rich and full harvest despite such seed as falls on thin or rocky soil. Be content with the fruits which come forth from that which falls on good soil and know that you are serving the cause of Truth and of God in worthy proportion.

Results are never that with which we are to be concerned. They take care of themselves when each spirit does the work which is allocated to him in loyalty and devotion. The same law holds and is part of the fundamental law of the All-wise Creator.

Know that your business is to prepare the ground, plant the seed, and cultivate the growing awareness of Divine truth whenever and wherever you find it. Then you can safely let results take care of themselves.

I am saying all this again and at somewhat greater length because it was necessary to fortify your spirit against the day when you may feel a sense of discouragement in this special mission which you have been chosen to perform. You will not be left alone at any time. Always there will be celestial guidance for your help and you will know that all is well. Take whatever comes in this way and be grateful.

The electrical vibrations are not as clear today as sometimes and you may feel a sense of interruption in the coming through of the message. That is temporary and should cause you no distress. They are to such communications as these, what superficialities are to real things in life, either on the earth plane or here on the Ether Planes. They do not distress you now as once they did. Such is the process of growth through experience. Growth always has its price, in the world of natural law or in the realms of the spirit.

The saints of God who come hither through great tribulation, paid the price of their spirit stature beyond what earth could understand or appreciate. That again, is the law in its working. But with the paying of the price, there come great joy and satisfaction in the inmost places of the spirit. The world today pays the price of the growth of temporal and material power, which was so out of balance as to throw the scales of modern civilization completely awry and threaten the existence of world governments for many generations.

Ungodly growth this has been. Like a noxious weed which spreads and grows up with speed, beyond the power of careful conservators of life to prevent. Its roots grow deep and eradicating them is part of the peace program that must come to acceptance.

These roots that coil themselves around the human heart and stifle impulses of love for the Father and for all things sacred and good, will be eradicated only at the price of agony yet to be suffered and at the price of such growth in spiritual power and understanding as now does not seem probable.

That is part of the reason for these messages. They will contribute to the development of spirit growth that will make itself felt in the gardens of men's souls where weeds of materialism and militarism and lust for unholy physical power must be cut down, not to grow again; but completely grubbed out and utterly destroyed until not even a vestige of them remains to sprout or take root again.

Here on the Inner Planes we watch carefully and see clearly evidences of progress along these lines. There are heartening signs in some places, of the rising power of truth in spiritual understanding. It is, as I said the other evening to you, like leaven. But the whole mass of the human problem is so vast in extent and so deeply entrenched in strength of root that there must be much greater growth in things of the spirit than now exists before this eradicating of evil roots will successfully be done.

Peace on earth cannot come by a treaty. It can come only through understanding the law of the Divine where peace is founded on justice and honor and love and goodness. There is no other way. Nor can there be!

To bring mankind to a concept that the world of the spirit is more real than the world of the physical and that the two are separated by a fine line of demarcation, is a long step toward planting seeds of the peaceable fruits of righteousness in the hearts of the nations of earth. Do you see more clearly than formerly how closely interlocked this entire plan of the universe is?

When men really know and accept that what they sow, they reap; that their earth power stands them in no stead when they make the Great Transition; that they take with them to the Spirit Planes only what they have built within themselves while they were residents of earth and that such lessons as they do not learn on the earth plane, they are yet to learn on the Higher Planes, their hearts will begin to change. They will see more clearly the uselessness of the material beyond bare needs of earth and eternal values of the spiritual power which they have often despised as effeminate.

Let this sink deeply into your consciousness and know that it is absolute truth. At present the prospect for enduring peace and justice for all, is not hopeful. But we see beyond the present. We know factors that are operating. We see growth that is developing, sorrow that must first be endured, disappointments that must be experienced. We see crucifixion of unwieldy pride and greed for power that must take place in many a human heart. We see shifts from the basis of selfish greed that must come and substitution of fairness in the plans of nations, before there is prospect of a just and lasting peace.

Many hearts will come to see the truth of the Divine law as it must operate in the affairs of men and governments before plans for peace programs will be other than ephemeral, something that will pass away as suddenly as it was promulgated.

There is no fooling the Almighty! Mankind takes the reins in its hands and tries to run away with its own will for a while. And like a wise earth father, full leeway is given to the runaway to let him see what is happening and how far he is getting from what he really wants or seeks. Then comes the lesson of following the law that is higher than personal wish or whim, and the necessity of adapting to its requirements, unless one would come to disaster.

The world of nations has faced that lawlessness, that irresponsibility of the runaway now for years; that disregard for any but supreme selfishness and greed for more power than the balance wheel of life permits to any nation or man. Always the pendulum begins to swing back. Mankind has that lesson to learn and to interpret in terms of nations and governments and of his own personal relations to spirit growth.

This talk seems to have centered largely around the ideas of seeds and harvests and soils, all centering in the vital fact that only as the seeds of life and service and peace and rightness are planted in the good ground of God's will and His plan for mankind, will the harvest bring satisfaction to the nation or the human heart. It is a hard lesson to learn. It is Divinely worth its pains. God bless you now as we complete this message for today. You have much to think about and to incorporate into your own heart life.

October 22

No influence of earth except your unwillingness to cooperate, can militate against the wide-spread usefulness of this truth which comes directly from the Spirit Planes. It is ordained for such purpose and to that end it moves irresistibly, as you perform the functions of channel from Ether Planes to earth people. It is not necessary for earth people to know how it is that we who are ministering spirits to the stricken of earth, can sometimes serve as invisibles and other times go in physical presence. That provision is determined by our instructors and matters not the slightest to us. There is no more mystery about that than about many another provision to which we here are accustomed but which is not revealed to minds of earth.

You see the two realms are different in their very fundamentals. Our vibrations here are on a much more rapid rate than yours of earth. Our vision is wider. Our knowledge is larger. You are hampered while you are on earth by the physical. We have shed the weight of the body and are open to much keener perceptions by virtue of that fact. It is something which you will learn when you come to reside in one of the many mansions, speaking in Bible terms. Until that time, it is better for interest along these lines to be curbed. Trust me as I say this and be grateful for the truths which I am at liberty to share with you. Many mysteries must remain mysteries until the human crosses the border into these Regions of light and life eternal.

Many another in years past has been privileged to impart to earth something of life and duty and God from these Planes. They are all carriers of Divine truth to certain hearts of earth. Quite naturally these follow a certain line of similarity in that they all seek to show something of what life over here is, and more of God's nature and love than earth minds have known.

It has been long since any considerable series of communications has thus come in responsible form and through an accredited source. The field is thus ready and ripe for a truly spiritual presentation of man's relation to God and to his spirit growth. Be not deceived about this. It is man's highest responsibility in any age, to know God and to live the earth life on the basis of God's truth and in harmony with His teachings. Nothing else matters. Nothing else counts in the finality of life. All else is vapor, gone as on a light breeze. The church and the world have distorted much truth about God. They have built up legends about Him and have pictured Him this way and that way. They have feared Him and have gone with no love for Him as the animating motive of their lives. They have wandered away from Him and wondered why they lost their way; why they stumbled and fell; why they found life flat and without savor!

The reason is so plain, so direct and so true. Nothing in all the universe can take the place of God's love and guidance and wisdom and power in the human heart. When He is thus accepted and when His will is guide in even the smallest things of life, the heart expands and life becomes a wonderful adventure of service and growth. When man insists on being his own guide, refuses the motivating love of the Father and wants his own way, life becomes as salt which has lost its savor. Inevitably so!

Earth people are wanting peace. They will get it on foundation of enduring justice only when it is based on the plain and simple teachings of Jesus Christ, the Son of the Father and One with the Father; only when truth and unselfishness and honor and the good of others all shot through with love of the Divine and willingness to follow His wishes, dominate all other desires of those who essay to be earth leaders.

Some of these will soon be removed from the seats of the mighty because selfishness and greed predominate in their plans. Some who appear in relatively humble positions of trust at this time, will rise to leadership for the reason that they place the wisdom of God above earthly wisdom and count themselves worthy of being followers of the Divine Creator. Watch the outworking of this which I tell you, as currents of life and war and government and peace proposals and plans for renewed government authorizations and sanctions occupy the minds of mortals to so large a degree.

Nations are building on the shifting sand that try to build a civilization—and base it on the human! Only God and His will and His way and His guidance can bring about a peace that will credit to the permanent good of the human race, after all the bloodshed which came because men tried to put Him off the throne of power and to guide nations and individuals by earth standards. What followed, was to be expected. And will be again, until the human learns his lessons.

You remember how clearly the Scriptures say, "Except ye become as a little child, ye shall in no wise enter the Kingdom of God." That still prevails. But it does not sit well with many who think they know better and who have no desire for the simplicity of the child mind. They think they can pit their wisdom against any other and come out victor! Think they have grown beyond being as a little child and pride will not humble itself to acknowledge dependence upon God.

There again free-will of which I spoke some time ago, enters in as determining factor. They need not seek God as guide; need not become as a little child; need not seek wisdom higher than that of earth. All of this is theirs to determine. But the law works. And as they sow in mortal error, they reap in tares and grief and destruction and utter crack-up of that which they try to build on foundations which had no enduring qualities.

No power of the universe can prevent the working of that law. He who obeys and follows where the all-wise God leads, reaps joy, and peace and permanence of satisfactions. I hope you will stress this to all to whom you may. It is so fundamental to the good life!

Turn now to another theme on which I desire to talk to you this Sabbath morning. Much of these messages from the Inner Planes is not spectacular nor revealing of some great mystery for the solution of which the human heart longs; not telling of things wholly new to mankind. Much of them pertains to simple teaching and precepts men should follow in living aright. There are many revelations in this series which have never been made to earth minds before and which will touch them with deep interest. Trace them to their sources and you will find that all is founded upon the word and the will of God.

They are the supreme influences of earth. Does the world think it has outgrown these and gone on to higher levels of intellectual power? Let the world-shaking holocaust these recent years attest whether these levels of intellectual power have justified pride of ownership!

Does the world think it is too modern to show concern about the things of religion, to use the word which has discredited itself and which I wish I might throw into the discard? What else has the world to put in the place of God and goodness and love and life eternal? The questions answer themselves!

Great things of earth are simple things, so simple yet so profound that human mind has not nor ever can expound or explain them. One—the love which prompted the Father to send His only Son to earth and to the death of the cross that mankind might better know and love the Son and the Father. The love of God is source of all right human love and is so simple that even a child may share and enjoy it; so profound that the wisest man stands confounded before it in utter inability to understand or to explain. So it is through all of life. Great people are simple people. Only little minds surround themselves with pomp and ceremony and display. In that greatest of all books—the Bible—all of this is vividly set forth. The Bible is not outgrown; not outmoded; not out of its place as guide and guard and compass for the safe living of daily life.

Why do humans forget it and think they grow beyond it? Let that question ask itself of all who read this message from the Inner Planes. Call it by what name any one wishes, it is the medium through which Infinite will is made available to mankind and Infinite love revealed to any heart.

Such messages as it contains are precious beyond earth words to express. And that one is wise who incorporates it into the fiber of his being; shaping the living of the days by its precepts; filling his heart with the love it offers and forming the judgments of life by the standards it sets up.

Let not mystery irk you! There is so little that earth intelligence really understands or is designed to understand. We know while we are on earth that certain situations bring certain effects or reactions. But why, is another matter. Earth minds acquire a creditable measure of knowledge. Few, except they base it on spirit, gain that wisdom which comes only from the Father.

Do not be fearful of mystery that is associated with what is good and true and related to things of favorable report. Let not the fact that you cannot understand it, hinder you from accepting that which comes from the manifest wisdom of the Highest. Understand what you can of it all and accept the rest on faith! Faith! Without which man is undone. With which man is empowered to reach magnificent heights of spiritual grace in the name of the Father and of the Son and of the Holy Spirit. God bless you! Soon I will come again for further conference.

WHEN THE DOOR OF THE SPIRIT IS CLOSED

October 25

Your world seems so confused at this time. I speak not alone of nations and governments which are more distraught than America can understand or appreciate. None living in that land of comparative ease and plenty, can imagine what it is for whole nations to be on the verge of starvation—beyond the verge into starvation itself!

Neither can you picture what it means to see those around you by thousands lying dead, unburied, mutilated, desolation inconceivable staring you in the face all the day and the whole of the night. Much of the rest of the world knows just what this means. For the most part, they are heroic about it, wonderfully brave, often numb with ordeals through which they pass.

Things like these make a background for life in many parts of the world today and it is not strange that the sense of distraughtness permeates the remainder of earth people with disturbed and disquieting symptoms on every hand. It is in the very air of earth. Scarcely any one escapes that atmosphere of disturbance which attends almost every avenue of living today.

You sense it strongly in the busy center where you spend your working hours and into which come so many lines of influence. You wonder why everything is so much more disturbed than it had been. This is the reason and there is no way out of it except through spirit power and by the exercise of prayer.

Very few know what it really is to pray, except to beg God for something and to lose faith when that something does not come. No.

Not faith. There was no faith in it; just a vague hope that something good might happen to them because they had asked. That is not faith. And that is not prayer.

Prayer is the losing of one's self in the atmosphere, the love, the power of the presence of the Divine, asking nothing except to feel that Presence near and to know the love and peace which pass knowledge.

Prayer is sweet communion. I have told you that before. I say it again because I want you to let it sink into your heart that prayer is refuge and a strong tower. It is the living fountain from which your parched spirit may drink and be refreshed. It is the dynamo of spirit power where your life battery may be recharged and where strength and energy of which you stand in need, may be gained.

Prayer! It has nothing to do with long and formal petitions heard in public worship and which too often find no outlet beyond the earth ceiling; no relation to the petition which is full of formal phrases and falls short of touching the heart which needs help.

Real prayer, the kind I covet for you, is in quiet, with the door of the spirit closed to the outside world, where the spirit opens itself in joyful surrender to the presence of the Holy One; not speaking; just listening; just waiting for whatever word or spirit of comfort or peace or love the Mister has to give to the one who seeks His presence.

From such sweet and restful communion, one returns to the conflict of living with renewed strength and courage, confident that the day is not being lived alone but that the peace and joy of the Comforter are present and suffice for any time of stress. Without such frequent periods of communion with the Comforter, there is not much possibility of calm or poised living in these or other difficult times.

I urge upon you the habit of such quiet times, when your spirit can turn from things of disquiet and seek refreshment—seek it and find it! This is the only way of growth and poise, of peace and satisfaction. As you look about you, on every side people are dissatisfied; rather, they are unsatisfied. They wonder why. It is because their own small fountains have run dry and their contact with the perennial fountain of Living Water is not in working order. Thus the flow is interrupted and the human heart is thirsty and parched.

It is serious. We watch it from our Higher Planes and in our worship intercede for you of the earth planes, that you may seek and find refuge in this quiet sanctuary when you and the Spirit God are together, where He imparts strength and wisdom and calmness amid the storm, which are so essentially needed.

Never let yourself be deprived of the opportunity of prayer. Never let the hours go by without stretching the wings of your spirit upward toward the God of love, Who has power for your every need. Never delude yourself into thinking that you are sufficient for a single hour, unto yourself and your needs. You are not! No one is. And there is no earth substitute for the rich consciousness of the closeness of God to your inner life which comes from the prayer of communion. Practice it! Love it! Grow by it! Thank God for it!

Some experiences of which you are learning these days, are sources of wonder to you. And you are perplexed about them. Your only experience with the invisible world has been in the messages which have come through from me on the Ether Planes. To you it has been a satisfying and strengthening experience. Letters from others on the earth plane tell you of their types of spirit communion with their friends and families on the other side.

These are so different that they cause you concern. They should not disturb you at all. For these people—and they are good people—such types of messages may be all right. Voices speak aloud that such kinds of communication do exist between the worlds.

But they have not been ordained for you, neither the other varieties of which your friends tell you. Let these be! They are not in error of themselves. But they would not meet your need nor would they qualify you to do the work which is expected of you. Not all souls are fed with the same food. Not all spirits need the same type of stimulation and of education.

This sort of message with its food for the spirit is that for the receiving of which you are specially ordained and chosen, that you may carry out your mission upon earth.

Let others have what is theirs. But do not be anxious nor fearful lest in some way you are falling short of your highest privilege. You are not. There is no gift within the power of the Inner Planes to bestow, greater than this one of receiving the Bread and Water of life which in turn you may share with those who hunger and thirst. Thank God for it! There are many ways of manifestation between the two planes. Some are as yours, filled with loftiest spirit substance. Others are adapted for spirits of different caliber. You have no occasion to be anxious or other than grateful that you are a channel through which flows the teaching of the Masters of the Inner Planes, voiced by me whom you knew so well while I was on the earth plane.

There is yet much more to give you before the series will be rounded into the complete whole which the Inner Planes desire. When it is finished, it will be a satisfying presentation of all that was contemplated through these messages, nothing necessary left unsaid. People of earth ask many questions, prompted wholly by curiosity. They will ask you questions related to these talks, which are not explained herein. That matters not. These talks are not a compendium of answers to every question, foolish or otherwise.

They are safe guides for living under the direction of those from the Inner Planes who are devoted to helping mortals who seek. So, do not be concerned when you must say you do not know, if questions are asked of you to which you have no bona fide reply.

There are all kinds of people in your world. You have been sheltered from much that was hard. But you are learning these days as you work through currents that swirl around you every day. Be quiet and composed. Remember that in quietness and confidence shall be your strength. That old word does not pass away nor lost its power. You need to put it away in your heart and turn to it many times a day when difficulties come. Draw upon it for such comfort as you need, even as you draw upon a bank for funds with which to negotiate the affairs of living.

It is always current and never is there absence of enough to meet the demand. This quiet; this confidence in the power and love of the Father, you need. Everybody of earth needs them. I beseech you to use them, nor let the strain begin to tell upon your courage or your esprit de corps.

You will be revitalized with the sense of the all-power, the all-love, the all-grace of God the Father, until it will fill you and thrill you with such confidence in yourself and your work as is beyond any doubt or uncertainty. Look forward to that day and work toward it in the confidence of which I just spoke. This is the way to carry through every hour of life, no matter where it is lived or by whom or when.

For God is not limited! There is nothing which He cannot do for you in any emergency as well as through the working out of every routine problem. Why do not, why can not earth people learn that wonderful lesson and find themselves free of the limiting burdens which are so unnecessary?

We see so much in every quarter of earth here and we long to share with you in the flesh the power which is available for the taking. And now, good night! God's blessing be upon you and give you refreshing sleep, with surcease of anxiety.

THE ESSENCE OF TIMELESSNESS

October 26

Our talk tonight concerns one of the greatest virtues which living on the earth plane calls for and which is not easy to cultivate or to practice. Here in the Spirit World we see and appreciate all that it means to earth residents to abide in kindness and to live and work in the spirit which is characterized by that term.

Sometimes it seems an over-worked term. There are those who think it is effeminate to admit kindness of spirit or motive. The word may be overworked. But the thing itself is neither weak nor effeminate. Certainly it is not overdone in the daily grind of life on earth. Kindness is one of the qualities of mind closely akin to love and tolerance and patience. Could any quality of spirit related to these three be other than a cardinal virtue?

Kindness comes hard oft times, when it would be so much easier, so much more humanly natural to lash out and speak one's mind, regardless of feelings; easier to wound; or even to be indifferent to others.

But kindness does not permit indifference to others' feelings. Always it sees responsibility for doing the strong, constructive, helpful thing, instead of brushing away a situation which is inconvenient and which selfishly does not interest one. The way of kindness is not the easy way. Rather it is the way of self-effacement, of self-forgetfulness and of putting one's self in the place of those who need consideration, and doing whatever is called for to help and comfort and heal and set right.

If qualities such as these are effeminate or weak, outmoded even, then living is turned far from what it once was. These qualities are the essence of strength and self-denial. As such, they are closely related to the Divine both in the forms in which kindness manifests itself and in the ways it takes shape in thought and speech. To speak kindly always in the heat and stress of modern living, or in any age, is test of the degree of Christ-like spirit and of the extent to which one is living and showing forth His qualities.

Kindness is part of Christian discipleship. It was part of our Lord's ministry on earth and entered in no uncertain degree to making Him beloved and believed, trusted and accepted.

Just plain kindness to your fellow human, regardless of color or age or condition, Christ-like kindness! Many a time it has brought smiles to weary faces and courage to hearts that were ready to falter, to fail and yield up the ghost of life. Does this seem to you rather flat and a bit stale after the things which have come in these messages from the Inner Planes, things of rare knowledge about our lives over here? Believe me, this simple quality of which I elect to speak a short while tonight could revolutionize the whole world; make wars to cease; go far toward setting up governments that would endure; advance the degree of civilization and make the world and all of its residents more like the Master of the Universe. Does that seem a slight thing? It is one of the rich elements of the human spirit which is dedicated to growth in the things that abide.

Nothing is small or insignificant or flat that can help someone carry a load and ease it in the carrying. No aspect of mortal life is more closely related to self control where instead of the hasty word or unkind act, kindness steps to the fore and the gracious word is spoken, the helpful act performed.

It is of the essence of timelessness, as all virtues are which are of the spirit. For you remember time is not a factor with us on any plane of spirit living. We have progressed beyond the arbitrary limits of your earth time and find it hard sometimes to bear in mind the metes and bounds of days and nights; of weeks and years with which your lives are bound about.

To us these time divisions seem crippling and confining. It is so good to be out from under them, free and without the limitations to which these divisions of sidereal time subject you. When you come over to our side of life, you too sense the perfectly marvelous freedom from all things material and physical and know how worthwhile it was to discipline yourself on earth to the acceptance of only such things as would advance your spiritual growth, to the end that you find yourself adapted to our life and ready to begin a life of great joy and service and understanding and love and adoration.

This homely quality of kindness in every walk of life reveals itself in the fabric of the spirit and is no inconsiderable factor in developing the spiritual nature to the point of being ready to make the Great Transition from earth to the endlessness of eternity.

METHODS OF COMMUNICATING

And now I am permitted to tell you more than usual of some aspects of our living over here on the Inner Planes. You have never become addicted to idle curiosity about the things of life beyond the Veil. You have refrained from asking questions that were not pertinent to your highest good. All of this reveals a growing spiritual discernment which augurs well for you, as for anyone who restrains useless questionings and devotes the energy of mind and spirit to matters of permanent moment.

You have wondered many times at that which others have told you, concerning our modes of communication over here. You heard me say once to Tim that I thanked her for the use of her vocal chords in speaking through her for your help. That of itself tells you that when we lay aside the physical body, old and out-worn or young and scarcely developed, we generally depart from the earth fashion of speaking through the mechanism of the throat and other organs of speech.

Instead we communicate by the power of thought which is far more effective, simpler, and once one is accustomed to it, is very beautiful. Again it is that earth restrictions are laid aside and the way of greater freedom becomes ours.

As I am speaking to you through this series of talks, I am energizing your mind with the power of my spirit, pouring these messages into your mind through the conscious medium of thought, so that there is no slightest doubt of your accurately receiving that which I send.

I would not be misunderstood or misinterpreted into meaning that we have no powers of vocal speech. We do. Tim has told you that she has heard my audible voice. Often she hears with her physical ears which for years have been attuned to catching voices from these glorious Planes of Spirit Life.

Others of your friends have the experience of hearing from their loved ones on these Planes. They hear, as they assert and as is undoubtedly correct, with their physical ears as ones from our side of life speak words of guidance and comfort and inspiration to them.

But for the most part and as we communicate among ourselves in the busy activities of our learning and serving, it is by the powerful medium of thought transference. It is not given to me at this time to explain the method to you. You do not need to know that. Nor does any one of earth need to know. Therefore we pass over it for the sake of speaking of relative merits of different methods by which earth residents gain the power of receiving the spoken word from our Planes.

Some of you feel that that which is heard by the physical ear is evidence of stronger contact with the Spirit World. Others tell you, as some already have, that the power of thought which flows through your mind and guides your hands as you fashion those thoughts on paper, is more convincing.

I tell you that whichever way the message comes from the Planes of Spirit, once you are convinced of the one who is speaking to you and of the genuineness of the message, is the best way for you. There is no reason for thinking that one way is the only way when we have at our disposal all the powers of the Mighty God.

In this as in everything else we do, we seek to adapt our service and our helpfulness to the highest standards of that which we are getting across to the mortal mind. Now isn't that reasonable? You know you can believe me. And you know that it is I who speak to you. So rest that doubt, which is merely a question within your mind.

With us, so should it be with you in every problem of daily living,—choose the way that is most favorably adapted to the purpose for which it is being done. Lay aside clumsy ways in any line. If you do not know better ones, ask us! We can and will suggest to any who ask, more approved ways and methods for transacting the work of the world. That is kindly service as much as any other thing which we are privileged to do. But remember that in the spirit, there is no great nor small!

Any work which is honorable and worthy of doing, is worth as much to the heart of the Father as the most spectacular act of leadership which ever received acclaim in the eyes of the public. Again I ask you to remember that whatever is done in honesty of intent and purpose, with the best of one's ability and all of one's powers, is as great in the eyes of the Divine as what is loudly applauded and seen of all men.

This should take away all the sting of feeling that sometimes your work, anyone's work, is out of sight and more or less insignificant or mechanical. It is not. It is part of the discipline to which every earth soul is subjected on its way to these Higher Spheres. So take everything which comes for your doing, put your most loyal and best into it and know that it will receive the blessing of the Father in Heaven.

Our visit for tonight is over. Bless you and may God rest and help and comfort you. Good night!

THE FEATURES OF OUR COUNTENANCES

October 27

Thank you for your loyalty. It is a basic element in all true living—loyalty to the highest one knows in his own heart. If earth people accepted such loyalty in daily life and exemplified it by their living in all ways, large and small, patterns of life on your earth would be made over and glorified in the twinkling of an eye.

Many earth residents who have proved for themselves the authenticity of inter-world communication and whose inner ears frequently receive messages from the Higher Planes, wonder about many things on our side of life. Some of them—many of them—I have discussed with you in this series. One question frequently mentioned is whether we who have left our earth bodies behind us and have come over to the sunny side of life, bear the same features of countenance as when we were robed in our garments of flesh and walked the highways of earth.

Really, it is of small consequence as far as our service and our values to earth people are concerned, how we appear. But I am permitted to tell you for the purposes of this book, that our spiritual countenances do resemble the features which were known and loved by our dear ones on the earth plane. No other way would be reasonable, would it? For I have told you that friends coming over the Shining River from earth, are so glad to be greeted by those whom they have known and loved on the other side of life!

If we did not look as once we did, how would we be recognized? And how would their hearts rejoice if we looked so different that we were to them as strange creations with whom there were no close bond of love? Of course! It is all as reasonable and as right as everything which the Creator has made. Only when the human meddles and muddles do the lines cross and things go awry.

You will remember that time when Larry came and spoke to Tim there in your earth home, that he spoke about his sister who had been ill so long, had lost flesh but had regained it and was very beautiful over here on these Planes where they see each other often. Would Larry have spoken that way to Tim had it not been true? Would I have told you that I was met by the surgeon whom I loved as my own son if I could not have recognized him when I made the crossing from earth life to spirit life? Could I have recognized him if he did not look as he did the many years when I knew him and loved him tenderly? And yet there is a difference! Every one through all the ages who lives the earth life carries the body of the physical as the casing of the soul through the earth years. Live as best one may, even the ascetic, the saint, the one wholly devoted to spiritual phases of life, it yet remains that on earth, it is the earth life that must be lived and earth conditions that must be faced.

The food one eats enters as a factor in the appearance of the body. The climate in which one's habitat is located, contributes certain qualities to the texture of the body. The kind of work one is called upon to do is involved in the general appearance of the physical, both in muscular structure and in facial features.

But when at time of the Crossing, one lays those physical factors aside, their work done, the physical no longer needed as abode of the spirit, do you not see how and why there comes inevitably a marked change in quality of features without changing the form of them or without removing those elements which designated or set apart from all others, the ones who are so dearly beloved?

What I am saying is that on these Ether Planes, the inevitable grossness of the flesh due to the work one does and the life one lives, due to the fact that the body is composed of physical and material substances unrelated to the spiritual qualities of these Higher Planes, disappears. It is sloughed off as rapidly as one develops spiritually and comes into power to live the spirit life exclusively.

Instead of this for which there no longer is any use, there comes the pure radiance of spirit in which there is no grossness whatsoever, changing not form nor features, but purifying all until there is finally no vestige of earth clay remaining to hamper the spirit which has come to this higher level and from which he will grow to always higher levels of knowledge and power.

It is a marvelous provision of Divine wisdom. We marvel at it continuously. For here in these realms there is no failure of perfection in plan or in outworking. All is the glory of the Perfect in which even our appearances share and in which we come by our steady development in graces of the spirit, to participate!

I hope this covers the question with which earth minds have been more or less concerned. Since we are speaking today of these things about which earth people are anxious, let me be a little more specific than I was awhile back when you quoted a question from someone with whom you had talked, wishing to know whether as we go about the earth in the capacity of ministering spirits, we go in recognizable form or as invisibles.

At that time, I dismissed the question as negligible. It is so in fact. But if by a more explicit reply I may be of more help to anyone, it is my privilege.

The highest form of life is spiritual. To that death has no relation. It is eternal and immortal. The most important work which we here on these Planes do, is done in the invisible, spirit speaking to spirit, taking comfort and inspiration, guidance and power.

To that form of service there attaches no question. Neither are we subject to difficult conditions of earth living. Not that this is much of a barrier. For it is not. When we do take on the form of the physical for some special piece of work which is needed on the earth plane, it is some other form than that which we carried when we were residents of earth. Do you not see the Infinite wisdom in that? We take it on, we serve, we accomplish whatever the mission is and we lay aside this bodily form which has enabled us to do the work we were called to do.

Just the technique by which this is done, is not in any wise necessary to disclose. Nor would it be helpful if I did. You and others will be satisfied to know that we are empowered thus to go about our work equipped to do it at the best level. That is sufficient for us. It is fully sufficient for you!

Much in the order of life over here on these Fair Shores is different from earth life. Naturally! The basis is fundamentally different, different as the physical body is from the spiritual body. That basis of difference runs the whole gamut, as you so readily understand. As long as you are of earth, it is unnecessary for you to know, indeed unwise for you to know, details of the differences.

You could not comprehend them, if you were told. I was a stranger to them before I came over and afterward, until I became adjusted and familiar with the new and better ways in which life is ordered on the Spirit Planes.

To crowd life back into the restrictions of the human, if once you glimpsed the radiance of the heavenly, would be all but impossible. So for the most part, except where it is helpful in the struggle of living and overcoming the problems on every hand, you of earth are wiser to live in one world at a time.

And now your hour is late. Perhaps tomorrow will open the door to more things which I would like to say on this general theme. God bless and keep you in His sweet peace and under the comfort of His overshadowing wings of blessing and protection.

October 28

Your day has been broken up beyond any idea you would have thought. But it was for your own good and for the furtherance of your knowledge of things of the spirit world. Remember that you may learn from every one you meet and that no time is lost in which you are open-minded for knowledge, even though you do not see its value at the time. Do not fear! Go forward in the faith and confidence which will bring you to your best and which will further the values of these messages more than now you can know.

It is very wonderful to know how clearly the way is opening for you, though you do not yet know anything of it. Trust it to us of the Inner Planes and go on about your work for the present. What I said to you so many times when the first messages came to you, I repeat with strong emphasis—that you are to have faith and more faith in the power of the spirit world to meet your every need, both of substance and of bodily strength, as also of direct guidance for the issuance of these messages to the world at large.

And now again, God bless you! Sometime ere long you will hear my familiar voice with your physical ears and see me with your physical eyes! Good night now!

"AS WE FORGIVE"

October 29

When I first began this direct series with you, I said that I was eager for them to grip you with their significance. They have done just that! Therein lies much of their power from the human side.

For herein contained is material abundant for hungry hearts and thirsty spirits, on which they may be nourished.

You are a bit anxious lest when this series is completed from the Inner Planes, I may not again speak to you with help and confidence. Do not fear! The contact has been established and will not be broken unless from your earth end.

It is now your Sabbath. The atmosphere in your home is right for me to speak to you about an important phase of living that must be cultivated against the day when the human will be transmuted into the Divine, the material body sloughed off for the spiritual. It is one of the hard things in life of which I desire to speak—the place which forgiveness holds in the well-developed soul and the power of forgiveness toward the development of the soul.

The model of course, is the prayer which our Lord prayed, "Forgive us our debts as we forgive our debtors!" It has been so simple through the centuries since He walked the earth and taught His disciples that prayer—so simple to repeat. I was about to say, "To repeat glibly." I am right in that, though it may not sound quite right for such messages as these. But it is truth—glibly!

Tens of millions of earth people pray that prayer, some thoughtfully, reverently; many as thoughtless routine. Some seek to square their lives with it. And their lives shine like burnished gold as they practice that admonishment of our Lord.

I speak today only of that one phase—"Forgive us as we forgive others!" It is one of the supreme tests of discipleship; one of the hardest lessons for the human to learn in his preparation for the higher world. Yet it is essential. Without it, there is practically no progress in spiritual living.

It is human to say to the teacher, "You say do this. You show us how." Our Lord, teaching those who were to carry His message on through their world, knew that He was to exemplify anything which He taught. And when the time came, in the extreme hour, in the most difficult way, He did show His disciples all down through the centuries, how to forgive even them who were crucifying His body.

"Father, forgive them!", He prayed. He and the Father were one. Even as the Father forgave, did He also forgive. And thus by example which is the most convincing form of teaching, He proved the efficacy of His prayer.

Always there are those in the human who say that it was easy for Him to endure whatever came because of His closeness to His Father. That is not true. He had taken on the form of a man. He hungered and thirsted; was weary and would rest many a time. He grieved when His message was not accepted. He was tempted and did not yield. The agony of the crucifixion was as real to Him as to any other in the human. Yet He prayed, "Father, forgive!" Than which there is no clearer evidence of His own forgiveness of those who were doing Him to death.

There is a phrase which was current while I was on the earth plane, which says, "I'll forgive; but I'll never forget!" He who says or thinks that, knows not the first iota of what it means to forgive; knows nothing of the spiritual discipline involved in forgiving and hence nothing of the progress of the spirit which comes from forgiving.

He who forgives any act of harm, any experience of injustice of whatever kind, has all but forgotten it when the forgiveness is completed. It is wiped from the slate of his heart and is of the past, leaving only such sense of rightness and lightness as must naturally follow a spiritual experience of that supreme sort.

In daily routines, there come infinitude of such occasions when slights, misrepresentations, falsehoods, betrayals and kindred experiences hurt the heart. Two ways are open to the one suffering them. Only two ways. To carry the load of revenge or hate or spite or remembrance of all that has been done and bog one's mind down to the mire of these levels; or to commit them immediately to the Lord, throw off their load of intended harm, pray for forgiveness to fill your heart, accept it as given the instant it is asked and go free from the load that will swamp anybody who is foolish enough to carry it. To carry it does only one thing—brings bitterness which fouls the spirit and keeps living at low earth levels.

To slough it off, committing it to Him, leaves the spirit free to go unhampered, with a song of thankfulness that it need not be carried and never again be remembered. The corollary of forgiving is always forgetting! Don't forget that ever!

Often from these Inner Planes, we see those who struggle with the problem of forgiveness and how to accomplish it. Not infrequently we offer ways to help bring about that spirit of forgiveness which frees the heart and lifts the load, leaving joy and freedom in place of that which could crush and destroy. It is wonderful to serve that way. How I wish earth people could see the direct relation between that and the joy that transforms when the spirit has been freed.

Joy is such a word with us here on the Ether Planes. Not only such a word. It is such a continuing experience. It does more than earth people can imagine toward forwarding growth in spiritual life. You may find it difficult to believe because there have been many people down where you live, who claim much spiritually and whose lives fail to show forth much joy. Here as upon earth, it is not yours nor ours to pass judgment upon another.

But let me say that on the plane where you live and on the one where we live who have passed the Veil, joy is one of the supreme experiences of those who most closely exemplify the life of pure spirit. How could it be otherwise? For God is good. He is love. He is light. And power. And life unending. He is everything which any one at any time in the endlessness of experience, can desire. And wouldn't that bring joy to anyone who asks? On earth, that person is at his best whose heart is filled with joy. Crimes are not committed by such. Harm is never done to another when joy fills the heart. Discouragement could not load its burdens upon any one whose heart rejoices. There can be no long face, no sense of depression or oppression when joy fills the heart.

However hard the task, joy makes it lighter. However stiff the grade, joy is strength to the heart and stimulus to the body. Joy transforms daily living. When one comes up here to these Planes of Spirit Power, it is one of the first characteristics which he sees. So different from what he has been taught to fear and to dread! Nothing cold or damp or lifeless or forbidding! All joy and light and love and welcome and service and music and busy working at the problems which we are to help earth residents solve; working too, at learning more of Infinite wisdom, and how to use this for the service of those who need.

It is beyond my power to imagine these Spirit Planes without the radiant joy which is on the countenance of every one and which characterizes our every deed and thought.

What joy does for us who have come up through many trials of earth; who know what they mean and what it is to conquer them, joy will do for every earth heart. Why won't you there—I do not limit this to you personally—get this sense of joy and know that it is the finest specific for the solution of any problem that earth affords?

Joy puts physical strength into your body where fear or dread tears down the functions of every organ. Joy so vitalizes your mind that things impossible under the weight of doubt or discouragement, quickly come to correct solutions. And you find there is no problem at all!

Joy sharpens every faculty of mind and body. And it is to be had by anyone anywhere. It is a spiritual possession and does not depend upon money in the bank nor any other physical possession.

Drop forever the thought that it is easy for those who have plenty, to know joy. There is nothing to that. It does not work that way. Joy does not come as a result of riches or magnificence of living or of any earthly thing. Joy is wholly of the spirit and comes from closeness to the Divine. It is free; without money and without price; to be had for the asking!

When joy comes to your heart, you can put it to work at once for you, to solve perplexities, open doors to opportunities of service, and to friendships and human relationships which are among the richest experiences of human life. All of this and more than I can express to you, joy does for you.

The entire atmosphere of living is changed when joy takes the place of gloom. It gets you nowhere, physically or spiritually. No one has the right to go about with a long face or a heart from which the sun of joyfulness fails to shed its warmth and comfort.

Does anyone ask how it is possible to have this joy in the face of such agony as fills the theater of earth today?

Spiritual qualities born of Infinite goodness are not dependent upon earth conditions, as I have explained to you before. Joy is a spiritual quality and is possible because it is of God Who never fails and never changes. It will bring influences of peace and of reorganization of earth governments more surely, more safely and permanently than its absence. For it is of God! Try it, I beseech you, any who need it! I bless you now with God's love and peace and joy unspeakable.

THE PARADOX IN SACRIFICE

October 30

While we are together this afternoon, I wish to talk to you on another theme without which this series is not complete. It is the spirit of sacrifice of which I would speak. It underlies all of the richest and best in life and runs the entire gamut, from the Gift of the Father, through the patriarchs, the prophets, apostles, saints in every age and place.

It is fundamental in the teachings of our Lord and in His practice. He came never to be ministered unto. But always to minister. The final great sacrifice was death on the cross. He sent His disciples out to face a hostile world. Many came to their death in violent ways, sacrifices to their loyalty to the faith which shone in their hearts.

The major fact is that they placed others first in their lives, reserving no right to take their comfort nor to hold tight to their advantage. They saw only something which they could do or give that would serve another. That was their test. And that is their glory. Not always is the motive spiritual. At least, they are not always conscious that it is. But always the spirit of the desire to do for others is uppermost. By it souls grow, lives develop, hearts grow richer and life is wonderfully satisfying.

The one who sees always self first has none of this uplift, none of the outreach of spirit power that comes with the sacrifice of self. In smaller ways where life is not hazarded but where comfort or one's own desires are at stake, the spirit is the same of being willing to let go of self and to sacrifice comfort or convenience or desire, for others.

Here on our Spirit Plane we see how it works in earth lives. The one who clings to his own way, not willing to give in or give up for the joy of helping others, comes through earth life wondering why joy eludes him, the joy which possesses those about him who find ways in which their self sacrifice may help.

There seems a paradox in it. But the principle is sound. And it works wherever men try it out. It is a cardinal factor of the great life. It squares with the principles of all that is great and good. The heavier the sacrifice, the greater the reward. That never fails either on your earth plane or in these Higher Realms.

While it seems that one loses who gives up his own advantage for helping someone else, in the last analysis and in the final shocking up of values, as in a pair of scales, the weight of advantage is always on the side of the one who forgot self for the sake of some other who needed help. Never be afraid that you will lose out, speaking freely as far as language is concerned, when you give up your desires, your pleasures, your seeming good, for the sake of another who without you would suffer lack.

The one who does that always gains, not always financially or in the things of earth. Sometimes he does. But always he comes to experience the satisfaction of knowing that from his sacrifice of self, he has reaped a reward far deeper and richer than the other way of self could have brought him.

I commend this to you. It is the way of rightness and of spiritual reward.

There are yet some things about which I wish to talk with you. One is the tendency of people to jump to conclusions and to reach decisions on premises which are not substantial enough to bear weight. Sometimes you jump just this way. Not as often as you did. Many people do. Almost always the issue is unfortunate, the conclusion in error and results are not so good.

The better way, as we here know, and as you of earth know when you pause to think, is to think carefully through such evidence as presents itself, evaluate the situation and reserve judgment! Therein is the difficult part for the earth mind. It is hard to reserve judgment. It is easy to arrive at conclusions that as often as not, are incorrect. It is the way of spirit power to wait with open mind and heart and always to give the situation the benefit of the doubt.

Much heartache would be spared to people of earth if that lesson were learned and lived! In thus gaining control over one's spiritual forces, there comes always that quiet which is mark of firmness of soul fiber and witness of close contact with the One in Whom is All-power and All-quiet.

Real power is never noisy; never blustery. God-power is always the essence of utter quiet. Mark well that difference and take it into the depths of your consciousness. Live up to its truth in your own life and commend it to others by precept and example. Passing judgment on others and jumping to conclusions about them or something they do are practically the same thing. These are dire enemies of spirit growth. There is no finer standard than that of St. Paul when he said, "Let this mind be in you which was also in Christ Jesus." There you and every earth person have the model of perfection. For in the mind of Christ Jesus is nothing save love and peace and joy, with the calmness of utter faith and Infinite power coming through from His Father.

Always remember that the person who makes a big noise in working and doing, is not the person of deep reserves or of solid fiber of character. Know too, that with patience and perseverance these can be cultivated to the great gain of him who needs the lessons.

Power that fritters away in noise, is wastefully harnessed in relation to achievement, whether one thinks of the human or in the realms of mechanics.

The day is coming and is not far removed when you will be more favorably situated for doing this greatest of all work in your life. It will have vast outreach into human hearts, supplanting despair with courage; weakness with strength; half-heartedness with strong determination; dread with calm assurance; fear with joy and the down-pull of life with all which up-raises and motivates with the Highest. I beseech you to look forward to this with the surge of enthusiasm which always characterizes you and gives you much of your power.

Whether you can see your way or walk by faith, just know for a certainty that you are definitely guided by us and that in no wise will you be allowed to stray.

THERE IS GLORY IN THE TRANSITION

Again I wish to revert to the basic theme of these messages and speak tonight of the glory which abides in the transition from physical life to the life of spirit when one is no longer hampered by the material aspects of existence. Of course you cannot understand it. No one can until he experiences it for himself. But you always found that my words to you while I was among you of earth, were true words. You believe me now that no longer am I with you in physical presence. So I know you do believe me that far from being fearsome, death is a blessing; a boon; a translation from limitation to utter freedom; a promotion from primary knowledge to contact with Infinite wisdom; an opening of the door to such brilliance and beauty of life and love and service and joy as the human heart cannot conceive.

Death, were its name changed to one with happy connotation and without the painful phases of material decay, would not stand in human thought as the arch foe, the destroyer of families, of achievement, of life. It would be known for what it is, the avenue along which one passes from one level of experience to another vastly better, more advanced and lacking all things of suffering and privation, uncertainty and loss; to a life where one may see the end from the beginning and where all is determined by standards of unselfish love; where there is no end to the growth one may make in all things enduring and worthwhile; where one is enveloped eternally with the glory of God's love in conscious presence and power.

Does this sound fearsome? Something to dread and about which to weep? And to drape one's home with signs of mourning? Smiles all withdrawn? No, oh no! These customs are at complete variance with God's way of light and life and with the truth about the merging of earth life into spirit life. The customs which have grown up around death are barbarous. They are not in harmony with the faith which Christ came to impart.

The home from which one has been counted worthy to be taken to a more beautiful home and a larger life without sickness or tragedy or frustration, is a home where lights should glow softly and beautifully; where there should be sense of peace and confidence that the Valley is not one of shadow but of light; that the passing is a bright one; the River, not a dark river but the River of Life washing the shores of the Shining Strand; where one sees and knows and is welcomed by dear ones who have made the crossing a little ahead and make the new life in the new world a friendly and comfortable beginning. Above all, the atmosphere and love of the Father predominate and fill every heart to overflowing.

Is this occasion for sorrow and mourning? Rather for holy Joy. It is human to suffer physical loneliness. No one knows that better than you. But even that can be transmuted into life that is richer in all things which abide eternally. So not even the aloneness is cause for the garment of sorrow or the spirit of heaviness.

The disposition of the earth body has terrors for many who find it impossible to look beyond to where the spirit finds joyful abode and eternal satisfaction in the life of the Inner Planes. Someday earth people will learn better ways for care of the body after life has left it. Even so, it is wholly a superficial matter. The growth of the soul is all that matters.

With this earnest word to you as seed for the planting of which you are enjoined to be earnest and active, I leave you now for the night. I give you the blessing of Almighty God, the Father, the Son and the Holy Spirit, than which no greater boon may be given to anyone.

November 2

God bless you tonight as you come from the duties of a busy day to your part in this series of cosmic communications. I wish that everyone who reads them would come under the spell of their truths. But such will not be the case. Unanimity of approval never follows any presentation of belief. It never has. As long as the human is as it is, probably it will never accord unanimous sanction to whatever the cause.

In such matters as these, likelihood is less. For the themes, indeed the fundamental possibility of communication between the two spheres of life, is filled with that which the human will debate and many will discard. Many though, will accept and rejoice at the largeness of life which has grown up within them because of the truths herein contained.

It is never easy for the proponent of any cause to witness that which he sets forth, turned aside as untenable or unworthy. Such experiences are especially hard for one of your temperament. But you must steel yourself to knowing that you will face such, in person or through the mail or in roundabout ways.

Be not discouraged!

It will help you if you will take the position that you are a sower of eternal seed some of which will fall on barren soil or in rocky places or where earth is unequal to producing harvest of depth or richness.

As a sower you must know that much seed will be scattered where soil is fertile, where rain and dew and soft winds will help in the springing up and growth toward harvest. Having done your part in scattering where soil has been prepared, you are not responsible for the seed's taking root quickly nor for the harvest yielded.

You will find, if I may pursue the figure of speech a little further, that one of the most fruitful methods of cultivation of this precious seed, is through prayer, that seed and soil may work toward richer soul life on human and spirit levels of living.

Are you content with this explanation? And will you take it in faith knowing that it is not yours to "grow" the seed but only to plant and water it with faith and prayer and assurance that the Powers which gave you these truths will take care against their being lost through unbelief or hostility or even harder—a closed mind?

In all the realm of thought there is nothing more discouraging than to work with a mind that is closed to the reception of truth, the walls of the mind like solid granite and the entrance door locked and barred against the admission of any truth new or different.

Wherever such a situation confronts one, it is useless to try to force the mind or soul against those barred doors of the spirit. Someday the bolts will be drawn and the doors of the mind thrown wide open that truth may enter and do its transforming work. Prayer and faith contribute to the day when the mind will be receptive and the truth which now may be scorned be eagerly sought and assimilated into the fibers of being.

So do not fear lest you are furthering that which will be too largely withstood. Rather know that to a degree of which you do not now dream, earth minds are hungry and eager for what will dispel fear of death and assure themselves of the continuity of conscious existence under conditions of joy in growth and in the atmosphere of God's love and peace and power.

There is nothing which the human, on the whole, dreads more than the inescapable fact of physical death. He sees no way around it. He must face it and experience it. And largely he is possessed with dread at the approach of it because he has had wrong teaching concerning it and because the race thought with relation to it has been totally in error. Thus there are countless people who will reach out, as everywhere they are doing, for a satisfying philosophy of life both here in the spirit realm and on the earth level.

These will read and meditate quietly, carefully, thoughtfully and rejoice as they feel their hearts warming to the clear truth which permeates every word of these cosmic communications. There will come to you from all sides their gratitude, comfort and satisfactions replacing the old, downward-pulling fears of the darkness and dankness of death and a philosophy of existence in the next world which lacked vitality and clear consciousness of Infinite wisdom contained in these messages.

To be a sower is great business, when you are handling fertile seeds of spirit life. Never before has so much pure truth as the Masters of the Inner Planes are entrusting to this handling of this series, been sent forth for the nourishment of human hearts. You will not be left to your own devices in carrying forward this task. You will have the conscious presence and guidance of these through whom, in the form of my voice, all of this has been entrusted to you.

A SWEEPING PICTURES

You have wondered and questioned in your own heart, why there has seemed such tumult in the atmosphere in which you work while there appears no tumult at all; why the tension is much greater than formerly when largely the same set of factors is at work. You wonder whether you imagine it, or whether you are at fault.

You could sometimes dissipate part of this if you took things more lightly. But on the whole, this which depresses you is part of such unrest throughout the physical creation as never has been imagined before. We who go and come on the speedy wings of thought, ministering to all races and kinds, see and face it everywhere to a degree unprecedented.

It is part of the upheaval which is destined to precede and to usher in an entire new epoch of civilization with changes so vast as now no leaders in any government are even conceiving. It will mean the readjustment of nations, of races, of education, of religious rites and rituals, of forms of government and economic foundations of government, until comes the day when the madness which has filled the earth for aeons is passed away and mankind has reached the place of willingness to pattern his life after the Divine. Therein every man shall have his fair opportunity; no more shall there be exploitation of one man by his more favored brother and the good of life shall be open to everyone. And there shall be war no more!

There are those whose sight is limited and whose penetration is not keen, who think that such basic changes will be in evidence shortly after the peace treaties following this second great war wherein the whole world has suffered and bled.

It is not so. The time for these sweeping changes is not at hand. More must be learned by leaders, more willingness to accept Divine guidance; more consciousness of human limitations which must be supplemented by the All-Power of God. More must be learned by those who are of the rank and file whose lives are as precious to the Creator as any ruler's who ever lived.

A truer balance must be sought than now is likely. There will be much more suffering by nations and peoples with farther-reaching purification of hearts and policies. The great era will not come to earth manifestation until earth people are ready and willing to accept the revised bases of justice for favoritism; of love for hate; of righteousness and the goodness of God in place of man's seeking for individual riches; not until the welfare of all is the goal of each man and to it each strives. Then will this era of progress and prosperity in things that are real and enduring, come to fruition.

Mankind has large part to play in bringing all this about. For his defaulting has bathed the world in blood and sated life with crime too dark and loathsome to mention. Mankind has brought all this upon the world and upon this age because of the errors of his thinking, and because he has supplanted the will and the way of God by his selfish desires for aggression and riches, for power and yet more power.

Remember always that this debacle which has held earth in its grip now for years, is in no wise because the Almighty is punishing races of men for this or that. It is none of God's doing. Man has brought it upon himself and will again unless he right-about-faces, re-gears his ambitions, renews his vision of goals toward which it is worthwhile to strive; unless he realizes afresh that he is responsible for his brother as always since the day of Cain and Abel. There is no shifting that responsibility! It is a long road yet to travel before hearts of mankind are turned round about to these goals of truth and unselfish living.

Gradual changes for the better as preludes to this coming epoch will reveal themselves and their power for good, finding acceptance in the lives of men and thus lay foundations that shall endure for all coming ages.

We wanted you to have this sweeping picture that touches more or less the whole field, for the vision it affords, the comfort it gives and the inspiration it will mean to you. When you share it with others, you will sense the eagerness with which many will accept and be ready for their part in preliminaries.

It has been wonderful talking to you tonight. Peace be with you and joy crown your life!

November 4

It is difficult to get this message through tonight in the face of conditions. The thing that so deeply concerns you about accomplishing this world task, need not concern you. The time is not yet ripe. Do you not remember that last night you consciously saw a door open suddenly before your inner eyes and a voice said—not my voice—"This is your open door!"?

The thing that disconcerts you is that the door was not a lighted door. It was dark. But there is nothing sinister in that. It means merely that the time is not at hand for the light to shine and your way be made clear. It is coming. There will be abundant light on your path. And there will be strength sufficient for every need. I beseech you to have faith!

FRUSTRATION OR FULFILLMENT

November 5

Conditions have righted themselves and it is privilege to talk to you about some things humans need to know for their lives on earth and to be at their best when they reach the Planes where spirit alone abounds and earth cares are left behind. First, I want to say something about what earth people think of as frustration. By it they mean that plans which they hold dear, which they especially desire to see fulfilled in their lives, never come to fruition but always are denied culmination. This underlies much worldly unhappiness and sometimes resentment at life. It eventuates in definite feeling that there is no use trying;

that what is granted to others is denied the one especially concerned with this matter of frustration.

Often a feeling of inferiority develops on the part of that person when no inferiority is involved, when actually the lesser is denied for the sake of opening the door to greater good. It is hard to get that across to the one whose wishes and ambitions are closely tied into the refusal of things to work out as it seems they should, humanly speaking.

Multiplied thousands of human lives have all but been wrecked on the rocks of this matter of frustration of what seem like desirable goals and ambitions attained by others no more worthy, no more capable, no more loyal to the highest. Sometimes it is related to selfish desire to shine instead of unselfish desire to serve. Not always. Often—and these are the instances where the hurt to the heart is the hardest to bear—it is because there is guidance from the spirit side of life where it is clearly seen that the individual's finest values and highest service will work out for ultimate satisfaction and better world values, if his plans and desires are diverted into other channels.

You do not wish to take this paragraph. You say it is too personal. Yes, it is personal. For that reason I am over-ruling your wishes and asking you insistently to record just what comes from me over the ether waves which do not fail nor falter in carrying the truth.

Always you have wished for earth success. That is not strange. You have had much of it in the work which we did together over a span of years. But your ambitions leaped to other fields in which you craved success which has been denied you. There are reasons why! Please go on with this which is hard for you but which needs saying, for thousands whose experiences are similar to yours.

You definitely wished to succeed in the fiction field, primarily to show that you could do what others whom you admire do with preeminent success. Fiction is not your field. And you have definitely been prevented from entering it. Other highly remunerative fields have tempted you. I say this in no spirit of criticism. But you have been inhibited. So have others who have not understood why any more happily than you.

Those who have succeeded in the lists in which you have not been permitted to tilt, have in some cases quite looked down upon—without saying so in words—work of other sorts which you have done which brings its mede of appreciation but not that accolade of applause which your soul craved.

That hurts you and all these others of whom I think as I dictate this message to you. It is hard to take, no matter in what field the ambition lies or what the motive is that goads one on to goals that are denied. Sometimes all of you think that life is geared against you. And you say that frustration is your lot. For the most part you feel that it is unfairly so! Do I not speak truly? I thank you for being honest enough and loyal enough to take this exactly as I give it, for the service it will render to others on the earth plane who suffer much of what you have experienced—and yet do.

There is nothing wrong with fiction, speaking now of you as an illustration, when the fiction is decent and clean, done with worthy technique and laudable presentations of life's problems.

Generally it is profitable in monetary ways which of itself and fundamentally, makes it attractive to many. It calls for qualifications of imagination, interpretation, analysis and synthesis of character and life and thus is highly attractive to the many who are endowed with ability for it.

Do you see toward the close of that sentence above how I have touched the crux of what I am getting at? "The many who are endowed, etc." Don't you see how that explains why you in particular and others in their fields, have been inhibited from the field in which are so many others, and held free for other and greater work in which there are not "many who are endowed for such service"?

Through long years you have been under training which you did not recognize and did not enjoy, training which has tried your very soul and tested every fiber of your being. It has been a hard road to follow along which some encouragements have met you. All of them you have appreciated. But they have not satisfied you.

You remember in the first of these messages which you resisted beginning because you thought it could not be that you were equipped for receiving anything so stupendous from the Inner Planes, how I made clear that this was not what you wanted; but that it was what the Inner Planes had decreed for you? Do you not remember? I repeat it today and I beg of you to leave now and for all time behind you, any desire for lesser rewards of popular applause, to others.

And just thank God, Almighty God, for the privilege denied to most of being a channel through which words of everlasting truth have been flowing now for almost two months of your earth reckoning.

The day will come at no distant time when you will see that you have not been frustrated but promoted; held for the thing so much better, rather than being let go free for the smaller rewards of life!

What I say to you, I say to all who have suffered similar experiences and have classed them under the generic term of "frustration." Wherever and whenever you can help others to better acceptance of the truth which I have imparted this morning, you will be doing something substantial.

I have now covered in full sufficiency this important and difficult matter without which I should have left this series incomplete. Do you not see that anything which touches the main springs of life for the human, is by that much an integral part of eternal interest? The reason is that the human and the spiritual are so closely interrelated that there is no line fine enough to separate them. Life on the earth plane is not segregated from life on the Spirit Plane. The two are closer than breathing and those who understand and accept this significant fact, are wise. It changes the face of all living and helps to obliterate all sense of this frustration of which I have been speaking this Sabbath morning, by your earth reckoning.

I wish now to speak briefly of another phase of life of which I have talked to you before, but which we here think needs emphasizing. It is the consciousness every hour of the day, that we of the other side of life are serving as ministering angels to you all of earth.

Some few there be who understand that and live in the glow of these presences; who know that a prayer breathed, in a second brings spirits from the Inner Planes to help and guide and comfort in whatever the emergency may be. They know that no problem can come to any one of earth for which there is not a spiritual solution and that help is available to anyone in return for a breathed request for help and courage and wisdom and strength. Those who do know this in daily experience and who live in the atmosphere of the knowledge find themselves lifted above bitterness of physical disappointments, of material matters, and living more really in the atmosphere of the spiritual. Some glad day they will experience it in constant participation, even as we do who have left the grievous weight of the body and glory in the lightness and freedom of the Spirit World.

There are some, perhaps many, who shudder at the thought of spirit presences surrounding them as they live their earth lives. They speak of this as "ghostly," as something which they do not appreciate.

This is a misinterpretation of the wisdom and love of the Father Who planned the minutest detail of existence to be helpful to every human who understands and accepts the provisions which have been made for his help.

If only earth people would abandon use of the word "death" and substitute some other which has no unhappy connotations and associations, it would go far toward easing this other situation.

And now my time is up. The conference with you has been grand. I thank you and I bless you, assuring you that God's Infinite blessing rests upon this service which you are to render. Let joy reign within you. And be content!

LOVE'S MAJOR MESSAGE

November 6

I thank you for coming so willingly and promptly to this joint responsibility between you and us on the Inner Planes. Many matters yet remain to be presented before this series of talks may be considered at a close.

If I were to condense into one word the predominant characteristic of life over here, to name the quality which more than any other colors our life and service, I would without hesitation say, "Love." It motivates everything we do and think. It flows from the fountain of Infinite love in the heart of the Father, which from the beginning of the world has been the mightiest influence the human knows. Love makes the difference between darkness and light in the human heart; between conflict and peace; between strife and quietness of heart; between envy and malice and the purity which knows not these negative qualities that wither and sear the spirit.

Love makes the heart sing. It fills the spirit with joy and peace and the desire to serve wherever need exists. Love has no partnership with sordidness nor evil thinking. It is never allied with jealousy nor false witness. It is the essence of purity and goodness and holds within itself all which is most like God.

Only as the human spirit is filled with love of beauty and purity and fair play and justice to all men; only as the earth person is willing to sacrifice himself that good may come to others without thought of reward for himself; only as he sees life and living through the softening gleam of spiritual love, interpreting the affairs of the world through the medium of unselfish love, can he come to his best possible self. As one of your writers long ago said, "Love is the greatest thing in the world."

As always, that which is valuable costs proportionate price. Love does. Always. It is not easy to follow these mandates and sacrifice one's self for the good of others, nor to appraise conditions of life through the fair-mindedness which characterizes pure love. Love is a rigid task matter, the while it pays richest gains the soul could seek.

Love fills the beautiful atmosphere in which we dwell on these Planes. It is impossible to put into earth words what it is like. As I could not have understood it nor accepted it while I was on the earth plane, no more could you or any other one amid the conditions of earth. So there is nothing but futility in trying to reveal to you what it really is from the viewpoint of spirit.

But I must discuss it tonight in its relation to that which was said centuries ago by the Master: "Love one another." There you have the crux of much that enters in to lifting life to higher levels, or dragging it down if the mandate is refused.

This is one of the severest tests of the degree of God-love in the heart, as it is one of the avenues through which the richest of life flows into living. Easy enough always to love those who are congenial with our tastes and whose vibrations harmonize with ours. For that we deserve no credit. But the Master did not distinguish. He told us that we were to "love one another."

The one who rasps, whose tastes are uncongenial, whose personality is distasteful—"Love one another!" That is severe test. It would seem unnecessary to make plain that this love of the command of the Master, is not the impassioned love which those know whose beings merge into one. Not that. It is the love which thinketh no evil, which never bears false witness, does not harshly judge, nor misinterpret nor criticize. It is the love which in the highest sense is the personification of the Golden Rule and which, if once really tried with the problems of your world, would bring solutions before mankind would think it possible.

Nations could not go to war if men "loved one another." There would be nothing to war about. Litigations, misunderstandings between groups or individuals could not last, if those represented in them "loved one another!" Harsh, personal feuds of which the world knows far too many, would pass away as with a breath, if earth people "loved one another."

As between members of earth families where often there is lack of understanding and of unity of spirit, this standard of loving one another in the full and complete sense in which He meant it, would sweeten home life as nothing else could.

It is not a matter of luxuries nor of lavishness which makes home what it should be or keeps it far from the ideal. It is this loving one another which works to its own beautiful goal. Failure to follow the Divine mandate results in strife and discord and standards below those which Jesus Christ intended as models for the families of earth.

It is worth thinking about. For everybody associates with others on the earth plane. Of great importance is the way in which spirit influences spirit, whether for joy and peace or rubbing one another the wrong way; of barely enduring the presence of the other and figuratively gritting the teeth in effort to put up with what might be a pleasant relation if they "loved one another!"

Therein lies the difference, human to human, group to group, community to community, nation to nation, until the whole world is included; the difference between life in the spirit of love which the Divine intended or without it in constant irritation.

When that irritation is big enough to involve nations, what results we call war. When it is between men, it is a quarrel or a misunderstanding. The principle is the same. The general result is the same. Either love is given its opportunity to sweeten and brighten life; or it is denied. According to which, the result works out favorably or with tragedy to the human heart. So with nations. So with the world at large.

We are told that "Love vaunteth not itself; is not puffed up." If daily living of men and women on the earth sphere patterned itself by these words, how quickly much of the disharmony would disappear! How easily the wheels would begin to move!

There is no solvent that equals love in every affair of life, from the least to the greatest. It is the sure preventive of war, of aggression, of injustice to man, of that which breeds discord and unhappiness between families and between nations.

Here on these Higher Planes from which these messages are sent to you, we see so clearly the wonder-working power of love in the heart. And we marvel at the slowness of mankind to realize that the solution to his hard problems, is within himself; just there in his own heart. There or nowhere. In his heart attitude to others lies the solution of what pulls him down or lifts him God-ward. Only when men see this and practice it with all their hearts, will living satisfy and life be a glad song, instead of bitterness of strife and unhappiness of discord.

This message has universal bearing. No one living on earth since the creation of the universe but has faced this truth and either proved its rare fruits of blessedness or failed to prove its sweetness and automatically tasted the bitterness of the reverse side of the truth.

That is the law. It works one way or the other according to the one who is willing to prove the power of love in the business of living or to discard it without trial, to suffer the consequences through permitting the law to work in reverse; against him instead of for him.

Love is not weak. Not effeminate. Not evidence of undevelopment. It is the strongest, mightiest, most courageous influence of the heart. There is nothing which love will not undertake; nothing it will not suffer; nor endure. Nothing which it cannot accomplish. Love is of the very heart of God. Within it are all qualities of greatness and goodness, long suffering and peace and joy and things of good report.

And so I say to you tonight and to all through you, "Love one another!"

When love comes into the heart, fear, arch-foe of happiness and power, goes out. The two do not live together. They have no affinity with each other. Man may choose in this as in everything whether he will live under the bondage of fear or with the flying banners which love holds over him and beneath which he rests at peace. It is a wonderful choice to make. Momentous choice. And open to every human.

In these messages, I have not talked of fear. It is a negative quality, composed of darkness and doubt and suspicion and lack of the faith without which it is impossible to live on one's best levels.

Fear does nothing but destroy. Tear down. Defeat. Deplete. In bodily health or business success or in ambitions of other sorts. Fear is most to be feared. We see its ravages on earth from our spirit vantage point, more clearly than any one of earth could see. Never does it do one thing that is positive or constructive. Fear is not compounded of elements that achieve but of them which bring loss and destruction to anyone who keeps company with it.

In your Scriptures, I beg of you to read how many admonitions there are that you "Fear not!" They did not just happen. They are there because from the earliest experiences of man on the earth sphere, his most dreaded enemy was fear that invaded his heart, turned his courage into water and his power into weakness.

In whatever realm of life, oust fear as assiduously as you cultivate love. Refuse to hear its words of defeat, or its dictates of dismay. It never does anything for you that is good. Thank you for this message tonight. God's blessing be upon you; my blessing too. Good night!

MISSIONS TO EARTH

November 7

We are coming through tonight with help which you and others need, who find yourselves storm centers suddenly and unexpectedly because of the crassness of others. That sort of situation is something which life experiences every once in a while, part of the discipline of the human, trying and faith-testing as it is.

So it will be well if I review the scope of what I have outlined with relation to spirit service throughout the world, wherever any one specially needs in ways that we of the Higher Planes can meet.

I have told you how sometimes we are in physical form though naturally not with the same stature nor countenance which we used while on the earth plane. You see clearly why that change is made, do you not?

I am not at liberty to discuss with you how the choice is made nor what body is chosen for any of us for a certain mission on earth. That matters not to you. It is for us to determine according to the judgment of the ages which prevails here and in which there is no lapsing because of error.

It was surprising to me when I first came hither, to see ways in which these matters are adjusted without friction or allowing for errancy—because there is no errancy! It is all just as it should be for gaining the right results in human adjustment and satisfaction.

I count myself most favored to go on more of these missions as I become adapted to them and have larger knowledge in handling the delicate situations which exist. Nothing I ever did while I was resident on earth, equaled the satisfaction which being of this varied service to earth people in distress, brings me.

We who minister thus in the physical are looked upon as earth media, sometimes wearing the familiar countenances of those whom they have known. Always the door to the confidence of the one at interest has been opened and we enter on a basis of understanding. There is never a feeling of strangeness nor tautness. Somehow the consciousness of the spirit presence makes itself felt in such manifest ways that the service needed can be rendered with ease and dispatch. There is never any thought on the part of the earth person that a visitor from the Inner Planes has come to help! If that were so, our power to help would be gone.

When, as is often the case, we go in spirit form only, the technique is different and we render our service through the consciousness upon which our impact is made without physical presence. It is strange to see the wonder-working power which we are allowed, when an earth person's whole attitude of mind and soul under certain conditions is completely changed, almost in a twinkling, under the influence of that presence and power which we are able to impart.

We can supplant their discouragement with confidence; their gloom with good cheer; their ignorance of how to proceed with a clearly outlined method which came from they do not know where; with calmness of mind in place of great disturbance of spirit. Isn't that worth doing?

And of course you know what reward there is for our spirits when we feel that we have helped another over the hard stretch of life's road. Many difficult stretches there be on that road, as I attested myself many a time. I know how sorely the human needs the sort of lift which I understand often came to me when I was unknowing of the source and did not comprehend while I was of earth. I only knew that help had come and that the problem was solved beyond my expectation.

Always help from Inner Planes is beyond earth expectation. Nothing from here is done half-way. That is one wonderful satisfaction—the eternal perfection of the life, the peace and joy and service on these Planes! How I wish I might share them with you of earth! The day will come when you do share them, you and the many who now are meeting and solving your perplexities as they rise. The complete fulfillment which you will experience when you come hither, will consciously atone for all the hardness of earth and its dispensations.

You ask how we know where we are to go and what we are to do to help some earth person. The call comes from spirit to spirit, on the wings of thought, as quickly as thought can fly from the heart of need to the heart of help! The cry is breathed by someone in trouble. And we hear. Someone among us here, is assigned to help meet that heart's need. And we are instructed by someone far wiser in the Divine economy, just what our method is to be and how we are to help.

Then we are off, unhindered by any material limitation. It is marvelous service, reward for all the faithfulness which we sought to maintain while we were on the earth plane.

Understand this! God never does anything half-way. He does for everyone who will let Him far more aboundingly than is dreamed. I found Him that way while I was of earth. I found Him more that way now than I then conceived. His power, His might, His love, His wisdom transcend all understanding.

This being true, as you know it is true you wonder and ofttimes grieve because that which you think you need and can use to advantage and for which you ask in what you think is faith, does not come to you. I have heard you grieve to this end while I was of earth. You wonder what is wrong with your asking or your faith as backbone of it all.

At times you, as most people, have felt that it was no use to try to prove God's goodness and His willingness to come to your assistance. And sometimes you have wondered whether, since nothing appeared to come of your loyal efforts, you would not as well give up and live along as best you could and trust to luck.

This applies to need for physical healings by the power of the Divine, to relief from necessities of many sorts, to the appeal for doors to achievement to be opened, to the whole round of experiences which mankind knows and often suffers as he journeys through earth life.

I speak with deepest appreciation of all that you and many others have suffered in this way of apparent denial of that for which you have asked, which seemed to hold nothing but good for any one and yet which has not been granted to you.

Nevertheless I speak truly when I say that the reason is the same as for the failure of the flower to grow which is daily lifted from the soil to see how the roots are sprouting.

At the back of the desire to look at the roots is lack of faith that the flower can take root and grow without help from the one who did the planting.

In whatsoever realm of the human, the master difficulty is unwillingness or fear to leave the issue with the spirit powers, having once committed it to them and their care. The flower must be uprooted often to see whether it is growing! What seems like faith is intermingled with questioning, even with doubt, though often it is unconscious doubt, whether the help which has been promised by the Almighty, will really come through in practical terms of meeting some specific situation.

When the flower is uprooted, it does not grow. When doubt or questioning is mingled with faith, results are not what the heart hoped for but was not willing to hand over entirely to the Divine for His handling. Only then can results come that are amazing in their satisfactions and completeness. We here wonder why earth people do not learn the secret of spirit success in solving their problems. It is comprehended in that one tiny, gigantic word—faith!

There are many who hold that word old-fashioned. Perhaps so. But the fact is the solution to life's major and minor problems. Faith is the keystone to the arch of achievement both on the earth realm and on the Inner Planes. If you will take that close into your heart and live with it in absolute submission to it, nothing wavering, you will find, as any one will, such marvels taking place in your life as now you little dream while you continue to lift the flower from the soil to see how it comes on. If my illustration seems insignificant, I grant it. But it does illustrate.

Before our talk for the evening is concluded, I want to speak of the values of seeing the bright side of life, of seeing more brightness than gloom, of looking for the sunny side and refusing to think that the dark side is all there is.

I speak this no more to you than to others who are prone to think that night is longer than the sunshine of the days. Sometimes so. But in the cycle of the year, it balances. Sunshine, cheer, gladsomeness, brightness and joy have their full share. When this is not so, is when the human refuses to turn toward the bright side and to see all there is for him on that side of life. Nothing will grow without sunshine.

The human spirit will not grow in an atmosphere minus the shining of the sun. Turn to joy! See the good! Look for what is satisfying! Render thanks for untold blessings! Acknowledge God's kindness and goodness in unnumbered ways!

Seek out experiences for which to rejoice. Cultivate this habit of seeing the bright and shining side of every day and of every order of living. Bless all of it and begin to look for all the good your tomorrow will bring. You and all will find that such an atmosphere within the soul will bring uncounted joys and rewards. You will be amazed. The more you give thanks, the more you will have for which to give thanks. Add this constant looking for the good side to the developing faith in God's promises for meeting your every need—and you are indeed rich in things of eternal value.

What matter the temporal, the fleeting, the superficial, the frothy? They are bubbles which gleam in the morning sun but are pricked by some thorn and burst into nothingness before your very eyes. I am most grateful for opportunity to talk with you tonight.

Please God may you rest well and open your eyes upon a day of conquest tomorrow. His love and blessing be with you in overflowing measure. I am off now!

November 8

You are remembering that it was two months by your reckoning of earth time, since you were induced to trust your hands at the machine and your mind to me, for the reception of these messages. You did not mean to doubt the possibility of worthy result coming through. But did in reality doubt; seriously. With your earth limitations, you figured that it could not be that you were competent for such service.

You did not wish to undertake it, fearing lest you be mislead. With considerable emphasis it was necessary to require you to take your place at the machine and be willing to resign yourself to cooperation with us. You were hesitant about it from the first. And that is not strange. Indeed it is natural. You had to be convinced.

When you became powerfully conscious of the presence of spirit entities in your earth home and the influence of all this was making itself felt in your inner life; when my message never failed to meet you when you had leisure to offer hands and mind, you became sure of the genuineness of all this. Thenceforth your loyalty to this responsibility and privilege has been all that could be asked. You have left nothing undone.

These past two months have done much for you and for those with whom you have shared what has come through. They will do more, both physically and spiritually, as you come more warmly under the influence of their reality. Just now you must be concentrating on the mechanics of taking this from me. When you are free to concentrate on the lessons pure and simple, the magnificence of what is revealed will work marked change in your life and in the lives of all who come under the influence of these revealings.

And so even as you do, we here thank God for what these two months have begun and the months ahead will carry through. Do not despair. Nor even question. Surely do not doubt the marvelous outcome of this which was ordained from the Inner Planes and given to me by my instructors from the Seventh Plane, for the help of earth people. It is so much greater than any of the smaller things to which people give themselves, and receive therefrom tumultuous applause, that the two classes of accomplishment are not comparable. Just accept my estimate and judgment on this, as you always were glad to accept my dictum while I was of earth.

Shortly you will receive definite instructions about handling all of this. You will begin to find that relief is opening to you in ways of which even yet you do not think. You need not be concerned. Just go ahead! Remember I said that to you in those words the night when first you were proving that power had been given to you to receive these cosmic communications without the intervention of a third person. I say it again—just go ahead!

Again I say because I wish to repeat it, There is no difficulty, no need, no problem, no loss, no heartache which the Infinite Father cannot take care of, if only the human will ask Him; trust Him; commit it to Him; and committing it, leave it to Him, without fussing or fretting or doubting! It is as simple as that in the telling, not so simple in the handling of the human emotions. They fluctuate. They question. And with that, out goes faith. And the perplexity remains. The problem is unsolved. The need is unmet.

All because quiet, deep-down faith in the promises of the Father was not given a chance to do its perfect work. We wonder why. And yet we know why. Someday mankind will learn more easily than now. And it will be a glad day when faith is taken at face value and really lived!

Another phase of the whole perfect round—facet, you may wish to call it—needs mention and a little brightening up in earth minds. I refer to the power of concentrating the mind upon whatever is the problem at hand, to think through to the logical end and the worthy conclusion. Does this seem a strange theme for even a short portion of this talk? It is an important part of earth development. Mankind is prone to fuzzy thinking—much of mankind is; thinking that does not reckon with all the factors nor see their import nor the inevitable outreach.

Too often, where concentration of God-given powers is needed and available, it is not used. Then men wonder why they seem futile in their work and why things do not work out as they should.

Here is the reason. Magnificently endowed minds with which the Creator blessed mankind are not used at par. Just played with, used for superficial thinking and not applied to thinking straight through a problem, as far as earth conditions make possible, prostituted to lower ends and lesser results than the Father intended they should achieve. Therein lies much of the frustration of earth about which we were speaking the other evening.

He who learns to apply to the full whatever powers the Infinite endowed him with, will find that he is richer than he dreamed, looking at his life possibilities from the outside. It is all within! What the heart wills, the mind can accomplish. Life then comes through to vast riches of knowledge and wisdom and understanding and power. It is most worthwhile. It is part of that which will prove valuable to you when you come smiling across the narrow stream of life and find yourself on these hospitable shores ready to take up the larger, the harder lessons which the Inner Planes give to everyone. Through them, you will grow faster than earth conditions made possible.

So I adjure you to use your powers of mental concentration to the limit and to gear your mind to the highest. It will enjoy being stretched and will grow accordingly. It will serve you at its best only when you have accustomed it to doing its best work. Anything less is unworthy a child of the Infinite.

Never let yourself say or think that any problem is too much for you to solve. And now the message of the evening must close, the while I prepare for service otherwise, in the name of the Father and the Son and the Holy Spirit. Blessed service! God's sweetest enduement of peace and power rest upon you! Good night!

November 9

It is a wonderful experience to have such direct communication over so long a period with one whom I knew so long and well on the earth plane and to feel the response of appreciation and cooperation which characterized your service in the time now gone.

THE WHITE LINE

A matter I would like to talk about with you tonight by your earth reckoning, and through you with many others, may not appear closely related to the heavenly spheres. But you will see that it reaches down into the deep places of living in every human heart.

I refer to what men call "down-right honesty." There are so many shades and degrees of veracity where this bed-rock honesty is involved, that it is difficult to distinguish between them and to follow the sharp line of cleavage between utter honesty on one side and honesty that is a little frayed and fuzzy and not quite clear, on the other side.

In the world of material considerations where men barter and trade for gold and things of the physical, this fine line too often lies far down under accumulated refuse of things earthy. These have been used to cover that line and to keep it comfortably out of sight and out of mind.

But covering it up and refusing to think of it accomplishes nothing, except to deceive the one who does it. And him it does not well deceive. Too often that fine line pops up and demands attention for him who has drawn it to be at ease. Only those who keep that line open and clean and fine, can absolutely forget it, knowing there is not one thing to conceal.

In this so difficult day on the earth plane, when the grandest sort of sacrifice is being made for freedom and ways of living that are worthy of mankind at his best; when there is so much self-seeking and greed for gold and place and power; in this so difficult day when ideals seem almost god-like in their grandeur and beastly in their depravity, it is necessary to keep that fine, clear, white line open and free. It shows safety from all encroachment of that which is not utterly honest and upright in human living and in the record each man is making.

It is a record which he will face when he makes the Great Transition and sees himself as he is without covering of glamour or concealment. For you remember how I have told you that over here every one is revealed for exactly what he is. And he rates at just what he has brought over from the earth world.

Nothing material counts. Or helps. Nothing which he has acquired by concealing that fine line bounding integrity of purpose and plan, does him one particle of good. At the most, money or its equivalent even when acquired in impeccable ways, is dust on these Inner Planes. It has no value whatsoever.

But when mankind has side-stepped the way that is straight and narrow by even so much as a thought or a plan that appears to harm no one else, by that much must he atone when he reaches these Planes of Absolute Justice.

There are those who in their thought restrict honesty to things of money and fail to see how the fine line runs through the entire pattern of human life. On one side or the other, each takes his stand in questions of intellectual honesty. Either he is honest in his convictions or he juggles with truth and facts and thinks the line is covered by clutterings which will prevent his being known as he is.

It does work that way sometimes for a while. But not to his advantage—ever. Whatever veers one iota from honesty and integrity in money or mind or spirit in any relationship of life, must of necessity appear against him when he stands, as everyone does sometime stand on these Spirit Planes, known for just what he is!

It is a sobering thought, an inspiring thought, that every gain one makes in living on the earth plane, will help him when it reveals itself in the purity of strict honesty and integrity, come that day when he has shed the mortal and faces life on the Spirit Planes.

The little trick, the wee-bit peculation, the veering from honesty by the shade of a thought, cost too high a price.

There will be times and places with people of many sorts, when this lesson which I am giving tonight will help you to open their eyes to basic truth and honesty as they are known on these Planes of Unselfish Devotion to all that aspires God-ward. Take it this way and use it whenever you have opportunity. There is much in it that will have eternal values for all peoples.

That same white line of probity in every thought and ideal, in every action and desire is the mark which distinguishes the one of Godlike character from one whose spirit is caked with the mud and mire of the mortal and about whom is much that speaks of what is low and self-seeking and downward-pulling.

Only on the right side of this line does the spirit flame into the pure white light of likeness to the One Who is all purity and perfection; to Him Who is our Exemplar, Pattern and Guide. So you see this queer topic does have close and vital relation to the human striving through devious ways of earth life, to come to oneness with All-Good.

Like every other lesson set for mankind to learn, it is a hard one. But being a lesson to learn, it is worth learning to the last letter and living in loyalty and devotion.

EXPERIENCING THESE MESSAGES

And now you have wondered many times during the receiving of these messages why the experience which was yours on the first evening when my words came through the ethers to you and you felt the presence of uncounted hosts with you, inspiring and giving you confidence for the great task entrusted to you, has not been repeated. Why haven't you had that thrill again? Why, on the contrary, do you frequently find yourself possessed of desire to fall asleep while the words of eternal truth are coming through, your hands active, your mind refusing to anticipate me? Why?

It has disturbed you and you do not understand the reasons for it. I give you tonight a hint of the reasons. On that first night, you were initiating a great adventure; how great in its outreach and influence you even yet have no idea. You thought yourself alone. You doubted your ability. You must get started aright, your mind and spirit aflame with certainty that the thing given you to do, was acknowledged by those from the Spirit Planes; that they were in hearty accord with it and were assuring you of the sincerity of the plan of which no earth man knew or in which he was to have a part where the receiving of the messages was concerned.

Therefore the spirits of those who long since had passed the Veil and who are associated with me in this Infinitely blessed service, came to you, hovered over you, gave you the blessing of their presence, so that you knew for a certainty that this was your ordained task. Does this explanation satisfy?

Why not again? Why do you grow drowsy? Why do not these ministering spirits come every night? Why can't you hold your mind alert as in the hours of your professional work? The hosts from Ether Planes are devoted to tasks which occupy them continuously, even though they need not to rest nor sleep nor recreate themselves. They come only at rare intervals in such power of actual presence as you experienced that first night. That one experience was all you needed to assure you of the grandeur of your task. Ask no more until the hour is at hand. Then they will come again!

You become drowsy physically because you wisely refuse to permit your conscious mental processes to function, holding your mind open to receive only that which comes on electrical impulses along the ether waves from me. Thus your mind is largely at rest and the power of vibrations is tremendous. It is overwhelming. It weighs you down. Your head is inclined to drop for these reasons. Physically you bow under the pressure of strong currents of electrical impulses which connect your world and the one from which I speak to you.

In addition, the mind in relaxation, is a better channel for receiving in absolute accuracy, any message emanating from the Inner

Planes. And you to whom this technique was new, have been taking this long series at the close of heavy working days, giving yourself to this which the other side of life has given you to do. Do you not have your answer? And is it not complete enough to satisfy your inquiries? It is the truth as far as it is possible to explain from this sphere to your sphere. You will accept it and be gratified about it, I know. All day you have wondered what I would talk to you about this time! And here it is, as natural and as necessary as if it were the opening instead of almost the close of the series!

God bless you! Off now!

STEADY GROWING

November 11

It was hard for you to break into the schedule which would have enabled this evening message to move ahead a bit earlier with you, not delayed by outside matters in which you have little interest. But these things come along and are part of your general responsibility. Tonight I want to talk to you concerning power. There are so many kinds of power that to define or limit or discuss in detail, would be impossible. In the last analysis, my message tonight revolves around the power of the spirit to overcome whatever obstacles stand in the way of development of one's best possible self. You remember that as one of my favorite phrases while I was with you on the earth sphere—one's best possible self! I hold to it yet as approvingly as I did then, knowing that in it lies much helpfulness to man's progress.

To achieve, calls for power—physical and muscular, intellectual, intangible and the power of the spirit. Power in whatever realm, does not come fully developed as gift to any man. The germ of it is implanted in every human heart along one or more lines. That germ must be tended, cultivated, exercised and given many a hard wind to blow against it and strengthen it; many a storm to build hardness of fiber into its substance. Every such germ of developing power must grow through the steady processes of nature, following the laws of growth; never jumping into full-grown potentiality without time to ripen and mature.

When it is ripening and showing signs of becoming real power in whatever field, there must be exercise of its muscles, as it were, whether of body or mind. The law holds. It is the order of life. And it is a strenuous order against which the human often cries out in dismay at the rigor. Discipline is hard to take. Men resist it fiercely.

Power never comes easily nor quickly. Like wisdom, it is of slow and tedious growth. But it does come when the human follows the order and the law of growth—and lets it grow. Had you ever thought of that phase of it? That often men will not let their power grow as it would do? Why is this sometimes in the earth realm? Because inherently man is selfish and often unwilling for power of others to surpass his own; unwilling too, to give his own inherent germ of power the careful cultivation and attention required to let it grow. Selfishness enters into both of these conditions. This is a common experience among earth people, selfishness being one of the traits difficult to root out.

As a seed planted in the warm earth of spring or summer season must be watered and nourished with sunshine and dew and given opportunity to come to fruition of blossom or ear or fruit, so must the germ, the spark of the Divine in every man, be given careful, intelligent attention if he is to come to the full-grown size for which he was destined for his earth career and for the endlessness of immortal service.

It is pitiful to us here as we see so many earth residents satisfied to let themselves grovel on low levels of undeveloped possibilities, weak and impotent, all but useless, when they have it within themselves to be worthy children of the Highest, blest with Infinite power to achieve great things on the earth level; later taking this power to these Higher Planes, growing to vaster degrees of life and of service.

I remember from my own mortal experiences how easy it is to follow the path of least resistance; how difficult to hew to the line of steady growing, where one must be disciplined in whatever work he aspires to be his best. No one comes to his most potential without this difficult discipline; this climbing consistently higher; this denial of lesser things that power may come, to its finest and service be commensurate with the best of which one is capable.

In the realms of spirit where man's relation to the Almighty is at stake, it is the same law of growth as in the natural world. There are those on earth who do not hold with this thesis; who think that one may leap from sin and wickedness into sainthood by the simple act of faith in Jesus Christ, omitting the intermediate processes of cultivating the sturdy fiber of the spirit and the foundations of knowledge. This is the way the Master taught His disciples that life is to be ordered.

No farmer ever harvested a worth-while crop without obstacles to overcome and cultivation to give. No scientist but has toiled against heart-breaking problems before he found the way through to his goal. No artist, no author, no anybody of ranking skill but has earned it through discipline, this steady cultivation which often seems tiresome and unbearable.

In the world of the spirit it is the same. It is here where need is so great and reward is so sure. The power to overcome obstacles of alluring by-paths of inertia which beset even the greatest; of doubt and hesitation; of reluctance to launch out into deep waters of commitment to any cause or course—such power comes slowly. It comes steadily and answers a marvelous purpose in the Divine, human plan.

With this power to withstand, to endure, to take the discipline and not repine, and to welcome it as part of the order of growing, there is great hope for the material phases of the world's reorganization and readjustment on better lines than the human has yet known; hope too, for progress in degrees of spiritual power.

Weeds spring up overnight and make a big showing. They overshadow the slow fashion of corn or wheat or staples of life. But the sun of a summer day wilts many a weed. It has no enduring quality, no fiber nor fruit useful to man. Easy to grow weeds! Quick they are getting started. Hard to eradicate. Often the soil of man's spirit proves fertile for growing weeds which must be eradicated at whatever cost of toil and pains.

Life at best, is discipline, that power may develop from it and equip mankind to grow into greater value in life, wherever he finds it and whatever problems it presents. Without this of which I have spoken so often tonight—this discipline with which every earth person is familiar—the human garden would be overgrown with weeds of indolence, carelessness, uncultivation, all qualities which the world does not need and which lead no man anywhere.

I have chosen to limit this message to one simple phase of the mighty theme with which all men are familiar, that many who need the lessons it teaches may see and learn and grow into better understanding of what it means to develop power of body, mind and spirit.

It is no light thing to deal with things of the spirit. I have been cautious in this talk tonight, plain and direct, even some may think trite, in the hope that development of power for living may seem a grander, a more prodigious process than many have realized. At any rate I have been sowing seed for the soil of human hearts!

I would continue for a moment on this growing in power for whatever is your line of earth responsibility. When I say "you" I am not meaning you personally, but all who will read these messages. Always there are ways, more than one, in which a matter may be accomplished or put out of the way. Always, too, there are those who choose the way of least skill that calls for least effort, regardless of its being the best way. Beware of such intellectual or spiritual slovenliness. It is blessed to grow and to come constantly into larger power for accomplishment of work on earth; and later for finer values over here where we grow constantly.

Power calls for all the pains of growth, all the agonies of such discipline as is connected inevitably with growth. But it is worth more than words can commend.

DEEP ROOTS

And now I shall talk to you awhile on other lines of the life that is lived on earth and continued here through the ages. I refer to stability of character. It is like a stalwart tree whose roots go down deep into the soil and which is not uprooted however severe the gale or fierce the storm. Its roots are protectingly deep. So it stands! The human, likewise, needs his roots of life deeply grounded in things that make for goodness and rightness; things that abide; that are valuable to him when he makes the Great Transition and that he can carry with him; things that prevent his being blown about by every wind and having therefore no fine-grained purpose of character or spirit.

In this transient day on earth when most things are upturned and there is so little that has proved its power to stand, stability is a precious quality to possess and to cultivate. It is not a popular quality. For change is more in the order of acclaim by those who insist upon variety. Variety is all right where it concerns superficialities. But in deep and great things with which the human must be concerned, stability of character is worth its weight in gold.

There are those who veer from one interest to another with the passing of the season; who weary of anything which calls for continuing application and effort; unwilling to stay by an agreement when the going is hard and the work taxing; who find always more to allure somewhere else than in their own spheres of work; who prove this lack of stability in their relations to other humans and whose degree of friendship goes no deeper than the surface soil.

Such people lack one of the fundamental qualities of greatness. They will never acquire the greatness which they crave and seek because they are not prepared in spirit to gain or to hold this which they desire.

If they had it, instability of character and purpose would disqualify them for using it in more than temporary degree. Stability is not spectacular. It makes no show. It gains no acclaim. Many there be who think it is more or less stupid and quite old-fashioned. They discard it for the sweets of something new which promises much and fails to cash in on the promises.

Every truly great or worthy person has qualities of stability which make him valuable to his place in the world and which especially put him in prospect of high rank when he comes over to this side of life.

The stable person is to be depended upon, whether it is convenient or against his desire; his word can be counted on; his integrity of service does not require watching; he needs no time clock to measure his faithfulness in service.

He is not changed by passing whims nor altered by notions of an hour. His life gauge is set by eternal standards and he does not veer except as growth leads him higher in achievement and possibility.

To have stability does not mean to be stubborn. Quite the opposite. Stability is always willing to be convinced of better ways and higher standards. Stubbornness does not have a heart of willingness to learn. The two are far apart at opposite poles.

The person who has sent his roots of life deep down into the rich soil of fidelity and purpose; who lives to be of greatest possible service in life; who evaluates the issues of life and elects to accept such as are good and true, is always learning-hearted, open to seeing avenues of larger truth along which he is grateful to travel; highways of progress which contribute to making better time in reaching his goals. Not so the stubborn man. He is stuck to his own way. Nothing moves him. Nothing convinces him. There is small hope for him.

Often the person who can be counted on to do his task in life superlatively well regardless of whether he is applauded, suffers from feeling that he is taken too much for granted and not appreciated at his true worth. Sadly this is true. It is part of the unbalance of life today and has been for ages. But always it is figured into the reckoning that today is fleeting. Here. Gone. So with man. So with his work. Likewise with those rewards which he wanted but did not gain. They too, are speedily gone.

But the magnificent fiber of character that holds him to doing what is his to do, doing it at his steady best even when the outlook lowers and he sees little to cheer him on, that fiber of character stands him in good stead. It leads him ultimately to the land where his immortal qualities of dependability, high-souled goodness and stability are worth all they have cost him.

Are not these more worth striving for than applause which is as light and passing as a summer breeze? More worth seeking than ephemeral acclaim which is as a moth whose gauzy wings are singed by a too-bright light?

Qualities of stability are the roots which push always deeper down to feed upon richness of nourishment which the Divine has stored up in lavish quantity for those who go in eager search for it; nourishment on which mind and spirit may live and grow. Those roots hold firm and keep life in perfect balance regardless of the allure of superficialities.

They are the ones for whom the difficult tasks of life await and whose contributions to right living are appreciated above par on our scales of eternal values. It pays in such coin as outweighs any paltry pay which earth could give. And now I hasten off on another mission.

THE GARMENT OF FLESH

November 12

It is good for you to give more than the usual time to speeding up the work of these messages. It is the desire of those who are related to them on the Inner Planes who recognize the need for all possible haste.

The reason for this mention of haste is that we here who sponsor these informal talks on the mighty themes of the ages, know how much they are needed on the earth plane and thus wish to avoid any delay that is unnecessary.

And now I revert to a topic which I have mentioned once or twice but not in as much detail as I desire. It is necessary though, to make clear impact on human consciousness concerning it. Therefore I approach it for further discussion this evening.

Human customs that relate to the disposition of the body after the soul has winged its way higher, are responsible to large degree for the shrinking of the human from physical death and burial. Modern refinements purport to conceal the fearfulness of it. But burial of which I now speak, is at best a condition from which to shrink in thought, as one watches the placing of some loved body in the ground. I will not go into detail about what happens following interment. The order of nature brings ultimately "dust to dust!"

Human efforts to prevent physical disintegration are availing for a longer or shorter time. Ultimately nature has its way and the body becomes dust after a long period of decay. If one elects burial for family or friends, we from these Higher Planes urge that nature be allowed quick right of way, that disintegration be accomplished as speedily as possible.

From my early earth experience, I determined long years before the Great Transition, that my earthly house was to meet its dissolution purely, quickly, completely and wholesomely; fire accomplishing so rapidly and so purely what nature requires long to accomplish. From my vantage point of final experience, I rejoice and am grateful that I elected that method and that thus my spirit was freed from any restraining ties of the earthly habitation in which my soul had lived while I was of earth.

Please let me say that the way I chose is so wholly the way to be desired when one takes all the factors into consideration. In a sense the method is inconsequential. But in another way, there is a subtle holding of the body to the spirit that sometimes prevents its being free for its full flight; sometimes keeps it earth-bound in ways that are not desirable nor helpful.

If the depressing customs and traditions which have hedged in the burial of those who have been promoted, could only be done away with, and other customs be established that radiated joy and life everlasting, increase of glory and eternal absence of pain, what gain it would be to earth people!

Always there will be that sense of physical loss of the one who has passed from sight. But with increasing knowledge of the possibilities of communication between worlds, that is being diminished and will not be so black a wall of separation as formerly when the separation seemed hopelessly complete.

The body has no slightest value when once the spirit has taken its flight and should be placed where it may revert as soon as possible to the primordial dust from which it came. The quicker, the better! Modern methods which seek to preserve the contours of the body for long years after the Transition accomplish nothing that is good and much that is detrimental. Those who are left find it easier to adjust to the order of life when the disposition of the garment of flesh is promptly and completely accomplished.

That of itself is great gain from practical standpoints. The spirit that has been released from earth bondage finds its adjustment easier when the bonds of the body are loosened as completely and as quickly as may be. These factors are the only two that primarily are worthy consideration. And they are worthy of it.

From this vantage point and in company with these others who speak through me, we hope for the rapid speeding up of earth mortals to appreciate the value of prompt reversion to the original dust of the bodily residue from which the spirit—the only deathless part—has taken its flight.

If this has seemed an uninviting topic for these messages, please let me say that this is instruction to earth mortals on a matter of vital importance to those who have passed the Veil and who know the sufferings which they experienced because they were hampered in their freedom and held back in their adjustment to the new, spiritual way of life by misguided, though loving reverence of the body and unwillingness to permit its return to the elements of which it was made.

The theme is difficult. Feelings that cluster around it are intense. I speak plainly but with tender consideration of those who from time to time are in sorrow. To them and to all I commend the meaning of this talk.

And now your Sabbath is almost gone. I trust you to the sweet peace of God and pray His benedictions to abide with you, giving you joy and a feeling of closeness to His warm heart. My blessings I give you!

November 13

I have a message for you and for others who often need consolation in spirit, the assurance that all is well though material aspects seem to show otherwise.

You remember that verse from the Holy Scriptures which says, "There shall no evil befall thee." Take that for your help. Lean upon it. Believe it. Live it. And know that slight temporal disruptions are fleeting and of no consequence whatever.

All that matters is what concerns the soul. And your refuge is always under the shadow of the Almighty. He never fails. He never will. All He asks is faith! And He will see you through!

There is another word in Scripture which tells earth people to "Commit thy way unto the Lord, trust also in Him, and He shall bring it to pass." If mankind really believed that, if people really committed their anxieties and problems to Him and trusted Him to lead them through, life would be made over in the twinkling of an eye.

It is one of the hard things for the human to learn. Somehow he feels that he himself must find and make his own way, and take care of himself. Not strangely he finds himself bogged down often, wondering which way his path leads and how to find it. The other is so simple, so satisfying a way, that even though I remember with clarity my experiences when I was resident on earth, I wonder why the earth person cannot find himself willing to put his trust where it will never be betrayed and to go free of useless and devastating anxieties.

Give of your best, in ways at your command, to help yourself and others practice this command of committing your way, let it pass from your guidance into His hands, then trust, literally trust, and you will be surprised and comforted to see how wonderfully things work out for you.

You remember that the other evening I talked with you about the human habit of pulling the plant up by the roots to see if the roots were growing; then being surprised that they gained no firm place in the soil and did not produce in blossom or fruit or ear. Of course. They can't. No more can one find relief he is entitled to, when his faith is as limited as that. Faith, you know, is the evidence of things not seen. When sight comes in, faith goes out. And there you have a valuable lesson on negotiating life even when the stream flows among the shallows or through rocky chasms or on level ground. Sometimes in its course through every human life it runs that gamut from level ground to rocky chasms to shallows. Blessed is the one who learns that there is a Guide to pilot him through one as well as through the other; to Whom darkness is as light; One Who never is weary; never slumbers nor sleeps; and in Whom is all wisdom, all goodness, all love, all power.

The life that fails to learn the lesson of faith when clouds lower, is poor in its essence, when it might know the fullness and richness of the Godhead. Earnestly I commend it to you and to all who are willing to adventure to the highlands of faith under the guiding care of the All-Father Who will see you through perplexity or need or heartache.

Sometimes the earth person whose load is heavy wonders why faith does not accomplish what he expected of it and why he does not go free of his load. There is no promise in Scripture nor in life that any one will be spared trouble or discipline of mind or spirit or that his way through earth life will lead constantly amid roses or by quiet streams.

Our Lord's life did not. His was uphill most of His short life. But never, not even on Calvary, did faith fail Him. Nor was He left to go alone through the Garden nor to the tomb. The lesson is one of the stiff ones that life poses. But it is as rich in rewards as it is difficult to learn. I beseech you to learn it and to live by it to the last degree.

Faith is such a sweet experience when you have grasped its significance and its true value as a working agent in life. It is like trusting a loving parent who would never fail his child. Exactly like it! But in the realm of the spirit, mankind finds it hard to commit his way and to know that he is being guided safely over hard stretches of life.

The hour is late. I commend you and all to the tender mercies of our Lord Who is the Shepherd of us and Who takes unremitting care of His sheep.

That is a beautiful figure of speech and as I leave you for the night, I ask you to repeat the Shepherd Psalm for the quiet and comfort it will give you. Remember too, that "Peace I leave with you; my peace I give unto you. Not as the world giveth give I unto you." Thank you for taking this important message.

BOTH SIDES OF PRIDE

November 14

It is good to begin again the talk with you at your evening hour. I am glad the one of last night, short though it was, went deep into your heart and calmed your spirit, giving courage and buoyancy to your mind. So it is always when faith finds the door open and the way free for entering the heart.

You will find that last night's talk which was most carefully prepared here on the Seventh Plane for just such need as yours, will meet real response in hearts and lives of many who will seek to follow it.

I shall talk tonight of pride. You had not thought of that as a theme, had you? But you see how it relates itself to the whole fabric of spiritual life, don't you? Pride is like many another quality with which man is endowed; it is very good and it is very bad! That statement is in no wise contradictory nor inconsistent! Here from our side of life we see the outworkings of it both ways among people yet of earth. It is their support and their downfall.

Because it is interwoven through the spiritual fabric, let us talk first about the pride that is very good; that will not let a person slump from his best efforts; that will not allow him to reveal himself as less than his best; that keeps his discipline over himself in high gear even when it is uncomfortable and inconvenient; that never forgets that he is deeply ingrained with obligation always to do and be his best.

That kind of pride recognizes that it is cheap to give up and costly to continue the struggle in a high-souled way, that others may see the courage manifest as strong as the heart which manifests it; and seeing, may emulate it in their lives. The pride which is very good, oh, most excellently good, and for which the world pines, knows how essential it is to believe in all that God is and does and means to the human heart. That pride knows full well how God places responsibility upon the heart that trusts Him, to live up to its privileges and to represent Him in all ways.

Yes, this is pride; glorified, it is true. Nevertheless it is pride in spiritual integrity and in manifesting it in every phase of earth work and life. Often it is easier to let go and let down in moral and spiritual standards. But pride in the purity of the soul and in the cleanness of relations to the One Who is all pure, comes to his help. And he does not let down! It is a type of pride not too often found, yet revealed surprisingly in places and at times when one would not expect to find it. Always it seems to have a breeziness about it as of fresh winds blowing in the open places of the spirit, with room for the sunshine and fresh air of the spirit world that can come in and abide. The world can do with plenty of this type of pride. It partakes of the Divine and no soul was ever too proud for its own good in this kind and degree of spiritual pride.

Quite at opposite poles is the pride that is equivalent to show-off of all things superficial, like veneer that shines, catches the sun and sends gleams of reflection from some bright object. But nothing deeper than the surface. All polish and glitter with no more depth than the surface of polished wood. This is the pride that struts spiritually as well as physically and makes a show of itself on very little. Of itself there is nothing wicked about it. But it is shallow, when life is in need of depths of goodness, depths of conviction and willingness to serve. The shallow amounts to little when much has a right to be given.

I speak particularly of shallowness of spirit which skims only the top, caring not for being willing to delve into riches of mind and soul that, like pure gold, wait to be mined and minted for use.

The pride which is content with shallowness is equivalent to weakness of fiber, weed-like fiber, quickly grown up and with no enduring quality. What life and the world need is the oak fiber which will bend but will not break because it is possessed of strength and abiding sturdiness in root and in branch.

This kind of pride costs heavily to cultivate. But like everything else which costs, it is valuable in soul fiber and spirit firmness. I commend such pride which goes deep into the soil of life, to every person who reads these words from the Inner Planes. It is a quality worth cultivation.

There is another facet to this question of pride—the side which preens itself on being light and shallow, on being the show-off and never the sturdy oak type, that seeks irresponsibility, the dance of light and shadow as on a summer day, seeks only its own light way and craves only to be seen and applauded of men.

Harmless as that may seem, we here from the Higher Planes know how seriously such prideful minds undermine others who often are seeking to find and to follow higher-leading trails of life. They are deflected by these gauzy-winged creatures of only one night, then are done and gone. Much harm is done by them. Their pride is not alone their own downfall. They are responsible for the downward pull of others. Altogether this is a quality of soul experience to be shunned, deceptive and deluding and to those extents, dangerous.

Anything is which leads one lower than his best of mind and spirit. His best, whatever his best is, can be so wondrously beautiful if it is pursued as a spiritual ideal, with the God-idea dominating it. No shallow pride can blind such a one nor lead him astray. He knows the direction he takes. He knows his Guide. And he goes steadily in quest of his goal.

Someday he comes to the end of his earthly quest. He may be still very young—or older. It matters not. But he comes over here to this side of life, finds himself in a congenial atmosphere where adjustment is relatively easy, because his spirit has been geared to the highest; his fibers of being are sturdy and strong and his search is always for that which has true and abiding values.

Here he finds kindred spirits who like him have followed the gleam of pure purposes and have sought to share all they had with those whom they could help. Such a one rejoices in the beauty of this spirit realm—radiance of color, harmony in music, spirits akin and congenial, mentality developed to keener abilities when no longer is it shackled to the physical body, and the enveloping freedom of thought and movement and life in every richest aspect. Under such conditions as the Higher Planes afford, he comes to great loftiness of growth and power.

Do I seem to have digressed from my original thesis of pride? Not if you follow the fundamental thought all the way through, until it is easy to see where God-like pride leads, in using soul powers which are the gift of the Creator for living and working at highest capacity and in purest sublimation of which he is capable.

Earth people often limit that word which I have used tonight as my central theme to the tendency to show off, with nothing much to justify the show; the tendency to want the spot light on any occasion. That is one small side of the whole quality of pride which is as constructive as the earth mind is prone to think of it on the negative side. So if I have opened a new line of thought on a vital matter of development, it is well worth doing.

Turn the word around and see it from its other side, then see how much you can cultivate this highly practical and valuable quality for your spiritual good. To say you are proud is as splendid as the type of thing that makes you proud. Do you see?

As in everything else, the standard which you adopt and by which you measure your ideals, determines the levels of that which you are acquiring. This thesis will hold good in whatever line of endeavor you test it.

This kind of study is stimulating because it starts the mind off on many a quest in directions that are different from routine paths into which the mind often falls and follows along, losing the thrill of blazing new trails and unearthing new riches of conquest often in the most unexpected places.

And now again, our hour is done. It is a message which was needed to round out the whole and I give it to you with gratitude. May the rich blessing of God the Father rest upon and abide with you. Good night now!

THE DIRECTION OF YOUR EYES

November 15

I have a message tonight which is destined to fill a need of hearts that cry for help and comfort. Under the mask which many people wear are forlorn hearts seeking more or less blindly for that which will satisfy. We here who have completed the human span know that nothing can heal and fulfill and satisfy except that which is of the spirit. All of that comes from these Inner Planes.

The difference between downtrodden, gloomy earth people and those whose faces radiate joy and confidence and power in living, is the direction of the eyes. It is not related to the loads they bear nor the problems they face, the perplexities they must handle nor the weaknesses they must overcome. None of that enters into the difference that separates the two classes of people.

Some who are gloomy and unhappy, cynical and bitter, have the most earthly substance, with everything the world calls good. Their money, their houses and lands or stocks or bonds or goods heaped up in the vaults of earth, have no power to erase lines of discontent from their faces, nor bitterness nor woe from their hearts. They find no brightness in the living of the days; no anticipation of good at each morning's dawn; no outbreak of sheer gratitude as evening wraps its mantle of peace and rest over the world.

There are others whose substance is limited sometimes to the vanishing point; whose work is heavy and earth conditions difficult in the extreme; whose faces glow with joy that is genuine and whose hearts radiate peace that others sense but cannot understand; whose spirits are unruffled under whatever stress; whose power to meet and conquer life is clearly from an unseen source.

What makes the difference? Just what I said a moment ago—the direction of the eyes! One class looks down at the mire and muck; sees only the dirt around their feet; only what is material and physical; only earthly aspects and clouds that hang low over their segments of earth life. Their eyes are so turned that they couldn't see the sun nor the stars nor the glory of the firmament nor the beauty of the clouds that bring glory instead of gloom to the horizon.

Nor can they see anything except what lies close around themselves; no vistas; no far reaches of hills and valleys and God's glorious trees; because their eyes are turned in the wrong direction. How clear all of this is to us here on these Planes of Privilege! How we yearn to help them turn their vision upward to the hills from whence cometh all the help that any life could possibly need! Perhaps it will surprise you that we give much time and study here to finding ways whereby we may focus anew the eyes of earth residents, giving them better appreciation of what there is to behold in life—and how to see it.

This means so much to me because as you well remember, my earthly vision was darkened for years and I learned through that discipline what it means to negotiate living with little or no sight.

This message therefore, comes very close to my heart and is given to you for all the help it may be to others who need to gain clearer sight and better ways to focus their eyes. I may seem here to mix my spiritual figure of speech with my own physical experiences while I was of earth. But if I do, I nevertheless think my meaning is clear.

The many whose faces and hearts glow with cheer and joy which the world cannot understand nor explain, have learned to see true sources of happiness; to look beyond what is physical to see in everything and everybody all the good to be found therein; to look "not down but up." Looking to the hills and horizons gives always far visions of possibilities. It reveals the shining of the sun of joy even in the valleys of life and points out the rare and beautiful heights to which any life may attain.

Looking high one never detects the mud and muck which those see whose eyes are turned downward. They see the sapphire skies of noon time; the indescribable glow of the heavens at dawn and at the going down of the sun; the glory of the moon and the majesty of the starry heavens.

As this is true of the material world, so is it true in the spiritual realms where our real living is accomplished. When one stands on high land and looks constantly up and out, there is no limit to the possibilities of what one can envision nor of the direction in which one's feet should be turned.

The downward-looking man pulls himself in the direction of his vision. Always that is true. The upward-looking person lifts himself by the very fact and force of the direction of his vision. And inevitably he moves in that direction.

The one is filled with darkness. The other is radiant with the reflected shining of the sun in his life. Which way you look, is all the difference! And does anyone have the right to shed gloom when he may reflect joy and gladness?

It makes such eternal difference both on the earth plane and in these Spirit Realms to which everyone comes soon or late, in what direction you look; what you see; where you go; what you accomplish and how you do it! There is nothing fleeting about all of this.

For as you see in the earth world, so will you go. And as you go there, so will you find yourself headed when you make this Great Transition. If your eyes have been turned steadily to the heights of pure purpose and achievement, it will stand you in good stead when you reach our shores. If you have seen only the mud at your feet, you will have gone in that direction only to find yourself retarded when you come to the Spirit Planes.

Speaking as I am tonight from the Inner Planes on a message which has been reserved for this series, deciding what direction is of utmost importance, worthy of careful and serious thinking by every earth person. We leave it with you for use in the relations of these messages and their scattering abroad.

God's richest blessings be upon you as you carry a double load, looking to Him for strength for every need!

OUR FATHER

November 16

The theme tonight is of the majesty and glory of God as we know Him from these exalted Planes where we see without obstruction and serve without weariness; where we learn of His love and goodness in an atmosphere of which earth people can conceive in only limited ways. The figure of speech tells of Him as Father. It is a happy figure, seeing that in Him is all goodness and from Him come all good things. In Him is wisdom incarnate. Nothing is known that He did not create. Thinking of Him as Father has inevitably given the concept of Him as a man. Such of course, is not true. He cannot be limited. His power is almighty and radiates into every space that exists. His limitlessness is beyond human power to understand. He is pure spirit. Unseen. You remember how the Scriptures say that "No man hath at any time seen the Father."

It is impossible to see spirit. But His presence is felt and known and loved in ways of great glory, too powerful and all-pervading to explain in words for earth understanding.

It is at His will that all good flows out and that the worlds swing in their orbits; that men are given power to see the right and to live it in magnificent courage.

The consciousness of His spirit pervades us here until it seems that there is no limit to our power to worship and adore; to love and to serve Him. It fills this unseen universe with such love and glory; such visions of the possibilities of life as we lived it and as earth people are living it now, that we yearn almost unbearably to share this God with you of limited vision and partial understanding.

One glimpse, one sensation of what He really is, would unmake all the little earth ideas and concepts about Him and stretch the minds of the human for comprehending adequately the real nature and power of God the Father. Though of course, the spirit never existed that could fully comprehend Him. On these Planes of Spirit Life we come much closer to knowing and loving Him than has yet been achieved by men on the earth plane, devoted and adoring though many have been.

As we learn more of His ordering of the Universe with its multiplied worlds and its infinitude of created things, we marvel increasingly, knowing better with each revelation that from Him alone could come such power and wisdom and glory and love. It is impossible to compress Him into human words. He just won't compress!

Mankind has too largely thought of God as austere; as Judge of all the earth. Those are phases of His limitless nature. But tonight I choose to think of Him in the relation of Father with Whom Jesus Christ was on terms of such intimate love and understanding that the two were literally one.

There was never a moment during the earth life of the Son, when more than a breath of whispered prayer was needed to bring the Two together in perfect unity, strength and power, more than sufficing for earth emergencies.

The tenderness of relation between the Father and His Son is one of the most glorious phases of experience of which this world knows, world whose paths the Son trod for three and thirty years; whose storms He stilled; whose temptations He faced and overcame; whose lessons He learned and whose sufferings He endured.

If the hungry were to be fed, Jesus lifted His eyes to the Father. If the sick were to be healed, He looked to His Father for power. If the dead were to be brought back to life, it was; "Father, I know that Thou dost always hear me!" And the dead came back to the physical dimensions of life.

In the last earthly hours when the Cross was His portion, Jesus said, "Father, forgive them!" So close was their relation of love that His endurance was adequate. And His courage never flagged nor power to fulfill His mission to the Children of Men. The Son was equal because the Father was with Him!

This does not show the Father austere, does it?

Men have erred in that they pray to the Son. He Himself enjoined men everywhere to pray to the Father. It is to God that men should lift their hearts in petition, in praise, in intercession and in worship. The Son prayed always to His Father and the one perfect prayer which teaches all men how they should pray, begins to "Our Father."

If only earth people could overcome the sense of remoteness of God, of the fearsomeness, the inaccessibility of God, and know that He is closer to them in their every earth struggle than their hands and feet; "nearer to them than breathing," what progress they would make in their spirit life! In their power to overcome the down-ward pull of earth life! What sense of communion with Him Who is all!

If you say you have heard that before, we from these Inner Planes reply, "Yes, you have heard it before. But if it were shouted from every housetop throughout the world every hour of the day, it would not be too much emphasis upon these qualities of the great and loving God. His children are not on terms of as intimate relations as is their privilege and as would give them Infinite infusions of added grace and glory."

I urge you to worship God the Father; to pray to Him; to know the loving sides of His Infinite goodness; to turn Him in every hour of anxious concern, remembering that not even a sparrow falls to the ground without the Father's notice! I beseech you and all to accept His offered light in any darkness; His strength in any weakness; His companionship in loneliness. It is more than any human can conceive. But it is true. He never fails! Remember that! He, God, the Almighty One, the Infinite Father, is your God, your Companion, your Helper, your Comforter, your ever-present Guide and Friend!

What greater message could we send you of earth tonight than this? The very firmament rings with His glory and the ineffable love which reflects Him. It is for you and for all of earth!

The angels sing His greatness and goodness. The spirits of just men made perfect, worship and adore. And we from these Spirit Planes are tonight telling you of earth to look to Him, the great God, for whatever your need is any moment of your lives.

He will not fail you.

I give you His blessing now in His name, blessing that is worth more than all the jewels earth mines could afford!

COMFORTS OF COMPANIONSHIP

November 18

On this your more leisurely evening, we shall talk with you about the power that comes to human hearts from constant companionship with the Father and His Son, Jesus Christ.

The church places less and lighter stress than seems credible upon these themes of vast significance, seeming to think that matters of more modern acceptance attract and hold more people to the observances of the church. It is a mistake; so great a mistake as we here know better than you of earth can yet know.

As a result the fire upon the altar of the church burned low. There has been little or no power from the modern pulpit.

The church has become relatively like many another institution, a good investment in community life. But it lacks this deep heart of companionship with the source of all power for victorious living. This source is the Father.

To know companionship with Him is the greatest gift life could make. And it is possible for every earth person to know in the most real and practical way. You have only to ask! This companionship with the Father is the sweetest thing we here on the Inner Planes experience and we live in that experience. It is impossible to describe it to anyone. But it radiates light and warmth, gladness, peace and lightness to every spirit. It puts wings on our aspirations and lifts us to higher planes of knowledge and power. It enables us to serve better when we are sent on missions that often are difficult, for the children of men. It fills our hearts with rejoicing to know that there is no limit to the growth of this indwelling companionship which climaxes every other ever known on earth or on these Ether Planes.

Only as the church on earth comes back—which really is coming forward and upward—to dependence on this companionship with the Father and thus receiving the power from Him to live grandly, will there be a flaming message and a witness to the vitality of this experience.

Companionship is a wonderful word, a comfortable word, a clear and intimate word because it represents understanding instead of aloofness and warmth of love instead of indifference.

Companionship is such a restful word, where no need exists to explain or to be on one's guard; where one may always be one's self and feed on the congenial response and enveloping love of the dear companion with whom is no variance of loyalty.

Rare and wonderful as this experience is among residents of earth, uplifting and inspiring as it is, multiply it a million times and you will get a glimmering of what companionship with the Father may mean to any heart which is opened to Him. I wish it might be possible for us here to make it so clear that mankind would see it as we see it and know that in this companionship is light for every shadow that falls across every pathway of earth. This companionship is shelter and warmth against chilling winds of discouragement and gusts of disappointment which threaten to tear the heart to shreds; against devastating sorrows that sweep down across the heart and seem to put the sun out of the heavens.

All of this is just a hint of the glory which can fill any heart that seeks this Infinite companionship with the All-Father. Every problem of life can be solved in the intimate relations of this companionship by faith in His Infinite wisdom and power. You know by your own experience how doors opened to you at a time of particular difficulty in your life; doors which no man opened, but which spread wide for you to enter into this sacred companionship with the Father Whose manifestations of love you especially needed. And you found it, experienced it and your life grew, your vision enlarged and your horizons were set farther back so that you could see and know.

I have spoken before in this series of how sore an error it was when the church stepped aside from its healing ministry of the body. Fear stepped in and the Divine Healer found no longer a place for His work among men whose bodies were sick. But that stepping away from one of the greatest opportunities the earth plane ever knew, does not mean that the power of the Father to heal His children has grown less. It merely means that they are not taking advantage of what He offers by way of health for sickness; of strength for weakness; of sturdy bodies in place of frailty which fears to do or undertake. All of this is there in the heart of the Father for anyone who asks and believes and accepts.

Isn't that a marvelous triumvirate—to ask from the loving Father; to believe that He grants what you ask; and then in faith to take it? Nothing else quite equals it as an experience. These three simple things are exercises for the spirit by which faith is strengthened, courage grows stronger, power to achieve is increased and all of life is enriched beyond human power to comprehend.

Ask! Believe! Accept! These three! Yet the heart of mankind finds them difficult to prove.

Asking is simple enough. Believing when with one's eyes the thing desired cannot be seen, overtaxes average faith. Accepting when the desired is not manifest, breaks down what is a perfect prescription for the ills of all humankind.

The breakdown is on the human side; never on the part of the Father. He stands ready, able, eager. But the law must be fulfilled which says that when one asks, he must believe that he receives and he must accept as having already received.

That law is simple and very profound, going into the deepest places of Divine wisdom and testing that which is fundamental faith. Without it, this relationship between the Father and His child is not perfect.

I commend you again to read that masterful statement of Saint Paul as he said that "Faith is the substance of things hoped for; the evidence of things not seen." And there you have it in a nutshell. No finer, no simpler, no more profound statement of what faith is and how it works has ever been given mankind than that.

If only you and all of you of earth would test it with every earth problem! Test it; prove it; make it work! Find out that it means just what it says! By so doing you would enrich your lives beyond comparison and the stature of your spirit would increase as you prove things in the spirit realm of which you had no previous knowledge.

Over here where we live, beyond the power of death to touch us or to despoil any of the wondrous beauty on which we feed our souls, it is great glory to experience anew more of what faith can mean and to demonstrate its working perfection.

You of earth always think that we here have no need of faith or of many of the things which are part of our spirit equipment as truly as they are of yours and much more actively employed than on your plane. In that you will someday learn how mistaken you were and how definite a part of our soul growth and life expansion is this radiant quality of faith in the Father. It is the dynamo of the universe. Harness faith to Infinite love and you see the tools with which we are able to work for the help of people on the planes of mortal life.

This is so great a theme that it is impossible to compass even a portion of it in these messages. But it is a very important part of the entire picture which we are giving you and will accomplish that whereunto we send it through you, for all who need and whose spiritual eyes will be opened to see, to believe and to receive!

Faith is of the endlessness of eternity! It is so simple that the little child may use it and prove it; so vast that the wisest mind can only dimly comprehend it. Happily, comprehending it is not necessary. All one needs to unlock the doors to its incalculable riches is to use it; test it and prove it!

While I was on the earth plane, I used to think that faith was an austere quality, stern, relentless and something to be a little afraid of; so little did I understand its nature or its working. Perhaps it is because it is so majestic a force, so far beyond anything which the earth mind can conceive, so superlative a power that mankind does not quickly grasp it nor learn to take advantage of its help.

But it isn't austere. It is part of the wisest provision the Infinite Father created as law immutable in His universe, part of the complete satisfaction which comes with companionship at the Father's side, as warm and gracious as His love which fills these Spirit Planes with radiance. Let your heart be filled with this free Faith and this Infinite love. Then you too, of earth will find your heart radiant with the same glowing quality, the same essence of love that characterize the Father.

What more shall I say on this mighty theme? Nothing at length. But I would stress the vastness of the opportunity to make life as grand an adventure as the heart can crave; stress also the certainty that faith in the Father's power to grant and to do for any who ask, is beyond cavil. Using, testing and proving are for each individual. They are part of the completeness of companionship with the Father.

However dark the world round about may be, He is light and Power and Peace and Glory and Love. Isn't this wonderful knowledge for each to have and to experience in his own life? Could heaven offer anything grander? Think on these things and demonstrate them for yourself. Then with faith renewed and love increased, you will be equipped to give more acceptably to those who need the truths which the Inner Planes herewith offer.

And now, good night to you! I go on a mission of great significance to human welfare. As I go, I send you the blessing of God the Father. This has been a most important talk.

WHEN THE PHYSICAL PRESENCE PASSES
November 19

You remember, I am sure, how the other evening when you were weary and disturbed, that you sat some while at your machine, waiting, willing to take our message. Nothing came. It was not possible to penetrate the fog of your disturbed mind and the sagging of your body.

The next day when you had peace and quiet in your heart and your body had recuperated with rest and slumber, I spoke promptly and easily to you, to the point of a vital message. You want to know why and how this is. It is neither possible nor feasible to try to explain the process in full to the earth mind. That is one of the mysteries which is withheld from those on earth. But I am at liberty to tell you that since these communications come by electrical impulse from the Ether Planes and must harmonize with earth vibrations which are at a different rate, it is exceedingly difficult to penetrate the density of fog which surrounds anyone who grieves or is disturbed in spirit.

Just why this is true, in its fullness of detail, will be made clear when you come home to this Higher Plane and are receptive to wider knowledge and clearer penetration which prevail here. Remember this, that it pays for you and all to maintain a poise of spirit and a peace of heart, both of which make possible the reception of messages from the Higher Planes to those of earth.

Lately you have been wondering about those who sorrow with fresh grief and whose hearts find no surcease from earthly loss. Nothing seems to have power to substitute for the physical presence of the beloved one who has gone. How can it be faced and endured? Where has the sunshine of life disappeared? Will the clouds ever be dispelled?

This is one of the hard problems; one of its severest disciplines; one of its most frequent experiences which seems never to lose its poignant power to darken the skies of the soul and to slow down the eagerness of living. Not strange! For the earth person has been prone to separate the physical from the spiritual and to hold to the body housing the spirit, rather than knowing that the body is only the scaffolding due to be removed when the real person, the spirit person, has no longer need for the scaffold.

Of course it is not the body that is the dear person; not the body that thinks and plans and loves and achieves. Not at all. That body is merely the housing of the spirit which is of life immortal and never subject to ravages of death. That spirit has no beginning and no ending. It is of the endlessness of eternity, which no one may comprehend.

It is not strange that the human suffers when the physical presence is removed and finds it impossible to realize that the dear one has been promoted to larger life and higher privilege. This failure to realize is because most of the earth teaching has been wrong and has placed such emphasis upon the dark side of death and the dissolution of the body. So little emphasis has been or now is placed upon the translation of the spirit to these lofty Realms where life is unspeakably beautiful; where living is on a grander scale; and where learning is accomplished without the fitful down-dragging of the body or distractions on the earth side of life.

This seems cruel to say, but it is intended in the kindest spirit, that at the root of much of the sorrowing for those who have passed beyond the Veil mistakenly called death, lies a sinister factor of selfishness! The one who has lost a dear one often does not rise above the thought of selfish loss; of how life on earth is to be managed; or a living made; or a social plan carried out; or a physical life be maintained; or a family held together now that the one has gone whose earth work has been completed and whose spirit released for promotion.

If that one had received an earth promotion, even though it meant physical separation for long periods, there would be rejoicing that the dear one was thought worthy of such enlargement of opportunity and responsibility and grateful pride for the privilege of living in a country where beauty and joy and comfort abound, where the promoted one would never be sick nor in pain. This is so, in very truth.

But when the promotion is associated with that dark, dank word called "death," the human gives up to despair and such sense of bitter loss as makes the Inner Planes wonder whether the lesson of the Transition from earth to higher life will ever be learned.

But it will be learned, of course, with the growth of the spirit of truth which lifts the souls of mankind out of false teaching and concepts that are in error and clears the air of doubt about the process called death.

Increasingly though slowly mankind is learning to his comfort the true concept that passing from earth is the opening of the door to life infinitely better, filled with the most satisfying development and employment in the gracious fields of eternity. When that is accepted in the human heart, the worst of the loss and loneliness is gone and there comes a peace which is part of truth itself. Eradicating the factors of selfishness in so-called death, is difficult for the human. The one who has been translated may have been the breadwinner, mainstay of a family, the dependence of the community, head of a business enterprise. With him gone, what can be done? Who will carry the load? Who will earn the living? Who will find the way for the neighborhood to prosper?

It is scarcely possible to say without being misunderstood, that back of these questions often lies something of unwillingness on the part of those who should do it, to shoulder the load of breadwinning, to come from having one's way all day to the discipline of an ordered life on schedule through which ways will be found, livings be made and perplexities be solved in spirit of triumph.

The one who has gone triumphantly through such ordeals, knows that often what seemed impenetrable loss, the most impossible situation, is blessing disguised for the moment, but working through to unmistaken values to the one experiencing it. Is it not true that often a shock of loss is necessary to shake the human from his pleasant, comfortable lethargy into constructive, worthy attitude of life where he rouses himself and goes to the business of making the best of himself and his God-given powers?

I use you as illustration because you have gone through repeated experience of the passing of your dear ones to the Inner Planes until you seemed to stand alone within what appeared like an iron ring surrounding you. Nor could you find release of your vast creative powers. From a purely physical standpoint, it looked dark and bad for you.

But one by one, you came through these experiences, having grown by what your spirit learned each testing time. You might easily have given up to despair that earth would have considered unavoidable. But you were comforted and guided, your spirit was taught that the door would open and you would go free of that iron ring which figuratively surrounded you, and this standing alone prove to be the richest experience of earth for you.

It has put you through your spiritual paces and stretched every muscle of your soul life. This is part of your recompense for all you have undergone. You have proved that the scattered threads of earthly life could be disentangled and the weaving be renewed for a pattern of great beauty. What you have done, others have done. And can do!

Discipline? Yes! But it is the medium of growth, of unsuspected powers of body and spirit. It is the release of dear ones from restricting bonds of earth to unspeakable freedom and joy and peace here on the Inner Planes.

With the present earth debacle of bloodshed and agony, when millions are coming with such suddenness from the body to these shores of spirit life, this lesson which we have been giving you this afternoon, is most important. Like most lessons, it is not easy. But it must be learned now or later for the sake of the one who goes and the one who stays longer on the physical plane. I beseech you to pass on as widely as you can, the significance and blessings which attend this Transition from the body to life which is pure spirit and filled with unspeakable glory.

If earth people could look high to the beauty and everlastingness of the life which knows no death, no sickness, no loss, no disappointments, no privations, what revolution would come about in the earth atmosphere! Weeping would give way to praise and sorrow to gratitude! All of this will come some glad day. You will have a hand in bringing it.

So praise the Father; look upward always; never give up to loneliness; seek always the comfort of the Inner Planes; and you will be doubly blest. Farewell!

November 20

The word we send you tonight concerns that old and usually dreaded thought of sacrifice in the discipline of the spirit through which it learns heights and richness of experience not otherwise attainable; but necessary for growth that must be made.

The human shies off from the idea of sacrifice. It implies suffering which is never welcome; and loss and hardship. These mankind never accepts willingly. But there is a power thru sacrifice that cannot be denied; a willingness to surrender and to forego for the sake of higher good and richer experience.

The Scriptures are filled with illustrations of the call for sacrifice and the results obtaining from willingness to give up one's own way and one's personal wishes in obedience to higher power and greater wisdom.

Could anything be more dramatic than the Patriarch Abraham as he takes Isaac, his young son, up into the mountain? Against every impulse of his father-heart, against every impulse of love and pride, he nevertheless was willing there on that mountain top to sacrifice the lad as a burnt offering to Jehovah, since that appeared to be the Divine decree.

The unknowing, unsuspecting lad; his questions about where the sacrifice was for which the altar was being prepared; the protesting heart of the father; his loyalty in ultimate degree to the decree of the Almighty; then when it seemed that the hour had struck and the lad must be offered upon the altar, there came "the tangled ram!" How magnificent it was! How severe a test for a father-heart!

From it there came to long generations of mankind, lessons of obedience, of loyalty to higher powers, of acceptance of the will of God even though it cut across the grain of every desire of the human heart.

Abraham proved that he would hesitate at nothing which the Divine asked of him; that he would be dependable in crisis; that courage abided within him for any emergency, any sacrifice, any ordeal and that he had nothing to fear from his own weakness under stress.

What marvelous lessons they are! And what power they impart to the fiber of one's spirit. To know that one will not quail under stress; that one has the inner fortitude to endure without crumpling down in defeat; what grandeur such knowledge imparts to the heart!

The Master Himself Who came in the flesh as the Babe of Bethlehem, came knowing that He was to be offered as a lamb led to the slaughter. Every temptation was offered to deflect Him from His course which was in harmony with the will of the Father.

He surrendered all claims to joys of this world; to experiences normal to the human; all desire for power that He might prove "that good and acceptable and perfect will of God."

Sacrifice, when the spirit is right, holds within itself grandeur of power; sturdiness of courage; sweet sense of loyalty; willingness to surrender the lesser for the greater, that are part of the discipline of every life.

We here on these Inner Planes were all tested when we were on earth, to see whether we could endure the strain of giving up our wills for the will of a higher power. Our limited vision could not see why nor even that the sacrifice could work out for greater good. The greatest benefit comes to the learning spirit. We proved that. We know the value of those lessons. The closer they come to cutting into the quick of life, the greater the ultimate reward in spirit power. Does that seem anomalous and hard to understand?

It is part of the mystery of life. No man may escape this discipline of sacrifice on the earth plane or here on the Inner Planes. It is an integral part of soul growth. As with all discipline, the more firmly it is grasped, the more unquestioningly it is accepted, the more rapid is the progress. This is its own reward.

He who seeks to escape discipline, who places his wishes first, comes never to any size in the world of the human or on the Ether Planes. We give that we may have; yield that we may grow; suffer that we may rejoice; all under the law of the wise God Who orders the lives of His children for their good. From these Planes of greater vision and larger understanding, we beg you of earth not to be afraid of the idea nor the experience of sacrifice; not even when your dearest ambitions and possessions are involved. Do not fear it! At its heart, it holds vast treasure for the one who accepts willingly and loyally and does not hold back in seeking his own wishes.

We have seen this exemplified so often that we know what it means for the human to offer himself and his abilities; his comfort and ease; his ambitions and talents for other than selfish use. In the home, this law is in constant practice—or in denial. Where there is unwillingness to sacrifice one's way, discord prevails illustrating what we say to you tonight. In community and church, in state, nation and throughout the world, the law holds with never an exception.

There is no relationship of the human where this discipline need not be experienced. Daily it presents itself in the associations of ordinary human life. Where it is understood and the principle of it followed, there come richness and mellowness, sweetness of spirit, strength of purpose, that make life a marvelous adventure.

Thus you see how that which is dreaded and shunned, is really a source of blessing when it is experienced in the right spirit. How it contributes to possibilities of growth and might in meeting the demands of living!

All of this illustrates the wonders of the laws which the Creator implanted in His world when He brought forth the races of men and gave them the world over which to have dominion. He gave them each other and themselves over whom to have right dominion, to come nearer the stature of what God intended they should be. It is all a part of the whole creative plan!

Down where you are on the earth plane, you are so close to constant conflict, that you do not see these things in proper perspective. But here, we see them as they are. And we never cease to marvel at the inter-workings of Almighty plans for His creation and the perfection of functioning when the children of men yield to this functioning.

We wish you could stand off at a distance occasionally and see the real picture. How it would clarify much that is murky and little understood! But you will see it and understand it when you are through with your earth work and ready to come up here—not to rest, but to work with renewed strength and ardor, with clarified vision and stepped-up powers; to rejoice and be glad at the opportunities that surround you here for wider serving of those on the lower planes of privilege.

The time is not yet. Much remains for you to do for which you are equipped and which will yield you great satisfaction.

The mighty themes which present themselves in this series, seem to have no end. They all fit into a well-rounded whole for which my instructors who prepare these talks with me, are eager.

Do you not see—but of course you do—how these latter messages have changed from the first ones which came through your helpful "receiving station"? Without her it would have been impossible for this door of communication between your world and mine to be opened. As the talks have progressed, they have steadily reached up to higher levels and to mightier themes for which you could not have been ready in the first stages of this experience. You have come to it gradually through loyal acceptance of this responsibility which we placed upon you.

You go back in your thinking often to that evening, more than two months now according to your earth time, when you had been told that you were to complete this manuscript without any intermediate party, directly with me. You were skeptical. And a bit annoyed. You made no move to start. So the spirits from these Inner Planes came to your earth home and with their inexplicable power, lifted you from your chair, took you across your floor, seated you at the machine and placed your hands on the keys. Still you hesitated until my words began to flood your consciousness. That is the story. It has mystery. Yes! And that must remain mystery. But enough has now been told for you to understand the sacred origin of this series of lessons direct from us of the Inner Planes through you, to needy earth people. Again I congratulate you that you were chosen, even if it was hard to arouse your consciousness to acceptance of your part in this plan.

This message draws to its close. Its lessons are of utmost importance and significance. I beseech you to learn them with willing heart. I leave you now for other missions.

May the sweet peace of our Lord rest upon and abide with you as you make your way through the work of the days. I bless you with all joy. Good night!

THE POWER OF PRAISE

November 21

It is good to renew our talks tonight on things of immortal importance that matter most in the life of humankind. Transient interests come and go, mattering little one way or another. But these issues brought before you from the Inner Planes, do matter much.

In their observance, they are open sesame to larger life on the earth plane; and they further spiritual progress as one by one earth people come up higher to live without the weight and sag of the body.

You are on the eve of your Thanksgiving celebration and this forms the theme of our discourse this evening. Not the celebration. Do not misunderstand me. But the power and the spirit of Thanksgiving as it operates in the human heart and as we live it here on these Immortal Planes.

The heart responds to that upon which it is nourished. When it is fed upon gloom and dismay and displeasure, nourished on doubt and darkness of outlook, it partakes of those qualities and is depressed. Thus living is colored to match that which the heart accepts. It is serious when one realizes that the power of thought can change the whole complexion of earth living. But so it is. There is nothing more downpulling than thoughts of despair on which many people live; discouragement and despondency on which to make a life. No wonder they come through each day at so poor a dying rate, with little to show for the effort of living.

Turn the picture around and see what a difference it makes when one sees the sunny side; and gauges life after the pattern of brightness and happiness and gladness for everything that is good! Many earth people see the good side of the picture and profit by it. But they do not stop to realize their responsibility for expression of thankfulness for this good. Thus they divide and diminish the good that would be theirs if they took a positive attitude and realized their obligation to express thankful praise for the manifold good that comes every day.

There is no tonic for the body which excels praise and thanksgiving. It tones up the body and brings the spirit to higher levels than could be reached in a millennium of gloom. It starts circulation, stirs nerve activity, animates the brain cells and makes life over for the better.

It is a marvelous factor in large living. When Jesus Christ walked the highways of His Palestine, you remember how He healed those who had grievous diseases, yet only one returned to praise Him. That one had greater growth in real life values than those who took the good and went off saying nothing to any man. They lost for their spirits the tonic and the thrill that come when one gives heartwarming thanks for good that has been received. It doubles every good when one gives thanks for it because it opens the eyes of the spirit to clear vision of other good and tones up all the quality of living for receiving other good.

As I found it while I was resident upon earth, as you find it now, and as we here know that it is, the custom too often is to take the good that comes, be casually glad, say not much about it and go on with the affairs of life. That way leads to poverty of spirit and stunts the growth of spirit powers which otherwise would multiply and fill life with more for which to be glad. Why are earth people so loathe to express emotions of gratitude? If only they would see what transforming power there is in hearty giving of thanks, deep spiritual thanks for every good thing that comes with the days, they would change the face of their living and soon they would be as different persons.

Earth residents have become accustomed to concealing emotions that bear any relation to the life of the spirit. That is a mistaken notion, a losing custom which results in pinched, starved standards within the soul where there should be lavishness of joy and gratitude.

When instead of this stunting concealment of the buoyant powers of thanksgiving, there is full and free willingness to show, indeed to shout praise for innumerable gifts which God has made a part of life, the entire measurement of living changes. And life becomes a rare adventure in good which increases with every expression of genuine thanksgiving.

Here on these Planes of Spirit we shout and sing for joy to give vent to our gratitude for the inexpressible goodness and wholeness which surround us and make our work the ecstasy that it is. How this unrestrained emotion of thanksgiving fills our spirits to overflowing and doubles every joy! I wish you could feel some of the released power which sweeps over us from this spiritual exercise! It is not limited to life on these Planes. In smaller degree and on slower rate of vibration the same quality of growth in all good things fills your horizon when you lift up your heart and give thanks.

How we wish everyone of earth would put this to a thorough test. Try it out! Prove it! Anyone who does, will give thanks anew for this lesson which comes from the deep places of the Spirit Planes.

I would that I might show any who need, how mistaken it is to reserve thanksgiving until everything is prosperous and there are no heartaches, no problems of supply, or health, or placement. The one who waits until perfection in his affairs has manifested, will never know the joy of singing praises and shouting in thankfulness for the good things which no man can number

Does life seem more filled with burdens and sorrows, with loads and disappointments to bear, than with things over which to rejoice? It will always seem so when it is on these that the thought is allowed to dwell. But with vigor of spirit turn to inventory of the blessings with which life is filled, then see if the scales of a thankful spirit do not show a true picture for rejoicing, that will enlarge the whole basis of living.

We here on these Spirit Planes do not forget our earth knowledge and so it comes to me to remind you that when those first men and women of heroic mold came to settle upon the inhospitable shores of this your country, they faced hunger, disease and death, with cold and drought, famine and danger. Yet it was with them that the formal celebration of Thanksgiving began! So much more seemed against giving thanks than for it. But they were wise in their knowledge of life. They gave thanks in the face of tragedy and disaster. And they set the pace for all who followed, as the country grew rich and powerful in all things material.

Thinking carefully about giving thanks I urge you to see that good received is in no wise limited to material good. When it is so limited in thought, half the blessing is gone. The good of highest value pertains to the spirit, to that which is immortal.

Who can count the spiritual good that floods every life of earth? The love of God, Divine protection, ever present help in any trouble, the over-shadowing Presence with its power to bestow peace upon a heart overwrought with grief! There is no possibility of estimating this good which is as free as the air. Need one wait for more than theme, to lift up the heart in outspoken praise and thanksgiving?

Each time you raise your praise in loyalty and joy, your power to give thanks is increased.

Thereby your power to receive more of the greatest and best things from the Almighty Giver, is enlarged. Do you not see how it operates always for the good of the one who is willing to make a life of constant expression of gratitude until the heart seems unable to contain more of the good that flows into it?

Oh, think of this day after day. Let your life overflow with thanksgiving even when things seem hard and you do not see your way clearly. Just praise and give thanks that the loving Father knows your way. He knows your need. He has all power, all love, to bestow upon you of earth whose hearts open by the magic door of giving thanks.

The surest way to close the door of the heart against increased good is to close the door on thanksgiving and tune out all feelings of gratitude for good which has been received. That does indeed lock and bar the door.

I wish I had fully appreciated this wonderful lesson while I was yet a resident of earth. It would have meant enlargement of my spirit powers and made me more a representative of the Father Whom I sought to serve.

Not until I came hither did I realize the possibilities for growth and joy and service that abide in giving heart-felt thanks for everything, even for what seems misfortune! Often it brings blessing in its wake. Learn your lesson! Do! And may the peace and joy of the loving Father rest upon you now and evermore. I give you my richest blessing and I shall come again at your next leisure. Good night!

GLEAMING GOLD

November 22

You looked up with surprise when you heard me speak the theme for this evening—"A man's life consisteth not in the abundance of the things which he possesseth!" Weren't you surprised when that flashed through your consciousness and you knew that upon such theme the evening message would depend?

This is one of the glorious things in life, that what a man has is not related to what he is. Many will not agree with you. To such, money and its equivalents are the gauge and standard, the beginning and end of all values. To them, everyone is big or little according to the size of the bank account. How poor such people are! Let a little gale of economic instability come blowing around the corner of life unexpectedly and gleaming piles of gold are whisked away, gone as completely as the wind that blew from somewhere and is gone, no man knoweth whither.

It cannot be other than that such changes in earthly holdings come overnight on the wings of national disaster; poor management; from death; or a thousand causes. Funds that were the be-all and end-all of some, are vanished. What is left? To their viewpoint, not much. They have estimated everything by false and transitory standards. They have measured the fabric of life by a yard stick that could not be depended upon.

It is tragedy when such situations exist. I do not mean when money is swept away. Often that is great blessing. The tragedy is when that has come to be any earth person's standard of estimating life values. By those standards, so much that is truly great, is below consideration. So many that are of the great among the children of the Heavenly Father, are scarcely noticed, because the yard stick is false in its measuring power.

Money and their equivalents have their place. There is nothing inherently wrong with them. They contribute to the comfort of earthly existence and make possible to the temporary owners of such riches, many favors to others. Money can be used as one of God's rich gifts, a trust from Him for which accounting will inevitably be made when the steward of that money reaches these Planes of Spiritual Power. Here nothing counts except what a man is, beneath all trappings.

Money was not scorned by Jesus when He lived on earth. You remember how He helped some weary fishermen who had caught nothing all night until He directed their fishing. Then a fish with silver in its mouth! Many times He used the convenience of coin to teach His lessons and to transact the affairs of His world. The Holy Scriptures speak of "the silver and the gold which are His," and "the cattle upon a thousand hills." Of itself and for uses for which it was intended, money is one of life's great assets and the medium of good through many channels.

Trouble begins when it gets out of proportion, when instead of being a vehicle for good, it is made the good itself. Then there is the mischief to pay. Life tangles into snarls when that happens. Values become confused. Standards muddle themselves. Hearts ache and break when those standards are in false balance and money is given place of greater power than it is entitled to have. Turn again to your Scriptures and see how this statement accords with that familiar verse which says that it is the love of money which is the root of all evil.

There is the difference between what is good and useful and that which holds the seeds of much evil. I have used money as an illustration. It is typical of the lack of balance in other lines of life, where false measurements disrupt the order of living and man's trust is misplaced because of it.

Part of the trouble comes from putting the medium of good in place of the good itself. For life is beyond anything which material means can make it. Real life is of the spirit entirely, beyond the power of money or its equivalents to reach. Many lives which were firmly grounded and had in them to make a grand issue of the earth stretch, cracked up because the power of money got out of hand and came to seem like the real thing, master instead of servant!

Money makes possible many good things. But life can be grand and noble without any of them, grander far, if having them shifts the basis of trust from the Father as Source of All and as Himself All, and makes possessions the basis.

Trouble begins right there. Take the material goods which money makes available. Enjoy them for just what they are—adjuncts to living. But in no wise relate them to real living!

Many examples come to the memory of thoughtful people where life on a grand scale proved entirely independent of material comfort which money makes possible. Men have lived in the world but so little of it, that they had physical possessions in the minimum. Yet their minds ranged the highest levels of thought to which mortals can ascend. They literally "thought God's thoughts after Him," oblivious of false standards which the human has set up.

Their greatness depended not even upon physical wholeness. Some of earth's grandest have not had soundness of body. St. Paul, you remember, had that ever-present "thorn in the flesh" about which earth people have wondered so much. Surely he had nothing of earthly goods. But he made life a tremendously grand investment, above any power of the material to tempt him. He lives on because his spirit was freed to do its great work.

Much of the enduring work of the world has been done by those possessing not even the sight of their physical eyes nor the hearing of their ears nor means enough for comfort of their bodies. But their minds have soared beyond these superficial things as if they had not existed. Their lives consisted not in the abundance of anything which they possessed.

It is wonderful to live completely freed from bondage to things; from fear of losing the paltry medium of exchange for which often are traded the richest privileges to which the mind of the human is full heir. Again it is a case of false standards. From our conning towers here on the uplands of the eternal world, we see alarming signs of the worship of money and the power it holds over lives of men. Many have sold their souls for its transient glitter and have found that it was only dust which crumpled beneath their fingers. But they had made their choice. And by it they had to abide.

In the terrible disruption which is tearing the civilizations of earth to shreds, the power which gold wields is alarming, in that it reveals how far mankind is from being willing to accept a spiritual standard for the new world era about which men talk wisely and for the most part, they are not planning wisely. It still is in their finite minds that the might of money and of arms must be the foundation of peace. But the might of money and arms will not bring nor maintain the peace which the world needs.

That can come and will come only when men have learned in agony and in complete self-surrender that the will of the Almighty and His standards must be in control of the new world wherein men are to have freedom and justice, good for their bodies and opportunity for the upsweep and outreach of their minds and spirits. No longer should there be fear of aggression for the sake of earthly pomp and power; no longer desire for ungodly balance of power; but working and living, heart and soul, for good to prevail for every man; for righteousness and peace and truth and honor to fill the earth and no man's hand be turned against any other man!

This is not a utopian view which I am presenting to you tonight. It is the foundation of what must come to pass on your earth before the awful price of this destruction shall be justified. There is no other way. It means that many who are high, shall be brought low. Prevalent self-seeking which has cursed the earth for ages, will be diminished. In its place will be absorbing desire for good to come to the earth life of each person and united effort help make the earth bloom and flourish with richness of its products.

All of this grows simply and naturally from the theme of my evening discourse. It leads conclusively to sure belief in the rightness and inevitability of the word which forms the crux of this talk—"A man's life consisteth not in the abundance of the things which he possesseth." How rich you are that this is true! How free one is who is out from under the power of things, released for great living in the power of the spirit!

Not many yet are willing to accept this which I am here saying. Of itself this matters not at all. It does not alter the truth. It does matter in that it shows false standards prevailing with so many earth people. Your own attitude in this vital matter and help in circulating these talks, will bring others to see and to accept it. God the Father bless you!

GREAT DESTROYER

November 23

A glad good afternoon to you on this your Thanksgiving Day! How much the spirit of such day will mean to millions of earth residents! Many will be uplifted by the atmosphere and memories of the day. Others will be saddened, not able to rise above low-hanging clouds of loss and change, into the full, positive spirit of the day at its best.

You yourself have just had a touch of nostalgia—I was standing beside you at the time—when you came across some paper which brought vivid memories flooding over you, of the time when many of us worked together for the betterment of humanity, as we saw it. You will be neither surprised nor displeased to have me say that in some ways our sacrificial service was misguided. We were in error in thinking that all of our philanthropy was for the good of mankind. We followed the light as we saw it and did our best. We must let it rest there without worry or misgivings.

It is concerning that common, everyday word that I would speak this afternoon—worry! It is on the lips and in the consciousness of most people much of the time. It seems harmless. But it is a great destroyer. One of the besetting sins of earth people, worry has not one good thing to recommend it. It is negative from start to finish. It sees only the dark side of every situation. Where there is no dark side, worry trumps up one.

For the person who would live grandly, worry is not to be taken even into speaking acquaintance, much less lived with on intimate terms which so many people give it. What is it? It amounts to saying that God is overpowered by something which leads into morasses of doubt and fear; that bogs us deeper down with every consideration we give it. Worry is related only to fear and the dark things of that brood, to none of which need any earth mortal ever give a moment's harbor.

Worry is a modern word though the worry fact has no modernity about it. It is as old as mankind, companion of negative qualities of living with which man has struggled through the ages. Many who do not think clearly but who skim the surface of thought, often say, oh, so often, that they "are awfully worried" about this or that. What good does it do? What strength does it give? What light does it shed? What help does it bring? Think through the situations about which men have thought they had to worry. See if you can find one single spark of common sense in worrying about them.

Nothing comes from it save depleted courage; lessened faith; and diminished strength to pull through whatever the issue may be.

Never has a constructive thought or plan evolved from worry or from giving up to it—not one! It acknowledges no faith in one's power to win through. Not only is it sign and evidence of weakness, but it drains strength from others who are prompted to worry by hearing it so ceaselessly talked about.

Worry is a denial of God and His omnipotence! If God is All-Power—and we know He is; if He is All-Knowledge—and we know He is; if He is All-Love—and we know He is; if His ear is open to every human cry and His eyes to human need, where can worry possibly find a crack through which to crawl into human consciousness?

Much of the difficulty is that it doesn't have to search out a crack through which to crawl. Most of the time it finds the front door of the human heart wide ajar to admit it! Once in, it sets out to stir up doubt about God's being really a practical help. All right in theory. But here is something practical that mankind would better worry about! Leave God to theory and to the church for special occasions. And begin to worry about this particular matter.

If knowledge of how to meet an issue or an emergency is tempting any human to worry, why not turn to the One Who is All-Knowledge; Who made the world; Who made mankind and should know how to show the way through details of daily living? Isn't that reasonable? Isn't that what the Father would expect His children to do? And wouldn't the child do it where an earthly father was concerned? How much more certain earth people should be of the willingness and the power of the All-Father in however small a matter! For of course you remember that so-true verse from Scripture which says, "How much more shall your Heavenly Father give good gifts to them that ask Him!" Right there is the way out for everybody who meets the perplexities and problems with which the highway of earthly life is strewn.

First, lock the door of your heart against the ugly brood which worry brings. Then in glad confidence, ask the Father for light and wisdom and guidance. Leave the whole matter in His hands. That is hard for the human to do. He is so sure that he must solve the problem with the little bit of knowledge and experience which his few years on earth have given him. Is it strange then, that clouds gather and darkness fills his heart?

From these Spirit Heights we see this process repeating itself illimitably on the earth as mankind struggles with what the days bring and as talk circles from mouth to mouth, that "there is so much to worry about!" We know what many of earth know, that there is nothing to worry about! Not even in this distraught day! Not even in this day of awful suffering! Not one single thing to worry about!

But there is much to have faith about! To ask the Father about! So many difficult stretches along the road where there seem no guide-boards to point the way. At every one of these, He is there to tell you the way to go, when you ask!

Many heart-breaking times come to earth people when their hearts are torn with loss of loved ones. I speak the word "loss" only as earth people use it; not as we here know it for promotion. These bereft ones often take the conventional course and turn to worrying. How shall they find the way to go? How can they endure what has come to them?

I speak in tenderest appreciation of what these experiences do for earth people. But that is the way of weakness. It is the downward-moving, earth way, not the sunlit highway along which the Father will lead any child who asks Him how to go; puts his earth hand in the hand of

Omnipotence and walks courageously into the dark, knowing that the light will shine and the way be made clear.

You remember vividly that period of your life when you were in uncertainty; when influences were seeking to lead you astray, strong earth influences which had much to offer along materialistic lines. At the point of your greatest danger, there shot into your consciousness like the sounding of a clear bell, this guidance from the Inner Planes;"Your way will be made clear!" That settled the issue for you. And you went free from the sinister influence which was surrounding you.

It was clear, spiritual guidance sent you at a moment of great need by the spirits on the Ether Planes who serve the Infinite Father through endless ages. How gratefully you recognized the source of that guidance! How gladly you stepped clear of entangling relationships! Would worry have had the word of guidance to speak to your consciousness? Or fear? Or doubt? But a whispered prayer brought the light. Always it does.

Worry is the hard, the struggling way. Faith and trust are the sure way along which you will be guided and your feet set upon firm places.

I am speaking today of that which is a deeply rooted ailment of the earth mind; which keeps mankind bound down to dullness of spirit in which is no radiance of faith and no beauty of trust.

The earth mind so easily misunderstands and thinks of faith as something removed from daily living and needs. As if it were part of the ritual of the church reserved for special occasions, instead of the dear treasure to be held close within the heart; used in confidence day or night; the good gift of the Father to His child.

If only you would think of it this way, living would be transformed. Your loads would be lifted and your spirit go free to greater heights of experiencing God in His Infinite love and glory and peace and power!

What rich rewards those are! Earth sometimes seems to be indifferent to these mighty spiritual challenges. Yet we know the number daily increases in which the children of earth come to deeper comprehension of the relation of living to the will and the presence of the Father and His power in the human heart.

The nearer the day draws to universal understanding and acceptance of Him as All, the greater and grander an adventure will earth life become.

Often the earth man raises the specious plea that those who do exercise faith in their lives, have as many difficult experiences; as many losses or sorrows as those who lay no claim to following where faith points the path.

Yes! Let me repeat what several times the earth mind has been reminded of in this series and what thoughtful earth people know, that nowhere in Scripture is the spiritually-minded man promised freedom from trials. Think back to Elijah; to Daniel; to St. Paul; to the saints and apostles; to Jesus Christ!

No one of them spared the trials of earth! But Divinely strengthened and constantly guided; upheld and made equal to the ordeal. That is the glory!

The strong man does not ask to be spared. He asks to be strengthened. See it in this illuminating way of spirit and be grateful for all it represents.

And now I thank you for joyfully giving your holiday time to this message. It has riches for you as for all who will accept them.

The blessings of the Infinite be upon you now and always. My blessings too I give you as I go to other service.

November 25

You have been perplexed of late because you have seemed to feel a frustration in your life that is not justified. You have agonized in that you have not been permitted to reach out into material ways toward a career that would shock up with others whom the world seeks hither and yon.

This spirit of discouragement came upon you partly through too much aloneness; partly through things you have read; partly because of the atmosphere in which you work. You have been saved from all this for which you yearned, so transient and ephemeral; as unsatisfying as a wisp of cloud to a hungry man.

Those whom you know and who occasionally lord it over you for reasons of their present popularity, have their own troubles. They do not lie on beds of roses. Neither do they understand the underlying qualities of your life and work. They can't. You are wise in always giving them more than their mede of appreciation. There let it rest. And know within your own heart that popular acclaim is merest chaff on the threshing floors of life, nothing except for the wind to drive away and be forgotten.

You know all of this. And you believe it. But sometimes when things grind your spirit you need to be told again how favored you are that the Inner Planes claimed you, against your will somewhat, but nevertheless claimed you, for this work which will endure; uplift; bless; and be light in the darkness of many a spirit.

It is not for one of the earth plane to run ahead of Divine guidance and chart his own course. Almost surely he loses the way and there is trouble in finding the road back to the Father's companionship.

So, suppose you leave all of this, rewards and everything, in our hands. Rest assured that what you need, you will have; not always what you want. I told you that in the first of this series. Once or twice it has seemed necessary to remind you that this work is not your choice. It is our choice for you. And that is better.

THE WAY FOR NATIONS AND MEN

November 26

Whatever comes from the will of the Father, will make you content, you have just said aloud. I was standing here as you spoke those words. And it is well when you or any one wills to be content with the will of the Almighty. It is so far beyond the dreams of any human. Always it means only good for him who accepts in praise and gratitude.

We here, looking back on our earthly careers which seem remote and tiny in point of time, know better than the human can know, how tiny earth is in every way except as a school for developing character from spiritual standards.

All things else are as vapor which passes almost before one sees it. Material aspects of earth living, money, success, applause, popularity, are all right but only as means to the deeper, richer aspects of earth life; only as adjuncts to the growing of the spirit God-ward.

I realize that I have said this before, often, in these messages. It needs saying over and again until children of earth learn it; not by rote but by experience; until having learned it in theory, they learn it in close, personal experience and know that it is true.

It is impossible to know contentment if one is depending upon things which are material. They breed only discontent, grasping, jealousy, comparison of all things by standards which call for more discontent-breeding things.

"Things" in one or another form cause most of the difficulty on your earth. One of these is power. The one who has a little power, begins at once, often unconsciously to seek more power. You expressed it recently when you said that you wondered why holding a certain office, seemed always to go to the head. It does. And that is a sign of trouble, one way or another. That is what is the matter with your world today—more power over lives and resources and nations and government—power and more power of material sort!

There you have in a nutshell, the foundation of all that is out of gear from the human side of life. If those in power were content to exercise reasonable authority from deep desire to be helpful to ones over whom the power is wielded, without thought of selfish aggrandizement, your world would overcome its major problem. For in that one word—power—are rooted the evils which inhere in greed for riches, for the sake of more power.

Break that down in your human terms and see how it ramifies into social circles, business life, political ambitions, into the administration of the church! Power and riches are tremendous assets when they are harnessed to the will of the Father; devoid of earthy aspirations; sought and exercised for helping to bring about the Divine will on earth as it is in heaven.

That phrase which I have just used from the perfect prayer, is the foundation stone for the abiding civilization which ultimately will exist upon earth. It will never come through men of material aspirations who seek personal aggrandizement for themselves or their nations. That situation is prevailing now in alarming degree as leaders of earth are grappling with problems which must be faced, understood and solved before peace treaties will mean more than pieces of paper.

They are going about it from the wrong end. The soldier who has suffered every privation and agony imaginable, has for the most part, done it with altruistic ambition, to protect the world from dictatorship and to preserve the freedoms most desirable for earth living.

These men, returning to their homes in disability or coming over to this side of life, find themselves disillusioned and disheartened. I have been serving them upon their arrival on these Spirit Planes, welcoming them, assisting in their adjustment to this new order. And they have revealed their deep heart disappointment at the manifest absence of the pure idealism with which they endured and paid the final price with the laying down of their physical lives.

It has been hard for them to see old, troublesome ideas of government which have led to the bitter conflicts this world has known arising from greed for power and place, sitting in the front ranks today!

One nation is unwilling to give up its authority over a smaller nation because it would mean giving up riches and power; unwilling to yield advantage centering in governmental authority from which power and riches accrue; another nation bled white in the struggle for freedom facing the same situation of grappling with greed of larger nations! It is all wrong; hopelessly wrong! It cannot eventuate in peace which will justify the struggle nor bring the world nearer the ideals which nations announced as their goals—freedom from fear and liberty for man to live and to come to his best possible self!

No one ever reaches his goal until he sees the way he should go—then goes that way. The way for nations and men is the highway of unselfish, altruistic searching for terms of peace which shall be fair and workable. Along this highway every man may travel in confidence as he seeks to work and to achieve in ways that are right and useful, ways that will break down forever the possibility of man or nation usurping power with wealth that would permit his wielding the power for selfish ends. The only way this will be attained is through humbly seeking to know the way the Divine will approves; to see the outworkings of this will for races of men; then being willing to translate the visions into terms of agreement by which nations will govern themselves.

This will be a lasting experience through every day of which leaders and those who follow will recognize the dominance of good over evil. Honor and fairness will be placed above gaining advantage. Unselfishness will substitute for grasping. Only what is right instead of what is politic, will be sought. Personal advantage will be submerged for the greater good of the larger number, all in the spirit of God, the Eternal, King of Kings and Lord of Lords.

Does it seem to the earth mind a long journey to go to a just and lasting peace? It is! Formal peace will come prior to this of which I have been speaking. It will be a better peace than the former one. But it will rest upon demands and usurpings that are the offspring of this desire for more power; upon the too-little caring for those who have not the wherewithal to force their will at the peace table and so must accept what they can get.

Do you wonder that the angels in heaven grieve at what they see on earth? Can you wonder that the millions whose blood has been shed these recent years for the sake of a righteous peace and a civilization of freedom from fear, question whether the price they paid was too high? All of it comes from mankind's not being content with enough. Always he has wanted more; almost always it has been more for himself. This "more" has generally been in terms of power with which he could exert his will, whether as capital breaking the backs of labor, or as heads of governments, or manipulating the money exchanges of the world, breaking whomsoever fell beneath the sledge hammer of monetary power.

Countless ways in which this operates. It begins at the same source and tends toward the same purpose. When people of earth come to the place of praying for Divine will to be done "on earth as it is done in heaven," not merely mumbling it as part of a ritual, then will come very wonderful developments in life through peace which will envelop the world. It will blossom in unimagined glory and mankind will really know what it means to live under the shadow of the All-Wise, All-Loving, All-Powerful Father.

Why are men so blind? Why will they not see that they are following "wandering fires" which will lead them again into wallows of defeat and despair instead of toward the highlands of freedom and peace, of growth and beauty and satisfaction, where enough will await every man and when swords shall be turned into ploughshares, with no man lifting his hand against his neighbor?

As we see the holocausts that are burning up civilizations and treasures of the ages, destroying what had inestimable value, reeking fury upon races and nations, does it not seem inconceivable that humanity has allowed itself to come to this pitiable pass? Again I say it has come because man has worshipped power and has sought to grasp always more of it, instead of worshipping Him through Whom the life of the world can yet become a thing of priceless glory.

Many are seeing it as we see it. Great newspapers are urging people to pray for God's blessing and protection and guidance. This is revolutionary. But it is only the start. It does not yet go deeply enough into the being of humanity to become the motivating influence which can shape the policies of mankind in ways of such harmony with Divine will as to preclude forever the making of wars and the destruction of mankind in ruthless seeking after place and power.

All of this message I have saved until now. It is most important and will accomplish much as soon as it can reach the attention of mankind. As you work with it, I give you the richest blessing of God the Father in Whom is all power for good and for contentment. My blessing I add on this Sabbath afternoon which you have loyally given to receiving this message.

November 25

I want to speak briefly now on another topic which I have barely touched. It concerns willingness to work. Does that seem strange to you? It may to many people of your plane. For there are many who do not relish the working side of life. They wish others to do for them and never know the joy of exhaustive, constructive work that taxes them but inspires the desire to go on and do more. Real joy comes this way, provided working is done in the spirit of service. When it is done as drudgery, the blessing is omitted and nothing is left but ashes of a burned-out task. The need to work even for daily necessities, is good. It carries within its heart many unseen gifts that are worth cultivating: the obligation to lose no time; to make every minute count; to face doing what one would prefer not to do and doing it cheerfully; the things one learns about disciplines and spiritual riches that are part of all this.

Not one of these good things connected with work but is a seed of spiritual power when it is tested and proved with spirit growth in mind and exemplified to that end. When these lessons are not seen and not learned, then work becomes weariness, blessings are not earned and the glow is darkened.

I do not see how anyone who does not relish work can be happy in the life over here where we who have passed the Veil which separates us from earth circles, work incessantly and glory in it. To us, any work which is ordered in the name of the Father, the Son and the Holy Spirit, is joy unspeakable. Why should we care what it is, just so in the doing we may be serving some child of the Father who is in need, to whom we can carry comfort and perhaps sometimes the blessings of abundance?

No longer, since we left the garments of the flesh behind, do we care except to be busy about the work of the Father. There are many varied ways in which we strive to meet the needs, especially now with such unprecedented numbers of battle-wounded and worn, coming over in great throngs.

How busy it keeps us with the joy of allocating to them the places prepared for their coming and seeing that they are introduced to all of the new life which they can assimilate at one time. Of course, it takes time to understand and to feel at home under new surroundings.

But how they do joy in learning what a different place this heavenly world is, from what they had supposed! How grateful they are to find out firsthand that there is nothing to fear and that those whom they love and who will come after them, have nothing fearsome to endure. They glow with gratitude as they understand this.

They take up their own work quite promptly, beginning in small ways, marveling that there is no weariness, no shirking, no monotony, no clamor for favored places.

"How different it is from earth from which we have just come!", they cry out. It is almost beyond their belief when they are new-come here, to realize that they do not grow tired since they left their broken bodies behind. New orders of life they accept amazingly well. They are so grateful that when they are what people call "dead" they are so much more alive than they ever dreamed of being on the earth.

So it is not strange, perhaps, that I should wish to speak to you about willingness to work. Done in the uplifted spirit, it is part of the spiritual discipline to which each is expected to accustom himself while he is resident upon earth.

Any task which holds within itself the seed of good to any of God's children and which is done in the spirit of good, is worthy of being appreciated by the Spirit Planes and is so approved.

It matters not whether the human is conscious of the approval. But that he keeps on at an honest task in the spirit of doing his part in the work of the world and that he puts all possible loyalty of heart into the doing, are prime qualities for the character building which will enable him to rate high when he comes over to our side of life.

THIS SUNNY SIDE OF LIFE

That expression of what is truth—the other side of life—is one great fact which earth people have learned only in part. Mostly they yet think of the dark line which they call death as cutting cruelly through the life of earth and separating it by a vast mystery from the other life over here. True! It is mystery which may not now be explained and which has had such terror for humankind.

Though it is mystery, it is not cruel.

Sometimes physical pain accompanies it. But that is brief. Then comes the sweet cessation, the consciousness of passing earth limitations and the unspeakable experience of the beginning of spirit life to flood through and to supplant whatever weakness had existed with strength that is unbounded; to replace with joy what had been fear; to begin to sense something of the glory and service that are part of this side of life.

Oh! do let me stress this to you and through you to all who read these messages: there is no dividing line between these two existences. There is no death. Life is without beginning and ending. It came from God and it remains with God Who Himself is the Alpha and the Omega. The mysterious experience which is called death for lack of a better name, is merely part of the order of nature.

The tree is not dead when in glory its outward appearance is changed, the gorgeous foliage disappears and the tree stands stark and bare. It is not dead. It is undergoing a mysterious change for a time in the form of its manifest life.

But at its heart is the powerful life germ; resting in safe seclusion against harm from blasts of external nature is the life-giving sap. And at the order of nature, which is another word for God, sap again begins to flow; the same sap; through the same tree; and the same life goes forward. There is no death!

When sometime the sap in our tree no longer functions, every particle that was in and of that tree changes into other form of life and is not lost. There simply is no death! The changes that come in the physical organism when the living spirit is released from the hampering garment of flesh, frighten and all but unhorse those who are left of the earth circle. Their faith is not sufficiently grounded, their knowledge of things spiritual is not rooted deeply in the Word of God and in His provisions for the welfare of His children. Thus they are filled with dread at this process which disrobes the spirit from the outworn garment and sets it free to wing to realms where limitations are not known; neither sickness nor any lack!

Only the garment is left behind! Sometimes it would seem that the garment of flesh was too new; too beautiful; too useful; too beloved to be laid aside so early. That too, is part of the order of nature and of nature's law in one or another realm and is the medium through which the Great Transition comes to the young and gay just beginning their lives on earth.

But do accept this, that their lives begun oft-times amid beauty and in settings of dear love, are not interrupted nor broken into. They go on with finer sweep of spirit power, with magnificently increased ability to grow, to love, to rejoice and to serve both on the Spirit Planes and on earth. We all, at the right times, go often under careful instructions of our teachers, to help lift some one's burdens that are too heavy for earth shoulders.

Never for one moment is there death! Only the carrying on of life more abundant in more expansive fields and with adequacy that is beyond earth to provide. It is more blessed than I can explain to you to see the dawning glory of these shores; to catch the strains of celestial music that fill these Spirit Spheres; to feel the indescribable new lifeflow running through us; to surge with the quick consciousness of God and His presence; His life and love in us and about us.

To know that we shall never lose this glory; that we are to go on and up; to grow faster and more sturdily than earth would have permitted; to envision service of such sweep as earth minds cannot conceive; and to feel the powers of growth moving through us, is to know a majesty of joy and rapture which I cannot express to you in earth words.

It is so wonderfully worthwhile all the efforts we made while we were resident on earth; all the faith we developed. As I have told you before but as I feel strongly moved to say again at this time, we of these Inner Planes remember the earth life and we remember those we loved.

But as we grow to higher stature of spirit power, earth and its multiform problems seem so small. It is at best a very temporary abiding place for the souls who call it home a few short years and then fly away to be forever with the Lord. It is not good for any one of earth to let the roots of his life or love go down too deeply in the soil of this temporary home. For "where the treasure is, there shall the heart be also."

All earthly treasure is subject to moths and rust and thieves that break through and steal. Then the treasure is gone! From this High Plane of spiritual privilege, we urge you to lay up your treasure where loss never threatens; where joy never is diminished; where tears are never shed; where the heart never aches!

Can this be death? No! It is just the other side of life! The joy side; the glory side; the radiance side! I would share with you who know aloneness and desolation, this rapturous anticipation for you to carry in your heart. You and all of earth should be ready for sharing it when you lay off the old garment, to put on the glittering robes of righteousness. The Transition is so wonderful when you have made ready!

WHEN BRUSH FIRES BLAZE

November 30

The theme this time is one with which many residents of earth are familiar and yet would scarcely expect to see in a series such as this. Only occasionally is there an earth person whose spirit growth is not hindered by this of which I speak with you now.

It is a quality; no, that is not the word. It is rather a trait compounded of several traits which grow into a state of mind detrimental to one's growth in things of the spirit. This of which I speak is resentment.

How easy for it to flame and flare in one's spirit! How it burns like a fire which runs through dry brush and destroys all in its path; leaves behind it blackened ruin where freshness and greenness had been; brings no positive values but destroys much that is useful.

Many a day there comes into your own experience something which appears unfair or unwarranted or unjust, from this or that source. It cuts to the quick, inside. You blaze high, within, however well you conceal the blaze on the outside. But that destructive fire burns away your peace, your poise, your calmness and joy, often your sense of justice, until mind and spirit are filled with a welter of destruction out of all proportion to that which occasioned the conflagration.

What does it do for you? Does resentment bring you added strength for service? Does it give you fiber to endure the conflict of life with firmer spirit less inclined to yield to defeat? Does it bolster your faith in the goodness of people? Does it help you to shed abroad into hearts of others more love and yourself to live on higher ground?

When I address these questions to you, I am not being personal to you. But I am remembering because I was present when recently your spirit was afire with harshness of experience which you did not deserve. You were very self-contained externally. But your heart was a smoldering fire of resentment. You did not sense my presence consciously. But don't you remember how I said a long while back, that I would be present in any doubtful or difficult moment? And this was both doubtful and difficult as a battle within your spirit. With much determination you said within yourself—not a word aloud—what you would do and would not do from that time on. The flames of resentment were wrongly set blazing by what you did not deserve but you should have extinguished them before the fire got beyond your control.

The fire was extinguished before long. But it had taken too large a toll of spiritual poise and assurance; destroyed too much inward peace, worth a million times more than you fully realize. When the flames were fully died down, you felt as if you had lost more ground in the realms of the spirit than would be regained easily.

Resentment never pays. It is a losing investment from whatever angle you view it. It never gives any spiritual coupons to clip in the way of growth in values that abide. It faces you with loss and charred remains of a precious possession.

Resentment is a composite trait. Entering into it as ingredients, are self-pity which is a sure-fire destroyer for everybody; and hurt pride; close cousin to self-pity and not worth any more to anybody; generally a portion of jealousy or envy neither of which is good company for anyone to keep. Quick temper, easy to ignite and a fast burner, is part of the element which flares up often in resentment.

If it seems trivial for one speaking from these High Planes to talk of such influences of earth, I ask you to realize that whatever helps or hinders the development of soul powers in any human, is in no wise insignificant to us. or is any help which we can give that will be an impulse to overcome the negative and strengthen the positive qualities of good, too much for us to do. There is no large nor small where growth of the spirit is concerned. That is all that matters. For that is of eternity, with values that are immortal.

When you detect the first, faint signs of a smoldering blaze within your heart kindled by resentment at person or experience, won't you clamp down over the blaze some such unfailing fire-extinguisher as "The Lord is my Shepherd, I shall not want. He maketh me to lie down in green pastures; He leadeth me beside the still waters; He restoreth my soul; He leadeth me in the paths of righteousness, for His name's sake"?

Or this one—"Peace I leave with you; my peace I give unto you!" Or "He that dwelleth in the secret place of the Most High shall abide under the shadow of the Almighty!"

What chance could puny bits of resentment have of getting the upper hand when faced with such power? None at all! That is why I ask you to act quickly when the first sign of a licking flame of resentment appears in your heart, to see that no oxygen of encouragement is given it. Then it will die down before it is really started.

It will mean more to peace and quietness of spirit of everyone who will do this than I can express to you.

Believe me, it is most important for everybody who is fighting a good fight for spiritual growth. In my own soul while I was resident on your earth, I bore many a mark as a scar because too often my impetuous spirit yielded to these quick-leaping flames of resentment against influences which I should never have noticed and against people whom rather I should have been seeking to help.

Because I have learned my lesson, it is my privilege to be as explicit as this, for your help. You will be surprised how much faster your spirit will grow when it does not stop so often to fight foolish little resentment blazes that have no significance whatsoever.

December 1

In the brief time you have this late afternoon I give you my blessing of gratitude and appreciation, adding a few words closely related to our former theme, this time on that besetting sin of so many earth dwellers—self-pity!

This series is intended to offer to all who read, a cycle of certain cardinal graces of the spirit to be cultivated during earth residence by way of preparation for the higher life. In doing this, a few pointers are approached from the negative side as being perhaps a direct route to their real inwardness.

Self-pity is one of these conditions which often is chronic and generally acute with the one who permits it to remain or gives it any refuge at all. The person who pities himself is ignorant of the law which proves what goodness awaits everyone who believes in God and loves Him. Doesn't His word tell you that "All things work together for good to them that love God"? And is there in this Divine law any place at all for seeing life and its factors from an upside-down point of view, instead of clear and true, as the Father intended us to see things in the world He made?

Self-pity is morbid. It daubs everything with unnatural glooms and blues. It sees the world in wrong focus, everybody distorted and everything out of joint, because it reckons from a false hypothesis and arrives at incorrect conclusions.

Nobody in God's world has any right to be filled with self-pity. Suppose obstacles have beset the days and hardships have come. Everybody has them, one way or another. Suppose dearest dreams delay in fulfillment. Others' dreams have faded or been late in coming true. Suppose others seem to have more and better than you. Don't you know that no two people have the same work to do, the same purpose to fulfill, the same blessings to win, the same goals to reach? No two!

So you are not to gauge yourself—and I say "you" with entire impersonality here—by anybody else but wholly by the opportunities which abound for making life its best possible and you, your best possible self.

Where therefore, is any place for self-pity? It belongs on the junk pile of the spirit, fit only to be put out of the heart before it is fully inside—and the door locked against it!

BLEST WITH HUMILITY

December 2

We trust you with this so important task that words are not equal to expressing what this series of messages is to mean to the world of readers. There is such reciprocity of trust, by the very nature of the condition, that each party to it is enormously profited. You grow under this pact of trust in the task which you accepted at our hands. We serve more widely because we trust you and your willingness to carry this through to completion, for the sake of your needy world and the countless numbers who are hungry and thirsty of spirit. They find no satisfaction in short-of-truth teachings that are widely offered. They will learn much that will nourish their spirits as they read these messages. So they will be most grateful. That will be part of your reward for the grilling labor which is involved.

I want to speak to you tonight about one of the great qualities of spirit which does not have as much consideration or appreciation as it should have. But it is essential to a spirit life that fulfills its finest missions of service and of being. I speak of humility.

As you would know, I do not mean the cringing, artificial, make-believe type of humility put on for show, counterfeit and lacking all evidences of being genuine. There is no merit in that sham which names itself by the exalted name of humility. That kind is sounding brass. It seeks to draw attention to itself and to advertise its mock-modesty of spirit. Really, it is blatant in its desire to be seen and praised for its seeming self-effacing. It is not self-forgetful for a moment. It looks for ways all the while to blow the trumpet of self.

In such qualities of spurious humility, the genuine has no part, nor does it seek through ways like those, to grow in the graces of the humble of heart. So suppose in this talk we set aside the Uriah Heaps of your world, after whom I used to relish reading when sometimes there came leisure hours for browsing through books.

I would concern us this evening solely with the positive qualities of that great asset of the soul which your earth words call humility. The one whose spirit is rich in that grace, always strives to grow to taller stature, to be more wise and kind, more willing to do for others and less inclined to think of himself.

Never does it occur to the one of humble spirit that he should demand his way, so certain is he that others know more than he. And from them he would learn.

There is one outstanding quality of humility,—willingness to grant that under any circumstances there is something to learn; from every one with whom he comes in contact, something to learn; from every success, something to learn; from every defeat, something to learn!

What a teacher true humility is! The antennae of its spirit are always feeling for the new truth which it may take for service; for new ways in which it may use and adapt and adopt that truth for better value to himself and for every condition under which he finds himself in his journey through life.

How different this quality is from the spurious one of which I spoke a moment ago!

This one rings true, like pure gold! As indeed it is, the rare and precious quality of spirit with which one grows more God-like as he exercises the characteristics of pure humility.

The really great person is almost always humble, though never truckling. Because this is so, your great earth person is easy to approach, simple and unassuming, without artificiality or show-off. Such a one knows, however wise he is, that the sum of his knowledge is like the point of a pin compared to the vast universe of knowledge and wisdom which the Creator has at His command.

This does not make the man of humility discouraged or unwilling to keep on with the quest for more learning, more wisdom, more graces of knowledge and goodness. Genuine humility leaps to take advantage of every opportunity to extend the boundaries of his mind and to widen the bounds of his mental and spiritual horizons.

He treasures knowledge which he acquires and coordinates it with the rest of his precious store that he may have that much the more from which to make his life of service.

Nothing puffs up the one who is rich in humility. But everything makes him grateful. Every good thing that comes within his ken is cause for his soul to sing in gratitude to the Giver of all good. And he takes what comes in that spirit of deep gratitude that he may amalgamate each new good with the sum total of his knowledge, coming more and more to be a good and loyal servant of the Most High.

The gift of humility is one of the most beautiful in the category of spiritual gifts.

It lifts mankind high. That is such asset to the immortal spirit as cannot be over-valued. I commend to you and to all the richness of this quality which bends low to help; stands straight and tall in the integrity of its might that it may be the more able to reach out wherever there is service to render.

In appraising life, humility never questions motives of people nor vitiates their purposes, seeking always to find ways to emulate what is true and noble in every person and every situation.

Jesus was rich in the gift of humility. He knew His Sonship with the Father but never did He take to Himself anything which was not His for enriching His life or for equipping Him to accomplish His earth mission. He gave all credit to the Father and said more than once that of Himself He could do nothing.

That characteristic of great generosity distinguishes any one of real size in the measurement of the spirit. He does not seek to be thought as the source of these but is grateful for power to acquire and use them.

Only as earth people manifest qualities of true humility, can they grow in richness and goodness and Godlikeness. The sounding-brass person with aspirations to pass his counterfeit humility off for genuine, does not progress in the Kingdom of God. Counterfeit on whatever line, does not pass muster here where the white light of truth detects and reveals any flaw of moral fiber, any deviation from what is pure and good and unselfish.

Nothing is ever menial to one of genuine humility. No service is too lowly or too little known for the truly humble person to do in happy spirit of cooperating with the Divine. Here as elsewhere, there is no great nor small.

The entire test is in the attitude of the soul, whether it resents the homely experience or accepts it as a channel for doing good and for learning new riches of knowledge and experience.

Resentment is not a close cousin of humility. The two are at opposite poles from each other.

Too largely earth people misinterpret humility. Often it is taken as a synonym of lack of strength; the equivalent of weakness of character and personality; more or less a mushroom quality.

But it is not so. In true humility is all the hardiness of moral and spiritual fiber which one finds in oak timber, closely, finely grained, enduring, capable of heavy loads and susceptible of beautiful polish! The polish comes from friction, constant rubbing away of all roughnesses until there emerges so highly polished a result as reveals the fiber and the texture which endured the process of the polishing. Loose-fibered timber, coarse grained and quickly grown, does not take on this flawless, shining polish!

And so I commend to you and to all, the lessons which you can learn from acquiring and using this beautiful grace of humility. It will dignify every aspect of your life and direct your aspirations away from the superficial. It will point you from standards which are material to those of the Divine. It will show you factors that make humility of spirit a truly great asset to everyone who strives to make headway toward his best possible self in his daily walk and work. It will make him the more ready for the inevitable journey to this Fair Land of the Spiritual.

Here there is no counterfeit. Here the one in whose earth life deep and sincere humility has been cultivated and exemplified, finds himself rich in soul-readiness in proportion as he has lived the spirit of humility and glorified it.

It is not a light quality of character to exemplify from day to day. If it were easy, it would be worth less. Difficulties which attend the growth of this spirit quality are in proportion to its values. They should be highly valued and sought after by all who aspire for high rating when they come to share the life of the Inner Planes.

I wish I could make it glitteringly plain to all of you how important this character-building is, for the living of your earth days and for the life which will endure through the endlessness of eternity.

Only the spiritual counts. This of which I have been speaking tonight is a spirit quality and has immense rating in the inventories of external values.

Can you, can anyone, afford to overlook this factor toward a well-rounded and full-orbed character, ready for its high place when you and they come to us?

And who can tell how soon your journey may be begun? God Himself be with and bless and comfort and strengthen you! Good night!

ADJUSTING TO THE NEW LIFE

December 3

I shall speak to you tonight more at length concerning the interlocking of mortal life with these Planes of Immortality. They are so close together, separated only by an invisible line. Close, so close, are they, whereas earth people think of us as remote, beyond reach, out of any possible contact, retaining no memory of earth life, dead! Several times I have talked with you on this theme. But it lies so near to the deep desires of the human heart that I am repeating the general substance of some things I have previously said, in hope that repetition may help to convince earth people that we live and love and serve and worship and adore!

How true it is that "There is no death!" The only phase of the Great Transition which comes under the category of what earth people call death, is the change which comes over the physical organism when the spirit has left its earthly habitat, the heart has ceased beating, the life blood has ceased to circulate and the body begins its process of deterioration.

That is the only part of the Great Transition which can be called "death." And even there, it is only life in some other form. For nothing created, is ever lost. Often it is changed; but never lost. Nor does any living thing ever die. It changes. And that is all there is to it.

It is natural that the body which houses the immortal part, should come to be the symbol of the spirit and take to itself such love as rightly belongs only to the spirit in its house of clay. When the body is emptied of the spirit and the change begins which is the law of nature and the order of the universe, it seems like laying away the one who was so dearly beloved.

Not so! That which was life and intellect and emotion and power to achieve, is not being laid away. Only the shell which protected the kernel. Only the clay house in which the spirit lived and accomplished its earthly end.

Recently there have been many of my dear friends from the earth plane who have fought the good fight through to the glorious end and have come in triumph up to these Planes of Great Glory.

It was great joy to welcome them one by one and to see the glow on their faces as they recognized me, one of their earth comrades and friends! They had had no fear of the journey for their lives had squared with the teachings of our Lord.

Mostly their concepts of this side of life had been of the conservative, orthodox kind and they were not prepared for the glory which they saw as they drew nearer. As their ears caught the strains of celestial music, they expressed such happiness as they never before had known. As we communed together, our souls seemed to knit more closely than ever on earth. For now we had all shed the cumbersomeness of the physical. We were as free as the birds, nevermore to know weariness or limitation or unfulfilled desires; free for all eternity to worship and learn and grow in the graces of the spirit, the while we would serve in new ways of greater power throughout the world of needy people. It has been great joy to me and I share it with you.

The uncounted millions of soldiers and civilians from persecuted countries, who come from their unspeakable sufferings, are not able at first to comprehend what the freedom is. Neither can they assimilate the beauty and the glory which spread before their spiritual eyes. They are dazed in the presence of it.

These need much help in adjusting to the new life. And they are so grateful for it. Thus our service is indeed privilege as we minister to these in special need. Nothing which they have lacked on earth, but is here fulfilled. How their gratitude does shine forth from their eyes! Often there come those who have feared and dreaded the crossing from earth to the Ether Planes. As they experienced the rapture which awaited them and saw how without foundation their fear was, they fairly shouted with joyful relief.

Those who come illy-prepared for spiritual atmospheres, who have never accepted the teachings of our Lord nor loved His way of life, find much to amaze them. To them it is most difficult to find a basis on which to begin the readjustment from materialistic, even wicked and criminal lives lived in sordid atmospheres on earth, to these spirit-filled Planes where all is love and worship. These unfortunate ones find intense suffering in the necessity attending their readjustment. First, the will to change must be brought about. Often that is attended with great agony of remorse and rebellion. They find nothing congenial in the life to which they have come; nothing to which their hearts respond.

Yet here they are! They are the lost sheep of the Great Shepherd. They must be carefully tended and taught, nurtured in the spirit and atmosphere of love which completely fills these Planes of Life, until the old ways of evil and darkness, the old desires of wickedness are overcome. Then hearts that once were black with sin and falseness of understanding are transformed by Divine love. And they find living on these Eternal Planes one long, sweet song.

We all see that being accomplished here in many ways. Do not think that such transformation comes quickly. It is of the process of growth. When growth at first has to overcome a rebellious spirit, develop new soil out of which to grow and into which to sink the roots of new life, it is slow.

But the change does come and it fills our spirits with Divine joy as we mark each in tribute to the Redeemer Whose love transforms.

No one comes to these Planes of Privilege but finds just the occupation, the interest most adapted to his talents. It is wonderful to watch such things work out. The one with artistic talent finds here such opportunities to portray beauty as earth has never afforded. He learns higher laws of art than earth knows. Likewise with celestial harmony. No desire of the human spirit but here finds its complete fulfillment!

These many things I tell you that through you others may learn and come to feel that this is no strange place but is in beautiful reality, home! It is home for the spirit in ways of entire satisfaction, a condition which no earth home ever was permitted to approximate. Always something was lacking in the earth home. Here nothing is lacking! And so I tell you again that it is our hope for you to use all possible influence to free their hearts and minds from the engrossing fear which earth teachings and customs have built up, to the confident assurance of this home which will satisfy. More than that, could anyone ask?

It is so important that as you assemble what you wish to bring with you to this Home, you do not let any surplus baggage slip in; something which will not be to your advantage; which will stand you in no spiritual stead; something of worthlessness when gauged by the standards of spirit excellence which prevail here.

Be careful about this. No resentments, however strongly you have felt justified in them! They will weigh you down and you cannot afford them. No false sense of honesty; no false witnessing; no selfishness when you placed yourself more highly than your neighbor; no envy; no avarice; no covetousness of any good thing which someone else had!

These and all traits more or less allied, are to be cast off, while you are still of the earth, lest you forget and seek to bring them when you come to these Shores of Spirit Life.

It is not easy for the earth person to reckon constantly about future values of what he is assembling as spiritual wealth to take to the permanent Home. But he does well to remember that everyone who comes here is known for exactly what he is, in the deepest places of his heart—not for any single thing which he has. This does much to change the standard of measurements for a person who is willing to think about it while there is time.

God bless and keep you; enrich your spirit; hearten and comfort you and give you all joy in service. The work you are doing in your earth relationships is far-reaching and should be the occasion of deep satisfaction to you. I bless you now. And good night!

I shall come often. Sometimes you will hear me speak and be grateful for it. But when you do not recognize me, you will nevertheless feel your consciousness of peace and joy lifted higher. And you will give thanks for it. Our trust in you is implicit and we bless you with the blessing of the Most High as you carry on!

Remember, you are not alone! Call us; and we shall come!

* * *

Ambition, Destiny, Purpose, Goal,

All day march on with stately tread

Adown the highway of my soul,

Nourished by Him, our Living Head.

The day is ever opportune

To serve amid the storms of strife;

The way is ever purposeful

To magnify the grace of life.

Ambition, Destiny, Purpose, Goal,

Conserve them wisely, O my soul!

* * *

En route to San Francisco, The Counsellor composed the above poem, wrote it longhand on a postcard and sent it to me. It has since gone widely among his friends.

SEEING THE INVISIBLE

To each who travels
the upward-winding path
with open mind
and learning heart,
in quest of truth,
this book is dedicated.

FOREWORD

SEEING THE INVISIBLE is not a sequel to the preceding volume, *From The Seventh Plane*, though it follows in close sequence. The Messages for these volumes came to me directly along the ether waves from the other side of life as I sat at the typewriter in my apartment in Washington, D. C., and later in my home in Hollywood, California. I typed them word for word, as they reached me, the first few coming through "Tim."

Without fanfare or spectacular trappings of any sort but vibrant with the manifest power of spirit presences they came regularly whenever I had leisure to offer my hands and my mind, over a period of several years. The Messages included in this volume are a portion of all which came, selected with care and under the guidance of the Inner Planes.

The Counsellor though whose cooperation all of this came that is contained in these volumes, was for many years my senior associate and my partner in earth service. Then as now, his diction was unique, absolutely characteristic, as individualistic as he! Shortly after his coronation, his words began to come clearly to my inner ears. There was such familiar ring to them, such vivid reminder of his earth days, such clear consciousness of the validity of his words and of his actual spirit presence, that I could not continue too long to doubt.

I tried to! Some friends did their best to make me doubt. For a while, I tried to rationalize into nothingness the whole set of experiences that centered in the coming of these Messages. I tried to make myself think that no significance could attach to them, perhaps nothing at all save imagination and my desire to have them prove true. But at the sword's point of clear, convincing and cumulative evidence repeated many times and in many ways which I could not with reason continue to deny, I yielded! All of this was contrary to my previous prejudices, to my proud sense of intellectual dignity and to my mistaken superiority, also to my formal rearing as member of a conservative family circle and of a very orthodox church.

But under the continuing and powerful impact of these Messages from the other side of life, I came to complete acceptance of them, convinced beyond doubt of their genuine quality and their incontrovertible values to human living. I accepted them as my responsibility, my privilege and my high mission from the earth side of life. I gave myself up to them and willingly though belatedly, consented to be a channel for these Messages direct from the Inner Planes to us of earth. It was the best decision I ever made. To hold my normally active mental processes quiescent was not easy, nor to prevent their slightest intrusion into the lines of truth that were coming through from the Spirit Planes and thus preserving the integrity of each communication in the words and the spirit in which The Counsellor presented it for earth reception and use. Early in my experiences of learning to be a dependable channel, he said one evening with almost infinite patience—his words appear in the former volume, From the Seventh Plane—"Do not try to think ahead with me. My thoughts will flow more easily without help from the earth side!"

Gradually I learned. The Counsellor explained how he stood beside me while he energized my mind through the power of thought transference, with the very Message which he wished me to write. If my inner ears failed to catch the exact word or phrase, he repeated it that there might be no doubt of my hearing just what he desired to put into my care. Not for me alone have these Messages come, nor only for my gratification and my help, sorely as I needed that, but that through my relationship as a channel, I should go all the way from receiving his spoken words to carrying them through to completed volumes available to those many everywhere who are needing this truth.

It comes bright with the aura of the Spirit Planes and radiant with eternal wisdom. It is as a free-flowing Fountain of Living Water, for all who will drink and be refreshed.

From our many years of earth association, The Counsellor occasionally and quite naturally used me personally, to illustrate some lesson or other which he was teaching in these series which were coming regularly by way of etheric waves to the earth plane. Except for such purposes of illustration, his repeated use of the word "you," is universal. He seeks in each volume to make this clear.

Associated with him in the Realms of Spirit in preparing these lessons that mankind needs to master, are those who have been much longer than he on the Exalted Planes of Knowledge and Power. Their wisdom is close to the Godhead. From this Infinite source, they together assembled this which we humans most need to know and on which we may live spiritually through these chaotic and distraught days. Then through the method of thought transference, The Counsellor has been privileged to transmit these divinely human lessons in short and simple form, from their High Planes to me who was their earth channel. These Lesson-Messages have made me over! They have changed my entire life. No longer have I any fear or dread of the Great Transition which each of us faces. For I have learned that the passing is "not a dark river nor a time of great fear. It is the coming Home to the Father's House, to those who are so happy to, welcome you!" Could any one fear such experience? Or shrink from it?

I have learned the vast significance and importance of daily lessons, even those that are most irksome and difficult, which life poses each of us, and that if I do not learn mine in this earth cycle, I shall still have them to learn, lessons new and old which The Counsellor explains and interprets simply and helpfully in the Messages of this book. Blessedly I have learned that I am never alone! For they who have gone on beyond our casual physical sight are not gone at all. They are with us in close and often perceptible companionship and in comfort and helpfulness, coming to encourage us and to guide our feet over rough places where we do not see our way. Their coming in so many ways of practical knowledge, makes us absolutely certain of the continuity of life in radiance and growth and service and joy.

From the Spirit Planes, The Counsellor gave the name for this volume. In loyalty and faith therefore, I send it forth into the world with the prayer that it may clarify our vision for "Seeing The Invisible!"

WINIFRED WILLARD
Hollywood, California, 1950

THE MESSAGES

THE VOICE

In harmony with what you were just thinking, you are our accepted channel for these words of truth from the Inner Planes. There are those who will_underestiatate the difficulty of being a channel. But you and we know that it is not an easy role to fill. So to you this afternoon, our gratitude goes anew.

This morning when you answered the ringing of your telephone, you heard the voice of your first "receiving station," calling long distance. We knew it would do both you and her good and so we played our part in bringing that call through for you. How many times our Spirit Planes intercept earth lines for encouragement of those yet in the flesh who sorely need promptings, which reach them in ways that are invisible, inaudible and very potential.

Mostly they do not connect the help with Spirit Realms. Sometimes they do. And then they are especially blest when they take it for what it is rather than for what so many call a "hunch."

Where, we wonder, do they think these "hunches" originate? Do they not see them as promptings from higher sources of knowledge and inspiration? Do they not connect them with that vital force which is intuition, which really is the Still, Small Voice? It speaks from within and is inseparably related to the God-power within every man. Except occasionally, earth people do not take time or thought to interpret these messages. They have the experience. If it appeals to them, they follow the "hunch." And let it go at that.

For any one who does that way, the loss is considerable. For he misses the conscious contact with the indwelling Divine that has more significance to life than any other influence.

I beg you, my friend, never to pass slightingly by any such guidance from within, on whatever line it is. Stop when you are conscious of that power, that Voice which is not audible with the outer ears but which speaks mightily to the inner ears! Stop and hear what is being spoken to you. Then follow the direction that is outlined for you, though you may not always understand why.

The "why" is not always explained to the human, nor need it be. The exact guidance from the Inner Source is the thing of utmost importance. Often it is the difference between success and failure where either of them is important.

Your experience this morning was not vital but it was designed to bring a lift to your spirit as Tim spoke from the far south.

Relativity of importance is not the standard to apply in the case of healing and heeding the guidance that comes from within. Learning to listen for this Voice that speaks unerringly from the heights of all knowledge, is a lesson of earth life which one is wise to learn to its full.

Disregarding it, passing it by lightly, is equivalent to failing, in a lesson which has been set for the pupil and which some day must be learned. Take all of this seriously, my friend. It has values for the growth of any one who will heed all, that it holds within itself.

I go now. I shall come again and know I shall find your willing mind and hands ready for your share in this inter-world series. How close our realm is to yours! Strange, that earth people fail to sense it. We are are with you, in and out, protecting and guiding, leading your minds to new thoughts, filling your hearts with fresh inspiration. Yet so few recognize our presence or our power. To us, that matters not. For it is our joy to serve in the name of the Father.

For them whose eyes are holden and whose ears are closed, the loss is very great. Remember that the real world is of the spirit where values are abiding and where joy is without end. Some day, you will know in larger measure when you lay aside the lesser things of earth and learn and experience on vaster dimensions.

God the Father empower you with His conscious presence and fill you with sense of His glory, His Allness!

HOW IT IS ON THE SUNNY SIDE

I wish you could realize how it is with us over here on the sunny side of life where time is not! It simply does not exist! We have to make conscious effort to remember how you who yet are bound to the narrow confines of earth, must keep to hours, and days, even minutes. Of course we do remember how it was when we too were on the earth plane and had the same limiting barriers to reckon with.

There appears no better way for ordering life on earth where it is so manifestly an obstructed world, obstacles on every hand, hurdles that must be taken, all to the end of growth in initiative, in courage and in strength. We remember all of this. And we give thanks that no longer do we have those thing with which to contend since we are part of the Spirit Realms.

For here the obstacles do not appear, nor the hurdles. Nor any barriers of time. We are unobstructed in mind and spirit and service. It is a glorious realm in which to learn more of the love and the worship of the Divine Lord. There are those who make little of Him and His mission. Pay no heed, my friend, to those who would belittle Him or His relation to all of this. Without the Great God, there would be only blankness down where you live and here where I live. Live? O so much more really, so much more vividly, so much more fully, so much more satisfyingly, than was possible on the earth plane.

Live? Over here, it is everything that one's fondest dreams could picture. It is home and fellowship and service, the presence of those we have known and loved on the earth, it is consciousness of our stepped-up power to help them yet abiding on earth and to watch their preparations for coming home to be with us here. It is radiant love of the Father from Whom all blessings flow now and always. It is everything that is thrilling, inspiring and satisfying to the deep places of one's heart.

When you down there are lonely and hard beset, when you wonder why so many pressing loads, when you seem frustrated while you would be fulfilled, just look forward to the time when you too will come Home to the Father's House, to learn the meanings of life's problems, meanings that were withheld from your mortal consciousness, meanings that only here can you interpret in terms of best helpfulness for your soul's welfare. Here you will find these hidden meanings made crystal clear and the reasons for them will more than repay you for all that you underwent during your trial times on earth. The greatest mission you are to perform while yet little longer you remain among mortals, lies in helping other to get some of this faith-inspiring knowledge of what life is over here!

Equally important is it, for them as for you, to realize what death is not! Death is such a misnomer, even where the'physical body is concerned. Even that does not die, as I have told you before. It does change. The constituent parts undergo change in form and in chemical quality. But these parts do not die. They continue to do the work nature has assigned to them, though earth mortals continue to speak of them as "dead." It is most unfortunate. I beseech of you to continue your loyal and helpful efforts to show people, as opportunity comes to you, that the change which comes to the spirit is the Great Transition from a goodly world to a Realm so incomparably better and more beautiful, more satisfying and more enduring, than earth words can express. Let them know how we here retain all of our former identities save only the weight of the imperfect flesh which we were, for the most part, grateful to lay aside for the hindrance it was.

Tell them that here our spirits soar and sing with rapture, as we learn more of the Master's wisdom and of His ways and His will. Let them see and believe that we who are for a while invisible, are not forgetful of them, but that we remember and appreciate and understand and oh! so often come to help you all through tight places on the highway of your earth journey.

Sometimes those places are like bottlenecks. It seems as if there is no getting ahead. But we see more clearly. We understand more completely. We are at your command on the instant as quickly as you breathe a prayer for help. What does it matter that you cannot see us with your physical eyes? Nor hear us with your external ears? Nothing at all!

Those who are far advanced in knowledge pertaining to the Spirit World do often see with their bodily eyes and hear with their earth ears. But that is not of the essence of importance. The essential thing is that we know your need and are equipped with those powers of Divine help which can open doors apparently closed, turn aside obstacles that seem ominous and solve problems that appear to have no earth answers. All of these things we do for the help of any earth resident who asks us, in faith. Dead? Does this sound like it? So much more throbbingly alive than ever before! Sometimes I almost yearn for you to come Home here, that you may prove for yourself all of these things which once were so strange to you but which have now become incorporated into the fiber of your deepest belief.

Let the glory of this which beckons you, be as a beacon of brightness and an incentive to keep you at your best. Let it be a light to you when your way may seem dark and your path winding. Never fear any of these things which come to every one of earth. Know that they are part of the developing disciplines by which the soul grows until it is ready for larger lessons and the wider sweep of knowledge that will open in revelation when the body is laid aside, its work done, and the spirit is free to wing its Homeward way.

The freedom is marvelous. I never forget what that means to me who so long was hampered by many frailties of the body. Let all of this which forms the substance of tonight's message be warm comfort and cheer to you and let it confirm you in the faith of this which you have been learning these years since I came Home.

If it seems long to you there, do remember that the time will come when you will no more think of it as long or lonely. For you will know the vast sweep of life that is not confined or restricted, or limited in any way, but is the perfection of God-life that will meet every longing of your heart. I beseech you to let your heart feed upon all of this. And be grateful!

The tender mercies of our Lord rest upon you, keep you within the hollow of His hand, His peace blessing you and His love anointing you to your special service whose reward will fulfill your every desire. And now, good night! And Amen!

UNSPEAKABLE PEACE

Happily, time is of no consequence with us. We are never hurried nor wearied nor burdened with schedules. I spoke of this recently to you but mention it again tonight because I was standing beside you a moment or two before you were fully ready. Even at the risk of repeating, do let me say that one of the feelings of real liberation comes from release of all that sort of pressure.

We work steadily. But no one here ever feels the consciousness expressed of "working hard." That is purely an earth phrase because it is an earth condition. Even so, you who are still in the flesh, would do better if you could learn to omit the sensation or subconscious feeling of the "hard" part.

There is where the devastation of it comes in. Throw all of that feeling out of the windows of your consciousness and learn to take your daily dispensation calmly, with poise and assurance that there is time enough, strength enough and concentration enough to meet every need.

But the thing I especially wish to talk about this time is the attitude of earth people in the presence of what almost all call death. Won't you help us develop a sensitivity, a feeling for a better phrase for that experience? Some word or phrase that doesn't have the sting, the thrust, associated with sorrow and loss?

The attitude I speak of is represented by expressions of "how terrible that he had to die"; "why did it have to happen?" and equivalent forms of negative expressions that wring the heart and strengthen the erroneous interpretations that are the race thought concerning death.

These expressions are not Christian. They do not take into account what the Father told of the life He has prepared for them that love Him nor of the beauty of the spirit consciousness that will be freed when "the golden bowl is broken" and spirit goes glad and unfettered, to learn and enjoy; to worship and serve with amplified powers which the Creator bestows upon them who have passed the gossamer Veil the world calls death.

There is no death! Do get that so strongly imbedded into your belief that you increasingly can help to eradicate the feeling and fear of death. I pray you acquire such, affirmative power that you admit no single vibration of anything that death is supposed to be, into your mind.

Shut it right out! And know that the Great Transition is not a time of sorrow or pain but of promotion. So definitely is it coming up higher that I marvel at the lack of emphasis of the church toward this positive, affirmative phase.

Even relating to the physical, death is merely change. Nothing dies. It changes. It breaks up into other chemical and physical properties, goes on into other forms for doing the work of the world while the released spirit is free to wing its way to realms where life is so much more abundant that earth existence cannot be compared. Abundant life! That is worth seeking, isn't it? Not cramped and limited nor beset with suffering and uncertainties. Abundant! The spirit experiencing every joy and satisfaction for which it could yearn. The spiritual exaltation which comes when the bonds of earth are severed, is beyond my power to express. But it is real. It is abiding. It bestows the sense of conscious reward for life well lived and work well done.

Even when the body has been hard pressed with weakness, the time of passing from the material to the spiritual is one of unspeakable peace, as if the joy were too deep and vast to be taken in all at once, when there sweeps over the spirit the first realization of the Creative plan which has governed the two worlds and of which earth knows so much less than it might know if the earth mind were open and unprejudiced.

I beseech you to keep at your studies of all things related to this unseen universe which lies all about you, which touches your world and envelops your life and is closer to you than breathing. It is a tremendous responsibility which has been placed upon you to carry this word as far and wide as your life-situation permits. Be assured the door will open more widely as you are ready to go through it.

The riches of our Lord compensate you for all that has been hard and lonely in your life! Keep right on growing up in the life of the spirit. Then when the glad day comes that you join us here, you will prove how true a friend the Transition is for all who have lived loyally in truth and integrity and unselfishness and service, in the name of our Lord. His presence abide abundantly with you always.

OUR WORLD AND YOUR WORLD

Tonight you are asking me to speak to you of "the other world." My friend, do you not know by this time that what you call your world and what we call our world, are so close together that there is no separating them? The only medium of separation is the limiting human thought which places Spirit Planes far away beyond the stars, completely dis-associated from the material plane. What mortals call "the other world" is right around you, where you live and work. We are with you, wherever you go and whatever you do. We cover the universe in our missions of service.

We come and we go with what to you is incalculable speed. It is such effortless speed, such easy winging of our way from one place of service to another in remote quarters. To us it matters not one whit. For our powers are unlimited and we are not subject to the restraints of your sidereal time. This is just one of the blessed freedoms which we acquired when we made the Transition. For it we often give grateful thanks. We who have broken the bonds of our fleshly bodies wish you could realize the encircling protectiveness of presences from these Planes about you of earth. It is there that we do much of our work, there that we devote ourselves to energizing thoughts of men and women with new concepts, fresh visions and farther-reaching plans for the advancement of good among children of men.

Just as with you! When I speak with you in these messages, I speak standing beside you. I pour the power of my thought into your mind so clearly that there is no possible basis of fear lest you do not understand me clearly and correctly.

True, you have not seen me since I left my physical presence. But you know I am there. And someday while you are yet of earth, you shall see me and recognize me. This is of minor importance, however, compared with heart acceptance of truth coming from one spirit to another.

The closer your heart is allied with us of these Ether Planes, the more gracious is the help which we can render. Any one who disbelieves in us or our power to communicate with those of earth, closes the door against himself and shuts out our cooperation on terms of spirit power. For we do not go and we can not serve where we are not welcome and received in faith. Sometimes we are not recognized as being from the discarnate and faith, then, does not actively enter as a factor.

Get this clearly in your consciousness, my friend. The one who builds a separating wall in his thought and belief between your world and ours, shuts himself away by that self-built wall of false belief, from transforming experiences which he would have if he had not erected such a barrier.

Until higher knowledge comes to him through some channel which makes him willing to tear down what he built up to his disadvantage and limitation, he is shut away from one of the greatest sources of inspiration and faith and peace and growth and power which could be his for the asking.

Lines of communication between the worlds, yours and mine, are buzzing these days. I say to you that in these distraught periods of earth life, people in desperation are discarding many restrictive prejudices against the world that is unseen and reaching out with surprising eagerness to prove the validity of communication between the spirit world and your material earth.

We watch this breaking down of inhibitions with deep spiritual joy. For it is so distinctly in the line of growth for one who is open-minded to spirit truth. You have proved the factual veracity of these communicating channels in the years since I came over to this side of life.

If you had followed the traditional path of your conservative orthodox rearing when my first little message was transmitted by proxy to you, if you had turned aside from it in disbelief because it was different from anything you had before experienced or accepted, or because it was called occult and thus branded by many as unsafe and unwise, you would have defeated yourself in the greatest possibility of growth and service which earth life every offered you and you would have rendered impotent the spiritual powers which happily have united for your help and progress.

The initial approach to you was most carefully planned here on these Ether Planes, so that you would slowly, gradually be brought within the circle of influence where prejudice no longer prevailed with you but where increasing experience with inter-world communication made you absolutely certain of its validity and of the familiar source from which the messages were coming. It would have been easy to make the wrong approach at which you would have shied off from further interest in this greatest experience which has ever come to you.

At first, the lessons were short and easy, filled with much that was personal and of value only as supports for your untried faith. You passed from that beginning grade rather quickly to these higher ones where assurances are no longer necessary that it is I who speak to you. God bless you every way for all that you have learned and done! You have had opposition and criticism from those yet encased in the rusty armor of unyielding traditionalism, who accept nothing unless it bears orthodox approval and who thus miss some of the richest spiritual experiences possible to the human heart. The day will come when their eyes will be no longer holden, when they too, will learn and break away from their self-set boundaries of belief. This structure of orthodoxy is but a shibboleth to those who prefer to accept what others say than to quest with their own outreaching spirits.

I beg you to commit your every interest and concern to the eternal keeping of the Infinite. He will not allow you to fall short of life's best and richest development. You are very safe in His hands. Amen!

COMPENSATION

It has been stormy today down where you live; stormy in your heart; perplexities crisscrossing! And what about it? Was any of it important from the vantage point of the Ether Planes? Will any of it endure and have lasting significance? Any of it worth remembering or being disturbed about?

Then why not drop it from your thoughts like a hot poker that can only harm by being held? And turn your thoughts definitely to constructive work that is worth doing and out of which can be fashioned much that is enduring.

Always there enters into life that marvelous influence called compensation which holds the balances pretty even and does not let one side of the scales go too low nor swing so high as to be dangerous to poise.

Compensation is part of the great gift of the Creator when He planned that man should have dominion over the material plane. What the human lacks in one way, he makes up in another equally essential way. It prevails, this blessed law of compensation, in the realm of physical things and equally in the world of the spirit.

Sometimes when we are bound about with problems of earth, we fail to notice lines that compensate for that other something which we want and which we lack. Sooner or later, the balance reveals itself and shows us wherein we are more blest than we had known. Don't fail, my friend, to take cognizance of joys that belong in the blessing of the law of compensation. It will help you along many a stretch and keep you from taking things of life too seriously. A lighter touch will spare you many a heartache. Watch carefully to make sure that you do not contribute to this unbalance where you are concerned.

Take more to prayer! The prayer that is real communion with the Father God, within the silent places of your heart, when you are conscious only of Him and not at all of the surface of living.

This kind of prayer gives you strength for any experience. It leaves you always with serenity that nothing else can give, with courage that does not yield when a hurdle appears in your path. I wish I could show you from these Planes of Exalted Privilege what communion of prayer really is and can do for the spirit.

Does it seem strange to you that we who have passed the Veil pray and continue to grow through the fructifying power of prayer?

We pray for ourselves and our steady growth in Divine wisdom and in the power of the spirit. Also we pray for others, both on the earth plane and for those who have come hither but are not attuned to the atmosphere of Divine love that fills these Planes, who rebel against it here as they did when they lived on earth.

We pray for their eyes to be opened, their hearts to be mellowed, their spirits made amenable to the transforming love and grace of Him Whose creations we all are. To Him in due time, every child of His gives loving allegiance and worship and service! Sometimes ages roll before those whose hearts are hard and who do not wish to become absorbed in the atmosphere of grace and goodness, yield to Him. But always they do. So you see, we here have much intercessory work to do for them as for the ones who struggle against the obstacles of earth life.

Prayer is thus very closely akin to our deepest emotions and when I speak of it to you so often, it is on this account. Practice it often, my friend! There is such value in it as is almost unbelievable to those who do not know by experience what prayer can do. Nothing is more true than the consolations and comforts that grow in the heart through prayer that is quiet communion.

I am off now for this time. It is so marvelous not to weary nor to lose heart but always to feel the glowing strength from the warm heart of our Lord and to know unfailing desire to be about the Master's business in whatever part of His universe we work.

His comforting blessings make you equal to your days and happy with the consciousness of constantly higher vibrations that are more quickly attuned with our realms. God love you! And Amen!

EXPERIENCING GOD

You have been in close contact this evening with powers of the Cosmic. Influences have been playing about you that are not of the earth. They are mighty in the power of the spirit world and tremendously important in their significance for your life. As these experiences come, your intellectual and spiritual horizons are pushed farther and farther back, so that you see more clearly.

This has relation to the earth world in which you are yet living but far more to cosmic consciousness where the soul of man mounts to its rightful place and asserts its full power in the life of the one who is experiencing these contacts with the spirit side of life.

Nothing is more important, nothing more wonderful, than to have your soul eyes opened so that you see clearly and have your spirit purged of the little, the frothy, the superficial while it is lifted to heights where everything appears in true balance and in perfect perspective.

All of this is another way of saying that you are experiencing God Himself when you feel yourself lifted almost bodily from monotonous levels of the flesh higher, still higher, conscious only of God and know yourself in His hands with Whom is all good! Is any other earth experience comparable with this? One needs not answer by word, such question.

Such spiritual purging comes only through meditation and prayer and through losing oneself in abandon to the higher power of the Cosmic, letting go of the earthly, as a child outgrows some trifling toy and lays claim to finer worth.

Cultivate these experiences, my friend. They are milestones on your upward climb. You will look back on each one with profound gratitude to the God-influences which have brought you to where you are competent to receive and to grow by these liftings out of your self.

Manifestations of presences from the spirit world have not often come to you. Never have they come in ways evident to your material eyes, though you have longed for them. They will come when the time is ripe. But you have been richly blest in the surging of your spirit when you have been utterly conscious as you were tonight, of spirit hosts around and about you, lifting you high in consciousness, increasing the tempo of your spirit vibrations and enabling you to know again for a surety that the physical world and the world where we dwell are as close as consciousness can conceive, closer than the fingers of your hand. There is scarcely a dividing line between!

If you would step-up your spirit vibrations through more meditation and more prayer for absolution of worldly ambitions and come closer to the rate of spirit vibrations in which we live and move and serve, it would so much more quickly contribute to your seeing with your eyes and hearing with your ears those manifestations of spirit presences which are all around and about you, which infiltrate the fibers of your being and prove that the very least part of you is the framework of bone and muscle and tissue.

Even these are spirit since all matter is energy which is another word for spirit. Lines of radiant energy which band your world and that pass in and through your physical body, connecting with our spirit realms, entirely destroy old ideas which I held when I was of earth, about lines of separation between what we called matter and what we thought of as spiritual.

How heavy and stodgy that was, as I tried to think my way through it and to make something consistent with what I believed of God! How grateful I am for coming Home to these blessed Planes of Power and learning how different it is from those human interpretations of God! They were sincere. But they were incorrect.

They hold you of earth back, tightly bound-about with beliefs that are like restraining cords whereas your spirit should be free to experience the intermingling of the two worlds and the presence in your earth life of us who have made the Great Transition. Our mission is to serve all those of earth who need us.

You are learning incontrovertibly that heaven is not off beyond the stars in some inaccessible place, but right where you live and work and need it. You are knowing that there is no death, that those you love so dearly have gone just out of your sight until you are able to see them with the eyes of your fleshly body.

What lessons these are and how transforming! They literally make over the world in which you are to live until that great, glad day When you will leave your garments of the human and in joy and gratitude accept the robes of the spirit.

We are in the radiant atmosphere of the love of the Son of God and we long to share with you all that you are ready to receive of the luminous beauty of this life, perfection of existence attuned to the celestial harmonies of the Creator.

But words fail me! Gradually your consciousness will take in more and more of what it means until you are transformed into oneness with it and ready to come on Home to us who await you. There is much for you to learn and enjoy and experience in preparation for that glorious coming which will be rapture to you.

The joy of it all attend your spirit, the eagerness of looking forward to it lift you constantly higher in consciousness, the loving care of God the Father be with you in blessing and power as you see with clearer vision and feel the vibrating energy that is God.

THE OPEN DOOR

Blessed are you of earth when you hold yourself in peace and poise despite turmoil swirling around you. Blessed when you can get your sense of values straight and true and hold them in perfect balance, seeing as with the vision of eternity and judging righteous judgment as with the wisdom of the Infinite.

Blessed are you when you can look past the glittering baubles of the transient and see true values which do not pass away, which are of eternal worth and are in harmony with the Father.

Blessed are you of earth when joy sings within your heart despite whatever harsh notes sound in your environment. Joy need not go off-key even when discord is clashing about, you and you cannot hear the tones of celestial harmonies which sound amid the dissonances of earth life.

Let joy well forth! Peal out the reasons for such joy until it swells high above and beyond the low rumble of earth sounds. It will cleave the air as on wings of pure spirit that cannot be held to the density of earth while all the firmament resounds to its perfect notes of rapture in the love of the Father.

There is nothing fanciful in this. It is so completely the truth as we here on the Inner Planes see it, practice it and realize it on every hand. We yearn for you of earth to learn the convincing quality of this pure note of joy welling forth and overcoming the low, discordant notes of all that is earthy.

Joy is so ethereal that it seems to have no density, no earthiness about it. Yet it is one of the mightiest influences of earth for everyone who will give it an abiding place within the heart. All who open their hearts to this celestial visitor from the High Planes of Spirit will find life transformed, their horizons extended by the magic power of this beautiful joy. Pitiful is the life that knows not joy coming directly from the heart of the Father, in His purity and greatness.

Cultivate it, my friend, and give it always the open door into your life that it may sing its way through the days and help to irradiate all your living.

Blessed are you when you reach this high plane where joy abides and works its wonderful power through you, whatever problems you face. We joy too, from these Inner Planes as we see this perfect quality manifesting within you and driving away all murkiness of spiritual atmosphere or gloom of intellectual concepts. They are thick and heavy and no beams of light or joy can penetrate them.

Do not count the cost in discipline of spirit when you cultivate heavenly joy. Pay no heed to the leaden darknesses that black it out and overbear its singingness within your heart. Let it sing!

Its song of rapture and peace and harmony and understanding will grow into a beautiful symphony of blessedness within your life, when you give it right of way. Despite what materialistic men say, it makes no difference that loads are heavy and problems many. Joy will sing its way through and over them and lift you as it sings, until you find that loads are vanished and problems solved.

Let not worry nor fretful anxiety find place in your heart when, instead, this wonderful spirit of joy can sing you through any perplexity; nor confuse this ethereal joy with the things of earthy mirth which often is of the lowest density with no spiritual quality in it. You can tell the difference by the effects upon your own heart. Joy always comes singing, always brings closer the sense of the presence of the Father, always lifts your consciousness into those high realms where vibrations are pure and holy and where nothing registers save what is true and good and like unto God.

BALANCED RATIONS

When earth dwellers lift their sights and change their lines of vision, many things that are only as enduring as morning mist, will shrink to their normal vanishing point of significance.

Earth is terribly ridden at this hour of sidereal time, with ambitions for power and position. They have assumed inordinate importance and men give them such influence as is inconceivable. This reflects in social life which is as near as trash to nothing. Great numbers of people devote their time to it, almost to the point of hysteria. Money lies at the bottom and is one of the great contributing factors in what is wrong with your world.

Not that anything is wrong with money itself. It is the medium with which life is negotiated on your earth sphere. It has its place. Kept there, its values are indisputable. Like oceans. Like rivers. Like everything else.

In their places, they are good and helpful and designed to serve mankind. But out of bounds, overflowing their borders, they are destruction let loose.

So with money. Everybody needs it. You need it. Comforts and necessities come in exchange for it. Our Lord used it to teach some of His most impressive lessons. It is part of the human set-up.

Let it get the whip hand, individual or nation, and there is the devil to pay! In such a plight, payment is not easy. Many are paying now. Many more will pay and with interest, they who have rated money above integrity and spirituality or service to others. They who have sold themselves for money do the transient thing, to outshine, taste the dregs of bitterness which always comes with such a sale. They find only that they have made a poor bargain that must be carried through to the end of restitution to those who have been harmed.

Whether that restitution comes at once in the current life on earth, it comes! Please believe me! And the debt is paid before it is wiped off the account of spirit wholeness. Never is it forgotten.

One of the phases of this temporal orgy is wastage involved—waste of God-given time, of strength, of talents, of opportunity to do great and good things which need doing, waste of growth in which every one should be enormously concerned. All along the road which mankind traverses, it is waste!

And that has no part in the Infinite God's plan of Creation nor in His law of life. Waste never appears in anything He has done. All is utilized to the last degree. But with man, prodigal waste of the most precious human stuff comes at every turn. Man throws away things of priceless value in exchange for some trifling toy that like the balloon, floats merrily enough for a brief hour, then wrinkles down to a tiny handful of useless wreckage. Pitiful waste of gifts which mankind has received from the Great Giver, designed to be used in ways of enduring good.

The lesson will be learned. But it is pity that such high rate of interest must be paid in terms of human expiation. I charge you to guard against such wastage. I charge all who Will think on this theme and who will see in the world situation, much that is good within bounds, get out of bounds and take the reins to drive to destruction! Money and power are closely harnessed together. They are a grand team, under the control of a careful driver, otherwise a team of destruction and fearfulness that runs amuck and does awful damage wherever they collide with others. Collide they do!

All of this is part of that great virtue of moderation, of temperance in all things. In many ears, it sounds old-fashioned and very dull. But in it are seeds of goodness and fair play, of wise use of substance which is part of the Creator's largess, of investment of time which merges without a break into the endlessness of eternity. All of this is involved.

Can any well-balanced person throw to the discard these things for the doubtful privilege of a "fling"? It is done all the while in your unbalanced world. The more it is done, the more out of balance life becomes.

Many are conscientious investors of their substance and their time in things of lasting quality and goodness. Their reward is great.

The whole issue is one of value and balance. The issue can be followed easily when the scales of life weigh fairly. It is worth watching in even small details that enter into the total to be reckoned by every man and every woman. It is tremendously serious for every earth person.

Hold steady, my friend. Keep close company with the Father. Be sure to keep to balanced rations in your spirit life.

The Great, Good God be very sufficient for your every need and enwrap you with the consciousness of His abiding presence and His unfailing love. Good night!

GUERDON

The word for you tonight is, "Reach up and go forward!" Be satisfied with nothing less than your utmost. I care not what it is. Stretch to your highest in mind and spirit, in even little things. Though of course, nothing is little. It is all part of the masterly plan of the Creator. Could anything from His hand be called little?

Watch the snow flake. Is anything tinier, more fragile, more just for the moment? But what power multiplied flakes have! See the smallest flower that grows beside life's common way. Perfect in every particle. Study the smallest shells that dot the shores of oceans of earth. Are any two alike? Or made with other than the perfection of the Master hand? There is nothing little as compared with large, nothing but should command your utmost powers, if it is worth doing. So, my friend, from the heights of these Ether Planes, I urge you all to reach for the highest, and stretch for the finest in whatever ways it comes to you to manifest superiority of spirit.

Life on earth is short. It is important as the training school for the soul, essential as preparation for life up here where you begin where you left off down there. Nobody can afford to pass a moment idly, unless resting is the appointed portion for that time. For the most part, time is of the essence of immortal values. With it, much can be achieved and learned that will be your recommendations when you come Home to join us here. You do not want to have to see where failing to reach up, to stretch the muscles of your soul, failure to go forward in courage and strength, marks you on an inferior grade of soul power.

No! No! That is not what you want. It is the fine, pure-grade mark of the forward-straining spirit that is never content except on the upgrade, seeking higher levels of discipline and nearer perfection of lessons learned.

This which I am saying to you tonight, my friend, is personal to you only in the sense that you are not to be prone to rest on your oars. You are not! The life of the spirit-world is one of conquest. The guerdon is won by supreme performance of faith and loyalty and love and service.

It is sweet to hear "Well done!" when first we come to these Elysian Fields. But the first thing we learn after we are adjusted here and have begun to understand the ordering of life, is that we still wish to reach up and to move toward that perfection of life which is represented by the Godhead. Ages it takes to reach that sublimity. But every effort, every conquest over doubt and fear and unworthiness, every tendency overcome to let mediocrity suffice, every glory won by faith and every new radiance acquired by loyalty of service, sets one that much nearer the greatest goal that spirit can frame. Keep to it loyally, my friend.

How wonderful it will be when over here on these shores you see the real value of what pressing forward has brought you. How grateful we shall all be! For here no one is ever left to rejoice alone at triumphs won. No one need ever fear to stir jealousy into flame or to rouse resentment.

Those two deadly sins are left behind on the earth plane when, as with me that night some years ago, I laid my body down to rest. And immediately came sweet release when the bonds of clay which had held body and soul together, were dissolved and I was free from the frailties which I had suffered so long on the earth plane!

How gracious it was when I realized that I had reached Home at last! How many years I had dreaded that release! All because I had been taught erroneously. Not until the actual experience came to me, utterly devoid of the terrors which I had anticipated, did I see the Transition as it is—sweet release, strength for weakness, freedom for limitation, beauty for ashes and the "oil of joy for the spirit of heaviness"!

It was all of these, multiplied and magnified a thousandfold. Please believe me, my friend. It is even as I tell you, only magnified beyond your earth understanding. Why do I talk at such length about life on this side of the Transition? Because your earth is so ridden with sorrow, with uncertainty, with suffering and limitation, whereas there is strength for everyone who will look forward to this next step in the journey, as it was planned by the God of all Creation.

Not only strength but joy which always heals and peace which stabilizes and poise which gives the spirit its steadiness of purpose and its power to achieve.

Think on these things, think much on them, my friend. They are worth more than all the earth baubles that can be put together. For these qualities of which I speak will last through the unendingness of eternity.

I crave for you to become so inoculated in your spirit with this certainty of the reality of life over here that never will you have one moment of distress as you realize its inevitability, but that rather, it will come to have enormous challenge to spirit, that you will live in this upward-reaching mood of the spirit, moving continuously and conqueringly toward these highlands where spirit is all and God is the power and the glory forever and ever. Amen!

ELECTRICAL IMPULSE

I stand here beside you even as I said when we were beginning these inter-world messages! You wonder how, it is that I hear your call voiced only through your thought, when I often am in distant parts of the universe on service. This is one of the earth wonderments which it is difficult to appease. It is part of the infinite mystery which surrounds the Spirit Planes and which would not be explainable in earth words nor to minds still housed in bodies of the flesh. I know this is not satisfactory to the alert mind that wants to know clear, full reasons of why and how. That wish may be granted only in part, as I just said.

The power of thought is stronger than bands of steel, mightier than any physical substance. We here who have accomplished the Great Transition learn from the beginning to communicate by thought transference. Once learned, it is much freer, more pleasing, more satisfying and far beyond clumsier ways of speaking through the limitations of vocal cords and earth words. That is indeed limitation, as we here see it now, though once we found it good enough. That was because we did not know the better way.

As I speak to you in these messages, it is by thought transference. I energize your mind with the exact words I wish you to take. It is all on electrical impulse and comes with such power that often it is overwhelming in its physical effects. You have found it so and your material body has all but flattened out under the impact of power along whose waves has come this transference of thought direct from the Inner Planes, to you of earth.

You hear my voice with your inner ears wherever you are, on the street, at your home or wherever: You hear it when your mind is busily occupied wits earth tasks. By the same method of electrical impulse which in its workings I am not at liberty to explain in detail because it would accomplish nothing beyond gratification of curiosity, by which I command your instant attention wherever you are, do I hear your unvoiced call for help, your unuttered appeal for guidance, your urgent asking for light on problems of life.

Please get this very clear, that life over here is negotiated on electrical impulse which is beyond earth understanding but which to enlightened minds here is entirely comprehensible. Increasingly earth minds see how all matter is electrical energy and therefore it is perfectly reasonable that the two worlds should draw closer together and that many more of these marvelous lines of inter-world communication should open.

The greatest hindrance is the absence of confidence on the earth end, the receiving end of the line of communications. For your earth is yet in the fog of ignorance about the power of communication from our side to your side of life.

Currents of power run in both directions, from us to you, from you to us, and it is only in being receptive to what comes along the waves of ether from these Higher Planes, that you of earth receive what is sent, and may send what is desired for us to receive.

When it seems like too great a mystery for human understanding—and it is if one would wish to know details of functioning in the Spirit Realms—just take this for your comfort that you hear my voice in whatever activity you are occupied, you recognize it instantly, you receive these messages without a shadow of doubt as to exact wording, yet no audible word has been spoken, no syllable that the outer, physical ear could detect.

What matters that? This way is so satisfying, so dependable, so unerring that it answers every possible need, doesn't it? Wherefore then be anxious lest in moment of special need or doubt or weakness I may not hear your call? I always have! I always shall! The method is not the matter of importance. The message is all that really has significance. And that is its own carrier. So don't be concerned about techniques, only about spirit essence. No word cones through from our Planes that does not have vital truth for those who are struggling with earth problems. I speak not of lower astral planes.

So it behooves you who yet abide in the physical to keep attuned to the right wave length from this side of life, to receiving any word of truth and power that comes. It never fails when the right attunement is in force.

I say this for your comfort and that you may know that further explanation of your question would be confusing to earth minds. Someday it will be clearer. But this is enough now. So give thanks for receiving what you need and for knowing to the limit of your necessities.

Your way is opening. Be patient. The darkness gives way to light and you will see whither your way winds. And you will like it. Rest assured of that. Meanwhile, give attention only to those things which are uplifting, to none that depress. Let go the little. Take firm hold of Almighty power adequate for every emergency.

May the abounding grace of the Father dwell within you in conscious presence of peace and satisfaction and light for every step of your earth journey. Amen!

TESTS AND STANDARDS

Yet another hour of conference together concerning things of spirit that do not pass away! Neither do they lose their significance nor their power in relation to realities of life. What is physical, is transient; quickly come, quickly gone. All that is of spirit endures forever. Seek therefore the things of spirit with much avidity. Seek to know the powers of spirit, that transmuted into your life, can multiply your values, increase your service, change your ideals, lift your sights and literally make you over into the spiritual person God intended you to be.

What all of this means, you may not fully understand now. But understanding will come and it will be as light in the darkness, light that will illumine your mind and show you the way your feet should travel. It will be strength to you and wisdom to you and power for overcoming.

Hold everything up to the light of spirit. See whether it stands the test of the genuine, whether gold or dross, whether its threads are evenly woven of honor and integrity without any marring of the beauty, whether in the bright shining of this light, it glows purely or shows substitutes for the pure product of the mine. Test whatever it be, by this light of spirit. Then follow where it leads, accept what it reveals, trust whatever its verdict, know that spirit is of God and that He never makes mistakes.

Spirit seems intangible. It is. No man may touch it. It seems evanescent. It is. No man may see spirit. It seems fragile as a dependence, as stronghold in time of need. Be not deceived. Spirit has a thousand times more power for bringing to pass the help the human needs, than he has with all his earthly tools and ways of working, more strength than all of the steel of the world for mastering earth problems and bringing help for time of difficulty.

Study to grow in ways of spirit. Let nothing turn you aside into alluring by-paths of human limitations, into ways of questionable wisdom and doubtful judgment. Study spirit. Learn its lessons. Put them into daily, hourly practice.

Come to the place of testing intuitively and unconsciously every thought and act by the standards of spirit. Discard what does not measure up to the highest. What reveals itself as worthy, incorporate into your inner being and let nothing distract nor lead you away from its clear-shining guidance.

Spirit will flood your heart with peace and conscious power as nothing else in the universe of God can do. When spirit comes to abide with you, the wonder of its quiet guidance and the satisfaction of its deep, wisdom never leave you. There is permanence with spirit and power of understanding life and of accepting those things which are of good report.

Close companionship with spirit quickly changes one's desires for the gaudy, the passing, the light and frothy, giving in place deep hunger and thirst for eternal values. O my friend, I beg you to place all things else in the scales against spirit and see how lightly they weigh, how little substance they have, how fleetingly they abide and how soon they wither as of no account.

It is illuminating to make such a dramatic comparison within the secret place of your own heart. I beseech you to make it and always to hold to the inviolable standards which there reveal themselves. Then indeed shall you be rich in those things which abide through the ages, to give you wisdom and strength and peace divine.

Spirit never leaves you without help, never fails to answer your call nor leaves you without sense of direction. Spirit is never blind to your needs nor deaf to your cries. Earth things will fail and fall short of satisfying. Spirit goes to the very center. Earth toys fall apart with a breath, their satisfactions gone. Spirit is cosmic, unfailing and unchanging.

Again let me say that spirit is God. And God is within you. Get acquainted with Him. Fellowship with Him. Trust this spirit which is Infinite and is part of Him! Nothing else is half as important for any man any time any where!

Another theme was in my thought for this evening's talk. But this one superseded it and therefore I know it was divinely intended for putting into your thought at this time. I am near you often these days when sometimes you are conscious of my presence and when you do not recognize me. It is all right either way. I go now for the night. God's spirit be your constant companion, friend, comfort, and inspiration. Amen!

DEEP PLACES

That which is greatest is invisible. That which is material is of smallest consequence. Spirit is all that matters in the long run. It alone endures. The physical and all that belongs to it quickly pass into other forms.

Spirit is without beginning and without end. Of course you cannot comprehend so vast a span. Not even the hosts of invisible Realms can comprehend. We only know it is true. After those dimensions of infinitude of life you should pattern your living. Nothing temporary or ephemeral should take strong hold of your interest, save in ways that pertain to the welfare of your earth days. This is so important for the earth person never to forget.

There is an insidious quality about the things of material success. Such things quickly and too easily possess one and come to be of more than desirable importance. Guard that well as you make your way through your world.

None of this suggests the ascetic life, eschewing good things or restricting oneself to what is purely spiritual. Not that at all! But a balance is what you should strive for between the physical and over-mounting needs of the spiritual. Watch to gain that fine balance which represents growth in values, as we here know them.

To learn theoretically is one thing. But to learn and then to live what you have learned, is another thing and of vastly more import. Acquire the one. Be sure of gaining the other. Then you have a solid foundation on which to build your spirit structure that will not pass away.

We were talking at our evening hour lately, about the peace of the Cosmic and how it may be experienced in the human heart, even when winds of earth blow and storms of life seek to destroy. It is not of quick experience that one acquires such peace within the heart. It is the slow, sure growth that comes when one seeks sources of peace which are the gift of the Father; seeks and gradually finds, proving their efficacy against whatever background.

This peace has nothing to do with the surface of things. It is of the deep places of spirit to which one penetrates by faithful search and with the patience that knows no giving up. What comes easily, goes the same way. What is rapidly acquired, is dissipated with the same facility. That which steadily grows to stronger fiber, is slow, oak-like growth.

I beg of you take time for cultivating this sense of cosmic peace in hectic days of earth living. I know what these days mean. I have not forgotten. But I have learned beyond what I can impart to you yet, the worthwhileness of studying to gain this sense of peace. It is power to you, to any one who so lives with open mind and inquiring heart as to gain possession of it. Then one is not buffeted about with adverse winds. As you approach it, you will be conscious of the sanctity of that toward which you draw near. It is the essence of the God-head, Beginning and End of all things, of all life.

Make much of your study of these things which are gaining more influence over your spirit life. You can afford to sacrifice trivialities, though you have few of them, for opportunity to grow closer to the heart of this true greatness and goodness. You will find it unfolding before the eyes of your spirit in ways of which you have not dreamed, worth more than all else in the world. Everything you gain this way you will find valuable when you come hither, to these Planes of Light.

Do not be discouraged when growth in these mighty matters comes slowly. It is certain to come that way, not by leaps and bounds. But it comes surely when search for it continues and the spirit assimilates each vestige of light and peace and power as it unfolds, and puts it to work within the soul.

Take your thoughts off of whether you are growing. Forget all of that. Keep your vision centered on the great goal toward which you aspire. And never waver!

This is so weighty, so mighty, that I have given you all for which you are equal this time. Feed on it. Grow by it. Remember always that the God of Hosts is with you, leading, guiding, keeping you. What more does one ask! His presence empower you each moment. His healing balm flow through your body until there shall be no sense of physical limitation in your consciousness. I leave you now. God bless you always. Amen!

ANTENNAE OF THE SPIRIT

This being your earth Sabbath, perhaps it is a favorable time to talk about what comes to one who is receptive. That word—receptive—means open-mindedness, willingness to learn and accept what is truth. Sometimes what is not truth gets passage into such minds.

It means keeping, if I may use such a figure of speech, the antennae of the spirit out for all possible contacts with the ether waves along which come and go such inconceivably great lines of thought and inspiration and knowledge and wisdom. Granting the appropriateness of this word from earth's scientific vocabulary, the antennae of the spirit need to be far out and sensitively alert to any message or influence that passes, detecting quickly whether it be allied with truth and goodness or tinctured with negative possibilities.

Being receptive opens magnificent vistas of thought and feeling allied with the action that is bound to follow. In a single idea thus receptively acquired, good often abides that is beyond power of man to compute. For in the idea, the thought, the mental concept, is the beginning of what develops into great achievement for mankind's good. However small the idea, one who is receptive will see the outreach in possibility and take it into active consideration for development that follows the animating motive. One who greets all such incoming thoughts with cynicism is heavy loser in the market place of the soul.

Receptivity is the builder of great and growing soul-dimensions. It stretches the mind and enlarges the spirit, brings riches from the whole of God's creation and offers them to the waiting soul. Great riches come this way, unannounced and unexpected, dropped into the open mind like a gracious gift from the Father.

He knew the gift would be received and nurtured by this open mind and carefully cultivated by this questing spirit. No limits are placed upon the receptive spirit. It is open to all the good which it will accept and use for the help of them who can be influenced by it. Do you not see how constructive a spiritual potency abides in this receptivity?

There come to the antennae of your spirit some concepts as have bewildered you, such as came just after I had crossed the River which flows beside our Heavenly Land. You were not aware that you could be open-minded to such ideas as were presented to you through your loyal "receiving station" those first few months.

You could not quickly nor completely accept that it was I who was speaking through her to you. You did not know that it could be. You wondered. You doubted. You feared. You hoped. But the antennae of your spirit did not fold down and refuse further impressions. On the contrary, you continued to seek, if haply you might find assurance that these things which were being spoken to you from beyond the Veil, were truth and were coming from me whom you had known so long.

The spirit of being willing to lay aside the old, negative, beliefs that "it couldn't be true" because you had never proved it true and to open your mind and heart to prove that the line of communication was running straight from me to you, with words of guidance and faith and life, illustrates what I mean by receptivity.

You might have been quite justified in your caution if you had yielded to your conservative tendencies and refused to accept this so-radical experience as communication from me whom your world called "dead."

But your spirit had that quality which was willing to test and to prove and then to accept, out of which came the deepest, richest, most transforming experiences of your earth life. They have literally made you over. Your spirit stands ready to accept whatever comes with the aura of truth encircling it, however different it may be from what you have previously believed. Because you were and are receptive, you are indeed blest.

Being receptive does not mean that one is to take up with any notion or foible, any propaganda and assimilate it unquestioningly. Far from it. Always one needs to separate chaff from wheat, true from false and being convinced of the quality of goodness in a concept which comes to the open mind, to accept and follow. This is self-evident. The quality of receptivity is a great reservoir from which infinite truth is received and service rendered in the name of the Father.

Streams of His beneficence are flowing into your life and out to others who, except for these streams, would find their lives parched and barren, no light ahead and no way through the quagmire of earth difficulty. Such is part of your reward which does not end but swells to the endlessness of eternity.

I have long wanted to speak to you on this theme and am grateful that my message is now safe with you. It will make its way to others who will find renewed hope and faith and courage and rejuvenating experiences for their spirits through it. God bless you. Amen!

FOR THEM BEYOND THE VEIL

It may seem strange to you that even as the messages of these hours together have built you into stronger faith and more stable dependence upon the All-Father, so have they helped my progress in things of God and growth.

The sense of sharing what we here have and see and know, with you all on your lower earth sphere, does me good.

Once before I talked with you about the value of prayer for those who have passed the Veil and who, as all of us do, need every possible help in adjusting and developing into the full stature of God. Believe me, there is great help for us in your prayers, even as it is our blessed privilege to send you spirit help and courage and light. While I was on earth, I would have thought such was a pagan doctrine. I would have turned aside from it because the Protestant church had no place for such intercession in its rituals. What matters that, except the loss which has accrued to countless thousands from the lack of such spiritual up-lift, if you of earth had joined to pray for their growth in things of the spirit, for power in overcoming errors committed on earth and for coming more quickly into perfect harmony with the spirit of God's love? Therefore it matters much.

As with many another teaching which I either espoused or turned from in ignorance, I have learned here and still am learning the great mistakes which people of earth make through that kind of ignorance which beset me in my earth career. It is one of the most mistaken ideas that there is no need to pray for those who have come on ahead into this more blessed land where the soil of the soul is richly fertilized with Divine love and every advantage given for soul expansion, where we see clearly instead of through a glass, darkly.

The power of prayer cannot be over-estimated in your realm on earth or in ours in this Better Abode. Power is released through prayer when it is used in simple faith, in mighty faith, that knows what it believes. Such power is available for the one for whom it is asked in that faith, be he yet in the flesh or on the Ether Planes!

This is vitally worth considering and following in all loyalty of spirit. One should never weary of such service which bring great recompense of reward to the one who faithfully employs the power of intercession in behalf of few or many.

Think on this, my friend. And live by it. Use it for me, for those many of your close circle who have come on Home in advance and who are expanding in the things of eternal life. It will be great joy to you when you come, to know how your prayers have helped all of us who will welcome you at your coming.

Of course, we pray for you, all the time and wherever we are. It is part of our sacred privilege to bear you and your problems in prayer to the Father Whose blessings we ask upon you.

You do not always know whence the feeling of rejuvenation comes nor why the load seems lighter nor why you appear to see more clearly in the realm of spirit things. But it is because from these Planes, we are praying for you and releasing power to you, faith to you, strength to you and all things great and good that will enable you to make such record in your life as will stand you in grand stead when you come.

This is of the greatest importance and I ask you to leave no loophole of carelessness in your pattern of prayer and of all things germane to enlargement of spirit power. We here, as I have so often told you, are carefully charting your course through changing scenes. To you with your sense of earth time, such outworking seem slow in coming. They take long when your nature calls for quick action and you do not like to wait! You never have!

But from our Higher Spheres of Knowledge and Vision in both of which wisdom abides, such changes do not come about with the quickness of your earth schedules. It cannot be. The tempo of the Ether Planes is different. The planning is different. And better. Your earth hurryings, your running around, your so great haste after every little thing of small or of no consequence, seem to us almost pathetic except as we remember that earth limitations bind you in knowledge and vision. We remember how it was with us while we were in the flesh, residents of earth.

But I pray you to believe me that the unhurrying, unhasting ways of the Spirit World are infinitely to be trusted and waited for in absolute confidence that the right issue will come when the time is right. And now, the blessing of the Father abide with you!

LIGHT

Let your light shine, that no darkness creep into your heart or hide the joy that rightfully is yours! The true Light eradicates darkness in which thrive all undesirable things which cannot take the Light of the inner life. Darkness is the spawning place of influences which do not make for heroic living.

Only the Light that is of God can dissipate this miasmic condition, bearing on its beams all things of good report. If there is dark or secret nook in your heart, turn the key quickly and let the Light shine in, to begin its work of cleansing, purifying and making like unto God again, as your heart was when you came into being through His creative Word.

I do not speak this to you personally, but to you as illustration of the meaning of this message that will shine out to people living all kinds of ways in all sorts of places and facing uncounted earth problems. They need this regenerative Light of God for clearing out the rubbish that clutters the sacred place where is the abode of the Most High.

With its myriad rays and colors, its healing powers and inestimably high vibratory rate, it needs only the door of any heart to be thrown open and kept open. Then this dealing Light will pour in with its blessed illuminating power for driving out whatever is dark and dank and damp with evil.

Every heart has some hidden nook into which the Light of God's joy needs to shine to restore perfect balance for the business of living. The human it is who holds the key to the particular place which sorely needs this cleansing, joy-bringing Light. It can change the sordid to the pure, the intolerant to complete understanding, the selfish into flaming forgetfulness of self that thinks only of others and of God in Whom dwells the perfection of selflessness.

His Light will show you that what had seemed a dire problem for which you are unequal, is not serious after all and needs only this Light streaming from the heart of the Father, to find the answer and to realize that the problem is completely taken care of. Jesus was that Light. Such Light it was! Like unto no other because it was the essence of purity that knew no evil accent but was the very garment of God.

All that any earth person desires of this Radiance which is beyond compare, is to be had for the asking, in faith. It will irradiate his body, change the order of his thinking and doing and implant within his being new ideals of spirit power and perfection that make one the more ready for the Great Transition when time is called. Open every nook and cranny of your heart. Withhold nothing. Ask His Light to shine on every desire and every act, revealing to you the way your feet should travel and the pattern your life should assume.

None of this can be clear while one lives and walks and tries to work in darkness. Only the Light can be the revealer. Never be afraid of it. Never think you do well enough with some of the rooms of your mental house in darkness of ignorance or false desires. Only by the bright shining of His Light within the heart can one come to the best possible, which is always the correct standard. Not man's best possible by his own strength and knowledge. Not man's best while part of him is left in darkness. But man's best possible when illumination comes through His Light shed abroad in the heart; when His knowledge and wisdom supplant limited human knowing and His Infinity substitutes for man's limitations.

Let your light shine! Bright and clear! Shine afar! No telling where it will reach and what darkness it will dispel. You shine! Let God take care of the rest! Amen!

BOOKED FOR PASSAGE

Tonight I would speak to you about being ready to come when your time is at hand, with no last-minute anxiety or sense of needing to balance your spiritual books. Does this seem a strange topic for me to use? Not at all. It calls for daily living of high order in which spirit is geared to the loftiest of which the human is capable, the eternal takes precedence over the material and nothing of personal selfishness is allowed to have part.

Thus you see, every person of youth or age, needs this spirit world and his coming hither in constant, constructive and happy remembrance, as he embodies into the pattern of his days those impulses and ideas and ambitions which will pass muster when he comes over to our Happy Land. There is nothing light or easy about such living. It makes one more keenly susceptible to spirit influences than to earthy currents that swirl about his feet.

Be ever ready to try to show those who know so little about the life over here, that it is a place of such development and joy and peace and constructive activity as is hard for the earth mind to conceive. The little baby who comes with its tiny body not habituated to ways of earth, may be a very old soul, may have gone through many reincarnations with their lessons and their triumphs and be fully ready to come quickly to high spiritual status, here where nothing but spirit power counts.

The earth parent needs to shift his thoughts from the little one who stayed briefly, to its invisible development and to its vast spiritual potentialities, here where nothing holds it back, where every impulse is toward nearer approach to the life that is hid with Christ in God.

None of this comports, you see, with the so-limited comprehension of earth people who think and mourn of their "loss" when one, old or young, passes from earthly circles to these Abiding Mansions of the Blest. Loss? Never! It is such gain as Saint Paul meant when he said that "to die is gain!"

Such gain! How I wish I could get that message across to earth minds. Everything about it is gain for the one who comes and it is of the highest essence of true love, for those who remain, to recognize the advancement that has been given to the dear one, to rejoice and never to mourn nor grieve nor wish that one back in the narrow limitations of earth living.

What a lesson this is to learn! I do not mean to learn on the surface of the mind as an abstract principle but to learn in the deep places of the heart, of the character and of the spirit.

You are moving out into clearer air where you will feel more freedom and better sense of the power that is in you. Go step by step. And the God of all grace go with you, bless you with His abounding love, fire you with His mighty energy and blessed powers to achieve. Amen!

THINGS THAT ABIDE

What a word that is—abide! In the physical everything is so transient, here a moment and gone forever. It is well that it is so. Transience is of the essence of the earthly. Substances that comprise the physical could not endure.

They were not intended to last beyond their brief time. Their value is limited and you of earth do well to bear that in mind. Nothing which is physical can abide beyond the small earth moment of time for which it suffices.

I thought I understood it when I was of earth. But now it is so clear to me. By contrast, things that abide stand forth with perfect clarity and beauty. They are of the spiritual which is the only quality that endures. Everything of the spirit has that quality. Why the earth person gives such overwhelming value to that which, like the grass, is here today and gone tomorrow, is difficult for us from these High Planes, to see, except as we remember how it seemed to us when we were of the human.

We knew better then. But the material loomed larger to us then as it does to you now and occupied more space in our thoughts than it should. All perfectly natural according to human standards. But not according to spirit standards. And in the phrase of the evening, they are the only ones that abide.

As from time to time I speak with you and through you, to the great numbers who will read these messages, I pray all of you to realize with deep sincerity that every word I send along the ether waves is directly related to things which abide. These words are to be taken seriously and incorporated into the fiber of your earthly life, for spirit growth and values. Nothing of these messages is said, save for that purpose. Recently we discussed the greatest of all themes, the love of the Father, love transcendingly glorious and available always to His children who need what that love can give.

Of course you cannot approach an understanding of it. Neither can we on these Spirit Planes who live closer to the Divine than is granted to ones of earth. But you can believe it and live on it and grow by it and be blest with it. You can learn something, of its sweetness and power and lean upon all that it means.

You can come blessedly nearer to appropriating its richness by accepting the truth of it and by learning to give out all that it means to you in service to Him and His children. Another thing you need to learn about this overmastering love, is that as you accept it, you learn by degrees to love Him as you never loved Him before! That is part of the prerogative of love. It is never one-sided. It gives and takes. As you take of this Infinite love, you learn to love Him in return through prayer and communion.

Pour out your heart to Him. Stretch the powers of your inmost soul to interpret Him in love and service. See Him as all the good there ever was or ever will be. As you do these things within the secret places of your soul, you will grow in ways that are wholly of the spirit beyond anything you would have dreamed.

STEADY REINS

I wish to talk with you about the discipline of the emotions of the human. There is vast power in emotions when they are properly ballasted and controlled by poise and sound judgment, so that nothing is permitted to run like wild fire against the grain of wisdom.

I refer to those waves of feeling that sweep over the human heart, that depress without reason, daunt without occasion and make the whole business of living more difficult than it need be.

Men and women are prone to be overcome by some unjustified fit of dejection. When they yield to it, as often they do, they dampen the ardor of their lives and lower the tone of their entire moral nature. Is that right?

Is God dead because discouraged emotions took the reins and decided to drive the vehicle of the human for a day or a week of your earth time? Where does he arrive when he gives the reins of his life into such run-a-way control? Just nowhere! Except into deeper dejection and a morass of greater danger than ever can trap him when he puts those reins of life into the keeping of the Good God and trusts His unerring goodness. The most casual earth word will sometimes throw a life off balance for days when there exists no foundation for such loss of power and such absence of the guidance which the Divine stands ready to give when the human asks for it.

Never is there loss of power when the Divine takes over! I wish you of earth could really believe that. And live it. And prove it. How rich you would be in your growing resources of spirit if you would refuse the temperamental upsetments and steady yourselves on the firm foundations which are in the Christ of God!

Think about it, my friend, and guard yourself against the defeat that invariably comes when you give in to negative emotions of disappointment or fear or discouragement. They are not born of the Spirit of God but are wholly of earth and abound in earth weakness. This is part of the constant choosing which the earth person must make, every one of which is momentous with eternal issues. For as you choose and as you live, as you give in or overcome, so your record will stand indelibly written and be your starting point when you come to these Beautiful Planes of Growth.

Give in to temptations of dismay or despair or come up over things with triumph of spirit and refuse to be downed! All of you who walk the ways of earth, make that choice many times every day, little heeding the significance of that which you do. It is time you do heed each one of these. For they are the stuff of which your spirit fabric is woven. You would not wish that fabric to be thin and poor with weakness of weaving, but strong and beautiful in design and in power to serve.

All of this grows directly out of your control of even the least of these things you call emotion. They are threaded through the whole pattern of your living. It is no light matter of which I speak to you tonight. It is of the essence of that which abides. Pay heed therefore to it. And watch your choices of emotion lest you be overwhelmed in unnecessary floods of dismay when you might be travelling the highway of conquest, your spirit rejoicing in the constant guidance of the Holy One Who never leads you astray. We here see this from our better vantage point of perspective and we know it for what it is in the quality of human living.

Learn more and more, my friend, to give thanks and rejoice at the innumerable goods and graces which come into your life. Study to see this side of the picture an acquire from it those powers for growth in spirit which come only as one gives thanks to the Father and absorbs the strength and sturdiness which stand one in stead both now and hereafter.

When you do not see much for which to give thanks, when you do not feel like giving thanks, discipline your heart to it with loyalty of conviction. And you will be amazed at the way your spiritual temperature will rise and at the ease with which you will recognize countless good things for which to praise, things you had not thought to notice before. It works like magic and always for your good. Prove it, my friend. The God of All Good be with you and keep you in the consciousness of His unfailing guidance and support.

GROWING PAINS

Do you remember from your youth-time how frequently you complained of pains in your legs or arms or back? Your parents listened patiently and told you they were just growing-pains which every earth person experiences when his body is developing rapidly and systematically.

It has been long since you thought of those childhood pains, for your body has come beyond them. But you are undergoing rather painful growing pains nevertheless. You yet are! These are of the spirit as it strives to leave its "low-vaulted past"—you see I remember that famous phrase from my earth days—and grow into grander dimensions of understanding and faith and love and wisdom. Of course these cause you growing-pains. For you are laying aside small ideals, childhood concepts of God and His ways, for ideals that are worthy of the Most High indwelling your heart.

Immature and inadequate interpretations do not challenge you to your highest nor lead you into your largest service of living as His representative. So you are growing in your spirit, finding, learning, testing and accepting new powers of faith and love and knowledge, adjusting them to your conditions of living. Sometimes they have seemed not to fit and have been difficult to live with in perfect comfort.

Occasionally you find that this or that teaching is no for you, man-made, instead of part of the God-plan for the children of His creation. It is not strange that this is so. When some creed or concept does not adjust to your highest life, take it off and lay it completely aside, looking in quietness and confidence for that which is perfectly adapted, God-adapted to your needs at the stage of growth in things spiritual at which you have arrived.

The teachings which come to you constantly from our spirit side of life have brought you radical changes of dimensions in your life and it would be strange if you did not suffer these growing pains. Rejoice, my friend, and be glad that the pains bring deeper understanding and deeper wisdom in ways of the spirit. Nothing else matters half as much! You are being tested, not because you have failed but because you have succeeded. Greater things are awaiting you when you have grown up to them, things of such magnitude in the spirit realm that when their grandeur has burst upon you, you will wonder at your distress over the slight growing pains, though now they seem aTmost beyond your enduring. Lay all that aside and devote yourself to whatever tends to this growth which prepares you for the way of greater service.

Take the growing pains! Let them hurt! Let your pride which sought other channels and rewards give way to these grander rewards which come with the greater growth. This thing of pride on the earthly basis can safely be let alone to take such care as it can of itself. At best, it is a transient, ephemeral thing of no substance and sometimes desperately in the way of a quality of spirit which completely outshines and displaces this temporary earth pride. Of course it is hurt at being ignored and laid aside. But away with it, my friend, and gear your life to those things which are being prepared for you and through you by the spirit world.

These cannot be given to you unless your spiritual growth enables you to meet the demands of those who are guiding you. All this it is that is the source of these growing pains that are blessedly of the spirit.

Our visit together this evening is based on eternal truth and on such spiritual understanding as is worth whatever the price. Take heart, good friend, and rejoice in your growing, in the maturing of your spirit fiber. It is all so entirely to the good, as you will see some of these days, more clearly than you see now. Blessings and peace and power and calm quietude be yours. Amen!

THE OTHER SIDE

Now that I am no longer bound by the physical body, isn't it wonderful that I may continue to speak with you and to know that you recognize the source from which it comes?

This is one of the great lessons which my coming across to this side of life has taught you. Taught me, too! For I had no knowledge of the possibility of such communication while I was of earth.

I would have discounted statement of such fact as spurious and have discredited any such power, had any one talked with me about it. Nobody did. Therein I was the loser. On account of all this, it behooves both of us to avoid any possible spirit of criticism of those who yet deny that this is possible. They too, will learn sometime in ways that are part of their life development. It is like being freed to a glorious liberty which earth words cannot express.

I understand how you feel about the wider horizon, the more extended view of life, the friendly feeling toward the Great Transition instead of dread and fear. I understand because I can read your thoughts as I used to hear your words and I am conscious of your gratitude for the enlargement it has brought you and for the growing awareness of spirit presences and the glory of God in every manifestation of life.

You cannot look now upon nature as so much wood and stone and material, lifeless substance. For you know that it is "afire with God," that behind the deadest-looking tree is the glory of God for those whose eyes are opened and who know that all matter is energy and hence is power, spirit power. In it shines the radiance that is God, to those whose eyes focus on the spiritual.

It is marvelous to bring the two worlds into such close relation in your every thought. For they are interwoven. Why, then, since matter has life and since there is no death, should not we who live more marvelously than when we were in the flesh, speak to you in your smaller, restricted, hedged-about little world? We do, as you know.

You have no idea to what extent these communications exist nor how varied are the channels which carry guidance and goodness to those of earth. Do I speak too often of this? Of course not. You cannot hear more of it than you wish. It is the great revelation of your life. It has done more for you than all other influences put together and your whole being goes out in constant gratitude.

Greater things are in store for you and will manifest in order as you are prepared for them. To you all of this is like a favoring breeze for a growing plant. All will fit into its proper place in your living and will bring you great satisfaction. Just know that I speak truly to you.

The God of Glory give you all that you need, His power speak to you through His every creation and His love enrich every hour of your earth living. He never fails when you ask and accept Him. Never forget that! Ask! Accept! And be doubly blest! Goodbye for this time. I am most grateful for this time of communion with you.

LIBERATION FROM THE FLESH

We here have watched you as often you have opened doors through which others might come into closer knowledge of these things of the spirit that center in the life of God as we seek to live it here where there is no hampering by things against which you of earth contend.

None of these should fret or irritate you because they are part of that discipline by which you grow and become ready to be at your best when the hour strikes for your liberation from the flesh.

Learn to think of it always in some such way as that liberation from the flesh. Never death or decay! Here on these Planes of Endless Life, the word and fact of decay are unknown, save as we hold in memory from earth days that process with which the human must so often reckon.

Thank God, my friend, that the higher you move in order of growth, the less you need to pay heed to such influences. Soon or late, you will leave them entirely behind you when you pass out from the physical scaffolding behind which your spirit was protected and in which it was housed for a while.

The scaffolding was only intended for temporary usefulness and it does seem strange to us that earth people cannot see the long-range view of it but, as I myself used to do, regard the body of more importance and significance than it really is.

Let not your heart dwell too much on anything physical or material. So fleeting is it, so transient, so little to be relied upon, so frail against storms that blow sometimes from more than one quarter at once.

The material is not designed to withstand heavy blows. Only that which is of God, which comes from Him by the high road of faith, is adequate when storms rage. The material gives way before tempests. The spirit holds strong and dependable always. Because it is of God!

We who have worked with charting the messages for you as the human channel, are deeply rejoiced at the eagerness with which many people are receiving them. They sense the life content and that quality of power that will strengthen them for living through tumult which makes so large a part of your present-day life on earth.

Oh, my friend, do not try to find your way through these jumbled times without the consciousness of the Infinite presence guiding and guarding you, strengthening you against every source of dismay that otherwise would unhorse you.

This is the most drastic time your world has ever known. Life is in flux and changing currents are churning and swirling. Swift is the current, dangerous the rapids and rocks against which many humans are dashing out their hopes and their lives.

No one need fear whose hope is in God, whose hand holds holds His and before whom goes that pillar of cloud by day and the luminous pillar of fire by night. It is impossible to lose one's way when eyes of the spirit are focused on guides which the Father has set for His children.

When darkness swamps the heart with gloom and defeat, it is because the one who flounders has looked elsewhere than at the true Light. It never flickers, never goes out! This is such vital truth that we bring it to you tonight as a refreshing draught for your spirit. Learn to take every problem to the Father. When you have asked for light and guidance, leave it with Him. The outcome will be made plain and you will be shown the way you should go.

We thank God that it is our privilege to help with the instruction that is given you, that is leading your feet higher and enlarging your heart interests.

The power of the Highest dwell within you and bless you constantly as by steady stages you journey toward this Land of Endless Day whither every human ultimately makes his way. Good night, my friend. I shall always come to speak to you when your hands and mind are free for my service!

SEEING HIM

Every thing upon which your eyes rest is manifestation of the Divine. Light is His garment. The firmament is His. The verdure, flower by the roadside, pebble along the foot path, all speak of the Infinite.

No place where your eyes rest but that He is there to be seen through what He has made and which reveals His power and glory.

How can the world of everyday affairs seem dull and drab and commonplace! It is crammed with God! See Him in every flowering bush and growing tree, in every blade of grass and tiny blossom tucked away in quiet nook, in running stream and ripening harvest, on the mountain side and prairies which stretch far and wide covered with mantle of His glory.

See Him and His everlasting love in all of this, see and know that the love of the Father is Source of it. And give thanks; continually give thanks! Nothing else will speed the rate of your growth better than constant giving of thanks to the great, Good God for all that He places at hand for use and joy and for stepping up the powers of the human. See never the dirt, muck, mire unless you can help to eradicate these.

Even so, keep knowing that behind every manifestation, stands God!

Worship Him in in the secret place of your heart and consciously offer Him your love in greatest degree of which the human is capable.

How you will grow this way under the spell of this love which Jesus came to bring anew to humanity when He walked with people of earth those years of His ministry in the flesh! It was always of the Father that He spoke, to the Father that He told His disciples they should pray. It is to the Father that I commend all of you for every need that can confront you in your earth life. Trust Him for everything. He does not fail nor ever fall short!

His blessing come down upon you now, making your life rich and abundant in those qualities of spirit that are most like unto Him. Amen!

AFLAME WITH POWER

On the earth schedule, everything vibrates in harmony with your time system, days, hours, weeks, years. To you it is natural while you abide on earth. We who step across into the higher life, readily forget these limitations and find it much more conducive to larger living.

Please get this clearly: Here we are without limitations as we grow in the strength and knowledge and wisdom and power of the Almighty. Without limitations! Can you picture that in your earth setting where all seems inhibiting and limiting? Here we are free and "unobstructed."

You are reminding me mentally that I have told you of the rigid schedules on which we study and learn and serve. Yes! The two are not inconsistent. We do keep to those schedules, of learning and serving. But while doing it, our spirits are as free as the wind to absorb, to grow to the full stature of men in Christ Jesus, to steep ourselves in the vast glory and bevy of these Ether Planes and to see how they reflect the CreaTor Who gave them their form and their spirit substance.

It is very wonderful. Your earth words are so impotent for expressing what I want to say to you. Yet they are the best there are at present until you come Home to your spiritual habitat. Then you will know and comprehend.

It will quickly be real Home to you, for you have studied so eagerly about it. You have lived so almost constantly in the atmosphere of it and been so loyal to these messages which have reached your mind straight from these Blessed Abodes.

We who send them to you would not have you disconnect yourself from too many earth interests while you continue there. But we are thankful to God for your responsible participation in this whose outreach is beyond computation in earth terms. When I say that, I sense in your mind a degree of doubt though you do not intend to doubt anything which comes with the sanctity of the Inner Planes.

But you see so many human complications related to this which you are doing with us that you wonder how it will work through. But it will work, my friend. Believe that! Do not let yourself see the hurdles. Do not give them that much power. They are nothing compared with power that comes from these Spirit Planes. From here we are sending power to you and to your work that will bring it to transcendent successes and to the questing hearts of the human, the Bread and Water of Life, for which they are perishing.

How many times I have talked with you about faith! And here I am beginning again! For you know that "without faith, it is impossible to please God." In whatever direction you turn in your earth life, you come to this, that you must have faith as a working partner, you must take conditions on faith, for faith is the absolute "sine qua non" of successful living.

Faith is the foundation stone on which you build the temple of your life. Without the foundation, you have nothing. Without faith in the Great God to do for you and through you, you are unhorsed and defeated.

Don't, I beseech you, let faith seem hard or foreign to your most common need. Nothing is too great, nothing too small for you to solve in the light of and by the power of faith. It will open doors when nothing else can. It will show you the way through the darkest night as nothing else can.

Faith is so wonderful that we here never cease to marvel at it, as we renew our victories of spirit through it.

To earth people faith seems stiff and hard to handle, a foreign substance, something with which one must struggle. I know. For I experienced it myself in earth life. I see it, from my vantage point up here and we who send you these words are eager to make it so plain that this stiffness and this struggle may be put off from your hearts, letting you handle faith as the radiant thing which it is, aflame with power, filling every heart which will give it room, with wonder-working possibilities. Life becomes blessedly free of struggle with faith in active operation!

We look to see every sign of growth in this understanding of faith in the lives of earth residents. Here and there, we see much that encourages. On every problem, test the working qualifications of this faith. And you prove its might!

But now! I must not talk at greater length. These are lessons for taking into the warp and woof of daily living. So they must not be too long. It is great joy to talk with you on these mighty themes and to feel the response which floods from your heart along the ether waves as you prove the presence of the spirit world and test the genuineness of these communications which we entrust to you.

Blessings of the Great and Glorious God be upon you now and forever!

SHORT WORD

You think often of that which I gave you late one night when you were not sleeping. I spoke saying, "You are heading into tight times!"

Just now you are going through those, to you, tight times, when you cannot turn the wheels of your earth plans.

You are learning in loyalty what it is to wait and not to worry, to trust and to know that your feet will not be permitted to stumble nor will you lose your way through the living of these important years.

You are learning a new degree and kind of faith that conquers doubt, takes strong hold of Almighty promises and rests there.

You are coming to higher level of awareness of the presence of God and of the sense of security which it gives.

Never falter nor doubt! Your way will be made plain. This is all for tonight. I hasten away to other service, the while I bless you with joy and gladness.

SOLIDARITY OF POWER

The "Abodes of the Blest" as often our Planes of life are called, are very close to you who walk the ways of earth. If the lonely-hearted whose homes are desolated by the going of dear ones, could be convinced of how closely inter-linked are our Planes with those of earth level, it would ease many heartaches.

I have told you before but I tell you again, that we are exactly as we were when we were in the flesh except that we have left the weight of the body behind us and have joined the Invisible Hosts of the Spirit. We are not far from you at any time. We watch over you all of earth. We comfort you when you are hard beset.

We yearn to tell you how much more help comes from spirit than from thoughts of the material and its power. It is a source almost untapped, available to any one who seriously desires to tap it for the help he needs. We long for you to know that we pass in and out among you as you carry on your daily living.

Often we stop beside you and long for you to feel our presence near and our help ready at your hand. The more you cultivate awareness of our presence, the more largely can we help you and the more stimulating the consciousness becomes. We like to be welcomed and appreciated as much as we ever did. It strengthens the bond between us and brings you and us much nearer together.

Think about all of this. Live it more intimately than ever you have done. Know that the cosmic hosts are with, you, that the ones who have gone from your physical sight are as grateful to return for a glimpse and for the "feel" of the former home they loved, as you could possibly be.

It is well to cultivate the welcoming spirit that invites those from our realms to come to you more often with confidence of welcome that means good both to you of the flesh and to the visitors from the other side of life.

Every outreach of spirit that increases your knowledge of these things is part of the divine surge of growth. Yield to it always. Growing is essential in every part of the created universe. Unless you grow, you stagnate. Never yield to that. Keep growing. Keep feeling out for more knowledge, larger experience with things bigger than you are. Familiarize yourself with them. Make them yours. Grow to their levels. Keep building wider, deeper foundations, strengthening your knowledge that will become wisdom some day and contribute largely to making you ready for the Great Transition.

Then you will begin life over here in a vastly advanced state. You will grow more rapidly because of all you have brought over to our side of life, as worthy material for use here. It is marvelous when one sees how it all meshes into one vast solidarity of spiritual power and achievement.

Those come to these shores who are sadly retarded spiritually and whose penalty is that they do not wish to grow in things of the spirit. They feel no close bond with any of the life over here that is motivated by love of God. They are at complete disharmony with all which surrounds them.

By slow degrees they must learn to evolve from that disharmony and merge it into feelings of oneness in all things with the Divine, oneness of spirit and, purpose, of desire and of service.

It is a transformation not easily nor quickly made and is one of the most marvelous dispensations of the Creator with Whom loss is never a part of any plan. With Him, growth and transformation and attunement with the Highest, even from the lowest, are in accord with His infinite wisdom and His Divine plan for all mankind.

This leads me to say something with which the church, my church too, is not in accord; that it is the duty and high-privilege of every earth person who believes in the power of prayer, to pray often and earnestly, with full panoply of faith for the progress spiritually of those who have laid aside the weight of the body and have come over to be here on the Inner Planes. Of this I have once before spoken to you. For as you there in the body need constant growth, we here also need the same continuing growth. As we can help you by inspiration of many kinds when you lift your petitions in prayer for counsel and help, so you can help us by the prayer of faith that all obstacles in the way of our most worthy expansion of powers, be removed and our rate of progress in life eternal be enhanced.

At another time, I shall talk with you more at length about this theme with which the church as a whole, has never been at agreement. What matters that? Except that the church is the loser for its unwillingness to learn beyond certain dogmas which it calls orthodox. Enough for this time!

The Spirit of peace and of power descend upon you and give you His blessing, lead you along the upward-winding highways of truth where vistas are larger and the sweep of Divine truth is beyond mortal thought to conceive.

THE HOLY SEVENTH

On your blessed Sabbath, it seems fitting for us to think together of the significance of the day as it is observed over most of the earth. The reason for bringing it into this series is that it has values which you and all of earth are obligated to observe, if you would live at your best.

Evidence is clear that the Great God instructed man to rest every seventh day and to make it "holy unto the Lord." Whether this should be interpreted as meaning the earth's Saturday or Sunday is, from our viewpoint of higher knowledge and clearer vision, utterly beside the point and entirely inconsequential. It is one of those moot matters over which human intellect has seen fit to argue and which has given much disharmony of spirit, to no spiritual good. The one thing of eternal importance is that there shall be that day, that every seventh day that shall be set aside "holy unto the Lord," in which man may rest and worship.

Two things there are open to disagreement when men wish to disagree. Desire to take opposing sides on almost any question is evidence of immaturity in man that leads to bitterness and separateness judgment. For the most part, nothing comes from taking opposing sides except gratification of human vanity which loves to parade its knowledge. Questions that have occupied minds of men through ages can never be settled beyond the point of further argument. And they are purely dialectical, without value to lives and hearts of mankind.

In such discussions, the crux of the matter is omitted and the heart of it takes a losing count. So it is with this question of the Sabbath. In its simplest form, it has not one thing to do with our Lord's creation of the universe and whether a day is a million years or twenty four hours. Men have fought bitterly with words over this phase which is immaterial and in the battling, have brought only schisms and discursive arguments. The question remains a potential battleground whenever men wish to argue. So much for all this!

The important thing is that there is a regular periodicity, laid down by the Creator Himself which mankind should observe for two distinct purposes. For rest. This the Lord decreed and used as illustration the creation of His universe. Again men have chosen to argue. What is rest? Should man be free to take what is rest to one but would be labor to another? Or should rest be set up uniformly and imposed upon the human race? Does rest mean change of occupation or abstaining from all labor, from all forms of pleasure?

Great unhappiness has arisen for many generations of the human race over this question and what earth calls "religion" has been very intolerant.

The Sabbath has often been made a nightmare by virtue of narrow-minded interpretations of all this, again losing sight of the heart of the issue. As we here see it, closer to the Divine than when we tried to do our best with the earth life, there is no real basis for any argument but definite need for man to understand that our Lord meant for His children to utilize this seventh day in such ways of clean, wholesome, individually restful living as would bring finest refreshment for body and spirit of which the individual is capable.

Can any body or any group decree how or what this shall be? How one set of activities is right and another wicked? What is rest for one person or group would be agonizing labor for another person or group. It has taken mankind long years and unlimited disagreements and penalties, to come nearer to this standard than any former generation has accepted.

The second question is closely tied in with the first. But there is a distinction about which again men have battled with words and emotions. What was meant by making the day "holy unto the Lord"? Must every one who claims close relation to fellowship with Him, interpret that literally? Does it mean that, against all odds, he must go to public worship every seventh day, spend it in formal worship or restrict himself to reading "religious" books?

This too, has been a fierce battleground. It was in my earth life, especially in my youth time when there was small middle ground. Either you did or you didn't; you were or you weren't. Grievous were the words spoken supposedly in behalf of our Lord and the meaning of His so plain words concerning the Sabbath "holy unto the Lord."

Men take the literal, the bare, hard letter of the law instead of the spirit in which are sweetness and light and life and growth. In the bare letter abides only dwarfing of mind and spirit. But the spirit giveth life, as the Scriptures have said.

One may make the Sabbath "holy unto the Lord" in as many ways as there are conditions in the lives of men. It may mean participating in public worship. Millions of earnest followers of the Nazarene observe that deeply spiritual way. And it is good. But it is not the only good. Who shall sit in judgment upon His loyal followers who do not observe it that formal way? There are those who walk closely with God, conscious every hour of His presence, who when the Sabbath comes, use it for quiet worship in which they reach out to God with as much devotion as they who gather in public places. For them, this seems the better way. Thus for them, it is the better way. I did not always think so. But I have learned larger interpretations of what worship and observance of God's Holy Day mean since I have been here on these Sunlit Plains of Power than I knew when I was living on earth with its so-often obscured vision. For each earnest open-minded person of earth, that observance of the Sabbath is best which brings him closer in spirit to God, the All Good. Beyond that choice which every human is at liberty to to make for himself, no one is free to pass judgment on any other. It is all part of the great issue of peace which is engrossing your earth just now. Peace, not warfare. Peace, not dissension. Peace, not narrow interpretations of laws which have no limitations. Peace, the spirit being free to take. God to itself in ways which bring abiding satisfactions. Peace, which lays aside that which is argumentative and accepts rich nourishment of joy and goodness from God Himself!

His interpretative power enlarge its scope within your heart. His essence of righteousness manifest within you and flower for the help of others. His grace grow constantly within the secret place of your life until He is so constantly your Companion and Guide and Comforter that never again do you feel alone. Always His glory shine in and through you. Amen!

SUPREME FACT

I have been telling you many things related to earth living, plain, homely things, vitally related to soul growth and readiness to make worthy entrance into these Celestial Fields. It is so vast that there is no compassing it. As vast as Infinity; as limitless as eternity!

I have spoken with you often about faith and courage and power for your life missions. But there is one supreme fact, one supreme theme that overlies all others, that permeates the whole of living here where I am and there where you are, the greatest thing of which there can be knowledge. Of this I would speak now.

Enveloping all else is the glorious fact of the love of the Father. The human had lost contact with the Infinite love. God had become awesome, Giver of Laws, of punishments and decrees. To restore to humankind this most blessed fact, the Son of the Father came in visible form to earth, witnessing for thirty-three years to this supreme love of His Father.

Nothing else in all the sweep of the universe transcends this theme. It compasses within itself all the radiance of the Godhead. Nothing else is God. For God and the Father are one. And the love of the Father is the supremest manifestation which even He can give. Within this love are contained all the glory, all the power, all the riches of the great I Am!

The love of the Father! If there were a million ways to express that love, a million forms in which man could count its manifestations, he would have but begun. Such love cannot be expressed in human terms. It is Infinity!

But through Jesus Christ, it is glad, free gift to mankind, as exhaustless as God Himself, as boundless as He is! How I would that I could make myself understandable. But I cannot go beyond the powers of limited human words and they cannot be adequate carriers of a theme that is of the very life of God Himself!

I wish you to take into your deepest consciousness this fact, that the love of the All-Father is for you, for any, for all who will ask Him to manifest it and will open their hearts to receive it. Can anything be more wonderful?

By the power of that love, you step-up the quality of your living. By, the majesty of that love, you build your own spiritual radiance. By the transforming beauty of that love, you make of your life so worthy an offering as to be acceptable to Him. By the steadying qualities of that love, you follow in His steps through your earth days and make yourself worthy of Him and of His gift.

Do not ever let your thinking on this theme be conventional or stereotyped. Let your whole being thrill to its power and its glory, your deepest soul powers exult in this most God-like of all facts.

Taste of the richness of it. Let your spirit soar into rarefied ethers in search of more and yet more understanding of the sweetness and the might of this love. Jesus was the interpretation in flesh and blood of the love of the Father, the incarnation of all that it may mean to the heart of any child of His creation.

Take this, my friend, and feed upon it. Let your spirit be nourished by the unfolding of this theme until it lifts you beyond the power of little things to disturb or annoy or to lead you astray.

The radiance of His Infinite love abide with you through the endlessness of the ages. Amen and Amen!

DYNAMICS OF PRAISE

Here on these Planes of Opportunity we rejoice that you are learning power that abides in giving thanks for every thing which comes into your daily life. That important lesson is filled with significance. It is a specific for many of the ills of earth.

Yes, giving thanks consciously and constantly, when the mind is free to remember. This gratitude will go farther in lifting loads of life and putting the soul into a receptive attitude for receiving more of God's good, than any other influence. It is not new to say how easy it is to give thanks when wheels of daily life move smoothly. It is part of spirit growth even then. But when the earth span looks difficult and the grade steep, it will clear away hindrances to your progress and open doors for good to come to you.

Not that the Great God asks praise for Himself! But the attitude of worshipful thanksgiving opens the soul for the ready receiving of all the best that the Father has to give. Ever more and more, learn to live by the dynamic power of prayer and praise. And you will come to higher planes of knowledge, into closer relation to Spirit Realms and finer accord with the heart of Spirit power.

Life has nothing better to offer, either on earth or in this rarefied life where we learn with greater ease because we are freed from the weight and weariness of the fleshly body.

Nothing will tone up a day for you like a burst of praise and thanksgiving first thing when you open your eyes each morning! Praise for the care and rest of the night, for safety and protection while your body rested, praise for sunshine and shadows that drift across the horizons of the days. They hold vast blessings for you to take by faith and be grateful for them. Praise and gratitude for sustenance for your body and spirit, for opportunity to show love and thoughtful kindness to everyone you meet, for ways in which you may serve with values to you who render and to them who receive. Praise, for each experience that comes into life! When it seems hard, more praise to the Father Who will carry you through by the power of His endless might!

This is so closely linked with the quality of faith that the two cannot be separated. They function together in miracle-working power. Only it is not a miracle! It is the outworking of the law of faith that believes where it cannot see and accepts that which has not yet come into the manifest.

Never think that nothing comes from practice of praise and expressions of thanksgiving nor think that things are going badly and what is there to be glad about! Then is the time to concentrate on this power which you can unleash by seeing through the darkness to the clear light of God's day as made known to them who live His life.

Wrap your every problem round about with this shining garment of praise to God, enfold every perplexity with this power of praise and prayer and faith, then see how quickly the problem is solved!

If sleep eludes you, cultivate anew the faith that all is working out for your good. Give ringing gratitude to Him for His marvelous provisions for your welfare and you will be amazed, my friend, at what this will do for you and enable you to do for others.

The Great God love you with His everlasting love that you may pour it out into thirsty hearts of others. Let all of this wash away every human passing of judgment on others, every tendency to be critical and let your soul ripen into the beauty that is a reflection of Him. Keep learning your lessons, my friend!

"BE YE THEREFORE PERFECT"

Tonight I wish to talk further with you about whether this one earth life is all, whether physical death is the end or whether there are yet other lives through which one may learn and grow into that perfect stature for which the Creator God planned. You remember the injunction to "Be ye therefore perfect as your Father in heaven is perfect." All thoughtful people have wondered how it could be that a few short years in the physical vehicle could accomplish even beginnings of such perfection.

Loss was never and is not now in the plan of the Creator for the world which He made nor for mankind whom He created to have dominion over the world. To put man in the flesh for more or less a short period of physical life in which he must learn all things which enter into the life of man upon earth, then expect him to be sufficiently advanced toward this perfect stature before he leaves the clumsy weight of the body, would score heavy percentage of utter loss. Man could not make such a grade, in the face of opposition on the earth plane.

It seems strange, from the heights to which I came so blessedly not long since, that the orthodox church does not accept the teaching of the reincarnation of the spirit time after time, in order to accomplish the sweep of knowledge and experience which will enable him to grow finally, after battling adverse disciplines, into that perfection for which God intended him.

It is so right, so reasonable, so in accord with that Which the Father does for His children! You want to know how all of this is provided and adjusted, how it is handled in the world of spirit, so that every human has his full opportunity to grow into the perfection of the Father. I may not go into that with you. If I did, you would not understand. No one would while he wears the physical garment. Nor would you be better qualified to live and learn and serve. It must be left until you come up higher to where these questions are revealed to the growing spirit.

Earth people allow fear of retrogression into less-developed physical garments, to out-weigh the wisdom and goodness of the Father, when conversation turns to weighty matters such as this one of reincarnation of the spirit. They think that such reincarnation has things of dread and suffering and affliction. They do not think of it, for the most part, as glorious opportunity to grow, to learn more qualities of spirit. Nor do they see the opportunities to overcome and to wipe out the old.

This matter of reincarnation is one of the most gracious manifestations of the wisdom of the loving God, whereby each one of earth may carry his spirit which was never born and never dies, through a succession of earth experiences, always moving higher, returning to Spirit Planes at each Transition to absorb more of the life here and to come closer to the heart of Divine love.

Then when the time is ripe, it takes on another physical body and again begins to learn from the earth standpoint, acquiring wisdom and grace and goodness which as yet, he has not made his own.

It is such a wonderful provision! So worthy of the Creator! So entirely something for which the earth person should thank God! Not until he has finished his course and learned his lessons, does he permanently lay aside any body.

Many want to know details of these wise adjustments between Inner Planes and earth plane. It is not intended for this series to convey more of the answers to these queries than I am giving you. But take my word for it, that everything about this mighty doctrine is good and right and as it should be. It is one of the most weighty and most blessed plans for mankind's development and for ultimately reaching that perfection for which the Christ bade him strive.

Know too, that there are no phases of it to dread. It is growth and joy and attaining of that stature which in the limited duration of one earth span could not be accomplished. I shall speak yet again on this theme in this series.

Whatever this explanation lacks of full satisfaction to the inquiring mind, please know that such questions as are not answered by these incomplete statements from the other side of life, are not for your good at present. Isn't that sufficient?

My profound gratitude to you for this evening of communication! It has much significance. But good night. I am off on a special mission.

POTENT PRESCRIPTION

Your spirit seems hungry and thirsty tonight for contact with Spirit Realms. When one is thus so ready, abundant sustenance is at hand. No soul ever went hungry when it was willing to partake of food which the All-Father sends.

Sometimes desire is for sweets when it is life-sustaining food that one needs for growth and power.

When frothy, alluring things of life do not appear, just know that your spirit diet did not call for them. One cannot grow on them. And life lived greatly, must be strengthened in its sinews by strong meat of God's Word. Take what comes therefore, through these messages and know that it is the right word for the time.

When the word doesn't come the moment it is asked for, when relief doesn't flood through just when it is sought, when the door doesn't swing wide at the desired hour, the human thinks a spiritual cog somewhere has slipped and that spirit forces are not functioning properly.

Rather, the one who experiences such feelings—I did when I was of earth—should realize the majesty of that word of the Lord when He said, "My thoughts are not your thoughts neither are your ways my ways!" From higher levels the spirit world sees the good that is needed, sees when the door can be flung wide to best effectiveness and when the one who seems bound can most wisely be set free from hampering limitations. The human kicks against those pricks of which Saint Paul spoke, kicks hard and often. But it does not get him far. Kicking is not the solution. Yielding is the answer! Infinite wisdom is guiding, the way will be shown and the door will be opened in the right way at the right time.

To learn such lessons, the spirit needs to be steeped in Divine love. This is the answer to the sick world's painful sufferings—Love! The love which thinketh no evil of any group or race or individual. When the difficulty will not yield to human formula, try love for what is wrong. It will win when nothing else will.

The dog that snarls at your strange feet will come under the spell of genuine love for it. The child afraid of the stranger senses the potent power of love and holds out its arms. The feud in a council chamber will melt away as by magic when love that thinketh no evil enters the situation.

Your world is grievously torn asunder over the race problems, problems because those who study them, for the most part, hold their necks stiff, feelings of understanding and of justice and of the love which thinketh no evil, carefully covered up and locked away. No wonder racial groups in conflict do not get far toward amicable solutions.

They never will until each issue is faced and solved through that love that is of God! Even after centuries of strife, the world of men does not like this prescription for what is wrong with its sick civilizations. Love appears to lack the qualities that dramatize themselves. It seems gentle to those who do not see its unmeasured power. It looks like a weak vessel where vast power is called for.

But put it to the test and it wins the mightiest victories the human knows. The sure way to prove this is to let it assert itself in full power of quiet strength. Until that is done, the world faces the inevitability of war.

Love can take hurdles of opposition, of misunderstanding and hatreds and first thing one knows, the hurdles are down, dissensions have vanished and hostilities disappeared. The lessons are for all. They are hard to learn. The issue is the same whether for one person or a thousand, one group or nations of earth. The principle is identical. The prescription is the same. The remedy is potent for any condition.

You wanted certain other things tonight. But that for which you hoped must wait a more favorable time. Do not be restive under this essential discipline. The issue will come clean and to your satisfaction before long.

Someday you will see the far-flung reasons for this that seems like a dry stretch along your highway of living. When you see the reasons, you will be glad and rejoice. I go now to other service in the spirit of this love whith conquers!

TWO WORLDS

You have wondered lately whether there is a period of probation after the spirit leaves the body before it reaches these Realms of Blessedness. Some one spoke to you saying that there is a time when the spirit is no longer of earth and not yet achieving the landing on the shores of the Ether Planes.

That would indeed be a state of suspension when the one making the Transition is neither here nor there. The two worlds lie so infinitely close together that there is just a breath between them. The interval required in passage is no longer than drawing the breath which separates the spirit from the weight of the flesh and wafts it across the Shining River of Life.

There is, as I have told you, the time of adjustment to the new order of life here. Sometimes when the body has been greatly weakened by long sickness, time elapses before strength has fully returned and the new arrival takes on the lightness of movement and of thought and of joy of consciousness that are part of life over here, just out of physical sight.

But not far! And there is no interval when the spirit is left uncertain or in straits of difficulty or doubt. Never a time when fear needs to possess the one who is making the Crossing. It is such a blessed dispensation of our Lord. There is not one conceivable way in which deeper joy or satisfaction could have been provided for His children whose earth journey is ended and whose battles have been won or lost, than His way.

For those who have made a poor showing with the struggles of earth in way of spirit, there is the necessity of beginning exactly where they left off when the silver cord is broken and taking up the unlearned lessons, not to lay them aside until they have been mastered. This is often a matter of considerable difficulty to the unwilling one in whom is no response to the atmosphere of love and devotion to the life of spirit. That does not matter. Nor does it change the order one whit. Slowly and very gradually, transition from hostility to Divine love and to the purposes of the Infinite, is made. It may take long. But it is made. And all the while, the frustrated spirit is surrounded by grace and goodness and the will of God.

To the one who comes across the River adjusted to the Divine order of life, to whom the atmosphere in His name is joy unspeakable, the adjustment is easily made and such a one takes up immediately the new lessons of life and growth for which he is prepared. There is no waste effort, no waste motion, no loss of power. It is one marvelous symphony of concord with the will of God in Whose creative mind is abundant provision for every earth spirit which comes winging its way from weariness of earth living to where such lightness of motion, such lightness of spirit prevail, as your earth minds cannot perceive.

How I yearn to share it all with you, to explain it fully to you, to make many things clear which now are mysteries. But my better judgment must prevail. One world at a time is the wiser order of life. If you knew all that I long to tell you, it would be an insupportable trial for you to continue in loyal adherence to your earth tasks. You would find your waiting time of earth much longer by comparison, so eager would your spirit be to come soaring to these Realms of vaster opportunity and privilege. So I desist from the intensity of desire to explain this and that, to clarify mystery for you. Please trust me as you always did when I was of earth and we shared common burdens and carried a common load. Trusting me, just know that this life which I live by faith, as I sought to live it when I was held back so mightily by the limitations of the flesh, meets the deepest desires, fills to the full one's every longing until there cannot possibly remain one unfulfilled aspiration, save to progress higher in the knowledge and service of our Lord.

You will be satisfied! What more can be said! The relatively small trials of earth seem so infinitesimal when seen in retrospect from this vantage point of spirit.

It has been joy to feel the harmonizing vibrations of our spirits as I have talked with you. The richest blessings of the Father rest upon you every hour; His peace and power be your guerdon always! Good night now!

SANCTUARY OF THE SOUL

I rejoice that our conversations continue about things of significance in spirit, life and power. There is small chance for development when the spirit is tense and in turmoil. But with relaxation, letting the load slip on to other, stronger shoulders, knowing that it is not necessary to carry it personally, quietude comes to the spirit. That is the growing time when as in fields of grain, cultivation of soil has counted and seeds spring into rich, lush green.

Times of quiet are indispensable for the welfare of the spirit and for gaining better grip on things of immortal value. Rushing, hurrying, doing, never stopping, are ways to make living futile and shallow, without depth of root or abundance of fruitage, the best way to keep from growing and to begin to deteriorate. Watch carefully when you are inclined to buzz around, in and out, busy with not much in particular, lest you dissipate this precious life potentiality of growth.

There is much talk these days on your earth about peace. Very little of the quality from which peace comes is found among earth people. Peace cannot come on nation-size bases until in the lives of the peoples of those nations, in individual hearts, peace has come and burning desire for greater growth in qualities that comprise true peace. Then nations will so administer their reconstruction policies that true peace may eventuate. It never comes with the heat of tense debate nor with the crack of an assembly gavel.

It comes, this peace which the world so sorely needs, from the hearts of men and women. To them it comes in the quietude of the private sanctuary when the soul lets go of the confusion and strife of the outer world and meets alone the Spirit Divine with Whom is all peace.

We have talked often in these messages about cosmic things and I refer you in this connection to the ordering of the universe. The stars and planets in their orbits swing through the ages, upheld by power too vast to comprehend. In absolute quiet. Crops grow without fanfare of noise or commotion, in silence that is pregnant with power to feed the world.

All vastness of power is quiet. The essence of God is absolute quiet. Noisy power is dissipated power, mostly waste, which never is God's plan for anything.

Cosmic forces are utter peace and quiet. Cosmic peace—nothing can transcend it! It is cosmic power than which nothing is mightier on your earth.

Peace that abides in power is so transforming, so transcending that nothing else in life equals it. Just contemplating it can make a restless spirit into such peace as cannot be disturbed by things of earth. Contemplating it, lifts one to sublime heights where Cod is seen, God and His ways all that really matter. There is no grating of gears in the operation of cosmic forces, no scattering of power, no distracting noise. The sun makes no noise. Just shines and warms. Mountains do not shout nor groan. Starry systems glorify the terrestrial universe without confusion or strife. I commend you to frequent meditation of cosmic peace which is possible for the human to emulate through communion with God.

Again I say, meditate upon this. Let the ideal of such peace grow apace within your heart routing confusions that are less than nothing. It is worth more than I can make clear to you of earth. The cultivation of this peace which comes from God and is of Him, surpasses aught this world can gives

THE POWER HOUSE

This business of living out one's term on the earth sphere is a great art and can be done worthily only when it is God-centered and God-directed. This does not mean church-centered, though I have as you would know, the most profound respect for the church which I served to the best of my ability while I was clothed in the flesh. But the difference is vast!

What a grand day it will be when the church, the whole great church on earth, leaves its man-made programs, its humanly-devised direction for the utter simplicity and beauty of the God life in which are no schisms and no selfishness, no jealousies and no strife! Does it seem to you that such a day is impossible to earth? Not so! It will come when man and woman, representing all humanity, seek pure truth, all truth, as it is in Him Who is Himself truth. In that center where truth abides, one finds no disturbances or disagreements but always the calm of adequate power for every need.

Truth, my friend, is too vast to be distorted. It is so great that it adapts itself to every need of every human who comes seeking it loyally and with sincere desire to bathe his spirit in the radiance of Divine Truth, to free his spirit of the little things that clutter and soil and mar the perfection of which it is capable and which finds that perfection only in Him. He is the truth that lights and guides and strengthens and protects and satisfies.

It is good that earth people are getting back toward God instead of seeking satisfaction in the outer frills of ritual and pageantry and form and ceremony. These are quite good of themselves. But they are as inconsequential, as unnecessary as frills on a working garment. The comparison makes itself and needs no elaboration.

To gain this truth is worth more than the gold of the universe. It comes through meditation and prayer to Him Who is the Source. I used to think that my earth prayers availed perhaps more than many. They were my human mainstay.

I spent many hours daily or nightly, in the most potent form of prayer of which I then knew. But how little I dreamed the reality of the power of prayer as I have learned it since I accomplished the Great Transition! It is that communion with the Father where is utter quiet, where the human merges himself with the Divine in spirit and purpose and rests from all labor, all fear, all strife, all anxiety while the Father infiltrates every fiber of being with that calm assurance that is communion with Him! Prayer so seldom needs to be uttered, save only in the silence of the soul. It is so much more potent when it is breathed only from the spirit human to the Spirit Divine, when there ceases to be any distance between the Father and His child and they become as one.

This kind of fusing is the essence of power sufficient for every experience which the human is called upon to share in the flesh. I commend it to you, my friend, in increasing volume, as you learn more and more to lose yourself in the folds of Divine love and to appropriate for your needs the quiet and confidence which He has promised for all who will ask and will take.

Be not anxious! In everything give thanks for His great goodness. The light is shining. God be praised and His glory irradiate your life, transform your days with His love and, the power of His might. Amen!

RANK AND POISONOUS WEEDS

Many lines of intellectual and spiritual concept have been sweeping around you recently. You have dallied several of them in your mind. That is right. All of them have some measure of truth and of stimulus to the inquiring mind. But be careful of too much dallying. It scatters the fires of concentration and keeps one away from such power as comes through carefully directed effort that knows to what end it is moving. Keep open mind at all times to truth under whatever guise it comes to you. But I beseech you not to be swayed by every passing breeze of strange doctrine. Not that you have been. For you have stood staunchly for the teaching that these messages from the Inner Planes have given to you. You have grown in and through them. You know in your inmost heart that they are truth.

I wish to talk a while with you now about all the doubtful brood of negation. It is an insidious thing, sees the dark side of everybody and every proposition, takes the doubtful view of every situation and misinterprets every issue of life.

Negation is like darkness in the physical world. It is absence of light. It is like cold in your dwelling. It is the absence of heat. In other words, negation, the spirit that denies, is both darkness and cold, holding in itself only burned-out ashes where it might be glowing warm with the fires of faith and love. In its gloom is no light whereas it might be filled with the light that always shines where the spirit is in full glory of kinship with God.

Negative thinking grows like any noxious weed, rapidly and rankly, flourishing on little fertility and gaining root in even thin soil. Once started, it is difficult to uproot and destroy. Beware of letting your mind run along lines that welcome any negative thesis, that see the dark side or look for the down-tearing viewpoint. Just accepting it, gives it power. Thinking negatively about any situation, helps it grow until it seems like something instead of the nothingness that it is.

Negation daubs the beauty and hopefulness and cheer of life and keeps one's eyes turned down instead of upward to the revealing of the brave, the beautiful, the true aspects of whatever one faces.

Negation is a cold wet blanket that makes one shiver and shudder. The other side of living, the faith side, the constructive side, looks for and finds warmth and light and hope and gladness that set the heart bounding with courage and ambition and determination to win in any battle.

The thing to do with negation in whatever form, it appears, is to oust it by a definite act of determination, of faith, of courage that knows it is the absence of those qualities that warm and cheer and help and help and heal.

Like a weed, this negation of which I am talking with you tonight, creeps in where there is the least opening and grows on any tiny thing, until before you know it, there is flourishing within you a great tree of discouragement and of downcast hopes and expectation of evil.

If any nourishment is denied it and if no space is allotted it, you will win your struggle over it and find your spirit free for the sweetness and light to which it is entitled, find that the sun shines into all the nooks and corners of your life bringing warmth and gladness where cold and darkness have been.

Not many enemies of the human are more insidious or determined than negation. The harder you attack it, the sooner you will be freed from it and the brighter your horizon will shine with the light that knows no shadow.

I give you my blessing tonight. You have been steadily companioned of late with special guidance and guarding. You are coming out into the clear. Hold that in your heart for comfort. The God of light and glory, of power and faith, lead your feet into paths of service that will be helpful and satisfying. I shall have a special message when next you are free for my working. Good night!

SPIRITUAL THERAPEUTICS

Great things are seemingly simple things, as earth reckons them. It is my privilege to talk with you this evening about some phases of giving thanks and ways in which it reaches out into ramifications of living.

More people are coming to understand the importance of giving thanks, as a sheer matter of psychology. That is one side of it, for there is a marked relation between expressing thanks and the brightening of the spirit, producing therefore a more wholesome condition of the mind.

If that were all there is to it, there would be no question of its value. That is merely a beginning. In finest essence, it is a spiritual service. For all things come of God and when our minds turn to giving thanks, naturally we think of the One from Whom the gifts came.

Thus directly and continuously, our thoughts keep turning to God, thanking Him for His good gifts. Our spirits become more highly attuned with each act of thanksgiving and our vision is widened so that we see more for which to thank the Father.

It is a process that increases in geometrical progression, bringing to each heart vaster array of blessings of all kinds for which to be grateful, than when we look at what we do not have and find our horizons bounded by minus signs of lack of what we think we want, instead of letting our spirits expand almost beyond belief with joy and rapture that the Father has given us so much.

The state of mind in which we view this is the difference between the darkness of ingratitude when we see only what we want and do not have and the radiance of light when we see how inconceivably much we have beyond what we could or think.

Perhaps you have noticed that I am speaking as if I were also of earth. Well, I am there so often on missions of service to those who need, that it might seem natural for me to speak thus. But the real reason for my mode of expression is that memory of earth life is very keen and tonight it seems the natural way for me to express this message of my heart.

We who have been deemed worthy of coming to this side of life, spend much time among the sorrowing and needy of earth and we see the vast necessity for teaching earth hearts to know the power that abides in thanksgiving. The physical reaction is undeniable. It quickens the flow of blood through one's body, vivifies all the physical functions and gives a whole range of new life to the one who learns to say, "Thank you."

Saying it to God is rare privilege that many earth people do not early learn. It is better than a tonic. As to the body, so to the spirit that immediately begins to be conscious of more for which to express the rich thanks that well up from deep, inward parts of the being.

It is impossible, I think, to give thanks for one thing without finding ten more that are fairly clamoring to be recognized as sources for which to give thanks. It makes life so rich, so beautiful, so expansive!

Little narrowness, inhibitions, petty wishes which come to seem puny as they really are, foolish cravings for things that pass like a morning fog, all fall into their places of inconsequence in the life that has become rich with continuously giving thanks for the good which the Father bestows upon His children.

So the therapeutic value to the body of giving thanks, is matched by the therapeutic value to the spirit which is cleansed of much that is unworthy by the flooding of gratitude which washes away unclean desires, replacing them with what is great and good and enduring. To body and spirit this spiritual exercise brings vigorous health and sturdiness of fiber with which to meet the exigencies of life and to come through them victoriously.

As the physical body grows in proportion to the wholesome food one eats, so the spirit grows as one gives it food that develops the whole personality.

The very features of one's face are changed through spiritually giving thanks. Not strangely, the material substance with which earth people negotiate living, things that are necessary for earth existence, come in greater abundance and from unexpected sources when one opens the door through gratitude.

That generally it is expressed inaudibly and said to God Who hears every whisper, does not hinder the coming of earth benefits to the thankful person. It is the working of the law that like begets like. So good comes to one who continually is seeing good in every phase of life.

This great theme is worthy of your careful study and of complete acceptance that you may come into full possession of understanding its outreach and relationships as you move through earth life and prepare for living with us here in these satisfying realms of spirit.

This has been a valuable talk. We entrust it to you for sharing with many who have not thought on these tremendously important lines of spirit knowledge. God bless you as you do all in your power to release it to others.

In every moment of your life may God's rich blessing be consciously with you. His peace be upon you as a benediction. My blessings of deep gratitude I add to this for the high privilege of this talk with you. Hasta luega!

FOR YOUR REMEMBRANCE

The Lord loveth His own! Don't forget that! Don't let yourself think that it is insignificant. It means the over-brooding of the Most High, His protecting wings sheltering in time of storm down there on your earth plane. Nothing in all the universe can surpass it for comfort and consciousness of being rightly guided.

It is light in the darkness and supply when you cannot see your way, companionship when you are lonely and all things good when it looks to the human as if everything has gone off awry. This love is the difference between drought and abundance of sweet, flowing water for the life of the spirit; difference between being hungry at heart and such abundance of nourishment that there is no desire for more.

The meaning of that wonderful verse from the Scriptures never wears out nor grows wearisome; never stales nor loses its power! The Lord loveth His own! Keep that in your deep heart, my friend, and live by it, especially when lowering clouds threaten to black out the shining of the sun. Once in a while, life seems dubious when you cannot see the way in front of your feet. But remember, my friend, the Lord loveth His own!

Let that do for you everything that it can. Then you will find that your need has been met, your way has opened and the darkness has become light about you. Isn't this like the Father in ways of great goodness? In ways of loving kindness and mercy evermore? Of course it is! There are no limitations upon Him and His ways of Divine goodness to His children. This sweeps over us here on these Planes of Spirit Light until we sometimes wonder how much higher it can carry us in ecstasy of worship and wonder. Then we call to mind what we have learned up here that those who have come hither, learn, serve, are disciplined in spirit until they come to wisdom beyond earth comprehension. Continuously, eons after eons, they move higher in those qualities that are of the Godhead. Then we know as we too aspire, and learn, progressing God-ward, we shall find our capacity for assimilating this love growing in proportion to our acceptance.

Let nobody try to tell you that this is not an Infinitely-planned universe, from tiniest atom to mightiest planet, functioning in perfect order according to His cosmic laws. We bow in humility as we survey the mighty works that He brought forth with His creative breath when He spoke the universe into being. The bad spots, as we used to say when I was resident on earth; show the mis-use of His great gift to man, of free-will. Having it, man is free to do as he wishes. But he bears the consequences of what he does.

These bad spots are man's doings and must be atoned for before man may move to higher planes to which some day he will aspire.

When the slate is cleaned, they who have caused these bad earth spots are free for spirit growth that was hampered until restitution has been made for the evil that was done. It makes life a matter of such serious responsibility but of great glory.

Blessings and honor and gladness and joy and sense of adequacy be to you. Someday all of this of which I am speaking will reveal itself to you at its true valuation. How you will then rejoice and praise Him Who loveth you as His own!

NOTHING SHORT

Discouragement is nothing short of doubt of God; of denial of God and His power; of God and His promises; of God and His love; of God and His plans for making His children like Him and worthy to be called the Sons of God. Discouragement amounts to nothing else than all of this and much more.

It is made up of hurt pride, envy, jealousy and mostly of fear that the future may not be able to take care of itself. All of these are compounded into the one word which earth people call discouragement. It is the thing which lets you down and does not one single other thing for you. It never carries you over a hurdle. It always leaves you in the middle of the mess which you yourself created and out of which you perforce must pick yourself up, get onto your two feet and start there by the help of God, to make your victorious way through each day, whatever it brings. And do it gallantly, too! Discouragement is nothing else than defeat. You are defeated in your spirit which is the important part of you, the moment you let discouragement get its nose into the tent of your life. Defeated for good and all you will be unless you turn yourself round and send this intruder out of your life. And keep him out! Mean business about it too, without any softness of manner. Make him see that your life is one place free from the abortive effects that result from discouragement.

This intruder worms himself into the heart by many subtle tricks. Once in, he seeks to establish himself safely where he can dictate the order of life and watch it fall to pieces under his negative influence. Then discouragement feels that it has done a perfect piece of work.

Discouragement turns joy to gloom; faith to doubt; achievement to frustration. This is the way it operates and it is a quality that is good only for ousting. Often a repeat performance is called for. Oust discouragement today. But in a couple of your earth days he is back again trying to work his way in through another door and to set up his work of destruction of all things best and most worth while in earth life.

Succeeding means to keep on turning him out, then locking the door against his return. When you have done some good piece of earth service, you let yourself feel that you have failed. Then discouragement comes round by some back door and finds that your once-locked door against him is unguarded and he walks right into your life again.

You have on your colored glasses about this time and see everything black and gone to smash, not one good thing to expect from the usually smiling face of the future. Take off your dark glasses. Let the sunshine of hope shine in. Realize that, the sun has always come from behind the clouds and by that token, it always will. It will not likely shine for you until first you have driven the intruder of discouragement out of your consciousness and locked tight the door against his return.

Many good locks may be used. Among the most effective is some promise of the Father that He will never leave you nor forsake you; or a Psalm which tells you of His over-shadowing wings of protection and love. So many of these there are which discouragement does not know how to turn to his advantage. So he leave you for a while. Then is the time for you to build up a barricade of sweet assurances from the Father which will make it ever more difficult for discouragement to break down and thus to sneak into your life.

Mark my word, every time you let him in, it is twice as hard next time to keep him out! He brings you nothing worth having. He is conscienceless. He is lying and deceptive. He tears down your physical strength and despoils your outlook on life. He messes up the colors that should be golden and bright and beautiful on your horizon and leaves nothing but glooms and sables, all dark, no ray of beauty or color or glory anywhere. Believe me, it is not smart to have any traffic with discouragement, ever, at any time or any place. I know full well and I remember with startling clarity how it was with me when I was on the earth plane, that one's physical condition, environment, temperatures, people around you and many another typical earth condition contribute often to helping this intruder find his way in through some momentarily unguarded crack in your door of life. You are weary. Your defenses are down. You are below par. He takes advantage of you and always leaves you worse than he found you.

Remember that and do not give him a toe-hold on your life.

DIVINE GIFT

Come with me in your thought a while this evening and let me show you some things which you need to know and understand. They concern vital issues of life and destiny and are of spiritual import wholly. Mankind has concentrated too largely on strengthening the physical sides of his being and has felt that the spirit side could largely be left to take care of itself.

Of course not! Spirit growth is much more important, much more essential. If man only realized it, he would give more thought to it than to ephemeral sides of existence which come and go in the twinkling of an eye.

These messages are designed to help the human see more of the outreach of human experience and the closeness of its relation to these Planes where death never strikes. I would talk with you tonight about the vision which comes with cultivation of the power to see what physical eyes see not but which is of supreme importance. Looking beyond matter, one detects spirit qualities and knows intuitively that their development must rate high in the scale of human importance.

That word, "intuitively" opens the door to much that is related to this range of qualities. Mankind frequently bandies that word about and does not think clearly of its full meaning. Intuition is very close to spirit. It is part of spirit life and is that by which man may recognize, if he is properly attuned, the voice of the Infinite speaking to the human heart. It is of immense importance and should be cultivated daily by one who seeks to grow in power and in outreach of understanding of life that is wholly spirit. Intuition when it is carefully understood, opens the door to inspiration that never could be gained save through this channel whereby the Divine speaks of many wonders to the heart of mankind. Intuition explains much that otherwise is unintelligible to the human and is such a channel as cannot be overstated in any description.

At any cost of meditation, it is worth man's effort to open the gates of study of this inward channel between the Divine and mankind, that wisdom and knowledge and grace and power may flow freely through and with the flowing carry light and abundance of understanding from realms of spirit to earth life.

Men have not often thought of intuition as a divine gift but as a "hunch" that is more or less something to joke about. No! No! It is part of the most God-like power which the Creator has implanted in the beings of His creation. It calls for that of which we talked together a while back under the theme of spiritual attunement and I sought to show you how the Divine can speak to the heart that is attuned, intuition being the provision along which it flows.

This does not come of itself into full flower but is the result of carefully tended growth, the germ of it being in the heart but needing to be cultivated until it comes to place of great dependability in meeting any opportunity or emergency which life brings so continuously.

Give time to the cultivating of this high quality of spiritual power. Sit quietly and in open heart. Let the spirit speak. Listen. Heed what comes along this channel from the Supreme Voice. Recognize its source. Ponder its wisdom. Act on what is revealed to you and continue to give time and attention to widening and deepening this channel between the Divine and the human. It is a secret place where the Great God speaks to the inmost depths of man's nature and is worth more than earth words can express to any who seek soul growth.

Remember in this connection that the channel clears only in proportion as the human is in tune with the Infinite. The one who is out of harmony will find that the gateway through which intuitive power is designed to flow, does not open widely nor freely. There must be this rapport of spirit with the Divine which comes only through yielding the human to the spirit.

If it sounds vague, it is as practical as anything I ever told you. If it sounds difficult, it is more worth learning and developing than I can possibly say to you. There is nothing light nor easy in these great matters of spirit growth. They are of the essence of timelessness and reach out into the eternities of God.

They are jewels to be mined with great pains and much care. They will repay in largeness of life all the study and sacrifice of smaller interests that help the human to higher ground and greater power.

It is time now for the good night word and I speak it in the name of the Father in Whose power I seek to serve wherever. I am needed. His illumination shine round about you and irradiate your life, making dark places light and the hidden way plain; His wisdom speak to you to supplement your every lack and His inner Voice give you all comfort and peace, now and forever. Amen!

BLOW UPS

The maelstrom, my friend, has an area of absolute quiet and calm at its center. Your life in the human, everybody's life, comes at times to where it seems that everything boils up and no firm footing is anywhere. At such times, realize that in quietness and confidence is your strength. That old word has the sanction of the Divine. It has been tested through the centuries. It has never failed nor fallen short.

You will remember how I said a while back through the channel of this communication, that God-power is the essence of quiet. The little mind boils over. It frets and wastes itself in fuming. The stalwart mind based on foundations of that quiet and confidence which come from God the Almighty, holds steady, anchors itself poisefully, restrains itself masterfully and comes through whatever the turmoil. It does not lose control nor waste itself in the bluster that blows furiously but has no calm direction, nor poised purpose at the center of each thought and activity.

It is well to beware of the type of mind that lets off steam every whip stitch, if you will permit the phrase which I often used while I was on earth. It is a serious loss of power which needs harnessing to a steady goal and used in purposeful reaching toward higher quality of living and achieving.

These latter do not come when the mind as tossed about with every little wind of displeasure or disappointment or lack of satisfaction with people or things. They come only when the human is centered deeply in God the Only, in God the All, when the motive power of each hour is geared to the control of spirit and nothing less counts one whit. Then the small turmoils cease to stir greater strife and slowly, surely, the mind comes to settle firmly on that assurance of peace and power which are in the calm of God! What enormous human power is lasted in the blow-ups of temperament and the lashings of temper that are not grounded in the quietness and confidence which are of

Him! When you are in danger of lashing back or returning tit for tat, remember that you are a child of the Eternal in Whom is all strength, all grace, all serenity, and that it is all for you, for the asking and taking. Let things and people bluster and blow! Real power does not abide there but in the inexhaustible resources of the Almighty!

NEVER A GOD OF LOSS

When first all of this was being opened to you shortly after I came here to the Inner Planes, you were unable to understand what I meant when I said that this was another channel of communication opening to you. But now you are seeing. It is marvelous in the ways it is working out exactly as the Spirit Planes decreed.

Times come to all people when changes come thick and fast and when the way dims before their mortal vision. You have been going through such a period, fraught with uncertainty to you. But not to us! We know the way your feet will follow. And it is a good way, though there will be plenty of times when you will need abundance of that royal quality of faith of which I have spoken so often to you.

The more you make use of that, the richer life will be to you, the higher the flood tide of power will rise through you and the greater will be the outreach of your influence. So, my friend, hold faith close to your heart now and ever, in all things large and small. Don't be afraid to trust every problem to it, really trust, I mean, and let your heart go free of any anxiety for the future.

The earth way is so frequently the stumbling way, with so many pitfalls, so many obstacles to test one's spirit strength and often not enough unlimited faith in those rich promises of God, to lift one high and carry one over the danger places. It is a lack of faith in Cod, never a lack in God's power, never lack of God's willingness, never lack of His Infinite desire to help any of His children meet the difficulties. Only the lack of the human to prove what He promises. Don't make that mistake, my friend. It is always loss!

God is not a God of loss but always of abundance of good and grace and glory. The more you prove Him, the more He will reward you beyond your expectations. I beseech you to believe this, though the human is prone to think that only he is equal to finding the way through. Small wonder that he loses his way and comes to grief. God is the one surety. I ask you to cultivate the consciousness of the presence of God every moment of your life and to realize that His goodness and greatness surround you, taking away all defeating sense of inadequacy to overcome whatever appears to stand threateningly in your way.

The earth person threatened by drowning, doesn't hesitate to hold tightly to a lifeline of whatever sort. The earth person who feels the ground beneath him give way, needs a life line in equal degree and with equal persistence. God is that life line. His help will not fail. His lifeline will not break. He will carry you through. Don't be afraid of change. Nothing is much worse in the earth regime than routine, from which mind and spirit do not break away into the free air of adventure where one finds new ways and new inspiration to make life over.

Change is part of God's order for people of earth. Few avoid it. Many are afraid of it. They seek every known way to hold to the familiar. They lack courage to undertake the new. The old is easier. To it most people cling.

But hardy souls welcome the stimulus of change, knowing how much it can enlarge their horizons and extend their spheres of knowledge and service, whatever the pains of adapting themselves.

Be grateful, my friend, for those influences that lead you into new avenues of living. Be more than grateful for the courage that took you unflinchingly through the suddenly-opened door of your great opportunity for enlargement.

These open doors come to many in earth life. Often they are not recognized. They pass unnoticed or unaccepted. This leads me to urge all who read these messages to be very receptive to every form of Divine guidance in whatever guise it comes.

Never does it come identically to two people, because no two people are alike nor do they face the same situations. Thus naturally the same door does not open to them. To each individually comes his own opportunity when the time is ripe and the season is at hand. Good night for this time!

THE POWER LINE

I was standing beside you just now and heard you think! It is so much more "limber," so much more pliable a way of communicating and when once one is accustomed to it, so much more expressive. On occasion, at our wish, we speak as you do. But we like the other much better, by the quiet power of thought transference. So it is entirely in character, to say that I heard you think!

Quiet power that abides in the deep places of your heart will function, when things are difficult, much better than other quality of power that stirs and stimulates you. It is the difference between the power house that generates what turns the wheels and the military march that stirs the blood with emotional fanfare.

Go deep into your heart tonight and see how frequently you of earth try to function on feeling alone instead of on this quiet power which comes directly from the Father God. His power is always adequate. It never grows thin and never is less than is needed for running your life.

It comes from that perennial fountain at the center of Creation and the only times in earth life when you appear to be short on its supply are when you fail to turn to it in confident faith that it is there for you.

You could not be separated from it if you tried. You are from the beginning of creation a part of God. Hence you also are a part of God-power. And that is Infinite power, enough and more than enough.

One never has to be economical in the use of this God-power. It never runs short. The more one uses, the more there is, for the channel is open and the current flows free. When it doesn't, look carefully within and see whether you have clogged the channel so the power cannot flow.

I beseech you to remember that never can any human separate himself from the great central source of all power, which is God. You can clog the channel so the power does not function. But it is there when the channel is free from cluttering things which have no value, trifling material junk that clogs and never turns a wheel of worthy human endeavor.

Does it seem out of character for one who has passed the Veil to use the word I just used? Why should it? We are as we were, save for the burden of the physical and higher grown in intellectual and spirit powers. We remember earth types and tendencies and we know so well the hindrances which "junk" puts in the way of spirit progress. Guard well the keeping of the power line free of all selfishness, all resentment or unforgiveness or impatience or niggardliness of Money or time or service which one can render.

Keep your steam up these days! Don't let the boilers of your intellectual processes get cold nor the fires die down. Keep going! Let others dawdle if they wish. But you grow. Keep out in the clear ahead of those who prefer to march to the rear. It's forward you should go. Steadily. Never let yourself lapse in purpose or in morale.

The day is too fraught with mightiness for anybody to be less than his best. There is a great, a magnificent pattern to it all, if only mankind will weave to the pattern, accepting a common basis for weaving, instead of flying off with tangled strands of individual patterns, without harmony of design.

Keep your thinking clear, my friend. Don't grow fuzzy because you are sometimes burdened with routine details. Keep the power line open to the Inner Planes. Know that all power is available to you for every need. It is all a question of this inner, quiet, unfailing power from which you cannot be disconnected and which is the gift of God to every human. The power of the Infinite flow through you, infiltrating your every thought and purpose and give you satisfying sense of adequacy in life. Remember His face always shines upon you.

WITHOUT BEGINNING OR END

Thank you for this hour of communion on themes pertinent to the life that knows no end. In that phrase is the thing I wish to talk about with you just now; the life that knows no end. That means just what it says. It came from God in the beginning and goes to God when on earth it appears to be completed. It is everlasting life!

Earth people use that phrase so carelessly, so unthinkingly. They do not savor its real meaning.

The casual person of orthodox teaching which frequently is equivalent to no teaching at all, thinks of the new baby that comes to bless a family, as being absolutely new-born, body and soul, without previous experience of earth or knowledge of life.

How does that comport with life that is "everlasting"? All life, as we here know, begins in and with God the Creator. When it comes to earth in the form of a little baby, it is simply a new manifestation of God life; manifestation of the soul that began in and with God but coming in a new body-form, for more earth knowledge and experience. Isn't that clear? Probably not, but it is as clear as my instructors from the Seventh Plane deem wise to discuss now. Think of this weighty theme with this new light, if it is new to you, that the portion called the soul is of spirit realms, was from the beginning and knows no end.

In one or another body housing through ages, it may return to live out different spans of experience on the earth sphere, growing in spirit stature with each reincarnation and moving ever higher by standards of spiritual growth.

As I have said before, I used to discredit such theory while I was of earth, steeped more or less thoroughly in traditional teaching, though always something of a revolutionary in my independent thought.

Now I know it is not a theory at all. It is fact, one of the greatest truths in all the vast creation with which the Lord of All invested His universe. It makes life great business and to be considered with every sincerity in every phase.

Who would handle carelessly that which is part of God-life? Who would bandy it about with little serious thought or fritter it away heedlessly if he believed that it is of God from the very beginning and goes to God for the endlessness of eternity? Life becomes, therefore, when seen in this light a very precious thing, gift from Almighty God for right use of which each person is responsible through all the reaches of endless years.

When you consider this matter in this light, it gives lucid answer to many interrogations otherwise inexplicable. It is not a pagan teaching, as I used to think. It is of the very truth of the Godhead, part of the vast plan of creation and too little understood by mankind whose interpretations have been made on the bases of slight knowledge and surface thinking.

I ask of you, my friend, to study this mighty theme so much misunderstood but needing wider acceptance by humankind, for the better understanding of fundamentals of life. Another time, it may be my privilege to go further into this, for clarification. Enough for tonight, however.

I leave you with the blessed assurance that God's omnipresence, His omniscience and His omnipotence are at your need any hour of any day. He holds back nothing which His children need to justify their best in life and come through their earth experience triumphant with His help.

From our vantage places here on these wondrous Planes of Eternal Beauty, we see these things worked out countless times and long to share with you the certainty that they will work out with you too, whenever you_make connection with Infinite power and love. His love enfold you. His guidance comfort you. All in His blessed name which is above all else.

SUFFICIENCY

"When you will let Him!" Do you wonder whither I am trending in this talk tonight? First, let me tell you how closely I listened today and silently participated in the important conversations which took place in your home. It was my joy to hear your work with the book of the morning and want you to know my gratitude for the lofty positions which you took. You are laying broad and firm foundations and I am grateful to see you building so firmly.

But now about that first sentence which you hesitated to take until I told you to do it. I heard said in your group this morning by your earth time, something about the work which God the Father does in one's heart. And now the qualifying reply is added, "Yes, when you will let Him."

This is great truth which you and all will do well to understand and to exemplify in your efforts for spiritual achievement. Of yourself, you can do nothing. Jesus said that, you remember. "Of myself, I can do nothing; it is the Father that worketh in me." Neither you nor any one can take the hurdles nor reach the heights nor learn the ways of wisdom alone.

But these things you can do through the years of earth life and afterward when you come to this beautiful Home, when you will let Him help you; let Him cooperate with you; let Him lead the way; let Him show you the course to follow; let Him reveal the truth to your understanding; let Him teach you what love is and what it does for the human heart; let Him explain what sacrifice is and what power is; let Him be all and in all to you. Then there is nothing impossible for you.

Believe that, my friend. Do not ever feel that you are sufficient. If you do, you are headed for a fall, as I used to say when I was among you on the earth plane. You are sufficient only when you are girded by His living grace and implemented with His love and peace and power flowing from the exhaustless fountain of Divine Life.

With that inflow which will never cease, you are sufficient, no matter what a day brings. He says that His grace is sufficient. And He proves it to everyone who will "let Him." This is, so important. It is not something to take lightly but very seriously. For He is the empowering of life. He can make it for you a thing of great beauty and service. When you will not let Him but keep the door of your heart closed against Him, it is no wonder that life conies to disappointment and disintegrates into weakness, a thing of shrunken worth. Let me say again how important it is to "let Him" be your implementing agency.

He stands waiting. But you hold the key. Either the key turns to open the door that "lets Him" flood the Divine essence and unlimited power into your life, transforming it into more and more a likeness of Him, or the key fails to turn! The channel remains closed. There is no inflowing power. Life shrivels, turns in upon itself because it lacks that great dynamic that could make it like unto the Father.

Don't ever fail to turn the lock; to open the door; to keep the channel free and clear for this transforming inflow of His life. Nothing else is half as important. Take me at my word, I beseech you. From here, I see so clearly with the vision of Spirit and I know whereof I speak. Willingness to cooperate with Almighty God in every last detail your is beyond my power to stress too strongly. Let Him in! Let Him shed His light upon you! Let Him make a new person of you with His love! He will not take the reins of any human life and drive, no matter how right that might seem to be. For that breaks down the validity of His gift of free-will to mankind. And that He will never do.

With renewed completeness and joy and gratitude, let Him work His will through you and bring you to loftiness of spirit stature which otherwise you could not reach. at is worth more than any other thing in all the universe:

God keep you close from all harm; lead you in the way of His understanding and wisdom and peace and bring you safely through to us here. Then it will all be clear. Blessings and Amen!

"ACCORDING TO"

It is good for these messages to make their way into permanent form for instruction of many who are not familiar with ways of life and kinds of service which we who are often thought of as "dead," are rendering.

Oh, so far from being "dead," we are more alive than on the earth plane, filled with vitality we never knew in the flesh, possessed with knowledge and power entirely beyond our scope while we walked the ways of the human, obsessed with the glory of transcending the obstructions of the material world and experiencing the raptures of this infinite sweep of thought and service.

Only to those who are left on the earth plane, is death a gloomy experience. To those who make the Great Transition and who have lived the good life, bringing with them their trophies of right efforts and their rewards of honest thinking and doing, the Transition is one of great glory and their hearts thrill at what they begin to learn from this side of life.

I want to say again what I have several times said to you that they sometimes grieve for those they have left behind in the flesh; especially if they see gloom and sorrow bearing them down. Often these newly-come visit their earth homes and yearn to see that their dear ones recognize their presence. Sometimes they do, though generally more by the consciousness of the presence than by mortal sight.

Sometimes they are not recognized in any way. That is hard for them. Nothing can help them more from the earth side than to see that the adjustment to their absence is being made in poised calm, with acceptance of the inevitable in faith, without mourning and gloomy atmospheres. If only earth people can learn this great way of helping their beloveds who have come to live here on these Inner Planes, they will make real contribution of service to them whom they loved.

And now I want to talk about a phase of faith that could almost be reduced to the accuracy of a mathematical formula. Does that bring a smile to your face, remembering my fondness for figures?

Last night by your earth reckoning, you were reading—I stood beside you while you held the little book in your hand and read its words of spirit wisdom—"According to your faith."

The first two of those four words I want to discuss. It is an exact proportion that works as inevitably as any chemical or physical or mathematical formula—according to! What do I mean? This. That when you ask of the Divine anything of which you stand in need, wondering whether it will be given you, thinking perhaps you can get along with part of it and you don't expect to get it all, faith of that degree and stamp gives you in exact proportion as you expect. Never any more. Nor any less.

In those simple words abides one of the mightiest propositions of the spirit world. To exactly the degree that your faith holds firmly, do you receive! According to! -If you expect little, you receive that way. If you take God at His great word and expect largely, asking in His name, you receive accordingly.

It is literally "according to" your faith. Unless of course, you have asked amiss for what would not be good for you or others. Anything asked in His name which is the way all should ask, is not likely to be asked in selfish spirit or for selfish purpose. Faith is like the rope thrown out to a person who is in danger. Holding securely to that rope, he is safe. Believing that the rope is the medium of his safety, it is literally so. Doubting its value and not holding securely to it, often he goes down by the pull of world undertow or the suction of selfishness or the quicksands of ways essentially earthy.

That never is the fault of the rope of Faith. According to the dependence put upon it, and the tight hold upon it, one is sure of all help that is needed.

Do I make this clear? It is one of the mighty lessons which the human finds it hard to learn, hard to grasp the working qualities of this faith which is more potent in earth living than could be expressed in words.

Take it into your every life experience, my friend. Let it help you. Never let go of it. Nor doubt it. Never take half a loaf when a whole loaf of goodness is available to you, "according to" your use of this power reach.

You are being especially companioned these days of unusual stress. Test this faith in all that they bring and keep on knowing that faith will enable you to triumph over any ill that appears to threaten. Let your heart enlarge and your faith grow as you contemplate anew the mysterious ways of God's working to accomplish His will, through the lives of those who love Him.

I leave you now for the night. I shall be busy about the things of spirit service as you rest. Tomorrow will bring you good. I leave you my unforgetting blessing and the blessing of the Father, the Son and the Holy Spirit in reassuring and renewing power.

LINES OF COMMUNICATION

Vibrations between your world and ours are intense these days. Lines of communications are in use day and night along which is passing wisdom of the ages for instruction of mankind struggling with gigantic problems.

I wish you could know what activity there is in this intercourse between the two worlds and how simple the use of this vibratory system is to those who have open mind to it. No problem or perplexity but can be submitted to the Inner Planes and receive wisdom and guidance and comforting assurance beyond anything earth knows. You understand this, for you have been the recipient of this knowledge now for years. There is growing appreciation on the part of earth minds, even those who are not attuned to spiritual frequencies nor interested in spiritual interpretations, of the power that can be appropriated through this universal channel.

However busy lines of communication may be, there never is a time when the call must be asked to wait for later help or when one is told that "lines are busy." Always this infinitely powerful help is open on the instant whereby Omnipotent God through His ministering spirits, gives help and counsel and love and abiding presence to those who seek.

Problems of every nation are counselled from here and amazing solutions transmitted on the quick wings of thought from our Planes to yours. This you need to remember, that the human having asked for help, does not always find himself willing to accept it or to use it.

That never turns us away from willingness to share this higher knowledge and wisdom with those of earth. For soon or late, there will develop the spirit that is willing to put into practice the oft-times startling advice sent out from the Inner Planes in answer to appeals.

I have not said much to you about this for a long time, and I want you to, keep your mind and spirit alert to it, especially as you are beginning deeper studies along the lines of which you and I have talked since I joined the Invisible Hosts who have passed the Veil.

Answers to earth's painful riddles are, on general principles, very simple. I do not mean simple in outworkings. But simple in principle. They follow the teachings of our Lord when He lived the earth life and told His disciples to "love one another!" He gave that Golden Rule which bids men do unto others as they would that men should do unto them. In these simple rules of the right way of life abide solutions of tangled skeins of national or international policies.

If only men would learn! They could use truth which is as available as air they breathe and be free from limitations, inhibitions, restrictions which now impinge upon life. If only they would take these forms of Divine truth and let their use transform life into a beautiful experience of freedom from turmoil and strife and seeking each to outdo the other! The law holds that if you know the truth, the truth shall make you free. It does and it will when men give it a chance.

Strife is rampant. It is deadly and holds within itself seeds of further conflict in which man will seek to outdo man, nation to overpower nation and purposes of civilization and God be further frustrated.

It goes back to that of which we have talked before, of man's power of free will which the Great God gave him and which, if man will, he may use for his undoing. If he will, he may use it for growth in those things which are the fruits of the spirit and of good report.

But men must make the choice. By that choice they must abide. We who minister to earth people, aspire always to help. But we are forbidden to influence them. Their power of free will must not be interfered with nor overridden. At that line, we stop, having delivered our messages in the spirit of true service.

Don't ever let doubt creep into your heart about the potency of help which the Inner Planes give. Nothing else in the universe has the power to achieve that Spirit has. No way is ever so dark but that Spirit can make the way plain.

You remember recently when you were hard beset and sleep eluded your night hours, there floated into your consciousness, into your mind and heart, that "The night shall be light about you." It brought you comfort and relaxation and peace of mind that no material help could have afforded. Don't forget it. Nor let your heart wander in allegiance to spirit influences.

I go now on assignment of much significance to human welfare, charged with privilege of carrying help and counsel where it is sorely needed. As we go on such missions, we know that the resources of the Almighty are at our hand and that we are freed from the limitations that used to hedge us about when we were in the flesh and went so clumsily about our earth tasks. How glad you will be when you see how wonderful it is, relieved of all that proved burdensome down there on earth.

Yet a while you must be loyal to your tasks where you are serving better than you know. Have no fear. No dread. No loneliness. No resentment. No weariness of spirit. Just go ahead, knowing that you are anointed for your task. And you will carry it through. The Good God pour out upon you the abounding riches of His power and glory, leading you beside still waters and renewing your spirit as He restores your soul. Good night!

SEED THOUGHTS

On your quiet Sabbath evening when you have just completed a difficult assignment from the Inner Planes, it is privilege to talk with you about things of lasting moment. Tonight I want to discuss the reality of thought and its significance in the life-plan of the human and here on these Higher Planes.

The average person considers thought as vague and immaterial, something that can be concealed and that has no direct bearing upon himself or any one else unless he expresses it or puts it into action.

He who thinks thus is in error. There is no greater dynamic in the universe than thought, expressed or otherwise. It is the food upon which man feeds in his inner life. According to it, he grows in usefulness and power to serve or shrinks in the scale until his balance in the bank of life is useless.

As a man thinketh in his heart, said the Proverbs, so is he, saint or sinner, selfish or unselfish, corrupt or clean.

It is impossible to think puny thoughts, to give them place even momentarily within one's consciousness and not be influenced in one's actions. To live with self-centered thoughts a day or an hour, is to feel their influence on the living of the day. Whether the thought be wicked or just weak, well-considered or a fleeting flash, it has influence on the one who harbored it.

Such is the power of thought that it influences the others who may never have heard it expressed but who feel the radiations that pass from the mind which admitted it.

So mighty is this business of thinking that no one should pass it over lightly. You grow to be like what you think. That is the law. "As a man thinketh in his heart, so is he!" Habit is closely related to thinking, which makes the whole matter more complicated and important. Get the habit of critical thinking, of negative, pessimistic outlooks, and you have a dual battle on your hands. For the power of habit is tremendous. It is no inconsiderable task to break the habit of unwise thinking nor to learn to replace unsatisfactory thoughts with such as will make life all that it should. The little thought means stunted life without the zest of growth, the dynamic of faith and the challenge of joy. Open the mind only to the good, the true, the great thought, seed from which will grow the good life.

Don't ever forget that, my friend. The good life! Worth more than all the gold mines in the world. It will prove its worth to you through the endlessness of existence over here on this Plane of life where one is filled with the surge of growth, of adjustment to spirit ways and spirit power, where the little is inadequate and the unworthy is its own pain and penalty.

I beg you not to tamper with little thoughts. Throw them onto the discard and fill those spaces with thoughts of God. Ask Him to fill your mind with only that which is germ-full of growth in ways of wisdom and understanding, with grace for those in need and willingness to subordinate self to purposes of farther-flung horizons.

I know perhaps more clearly than any human can, how significant even one thought is, taken into the mind and there planted! It is bound to grow. It will bear harvest after its own kind. Be sure what kind it is, my friend. For it is seed.

The presence of God surround and fill you. The patience of God possess you. The glory of God shine through you. Amen!

THE LAW OF GROWTH

Tonight I come to meet my part of this mutual obligation. How good it is for us who have passed the Veil to make the earth contact with you who also need the wider horizon which comes from close consciousness with this radiant side of life.

Because I know what it would do for all of you of earth who are interested in life over here, I wish almost overwhelmingly that I might describe it to you, modes of existence, types of companionship, systems of learning, atmosphere of adoration of the Highest, the Great God Who is above all!

Tonight the urge is strong upon me, perhaps because your earth is so terribly ridden with uncertainties, with all that is the opposite of peace, so shaken with strife and selfishness that you who reside in the flesh feel no firm foundation beneath your feet. The chaos that prevails roots from men's selfish greed for two things of great destruction: love, too much love, of money and power. These are roots of bitterness that is biting into every heart of human life.

Everywhere you find this chaos and things of ugly brood that spawn from the evil of which I have just spoken. The reflex action to all of this shows in tensions, strains and irritations like pins sticking into sensitive flesh. They need not be like pins. Unless you give them power over you, they lose their sharpness to hurt or to irritate. But of something else I especially desire to talk with you this evening.

Nothing here is static. Everything changes even with us. That is the law. It is the law of growth. And as you so well know, we here grow at a more rapid rate than those on the earth plane. Our growth is spiritual and intellectual through which we may help with earth problems.

The orthodox church thinks of this side of life as "finished." It is not so. We come hither. We learn and adore. We serve. We go hither and yon. There is no limitation to our presence. We are not established in the "many mansions." That beautiful concept is to be interpreted only as a figure of speech intended to convey the impression of vast comfort in our existence, complete satisfaction with our surroundings of goodness and glory. Please take it that way. And no other.

There is no stability of population over here. By that I mean nothing negative. But I want you to understand that the divisiveness which separates humanity into family units, neighborhood groups, city and country and continental assortments, simply does not exist here.

We do not cling to any when we reach this happier, more satisfying life which is without beginning and without end. We have grown beyond narrow exclusiveness. That means no lesser love for our dear ones. It does mean that we all have come to wider vision and larger aptitudes for wisdom that is of eternal moment.

Much that is attached to the small and dear idea of the family, was material and entirely transient. We are past that, as some glad day you will be. Then all of this will be clear and gracious to you. You will marvel at the restrictiveness of earth concepts, and at how you could have been satisfied with them.

We come from earth, our one set of lessons learned, after a longer or shorter time here, we return to earth to learn yet other lessons, to experience and to master yet greater soul disciplines that we may the sooner reach that spiritual perfection when by the grace of the Great, Good God, we shall no longer need the experiences of the earth plane and may have our abiding places forever with the Lord.

This is so radically different from what I believed while I was with you on the earth plane that it is difficult perhaps, for you to reconcile yourself to it. I want you to know that it is very truth and that it is in the order of the Divine will whereby life goes on from its endless beginning to its unending climax, a perfect cycle of growth, of glory and of power which come from the Infinite.

Thus there is constant interchange of personalities with whom we fellowship each other, from whom we part without pang, moving constantly closer toward the consummation of perfection in the eyes of the Most High God in Whom and through Whom is all life.

Do you not see how all of this contributes to the grandeur of living, to the worthwhileness of earth experiences, to the seriousness of learning life's lessons and of gearing every experience to the standard which is in harmony with the Creator, God? You are opening yourself to greater degrees of blessing from spirit sources than could have come to you along the ether waves if you had adhered to those former concepts with which the average earth resident contents himself.

Blessings of God the Almighty abide with you, His wisdom instruct you, His glory surround you, His life fill you with all of its fulness as you grow and serve. Amen!

WHICH WAY THE ATOM?

We who have made the Great Transition want you to know how practical a world ours is and how cooperative with yours. Practical in every high and lofty sense. For we are busied with our varied capacities at outlining and bringing through to finished detail many things which help you negotiate daily earth life.

Your atomic bomb that is causing such intellectual unrest and worldwide discussion, with its infinite possibilities one way of blessing and the other way of destruction, is of the creative stuff of which the world was made out of the void.

The power it represents is limitless and will be utilized in ways of great good, if mankind walks softly and heeds his way, if he remembers that he is his brother's keeper and is responsible for keeping the world at peace, instead of weighing in the universal scales things of war heavier than issues of peace.

Let mankind try that just once more and he has lost the opportunity of the ages to prove his supremacy and his spirit potency over lower orders of living.

Just now this is a race between two lines of things in the minds of many men who sit in seats of power. This terrifying thing of which we speak is material. But in more correct phrase, it is pure energy which of course, all matter is. Energy now is known to be allied to spirit and this atomic power comes closely to being a spiritual issue. Wrapped in its inestimable force is as much power for human good, as it holds of potential destruction. This brings into play in a most vivid and striking way the fundamental power abiding in every man—the gift of free will, the power to choose what he will do, which road he will follow, which course he will pursue.

I've discussed it with you before but not in such relationship. It fits perfectly into the situation which is bewildering the thought of the world and will, until the right choice is made. That hinges on the spiritual attunement which will enable mankind to see the potencies of his choice and to know in his deepest being which way the human race must follow in this greatest of all employments of pure, creative, elemental matter.

We here have watched this development with deep interest. I shall not say with anxiety. For on these Inner Planes we see from other viewpoints, than those which earth uses. Anxiety does not enter our hearts.

But the whole issue is a contest between the material and the spiritual, two types of power between which man will elect the use which he makes of this which the Creator used in building His universe.

I beg of you to take into careful and constant consideration this matter of free will. As in this atomic situation, so in others. It is one of the weightiest factors in life, entering into everything one does, into every choice one makes, into all of the organization of the world in which he lives.

Tremendous issues abide in it and results that flow from it make it worth your most prayerful contemplation.

Free will will function in this weightiest matter of atomic fission. Remember that from our vantage point, we watch the contest as it wages around the world and enlists the thought of all people.

We always seek help from the Highest for those who turn hither for light on every problem and strength for every need.

I leave you now and I ask the favor of the Father to rest upon you, to make straight your path and safe your going.

READINESS

Again you come at the appointed hour! I am so grateful that here we have no hours or minutes to figure, no being on time or being late. How gracious to be freed of all this which is part of the discipline of the human while he learns his earth lessons. It is a lesson that needs to be learned, this being dependable in times and seasons in the flesh.

To it belong qualities of the spirit which abide and are needed after one has made the Great Transition. You see the whole scheme of earth life is so blueprinted that whereas it seems to be related only to matters on the earth level of life, it really ties in closely with qualities especially adapted to give abundant entrance to our Higher Planes of spirit life.

This business of being ready when the time has come for seemingly insignificant earth appointments that appear to have no cosmic importance whatever, really has great importance on the large scale. It teaches the one concerned that he is obligated to be honest in spending time that belongs to some other person, as much as his property or money.

How few earth people understand and accept that! Or gauge life standards by such measurements! Time is eternity, as important as that, the endless cycle which earth people break down into seconds and centuries. They speak of wasting time, stealing time which does not belong to them and making it a matter of no consequence. Therein they will atone when they reach the Ether Planes and see every issue of life in true light.

Nothing which takes advantage in any degree of any other or that disregards the highest sanctities of earth life is unimportant. All of it is in the fabric which each individual is set to weave. Each broken thread in the pattern, each mar in the perfection of the weaving, must be amended on earth or later when one comes to these Planes where there is no dissembling.

Doesn't all of this give dignity to living? And isn't it important to realize the close bond between the two sides of life so that each may weave his stretch of the pattern with beauty and grace?

Not until I came Home, after crossing the Bright River of Life and had adjusted to the order of living here, did this unfold in its great significance of relationship for every human. I wish I might have had the cosmic interpretation of all this while I was a man in the flesh. I might have made so much more of myself and been the better Prepared for joys and responsibilities of service and growth on this Sunny Side of Life. Because I didn't know of these relationships between the two worlds, it is duty and privilege to make it as plain as possible to others of earth, while yet there is time.

None of these things is belittling. They are lessons for faithful and intelligent mastering. Then you will have greater qualities which will stand the test of spirit here. It is a wonderful interrelation of privilege and responsibility, whether the lesson be of honesty in use of time or of wise investment of talent for service.

Nothing but has all-important place in the infinite plan of creation. Nothing is left out, nothing forgotten, no cog but has its wheel, not one need but has that with which to meet it. Study all of this, my friend! It will repay you for every effort you make to understand and to assimilate it to the extent that is given the human to understand the high rate of spiritual perception and vibration.

I thank you for this opportunity to discuss this important phase of life with you. How glad and thankful you will be when you have fought your good fight, have finished your course and come Home to those who await in patience the hour of your coming!

The peace and joy and rapture of the Father be with you. I could wish you nothing else worth half as much as this.

DEEP ROOTAGE

Power to hold steady when winds of conflict or disappointment or discouragement blow, is one of the main channels of growth. For they do blow upon every human who stays any length of time on the earth. If these winds did not blow, he would be flabby, weak and coarse-grained in his spirit fiber and lacking in stalwart qualities of conquest over temporal things.

"Keep me steady!" That prayer I commend to all humans who are easily blown about by passing winds, who do not stand on firm convictions of judgment and ethics and principles of what is good and right. To hold steady is tremendously worthwhile in the development of character.

And remember, my friend, that every earth person is steadily moving toward the Great Transition. No evading that! Woe to him who goes with the worthlessness of transient, lightweight or spurious baggage which has passed muster somehow in the traffic of the earth world.

Over here, it is put at once into the discard of eternal worthlessness where it belongs. And the one who accumulated it with such fierce earth ardor finds himself empty-handed because things of character, of steadfastness and dependability did not seem sufficiently important to be striven for. How tragic it is when one sees it from the viewpoint of these Inner Planes!

Character is like the sturdy, deep-rooted tree that has sent its roots down past rocks, around obstacles and through whatever kinds of foreign soil stood in the way of its nourishment and water for growth.

Finding these things, its roots continued to anchor themselves in firm foundations of earth. And it is the rootage, not the waving of branches bright with blossoms and foliage, it is the rootage which holds that tree steady and unmovable when rains come and hurricanes blow and icy storms of sleet weigh heavily upon its strength. Its roots are deep. The tree stands safe!

That is character. The tree takes what comes and is not broken by it. When the Great Transition comes to one who has built strong, flawless character, what values it will have for him! What he brings over to this beautiful side of life begins at once to help him forward to higher levels of spirit knowledge and achievement, to richer experiences of worship and adoration of Him Whom we acknowledge as the All, the Creator, the Father. How can earth people fail to think these things through in clearness of vision while they follow the path of earth struggle? For they know all the while that toward which they move!

I wish I could make it as plain to earth minds as it is here to us, that spurious, counterfeit qualities of character that seek to deceive by their speciousness, do not pass a moment's muster over here.

They last for a brief earth moment and are gone. But the steady qualities of what is genuine and good and pure and faithful, that go deep into the inmost places of spirit, are pure gold. They ring clear and true over here, as they do on your earth plane. Keep sending your roots of spirit inquiry and quest for knowledge and for ever greater riches of sturdy character down and further down into firm foundations of understanding and belief that will hold your tree of life strongly in place despite winds that blow fiercely on earth, hold it steady and true for you when you come so gladly across the River of Life, your earth tasks laid down, well done. One of the qualities of spirit which Jesus taught and exemplified was this infinitely precious quality of character. Cultivate it happily, my friend, and with due appreciation of its great value. It will reward you even as it has already done. Remember, "Be ye steadfast, always unmovable!"

I am off now on some difficult missions for men who are in desperate straits. We are with you many times a day when sometimes your spirit needs the uplift of special tonic. How quickly you rally! God bless you for it. Amen!

UNDERSTANDING

Thank you for coming so promptly to this hour of communion on matters of spirit value. It is reciprocal gain that comes from the hour together, for you yet living in the flesh and for me relieved of its weight and blest with spirit freedom. How great a deliverance it is no one can conceive until he too, has come up higher to live on larger terms and to understand in richer values.

There are those who will say that it is natural for one who has lived his earth life to full maturity of years to feel the way I have just expressed. But for the younger person vibrant with unfulfilled possibilities and desires, it can be only tragic loss to go so soon from the physical into pure spirit.

It is not so! Our life over here is so radiantly filled with things of youth and its development, with service destined especially for the young and with joys that are part of the youth cycle, that for even the very young, the Transition is altogether gain. You do not understand it from your limited earth vision. So I ask you to believe it because I tell you it is very truth. Never did I tell you what was not true. I do not now.

This brings me to the central theme on which I wish to talk with you this evening. Understanding! It is one of the great qualities to be cultivated in the spirit. With it comes tolerance because there is understanding of motives and purposes. With it is patience because one realizes that matters of great moment are often slow in coming to fruition. With it comes mellowness of spirit because one learns that the richest things are not of surface shine but of spirit radiance which is hidden, in the deep places within.

With understanding comes largeness of thinking and expansion of feeling, because the far horizons are extended te include so much that never appeared before to the spirit until understanding opened its doors and revealed things of great value, worth acquiring at the cost of any pains.

Understanding is a rare jewel in the crown of one's life. It is the mark of a great spirit. It does not come easily, not quickly. It is the reward of deep living and thinking, of feeling and serving. Understanding judges righteous judgment. It does not mistake what is superficial for what is real, neither does it see the spurious as genuine. Its basis of estimating life is in the teachings of Christ where truth is dominant. Understanding always squares with this and is never at variance.

The understanding person is never arrogant, never aggressive, never self-seeking nor assertive. Always he separates what is good from what is questionable and lays the weight of his emphasis upon things of enduring quality. He lifts his eyes to the heights for inspiration and does not take guidance from what is of low design.

Understanding is of the rich fruits of the spirit and is compounded of those things which are of good report. It is like the richest, the ripest fruit which has come to its choiceness through the fulness of days of ripening in sunshine, of taking the rains and the winds that blow and the hours of darkness. All are in its order of growth and bring it to its finest perfection as one of the good gifts of the Creator.

So it is with understanding in the heart. Some days have been dark and sunless. Always the negative has had to be appraised and seen for the hollow thing it is, with the positive accepted in its place and built into the fiber of living. Love and sorrow and their acceptance without sting or bitterness are part of the understanding of which I speak with you tonight. It is great tribute to any one so to live that he is recognized as an understanding spirit, able to see behind what appears to that which is real and to manifest the gentleness of interpretation that is part of true understanding.

I would that you take to yourself the learning of this lesson, the acceptance of this commission to become familiar with specifications and dimensions of what understanding is, in its finest terms. Only great and good qualities enter into it and only real living in terms of the spirit can give to any human the grace that comes with understanding. It is like love in its effect upon life. Indeed it is one facet of love and as necessary to the good life.

It takes away all rawness and substitutes mellowed, tempered strength and graciousness of spirit, than which nothing is more to be desired in man's achievements. Let understanding grow within you, my friend. It costs to learn and to manifest. But it will pay you unfailing dividends in the standard currency of the spirit.

This has been a delightful talk, a vital talk, because its theme is of the essence of true living. Let it grow within you as a strong tree of rich fruitfulness.

The blessing of the Almighty rest upon you, blessing which is life's richest gift to you. Amen!

ERRORS OF DEVOTION

In the dark of your sleep hours as you lay restless and disturbed, we sent to your remembrance that which had been a lifesaver years ago, by human reckoning of time—"Thou art my strength and my deliverer." You laid it in the heart of your anxiety and it has eased your way through all of the day. Hold to it and never doubt!

Remember how often it has been said to you from these Higher Planes of Privilege that the spiritual is infinitely stronger than the human. What would be impossible from human standards is brought to fulfillment without strain or anxious concern by the spirit powers. Don't ever forget that. Put it to the test. Believe it with your mind, your heart, your soul and you will achieve many a victory on the field of life. Those who have no knowledge of such power, fail of more than they can estimate. It is to them a sealed volume, a source of power that does not exist. But you have demonstrated it many a time. You will again, to your great gain and comfort.

At its best, the flesh is relatively gross. It is material and is nourished by material things, though it houses the immortal spirit. This is as much of the reason as the earth mind can assimilate why continued adulation of and grieving for the body of one who has gone, retards the spiritual freedom of such an one and hampers him in the beginnings of his growth here on these Happy Planes. He is struggling to shed the things of the body, every vestige of the influence of the material housing that has served him but for which he no longer has need and from which it is his advantage to be free. The intangible relation between the two makes it highly desirable from the spirit viewpoint, for the body to be placed quickly where it may follow the course of nature back to the dust from which it came, leaving the undying spirit free to start in the world of spirit with no hampering influences restraining it.

Excessive attention to the body when the spirit has left it, has nothing good in it either for those who abide longer on the earth plane or for the one who has been promoted to our Loftier Spheres.

You see the logic of it, my friend. The actual working of it in terms of molecules and physical forms as interrelated to the spirit, need not concern you nor any one of earth. The principle is clear. Earth people should know and understand it. Adoring the body, the housing, the shell, merits no one anything. Loving the spirit well enough to set it free from every handicap of earth, is infinitely finer, form of devotion. Think well through this whole principle, my friend. It is worth more than gold in term of spirit growth, as we here know so well. Share this with others and you will be sowing good seed.

SURE SOURCE

I want to talk briefly tonight about our Far Shore, as so often people of earth think of it and as sometimes we here speak of it. I remind you again that it is nearer to you than your hands or your feet, that we who dwell on these Spirit-Planes are of you and among you, carrying help and encouragement through the hours of every day. When I say "you" in such connection, I mean all who live and work yet on the earth sphere. It seems far only because physical sight is restricted to material objects and cannot always see us. Eyes of spirit see far more clearly and catch radiant glimpses of us as we come and go in and out among you, rejoicing in the privilege of helping to lighten earth loads. Please never forget that our chiefest mission from here to you of the earth plane, is to help with loads so they never become burdens. Sometimes they do. But they shouldn't. For spirit power is equal to solving any problem that earth conditions produce. Learn more and more, to turn your heart upward in thanksgiving and supplication, asking for and knowing that you receive the strength, the light, the wisdom you need. Could any provision of the Creator be more precious to mortals than this knowledge of how to tune in to the power of the Cosmic hosts and be recipient of their infinite assistance?

It is worth more than all the gold of the universe at hand, for every one who asks and is openhearted, to receive. Test it when there is slightest need. Prove it whenever you ask it. And you will be girded with power beyond your farthest fancy. Gigantic problems which nations of earth face, call for much activity on our part, where millions are suffering for food and shelter and courage to begin again, to find the way without terrors of authoritarianism.

All of these need ministering spirits to help in this difficult time of adjustments when the human is insufficient. It is such blessed service when we bring comfort and consolation to hearts that have been desolated. How you will thrill to it when you come. Don't forget this, though! You must work loyally through the years until your lessons are done and your lifespan completed on earth before you ask to be released for coming Home to the Ether Planes. They will seem very home-like to you for you have lived so earnestly in them in your thought life. They will more than repay you for all that has apparently been denied you in the flesh.

Hold yourself as a daughter of the King! The protective garment of God enfolds you and no harm can come to you who wears it! God bless you and cause His face to shine upon you and give you peace. Good night!

"WHY?" HAS AN ANSWER

You wonder why it is that not so often as in the earth months past, do you hear me speak. You question whether it is failure on your part. The reason is that you are growing beyond need of constant reminder and to the point where direct contact between you and Spirit Divine is better tonic for you, better medium of power for you. Do not misinterpret this into thinking that you are left alone or that our fellowship is undergoing change. Just take this as I give it to you and know that it is in Divine order for your welfare and progress.

There will be no surcease in the coming of messages to you, for all who need and will be nurtured by them. In other words, change is part of the eternal, plan where nothing is static. You will hear my voice frequently and you will know that the contacts between your realm and mine are constantly possible, with the help from this invisible world available on the instant.

Take it all in your stride and know that greater things are in store for you, imbued with better values and larger outreach for mind and spirit, than you have for some time experienced. That too, is part of this change which is the order of life, which scarcely anybody likes but which all must accept. Otherwise, staleness and stagnation. Change is manifest in our Inner Planes too, for I have told you how we move from one level of growth to another, how we learn and serve, then go on to the next higher realm. It is all part of the perfect plan conceived by the Creator. It has no flaw in it save as mankind fails to permit its perfect functioning by his imperfect use of parts entrusted to his handling.

When you stop to ponder, you see how there is no dividing line between the two worlds except for the physical presence which we leave behind as we cross the Shining Waters and begin the life of spirit unhampered by the flesh.

The thread of continuity runs through all of life, on your side and on our side of the Veil. The same Divine laws prevail. The same spirit of growth. The same love. The same Lord!

I beseech for you an open mind, a willing heart, anticipation of all things good and satisfying, a constantly outreaching mind and heart, ever more pouring out to others the good which has come to you. All of this I beseech for you in the name of the Father Whom we love and serve.

PEACE THAT IS POWER

From Planes of Spirit
To the planet of earth
This eternal Truth is sent,
That it may be unto your hearts
His deep-flowing Peace and His Power!
—The Counsellor

FOREWORD

FROM THE other side of life, these Messages have come along the ether waves, from The Counsellor. Sitting alone in my home, I have received them, receptive to the familiar voice that was speaking the truth, as is herein recorded.

The external technique incident to this still-continuing experience, I have tried to make clear in the two former books—"From the Seventh Plane" and "Seeing the Invisible." But because sincere questions are frequently asked me, I seek again to clarify a few aspects of receiving these Messages and putting them on paper.

The voice which speaks is inaudible to outer ears but it is undeniably clear to my inner hearing. How this is accomplished, I do not know. But that it is, I do know. The Counsellor transmits these Messages "verbatim," as he used to say on the earth plane. I transcribe them, word for word, on the typewriter as they come, deeply conscious of the power that is operative.

When interruptions seem to break in while he is speaking, they disturb neither him nor me. Those who have read the preceding volumes from The Counsellor, will remember that he realizes my earth responsibilities and that I cannot control either the ringing of the telephone or signals at the doors. And he never wearies with waiting since he laid aside the garment of flesh, but stands unperturbed, while I fulfill my part in whatever it was that took my attention,

Some have wondered why The Counsellor entrusts these Messages from the Other. World to me. For many years we worked together, sharing professional responsibilities and carrying a common load.

Thus perhaps it is natural, and it may be simpler, for him to energize my thought processes by the electrical impulse which is his accredited method for sending these inter-world Messages to planes of earth.

I take no personal credit as the human channel for this far-flung service. But I am grateful. Occasionally people express surprise that he does not reveal new and startling truth about the nature of God nor tell in detail that which might satisfy normal human curiosity, concerning the ancient prophets and other great personalities who have been long ages on the Inner Planes.

The reasons he does not enlarge on these themes, are simple and clear. Basically, two major motives, both wholly spiritual, prompt the sending of this truth from the Ether Planes to mankind yet functioning in the three dimensional world. These Messages are not intended to gratify casual curiosity nor to be merely interesting reading. They are profound lessons set for us to learn.

The first one is: There Is No Death! It is a difficult lesson to learn with the heart! Recently The Counsellor repeated that millions of people living on earth today, are terrified at the thought of physical death and hold utterly incorrect ideas of what it is and how it is.

Thus, out of deep conviction, he seeks to teach clearly and convincingly from his vantage point of life on Spirit Planes, that the experience we have mistakenly feared, is not death. Instead, it is The Great Transition from limited earth life to unlimited development on those beautiful Planes of Power. It is never death!

Together with that motive and a part of it, come the illuminating lessons, bright with their auras of spiritual import, to teach us how to live day by day, as we move irresistibly toward the greater life that awaits us. The second reason is:

These lessons direct from Inner Planes, are designed to help us be ready, unafraid and filled with conscious anticipation, when our Transition comes due. It is a universal experience. To face it aright, reveals deep-rooted wisdom and grace.

These dominant reasons explain why The Counsellor confines his teaching thus and does not branch out to any extent into aspects that are not vitally related to these lessons which bear within themselves the greatness and the grandeur of eternity.

Please let me say again that which I have said in each of the former books from The Counsellor, that his frequent use of the word "you" is generally impersonal and is seldom restricted to me whose responsibility it is to receive what comes and to do my part toward making it available in printed form, for the many who hunger for it.

"From the Seventh Plane" and "Seeing the Invisible" have gone to England, Ireland and France, to Guam and Japan, to Afghanistan and Burma and South Africa, perhaps elsewhere abroad. In this country, they have made their way to remote woods of the north, to tiny villages and great cities, to university centers, to metropolitan libraries and less pretentious ones, to many hospitals and institutions of reform, in all of which are they who yearn for this clear-cut, dynamic, life-changing truth.

In loyal acceptance of all which is involved in putting forth this third volume from The Counsellor, I see it move out on the stream of life, into the world of humankind, to do its silent and potent work in pointing the way.

When the going is dark, we shall find the Light that shines. When earth's perplexities are baffling, we shall know the Peace That Is Power. And nevermore need we be afraid!

WINIFRED WILLARD
Los Angeles, California
August, 1957

THE MESSAGES

THESE THINGS WE TEACH

As I speak with you this evening, I am in the atmosphere of prayer, aware of the significance of what I bring. It is not a light thing to speak from Eternal Realms to people of earth whose burdens are heavy, their spiritual understanding often limited, many of whom have been misguided in their teaching.

From the Inner Planes we must first gain your confidence that these words come straight through the ethers to you and through you they go to many who are hungry for truth. Often they do not realize what their hunger is. They know there is a craving within their deeper nature, but until the truth reaches them, they do not find their hunger appeased.

After confidence has been established between us of the Inner Planes and you of earth, as it was shortly after I made the Transition, it is necessary to replace mistaken earth teaching with truth which is as clear as crystal. We approach this responsibility only as we are inspired with Heavenly Wisdom and filled with the Love of the Father.

Dread of death is something we seek to eradicate in which we earnestly ask your cooperation by prayer and earth endeavor. This dread is deeply entrenched in millions of hearts, associated with problems that concern those who remain on earth as well as those who have laid aside their physical garments.

We strive to teach all who will learn, the close interrelation of these two spheres between which we pass many times daily, and that only such spiritual gifts and understanding as earth people have gained while in the physical body, may they bring as entrance credentials when they come to these. Etheric Planes.

We help them to learn, though sometimes slowly, that death is not a magic wand which in an instant transforms a sinner into a saint. They must learn that they have their credits to earn while they are yet of earth. When one leaves the physical body, he begins to grow in spirit in ways of which he had no previous knowledge—but should have had! Learning to work with the powers of thought transference, is difficult for most who come hither. This is the medium through which we converse and carry on our work, using vocal cords only when necessary for gaining some earth interest.

Another lesson for them just come, is that Spirit Planes are places of intense activity in every form of earth interest and organization, where all study and progress as rapidly as they learn.

As little by little, knowledge is acquired, each one must exemplify it in his own activities, then use this knowledge for teaching others who have not yet learned it. We teach them that only as they work and study in the spirit of love, can they grow in spirit stature, for love is the great dynamic through which marvelous things are accomplished. These lessons should have been taught on earth, but rarely are. Many who come hither think of lessons as restricted to the more or less earth years, then no more lessons! We teach the necessity for returning time and again to earth to learn lessons not yet learned amid earth conditions, returning then to Spirit Planes to absorb the details of the life just lived, into the fiber of the soul. Sometimes this lesson is easily learned. Sometimes it taxes us to make it plain. The power and glory of service in His name, is stressed in our teaching, regardless of rank or position of those who need to learn this, also the close relations between the two worlds and the vast powers of intercommunication for the sake of scientific research, for transmitting vast ideas for earth to develop and use, to prove that the human does not die when he makes the Transition.

We strive to demonstrate the sweet peace that comes from communion between our sphere and the earth plane, with the light which is shed on darkness and joy which supplants sorrow. Above all, we seek to interpret the Father in ways which reveal His love and peace and power both to those in the flesh and here in Spirit Realms.

You look outward and fancy that what you see is reality. It is not. The outward is temporal, filled with unceasing change. And so you do not do well to look to the outer for satisfaction. You do not find it in possessions or in persons or in material power. These all are transient, visible or available a day, then gone!

Mankind has wearily struggled to gain outward things, thinking that this or that would surely give him satisfaction and be contentment to him. When he has them, they turn to ashes, and their power for his content is nothing. Outer things of course, are necessities for the convenience of the body, for nourishment and protection as the body does its work in the world. Not beyond that!

You think to find God in the outer. Yes, in a sense. For it is impossible to imagine any place where God is not. But for strength and courage and wisdom and grace, you find God as you turn inward to the deep places of your being, closing the door of your spiritual closet and shutting out whatever would intrude into that sacred place.

There in quiet and seclusion, you are aware of His presence. with you, that He never changes, never goes away, never is indifferent and never is short on power to meet whatever is your need. You easily meet and experience Him in the rushing fever of life, if you are familiar with finding Him within your heart. It is within that you turn for getting acquainted with God, with His fulness and His allness and His pervading presence, no matter how storms blow or foundations crumble.

Take this to your heart for comfort, a fundamental lesson which your development in spirit needs. The outer view of life is superficial and generally the wrong one to take. Get down beneath the surface when you can, to where people's motives are discovered and often they will prove sound and good. We see this from our vantage point, as earth people do not see. So we are freed from critical tendencies which so sorely blemish the pictures of living.

Guard yourself against all spirit of criticism, if you would know His inner peace and power. Learn to take any one of whom you are prone to be critical, at his highest valuation of merit and integrity. This will yield substantial returns in your life and keep the tares of criticism from growing wild in the field of your heart. They grow fast and despoil your enjoyment of His sweet peace within your heart.

When you seem about to break out in criticism of some one for some reason, pause and send a blessing through the ethers, a prayer for good to come to both of you and for what appears like evil to be overcome with good in the hearts of each of you. This will take no longer than the criticism and will go far toward changing him and you. The result will be so radical in terms of good that you will be amazed at the power which has been released for your development.

Try this! When I say "Try it," I do not mean as a venture that may succeed or fail. I mean learn to meet experiences with these solutions, never belittling any one who is doing his best. Be sure to believe that the one you want to criticize, is doing his best, even as you want him to think of you. That's a lesson tool not easy to learn but vitally connected with your growth in inward poise.

The peace of the Father which passeth knowledge be to you all that you need for every moment of your living. Amen!

TREMENDOUS TESTS

Man and woman of earth are so constituted as to want what they ask for, almost on the split second. If they must wait, they fret, self-control frequently losing out. They sometimes wonder where God is or even if there is a God. This is all very childish and unbalanced. But it is the way many mortals live their lives.

To such people, faith is all well enough and they like the idea of something on which to fall back when things go wrong; sort of a vicarious support to help them feel secure. But times come to everybody when asking is not answered at once and waiting is essential. Then what of faith?

Often it is laid aside as something which failed to keep its promises. Such quality of faith is puny, no good at all as a foundation on which to stand securely when winds blow and problems threaten ominously. Then there is need for the quality of faith that has power to endure.

This is more magnificent in terms of reality than to achieve some special undertaking. The power to endure calls for faith that knows courage and patience and love which are beyond man's ability to procure for himself. They come only from the Great One Who is the All-Provider of whatever is needed.

He alone gives the graces of courage that enable man and woman to endure and "having done all, to stand!" Remember that bit from Scripture? It is more difficult to stand than to run around, doing what may or may not be worth much.

But to have that granitic strength of courage to stand, to wait, to endure with patience, is evidence of Almighty power within, demonstrating great spiritual progress. Take this into careful consideration and meditate profoundly upon the values which are herewith brought you from the Inner Planes.

Then put into the other side of the scales of life, all impatience and unwillingness to wait and you will see the weakness, the lack of inner strength which is revealed in the life that does not know how to stand still and wait upon God!

Never-failing faith and the grace of patience answer your call as you look to the Father and ask for His power to meet in quietness and confidence the times of waiting that test the soul. The test is part of the discipline which life imposes and which always is sign of the processes of growth. God bless you as you learn the many lessons of earth. Amen!

HOW LIGHT WE ARE

I have awaited your coming to this communion time together. But I have not wearied. Can you realize what such freedom means, you who are bound about with the tensions and restrictions of earth, as millions of others are? To be free from these hampering influences is one of the amazing freedoms which one experiences when first he comes to the Inner Planes. You remember how I exclaimed to you long ago, at the lightness I felt as soon as my spirit had laid aside the clumsy physical body which so long had been its mortal abode.

This lightsomeness was remarkable after my years of being burdened with the body of flesh and I did not at first know how to adjust to it. Indeed I had to study to learn how to adapt to it, for its great values which I knew I would need.

This lightness prevents our wearying at anything which is in the order of our service and is one of the most gracious aspects of life here on the Inner Planes. My sympathy flows out to you all of earth as I see you struggle with the heavy demands of the body in your daily work of accomplishing the purposes for which you came into incarnation.

Then remembering how it was with me, my very soul glows with gratitude and I yield yet more thanksgiving and gratitude to the Father for relief from this restrictiveness which earth places around its residents. Happily you who are there do not quite realize what heaviness exists in your atmosphere and against what loads you work daily. You can not know until you come Home to learn by contrast what I mean by this marvelous lightness which we experience here.

Every influence which lifts and inspires you is worth much to you, for it gives the strength you need to overcome the downward pull of earth's heaviness and thus gives you something of this lightness of which I am talking with you tonight.

We here on the Etheric Planes are unhampered by any deficiency of a physical body. This is glorious joy to us, enabling us to accomplish our far-flung service throughout the universes. Think often of this and let it be fresh cause for anticipating the time when you will know by experience all that I mean.

But your service there comes first; "there" meaning earth and its work. Finish it completely, then rejoice! Amen!

GOD MANIFEST

We who send this series of Messages from the Inner Planes through you, wish to stress anew from a former talk, that you may put on the protective garment of His presence, becoming thereby impervious to dangers that threaten. By the power of this protection, you consciously experience God Manifest!

Use it! Daily, hourly, at every slightest need. The more you exemplify this mystic power of God Manifest in your life, the greater it grows for you and the vaster its helpfulness. Lay that thought up in your heart as true riches and feed on it in the silent watches of the night.

God Manifest! In countless forms and ways. And through you. Through every one who opens mind and heart to such manifesting. Could anything be greater? More transcendent of the narrow limitation of the human horizon?

Look out beyond all which sometimes threatens to close in around life on human levels. Thrust all of that away from you. Learn in every way and every day to experience God Manifest. In people; in the clouds and the sunshine; in flowers and the singing birds; in darkness and light; in loss and in gain; in joy and in sorrow; everywhere, God Manifest! Scan the wide horizons of thought and feeling, of His power and glory and His ways with mankind. As you do, you will feel yourself grow in deeply vital degree. And restraining shackles will fall away from your soul.

I bless you now as I go for other forms of Divine service which I am to render in His name. I leave with you the sweet consciousness of the unfailing presence of the Father. Upon you be the enduement of

His peace and His comfort as increasingly you learn the glory of experiencing God Manifest! Amen!

IN DAYS AHEAD

Be not affrighted nor disturbed nor fearful of losing your way! On the earth stretch it often seems as if the one climbing the pathway to life more abundant, were in a cul-de-sac where the only way through led to defeat. This is only in the seeming. There is always the way through when you put yourself in the care of the Father God and leave yourself there.

I can not over-stress how important this is at the present time in the ongoing of your world. Tensions become tighter and strains heavier. It is a conflict between the forces of right and the forces of evil constantly trying to tear down and despoil whatever is good and holy.

Millions of earth feel themselves caught between the two sides of this conflict. Sometimes they wonder whether they will be ground to pieces in prevailing processes which they do not understand. There are many explanations of the changes which are imminent and there will be until the Golden Age has come with its surcease of suspense and frustration and threat of impending harm.

In the meantime, people of earth are distraught. They do not know why. They are fearful of something they can not describe. All of you who know the joy of the conscious presence of God are needed at your spiritual best, in attunement always with Him, wishing only to do His Holy Will. Come what will, you need thus not be thrown off your spiritual balance. Remember, the most important thing is to keep centered in God, the Source of All Good. You will then be able to show others the way to that center and to prove the peace that abides there where is perfect calm. No storms, no disappointments, just the calm at the radiant center of your being where the Father dwells and whither He invites His children to share His unutterable peace.

You can find it in no other place. I repeat because it is a wonderful truth that only when you are centered in Him can His peace be found. In the trying days ahead, the one sure refuge is the Eternal God. He will be sought and found by those who have thought they had no special need for Him and that He was a bit old-fashioned!

In the times that are ahead, when things of sense and flesh over the world are undergoing radical change, the old-fashioned idea will not be very convincing! His power will shine forth as the one stronghold for mankind. His love will never fail those who seek and accept it. It will be as the sun for brilliance and its quality of comfort will be beyond compare.

I realize that you wish me to tell you when these changes will occur. If I could, I would not tell you. For people would be unhorsed if they knew particulars which are not for the human but are only in the keeping of the Father. In wisdom that is infinite, He withholds knowledge that would not be helpful to mankind.

Trust Him in this and in everything. Know that His way is best and leave all matters that are of natural, earthly curiosity, to the care of the Spirit Planes. It is better so. Your part is to stay attuned with Him, to keep centered upon the Rock of His strength and power and love. His blessings rest always upon you!

NO LIGHT

Dark outside, did you say? Often it is for one who is living his earth life in the midst of darkness that enshrouds. But outside darkness is superficial. It concerns only the material and the things of material nature. The life that really matters is not of the outside.

So the darkness of which I heard you speak, matters only transiently, concerned with things that of themselves are passing. It is the inside that is more important than you can dream. And never need there be darkness of any kind in the life that is within. For always the true Light shines, overcoming any tendency of the human to yield to appearance of darkness.

The life within is made perfect by the conscious presence of the Father in Whom is no darkness. There where He dwells the Light shines more and more unto the perfect day. The inner life knows the beauty and grace and deep satisfaction of those qualities of spirit that are true and good and honorable, in none of which does darkness abide. The darkness that is without is a matter of passing clouds that hang low.

So why be fretted about this which really is unimportant? A few lights visible seem to be companionable. But when they are not visible, you know that you may always function in the Light which never fails and that is not subject to mortal conditions. Release from your consciousness all thought of no light here or there in the outside world. Keep your thought joyously concentrated on the inner life within your soul where no gloom need ever penetrate or cast its shadow over your life. The Light that is God is the very essence of beauty and power and life. Its shining is radiance beyond compare. Your heart may always know its effulgence, save when you allow earth-born clouds to shut it away.

This you should never do. This you need never do. Keep your life open to the brightness of His shining that will dispel any darkness as it comes swooping down terrifyingly. When you see signs of such darkness, turn within your heart and let His Light have full sweep. It will irradiate every feeling of fear. And you will go free!

FREE!

Earth residents often say they "are so busy!" I remember how it was when I was among you. Frequently I was too busy with temporal affairs. Could it be that some of you may also qualify under that heading? My question is for your answer within your heart. What answer you give, is important to your own unfoldment!

On these Inner Planes, our every power is intensely concentrated on learning and serving. From these two, life as we here experience it, becomes radiant indeed. We wonder how to grow as rapidly as we yearn to do, to compass all which we wish to do and to be. It is most wonderful to be uninhibited by things and unhampered by time!

Where you live there on the planet of earth, how cramped it seems to us who have been freed from it. Nor can you understand what freedom for living really means until you come hither and feel the essence of it permeating every fiber of your being.

We are free of every obstruction, free to soar to heights of knowledge and wisdom and love as rapidly as we can absorb them. This is thrilling to realize and to experience. It is life glorious and significant in the ultimate, in eternal beauty, without littlenesses that clutter the living of earth and make it difficult at best.

These things I say that you who remain a little longer on the physical plane may understand why I so often say, "There Is No Death!" It is life transcendent here; to anticipate; to prepare for; and in no wise to fear or dread. The orthodox earth teaching about death is not justified. Please trust me about this. If it were not true, I would not speak these words.

If only people of earth would drop their incorrect concept of this marvelous Transition which opens the gates of Living to glory and radiance as earth does not conceive! Death? No! Life unending, active, progressing, filled with challenges and continuing development! You remember how I hated death while I was of earth and how I shrank from it. Much is wrong with earth teaching when one lives the years of my earth life and does not have the true concept of life beyond the Veil, presented so convincingly that he cannot fail to accept it.

No teaching was ever given me while I was in the physical vehicle to help me understand the wordless glories of this Transition which I made so suddenly and which burst upon my wondering spirit like a blaze of incomparable light. This is one reason why these Messages from the heart of the Inner Planes are put forth through you for teaching mankind who yet must face and experience this crossing from earth to Glory Shores.

They are of tremendous significance and carry the weight of Infinite sanction. Every time you relieve a human heart of dread of the Transition, you have rendered service worthy of more than earth can give. I bless you with joy and gratitude for your participation in this cosmic task.

ON TOP OF THE LOAD

I heard you as your thoughts framed themselves within your mind, though unexpressed in spoken words. Word for you tonight is, "Oh, rest in the Lord!" Let His promises uphold you; His love encompass you; His strength gird you for each day; His goodness satisfy you; His greatness lift you to higher levels of experience and faith! Let Him be all to you! And just rest!

While you are working in a physical sense, rest your heart and your spirit upon Him. And be content. Don't carry things of your earth world as loads. Don't let them weigh you down. Nothing of earthly life is worth that. You must learn to get on top of the load and rest while it carries you, instead of being underneath, where it bids fair sometimes to crush you. Just rest in the Lord. It will do wonderful things for your spirit and rejuvenate your body more than I can reveal.

The joy of the Lord is your strength. But where is that joy when you are down under some load instead of riding high upon it and knowing that it has no power over you? His joy overflows at slightest opportunity, fills your life and runs over in great, refreshing streams to fructify your spirit and make of your life one wonderful manifestation of His glory. It will work if you go about it right and keep on about it. His joy is such stimulant as earth does not know from other source.

It is like the freshness of a mountain stream on a sultry, heavy day. There is tonic in it and life in it and power to go on without giving up. It is like the cool, soft breeze that blows in when the day has been hot and evening falls. In that breeze there is such quality of strength that one forgets the heat of the day.

His joy is the best sedative of which I can tell you. So move up into more intimate companionship with His joy, my friend. Sense the warmth of it and the vibrant, thrilling quality of it as it fills your heart. Your body will be made anew and as your spirit sings, will respond in rhythm with all the grace the Lord gave it at the creation. Resting is not indolence nor lack of ambition. Resting in the Lord will mean more energy, more desire to achieve big things, more power in accomplishment and more lilt as you work, than could ever come with the stress of sheer will power.

He is a more wonderful Lord than the spirits of those longest on these Planes can conceive. How then shall earth people know Him except in the smaller dimensions which earth permits? It makes it so essential for you who are enwrapped with the garment of the flesh and who toil at physical tasks, to let His joy fold you close, His rest pervade your tired body and His peace be very real to you.

I know what it will do for you and what glad recompense it will be to you when you come Home to be forever with the Lord.

Leave everything with Him. He is equal! Listen for His clear, still, lovely Voice as He tells you the path to follow and the goal to achieve. He will, if you will! Never doubt that!

All of this has grown out of that wonderful sentence which I quoted at the first of my Message—Rest in the Lord. He is the most precious Companion you can choose and I commend Him to you in close and dear comradeship along the journey which will lead you here to us.

May He rest you and fill you with His joy supreme. I go now. So often I come. And I keep close guard over you. Amen!

CRESTS AND TROUGHS

Speaking sea-wise, between crests of the waves lies the deep, ominous trough whose walls of water threaten to crash down in awful deluge, if you are caught in the trough. In terms of life, I suggest you keep away from the trough, but remember the high and sunlit crest sparkling with myriad spots of light.

On the crests, sun and wind have room to play in the glancing beauty of grace of motion and inimitable freedom. If I seem to speak figuratively, I grant it. But what I am saying, applies as well to human life as to the open seas. Down under in the deep troughs, the going is dangerously hard. As you see this in terms of your earth lessons, you will make steadier progress upward.

Earth's problems, many of them perplexing, all have solutions that can be right and good. For back of these problems are definite purpose and plan. Sometimes it is difficult to find them. On our Sunny Planes of Life, we learn to look for inner meanings and apply what we learn to the next lessons that come to us.

When our solutions appear, we know we are the stronger for the part we played in finding them. It will be so with you, too. Nobody finds these solutions for us. Get this point! We do it for ourselves. Nothing is done for us on the Inner Planes which we can do for ourselves. Otherwise it would not long be heaven, for tedium would bear us down.

All of this is part of the greatness of life over where I now live, because we learn better than we did on earth, the glory of doing for ourselves and for others. In the flesh, it was temptation to let some one do for us what we did not feel like doing for ourselves. Many spoiled people, adults and children, result from this way of doing.

Here no one is pampered, though the most gracious help is offered where it is needed. On this side of life, we learn not to exaggerate difficulties. We do not blow up small issues into big ones, as often earth people do. The way it is here is better. I hope you of earth will earnestly follow it.

The benedictions of the Father enrich every phase of your life and His peace fill your heart. Keep always to the high crests where the sun shines and beauty abounds!

YOUR PATTERNS FOR LIVING

When you are tired of lessons and disciplines, change your thinking and rest your mind a while. Remember your school days when sometimes lessons were hard for you. But there they were, whether you liked them or not. Then came examinations that proved how well or how poorly you had mastered the lessons.

In the Realm of Spirit there are systems, teachers, studies, tests which everyone who wishes to progress spiritually, must take. Here you have the blessed privilege of studying deeply into Truth, at the Fountain of All Wisdom and Understanding.

As your soul grows, you become aware of vast reaches of knowledge and wisdom ahead for you. Raptures of grateful worship and love to the Father will swell within you. Even while you are of earth, the more you sing praises to the Father, the richer your life becomes. Do not fail in this. It is important to your spiritual life, while you are in the flesh; increasingly so the higher you move toward these Planes of Unhampered Understanding.

Whatever comes, give thanks for it. Be grateful because you are learning that it is what you yourself ordered. It is made according to the pattern of cosmic law. You are wise to follow closely the pattern that is divine. Rejoice in its perfect design, even when you do not understand it.

Give ringing thanks for His goodness, never letting any cloud obscure the vision of the goal toward which you aspire. Let your faith in Him flame forth, lifting you high in consciousness. It will be worth everything to you, now and eternally. Off now.

IT IS NOT ESCAPE

I stand here beside you as I give you a brief, important word. Life on this side of the Veil does not experience the heartaches and disappointments of which earth knows so desperately well.

We do know the deep regrets which result from realizing that we made less use than we should, of our opportunities for spirit growth and understanding and service to others while we lived in the flesh. This we see vividly and unmistakenly after we have made the Great Transition.

Life on this side though, is worth all the patience, the faith, the love, the willingness to learn that it can cost the earth person. If I could, I would gladly open it before your eyes that you might eagerly anticipate your coming hither. But I may not. You could neither understand nor endure it, if I did. It is with the wisdom of the Infinite that the line is drawn between life where we are and life on the earth plane. The important aspect of your life is loyalty to all which is yours to do, to learn and to be, while you remain in the physical vehicle, knowing as much as seems wise to tell you of life on this side, and trusting the rest.

There are those who would push off from the shores of time and head out for these Realms of Immortality, before they have learned their lessons there, hoping thus to escape the hard experiences of the physical and more speedily to acquire the larger sweep of life over here.

This is in error. Coming that way, they find they must begin exactly where the left off on earth, every lesson to learn to the full, every discipline to accept and to incorporate into the fabric of the soul. This which is often considered the way of escape, simply does not escape!

This lesson so seriously needed to be put before people of earth that we determined upon this channel for teaching it. As we have here given it, is the Divine order, right and good and perfect.

NOTHING JUST HAPPENS

There is no chance. Everything comes by a cosmic law that men call cause and effect. Many who are affected by what they say "happens," do not know this law nor do they have any idea of the sequence of causation. They see only the effects which either they like or do not like.

But in every case, a chain of circumstances operated, on material, mental or spiritual levels, moving from one step to the next and bringing the sure result. The cause is the thing which you should always watch because it is what sets up the chain of activities that bring the effect. No changing this law!

The word, the thought, the seemingly insignificant act or desire need gearing to the highest standard of which you are capable so that causes you set in motion through your daily living may bring effects you will rejoice to experience.

If you accept only what is worthy into the fabric of your life as causes, you will avoid many heartaches and sorrows that heap the shoulders of mankind so heavily.

Remember always that effect follows its cause. You need pay small heed to the effect. But pay infinite heed to each cause lest you set in motion influences certain to bring you misery and grief.

Bear this in mind constantly as you meet the problems of your world and it will step you steadily higher. Causes often seem trifling. But they bring momentous effects, for good or for bad. You can not change the effects. But you can change the causes.

From the Inner Planes we see men of earth unthinkingly set causes into motion; then we watch their impotent amazement when they see what they have done. They have not considered that every result comes from the working of unerring laws which they allowed to get started and which then got beyond control.

Sometimes, indeed often, effects are of the nature of light and joy. Sometimes they are as trying as a rash of poison ivy which gets a head start. Causes are often treacherous because by their seeming smallness, they look harmless, then get out of control before you realize what is happening.

Now I must be off for other parts of the universe where help is needed. May the richest blessings of the Great, Good God be with you day and night; and may you never lose the conscious sense of His presence and the sweet peace of His love. Good night!

YOUR PROTECTION

Daniel was as human as any man who ever lived. But there was a difference. He paid no attention to the lions even when he was locked in the den with them. They could have done with him at one swoop. And he knew it. He didn't think much about them because his heart was stayed on God!

Divine protection like a garment surrounded him because he was conscious of the Holy Presence with him every moment. He knew the God to Whom he prayed many times daily, was constantly with him. He was on close and intimate terms with his God and knew he was protected from all danger.

In this way of prayer, Daniel literally clothed himself with the might of the divine until the ravenous beasts had no power over him. If Daniel had kept his thoughts on the lions or feared them or given them ever so little power, they would have been at him like a tawny flash. And Daniel knew it!

But God was the saving factor. He is now. His power never loses the infinite all-protectiveness that avails. Get my point clearly. Because Daniel put his entire trust in his God, he was completely protected from danger that was very real. For you today, there is the same God; the same power. But you must use it!

Here is a word That will help you: "In all thy ways acknowledge Him," not acknowledging any influences that could harm you, giving them no least power over you and never permitting your inward calm to be threatened. Instead, "In all thy ways acknowledge Him!" Put Him on as a garment, and go your way in quietness of heart knowing that "He shall direct thy paths." Whatever turmoil swirls around you, you have the same God, the same power of protection that Daniel had.

I leave you now, praying you to wrap around your very self the glory of His All-protection and you go free of every anxiety through knowing that He does indeed direct your paths. Let storms rage! Winds howl! Problems of earth thrash about you! Pay no heed. Keep your heart centered in Him. Thus you will experience the secret of Daniel's protection against those hungry lions.

The peace of God suffice you; His presence undergird you; His glory shine round about you; His love rest your heart; His blessing be your benediction. Amen!

SUFFICIENCY

Please try to realize the tremendous scope of that word; then to know that the Father is sufficient; for your every need; for your entire life! Can you of earth ask more? Sufficient! It matters not what your need is, He is the sufficiency. That means that in Him there is no lack whatsoever. If people of earth would actually realize that, living would be transformed.

If fear torments your heart, He is the sufficiency of courage so that you go free of whatever might otherwise bear you down. If dread of the future stares at you like a specter, you may know that the Father is the utter sufficiency of protection and you have nothing to dread.

Think of it, never need there be any lack in your life, not any! Wonderful indeed is this Infinite provision for His children of earth. If sometimes you wonder how to make ends meet—I well remember that recurring problem from my years on earth—just know that His supply is ready for meeting the situation in ways that satisfy.

No child of the Father need ever lack any good thing, if he asks in faith, then opens his heart to receive that which meets the need. This asking in faith is part of the cosmic law and may not be overlooked. Remember how that vast throng hungered on a day when the Master was speaking to them of eternal issues and there seemed no food for them.

Then the lad's two tiny fishes and his few small loaves which the Master blessed in faith and lo, from the invisible storehouse came sufficient to feed the thousands and leave generous remaining resources for others.

Are you sad at heart, your days seeming wrapped in darkness of aloneness? His comfort is sufficient; He has balm for the wounded spirit and His Joy fills the heart that realizes Him as the Giver of all good. If your body suffers pain and refuses to function, you may remember how He said, "I am the Lord that healeth thee!" His love is the mightiest healing remedy earth has ever known, and never a shortage to plague any one who seeks the healing flow.

From these Inner Planes where now I live and serve, we rejoice as we see countless earth people whose supplies of many kinds run low, then we see them in simple, powerful faith ask the Father to open the doors of His sufficiency, that their needs may be met. The very heavens seem to open and good pours down upon them, because faith has knocked on the doors of His infinite storehouse. Where there had been distress and sometimes even despair, we see light hearts because the Father has again proved His sufficiency, His good has manifested and lack has been destroyed.

Whatever your life needs for perfect balance, He is your complete sufficiency. We see it here in such lavish and radiant glory and we long for each of you to prove Him in His way of perfect supply when with faith and your own earnest endeavor you ask Him to supplement your supplies when you are bond your depth; then you reach out to receive His overflowing sufficiency. He never fails!

WON'T YOU TRY IT?

Faith is your sure anchor, whatever storm rages or fear tears at your heart. Take faith for all it is worth. Depend upon it. Cultivate it. Give it opportunity to work its great miracles in your life. Beautiful radiance surrounds this faith which is at its best when you need it most.

Earth props do not work this way. But faith is of the spirit and blossoms into beauty and power when you turn to it as your mainstay. You are never in a place so difficult but that faith helps you through and brings you out into larger life.

Some day you will rejoice to see the honor roll—if I may speak of it thus—of those of earth who have proved the power of this faith. It is most wonderful to realize something of its greatness and the far-flung range of its values down the long ages. You just can't go wrong when you companion with this mighty spiritual grace. It is strong. It is always at hand. It never wears out nor wearies nor leaves you!

Faith is like the staff which mountain climbers use on stiff stretches of trail, comfortable and safe to lean upon, giving you complete assurance of such spirit help as you need. Nothing is ever too stiff an assignment for faith to carry through!

If you would stake every hope and ambition and need which life poses you, on the power of faith to see you through, marvels would come to pass in your life. Let yourself go completely where faith is involved. It simply will never let you down, when you meet it on its own terms of cooperation.

You can trust faith with everything of your life and know you will come through with spiritual banners flying. Do, I pray you! Off now for other work, my blessings abiding with you to help and strengthen you and all who read these words.

POWERS OF PRAISE

There is no greater tonic for your spirit than giving thanks and praising Him Who is the Great God, pouring out gratitude and adoration and worship through prayer and through your living and serving. Somehow this eliminates the dark forces of envy and suspicion, jealousy and intolerance and hatred and in their place, gives new power to purity and the glory of being true followers of Him Who is Supreme.

This way of life is the deeply grateful way, the powerful way that strengthens the soul for such living as can withstand the tests which earth imposes upon each one. Give thanks unto Our Lord even when days are dark and you can not see your way. Just know that He sees your way! Pour out your gratitude to Him because He said it was His good pleasure to give you the kingdom. And He never goes back on His word.

Being grateful even while your skies are dark with uncertainty, calls for mightiness of faith that will not be denied. But none other is the sure way to achieve. It is the way to progress along the ascending spiral of life from earth to celestial realms. To praise the Father at all times, regardless of clouds lowering above you, lifts you into the high consciousness where you know life is good and nothing else matters much except to be His efficient, loyal follower.

There are those of earth who yield Him praise and thanksgiving in a lukewarm manner as something that is their duty, without depth of feeling or genuine emotion of joy in it. So it is worth little less than nothing. Others choose rites and ceremonies that are formal expressions of inward feeling. Who shall say these are not good? Any thanksgiving is good.

But gushing springs of joy and gratitude and praise from a heart so full that it can no longer restrain its feelings for the Father, are springs of deep-flowing power that can meet and overcome days that are difficult, heartaches that are unexpected, and ways that are forbidding. The soul will surge upward when despite earthly setbacks, you wholeheartedly trust Him and praise and bless Him for His loving kindness and His tender mercies to you.

Use the irresistible power of faith to gird your spirit against halfhearted expressions of gratitude when you should be singing praises and glory to Him for His wonderful works and His unfailing goodness to you.

Make this expression of your glowing gratitude a vital part of your worship and adoration, be your day dark or light. And keep knowing that His infinite goodness manifests for you every moment in greater profusion of blessings than your mind can comprehend. Accept it all in humble gratitude and overflowing adoration. Live in the atmosphere of praise to Him and rejoice always in His unlimited power of grace and goodness to you!

GLIMPSES OF GLORY

I rejoice to tell you more about these Heavenly Planes where we live, who have come from the earth plane. I knew nothing of the highly organized and active life which is the portion of those who come to this happy side of life. In this series, I am omitting mention of those who come from the material body unprepared for spirit life. Elsewhere I have spoken of them.

I was amazed when first I came, at the atmosphere of divine and enveloping peace. It surrounded me and was as it were, part of the landscape. I could not describe it. I cannot now. But I thrilled to it. There was none of the tension of earth, none of the striving after something unattainable, but only the beautiful inward knowing of peace that comes from the Father God.

Everything upon which my new eyes rested seemed—how shall I say this so you can understand it?—as if it were softer than the silkiest velvet of earth, no harsh surface anywhere. Everything had a quality that "softness" does not describe but I find no word which does describe it; heavenly peace everywhere.

If only men on earth comprehended this peace within the heart, they would eagerly wish to slough off the harsh, strident, aggressive self-seeking and rest their hearts in this divinity of peace. It is neither negative nor weak, but has all the qualities of strength which one needs in this active world of spirit. This peace goes to the depths of one's being and reflects His infinite peace Who is the Fountainhead of eternal peace.

It is compounded of power and love and understanding and unselfishness and all the qualities that are like God. I wish I could make it clear to you as a foretaste of what you will someday experience! The more earnestly you seek peace and pursue it while you are in the flesh, no matter what the environment or the problem, the more fully will you open your being to this inflow of the heavenly, all-enveloping peace which fills these realms. Earlier in this talk with you, a phrase slipped into a sentence which I had not meant to use, but which tumbled out through the channel of my thought and came to you—"everything upon which my new eyes rested!—" Doesn't that give you insight into one of the most marvelous aspects of life here? It means that everything which on the earth plane has been difficult and imperfect, is transformed here into perfection of functioning in which all is as it should be.

You know so well how difficult my struggle was with the old eyes which performed so small a part of what eyes should do and for years, no part at all, and you know how hard that made my earth living the last score of earth years. But my new eyes! Instantly upon my arrival on these Blessed Planes, my new eyes saw clearly, completely, full-circle-round. You well know what I mean. I saw above and below, to right and left, visions of consuming beauty. Faces of my former friends stood out clear and distinct. The glow surrounding each one was easily visible and the glory of the landscape filled my new eyes so that I almost forgot how difficult it had been to see even a little while I was on the earth plane.

How well I remember that first day as I spoke to you through your first receiving station. You were so eager to know whether I could see again and I replied—I wanted to shout to you!—"I can see as well as a youth of twenty." I shall never forget that sentence, into which went pent-up emotions of long and weary years of my inability to see!

The eager, humming activity of these Inner Planes was another surprise which did not harmonize a bit with what I had been taught about the spirit world. It is gloriously true and never palls upon us. We work at many things we knew how to do with earth dexterity, then we move into greater skills using new creative power which here is immensely stepped up and aids us in every way we need.

Here we learn much of scientific knowledge which is hidden to us while we are of earth. The mysterious and wondrous functioning of mind and spirit opens to us here from the Source of all wisdom. Such surprise, such joy it was and inspiration beyond compare! All of it is another way of saying "God!"

THE MASTER'S WAY

The time is at hand to open the current channel of thought along which unchangeable truth may flow and through which life may be nourished and enriched. Advanced spirits on the Upper Planes from whom these Messages come, understand whither this talk trends. The present confused life of the world is a time when political and commercial propaganda flourish; likewise spiritual propaganda, if you accept that incongruous phrase. Anyone may easily be engulfed in what sometimes is pseudo-wisdom or esoteric interpretations which could sink one.

Remember! Spirit wisdom is simple in expression. It is easy of understanding, however vast the truth at the heart of it. "The wayfaring man though a fool, shall not err therein," you recall. The words of Christ were as simple as childhood's language though He dealt with eternal verities and was Supreme Guide for mankind. Simple. Reasonable. Helpful. Balm to grieving hearts. Light on darkened paths.

He taught of the will of the Father, of the wisdom of the ages since the creation of the universe, of the divine plan for mankind upward toward heights of unlimited spirit unfoldment. He illustrated by taking a little child in His arms. He taught this way to His disciples who were plain, simple men, more accustomed to manual toil than to splitting phrases.

He spoke no word difficult to understand sufficiently for human good. Take Him anew as your model, your exemplar. Follow the line of His thinking. Go with Him in all the simplicity of His grandeur of wisdom and life. Then you cannot go astray nor lose yourself in quagmires of systems which not always are based clearly on the words of the Infinite. It is easy to make the way hard! In His matchless power, He cut away much of the rubbish that had cluttered the minds of men for eons and pointed them to clear truth of Infinite wisdom.

Follow His way, always! It is this way, His way, which we seek to make plain to you through whom we speak from these Ether Planes of Higher Knowledge and Power.

Enough of this now. Other work awaits me and I hasten to it, knowing it is His service.

NO RESENTMENTS

Do you realize what it means when you ask to be freed of every unworthy and unjust thought, every resentment and taint of selfishness, every low motive? You remember when the Psalmist prayed to be cleansed of secret faults. It means major surgery now, as it did then. For these influences are part of your very life fiber. When I say "you" I am not being personal to any one.

You then, have held selfishness in your heart, saying whenever you thought of it, that you are just watching out for "number one." And you felt justified. When you have been unfair in your judgment of some one else, you say you are being frank and saying just what you think. When you blaze with resentment, you say so-and-so did something that was not fair and you do not care who knows what you think.

Am I remembering how the earth person often reacts? I seem to remember too clearly, for many times my reactions were similar to these I just hint here. Sadly I remember when on the earth plane, in the heat of feeling, I did not desire to be cleansed of those secret faults.

There were times when David forgot his prayer for cleansing. But those were not his high moments. Nor were they mine. Nor are they yours. Times when we mount highest in God-consciousness are when we see these faults as flaws in our souls; where the pattern does not run true; where dark shows instead of shining light; where warped judgment does not keep geared to truth and love and God; where earthiness shows instead of purity of the spirit.

When you see these places where threads of life are tangled and knotted and snarled, the weaving spoiled and colors blurred, you do not feel so sure that these things matter little. For they matter tremendously in the pattern of life which you are weaving and which will endure always.

These are not little things. Nothing is little which affects life and its standards, on earth or here on the Spirit Planes. Is there something which we here may say to bring these human patterns into focus for your clear seeing and deep understanding? Earth residents say so lightly that they are just upsurgings from fires of quick temper that set you saying and thinking what except for that sudden heat, you would not say or think. Deep hurts are inflicted and resentment begins to pound like pus in a wound which indicates poison that must be gotten rid of, for your safety.

Cleansing is often drastic. No surgeon cleanses a carbuncle by merely washing the surface of the skin. He goes deep to the core of the trouble and calls it a good job only when all poison is gone and the wound is surgically clean. The same principle applies to the spirit. Whatever the flaws of character, they need cleansing, so your spirit may grow in love and service and power.

Measure everything by His standards. Follow His way. Live by His spirit of love. Let humility and harmony, love and unselfishness and understanding and justice take the place of the negative qualities we have been discussing. Then resentment will not throb, puny impatience will not spoil your days nor unjust snap judgment be passed on any one.

This experience of cleansing gives far more to life than it takes away. God bless and keep you and may His joy brighten every day for you!

SOME ONE PRAYS

Relaxation of body, of mind and spirit, is a requisite for the successful functioning of these electrical impulses along the ether waves on which the Messages go from us to you. When the human is tense with anxiety or displeasure or grief or with just plain nerves, as I well remember, it is like a high wall that shuts out the potency of help which we would like to give. I know. For I recall from my latest earth span, how difficult it is to be inwardly calm when the circle of one's experience is in tumult.

But it can be done! The whole being takes the Father at His word and casts whatever the burden upon Him. Then the tempest quiets! The door to your inner life opens for the incoming of such comfort from these Spirit Planes as you need.

Sit in quietness and confidence the next time you feel life begin to churn within you. Open the door to your heart and ask for His Divine peace. Realize that always the spiritual is stronger than the earthy and that evil is overcome of good when your complete trust is in Him.

Marvelous experiences in proof of this abound, where apparently favorable outcome has looked impossible. But some one prays! Some one, with utter faith, talks to the Father and is assured that He knows the way to go. Some one lays the entire responsibility upon Him and quietly trusts Him.

Miraculously, men say, results accrue that seemed impossible. But some one has prayed! With faith; with abandon; with the power that develops from deep knowledge of the Father God! With implicit confidence in help from Spirit which transcends all other help in the universe.

In times of anxiety, remember: Don't worry. Don't fear. Pray. Believe. Leave it all to Him when once you have committed it to Him. When you think you cannot keep from worrying, pray instead. Pray as earnestly as you would worry. Results will amaze you. And they will all be for your good.

When seemingly some one proves disloyal or unworthy, let not that shake your faith nor turn loose a flood of pity of yourself. What should you do under such circumstances? Wrap that one round about with the mantle of your genuine forgiveness. Pray God's forgiveness of him. Ask infinite, continued blessing to rest upon his every good effort. And look for early ways in which you can offer constructive help to him.

Never preen yourself on your goodness. The human is prone to do it. Rather thank the Father that He has taught you how to overcome evil with good. Let this good build you up strongly in ways of Spirit. Never does good come from worry. All good comes of faith. And prayer. And committing the load to the Father. All good!

Suddenly you will find your clouds passed and the sun shining for you. We pray that all of you in the flesh will learn always to keep the wheel of your thoughts and emotions under positive and constructive control. When you let negative influences take hold, it is as if you pour fuel upon the flames. Put all your thinking on the affirmative side of prayer and you will starve out evil influences for lack of any oxygen of encouragement.

The God of all peace and all grace, of all love and all might, be with you in conscious presence. May He guide your thinking, your act-ing, your feeling and bring you through each day in closer walk with Him. Amen!

THERE IS NO DEATH

It is of life and the Great Transition that I would speak with you. Many earth people mistakenly call it death. While we are of earth, we often think it is the end of everything. We grieve. We mourn. We wear black, all smiles withdrawn. What may I say from these Inner Planes to convince earth people that this Transition is in no wise death? There is no death! Not even the body dies. It changes. The Transition merely means moving oneself and one's interests from one home to another, adjusting to a new life that is satisfying, stimulating and in every way glorious.

It bears no mark of death save that the worn-out garment which often becomes troublesome, is laid aside. Nature takes care of that in its wonderful way, altering the chemical and physical properties of that worn-out garment into other forms which are again used for the work of life in the material universe.

When the garment is new, the principle is the same. It is putting aside something frail and transient, subject to pain and distress and decay, for the priceless privilege of gaining that which can know no suffering, no lessening of strength, no slowing down of vital processes, no growing old.

The sense of separation is the heartbreak. But earth people are learning that we who have "died" are alert and alive since we left the narrow, limited life and began the new life that is growth and the glory of learning and serving, which we could not conceive while we wore our garments of the flesh.

You of earth are proving in increasing degree that heaven is right where you are and that we who wear our beautiful garments of spirit are with you, that we talk with you, protect and guide and inspire you.

This life on the other side of the Veil is infinitely radiant beyond what we called life when we were clothed in the old robes which often did not fit us nor give us comfort. The robes we wear now are of beauty and glory. As we grow in spirit stature, they become more radiant and shining, with colors beyond compare. None of this sounds like death, does it? Because it is not!

This life on the Inner Planes is the perfection of the Father's love, life at its best as the Lord of All created it, that His children may grow from one height of spirit understanding to higher planes of love and service.

Won't you of earth just know that your beloveds are not "gone," but are in and out among you as you work; and that you give them joy when they see you adjusting to the changed order with light in your eyes and courage in your hearts; when they see faith in your living and eager anticipation girding your spirit for the day when you too will reach these Planes of Light, laying aside the weight and weariness of the flesh, ready for the new joys that await you? For thus it is!

THE RULE OF LIFE

I would like to talk with you about something as necessary to the good life as breath is to the lungs. Obey this rule and you live joyously, with good coming your way. It is The Golden Rule, not of man's making, but spoken by the Master of Men on the Mount when He said, "All things whatsoever ye would that men should do unto you, do ye even so to them. For this is the law."

When this Golden Rule is the measuring rod against which all actions are squared, life takes on tones of rightness and fairness and God-likeness which lift it out of the dull and drab, into the bright shining of joy.

Think with me for a moment, what it means to obey this Rule of Life. It means never to take advantage of any one else in any bargain or transaction, business or social, which you would not wish some one to take of you; never to show jealousy toward any one nor give him occasion to suffer any unfairness from you, unless you desire your own heart to suffer the same way.

This Golden Rule which Jesus gave the world as He spoke on that famous Mount, is basic to all good living. No one can live at his best unless he is in harmony with it and with all that it means. You do not wish any one to shower hate or revenge or intolerance upon you, even though conceivably you might deserve it. Therefore are you at liberty to show hatred or vengeance or intolerance or pettiness to any one else?

What does The Rule say to you? It does not make any difference how sincerely you think you are justified in being hateful or intolerant or unfair or spiteful to anyone! Whatever you have sent to that other person in act or thought, you may expect to take as the ball of life rebounds to you.

This so-great-and-good Rule reaches out into your thinking and means that you should send to others only such thoughts as you wish them to send to you. This would change many lives if everyone would live up to it. For this Golden Rule is woven into every thought you think and into every act you perform, however alone you may be.

In the affairs of state and nation, there stands The Golden Rule which state and nation obey or refuse to obey. On one hand, it brings blessing and prosperity to that government which obeys it. With equal certainty, it brings discord and disharmony, dissension and strife upon any government which refuses to recognize this Rule of doing to the other person or nation, what it wishes to experience for itself.

The Rule works just this way. Always! It reaches out into every activity of every business and into the affairs of every family circle, bringing joy and peace and harmony when members of the family do to the other members what, in principle, they wish the others to do to them.

Domestic tragedy would not exist if people lived by this Rule, taking nothing from any one which they would not wish taken from them, living each day by this simple, powerful Golden Rule which is the foundation of all good living. At the bottom of the present world tension and unrest and bitterness, is the fact that people have not obeyed this Golden Rule. They have done to other people and nations what they did not want and do not want other people and nations to do to them. So as individuals and as a world, you take the consequences!

When mankind is willing to take this Rule of the Master of Men into their hearts, at its face value, and see in it the solution of what is wrong with the world, just and lasting peace will come to bless the world and end the warring fury which has blazed through the centuries. Take this to heart, all you who read. Let this Golden Rule in its radiance, work in your life. Then see what marvels come to pass within you. And in others!

ABOUNDING LIFE

Few people of earth see beyond personal points of view to Universal Principles that underlie all living. For them everything revolves around personal desires and ambitions. To the degree that this is so, life is small instead of ranging boldly into higher realms and taking on elements of true greatness.

When their personal viewpoints do not gain the limelight of prominence, the ego suffers and situations become difficult. I remember all about it from my days on earth. This is one of the littlenesses that complicate living. Otherwise man would develop on lines that are good, regardless of personal ambition.

The problem is increasingly difficult where the ego is overdeveloped and the individual thinks his wishes should be supreme, with small regard for others' desires and emotions. The one who sees beyond selfish desire and subordinates himself to the higher good that is in harmony with Infinite Principle, is panoplied with power and protected for service on every level of his earth life.

Little minds that see only themselves and their wishes, blow themselves out in great gusts whenever the personal is overridden, gusts that are not harnessed to power for great living or achieving. It is always your privilege to stretch your mind beyond the limited personal to the vastness of the impersonal where Eternal Principle functions in perfect impartiality and justice.

Helpers from the Ether Planes, invisible to physical sight, are potent in all such issues with great influence for good and right and God. They help you with your problems and seek to teach you to look beyond the personal and the selfish to the radiance of the impersonal and the universal. We of the invisible world are with you every day, touching every phase of your earthly experience and raising your consciousness to higher levels.

Count on us increasingly. It is our joy and glory to help you grow tall spiritually. And may the God of All Love be constantly close to you. Amen!

RACE TRACKS AND FURROWS

Life is like a race. The first few laps are easy. But the going grows harder and the running stiffer. Then it becomes a test of the endurance that stays in and sees it through. This quality of perseverance does not belong to those who look for the spectacular. It does belong to those who are eager for eternal values.

It means keeping at it until the race is won, making ready for stiffer races on Spirit Planes. To all of this perseverance is geared. You should see it as part of the Infinite plan by which the soul grows and takes on rarer qualities of perfection which someday will show like God.

I remember when I was a resident of earth, that we used to refer to this sort of thing as plugging. We demurred at it. We felt that plugging belonged to the slow-going plough horse while our gifts and powers belonged to the race track. There the going was swift, spectacular, brilliant. There applause would greet our running!

Well I remember those feelings. I remember the murmurings in my heart at the many furrows that were mine to cultivate out of which what crops were raised, must be by my keeping eternally at it. I failed in those days to see that the plough horse and the furrow were akin to the race horse and the fast track!

Each has his stint to cover, over and over, his schedule, a cycle of time allotted. One has as many hurdles as the other, each its own rewards. Winning depends on keeping to the course, plough horse or racer!

SUBTLE BUSINESS

Steadfastness is not particularly popular at present in your world. What does that matter in the long run? It has the essence of true greatness, its roots delving deep into the soil of spirit understanding, drawing their nourishment from springs of living water that never run dry.

On the whole, steadfastness is far better than the flightiness that runs hither and yon seeking satisfactions that are superficial. It comes into its own when the going is hard and the human yearns for greener pastures elsewhere. Then steadfastness is a pillar of strength.

This does not imply that it is never desirable to change from fields no longer promising. Take note of this difference, not letting yourself be too eager for winds of change to blow nor refusing to see the line between steadfastness and servility.

Steadfastness never means yielding to dry rot, neither does it fear to break away from the old when breaking away is clearly intended. Quite a point there! Wisdom is needed to see the median line between two "goods" so that you do not take the "good" when the "better" is open to you. This calls for careful discrimination while the human lives his earth life. It is subtle business!

Please realize that this is at the very core of the problem of earth living. Many of mankind's difficult adjustments Would not have gotten out of hand if he had sought for steadfastness and merged it with moderation in his human planning.

Some of the weightiest factors in the growth of the soul and the stabilization of the spirit are involved in this lesson. For the trend to extremes often leads mankind into dire straits. Do not let this steadfastness bog you down. Be willing to see when it is desirable to leave the good in favor of the better. Spiritual skill abides in that power of seeing and I commend it to you.

And now peace be unto you, joy within you as your consciousness of One-ness with the Father keeps you poised and confident in the steadfastness of His grace.

LIFE HERE AND THERE

Think life! Look life! Feel life! Be life! For all is life! And there is no death! As often I have told you, millions of earth people shrink from what they call death and they fear it is the end of everything for them. In reality, it is the beginning of what is more beautiful, more satisfying, more wondrous in every way than the slow, painful, limited uncertainties that mark life in the physical body.

There are those for whom the Transition called death, does present awesome aspects, when they have broken the laws of God and man on earth, caring not for goodness and tolerance, for justice or mercy or humility and for whom the greatest of all, the law of love, has meant only lust and licentiousness and unbridled passion. For such as these, laying aside the material body is fraught with darkness instead of light, with surroundings of evil instead of the lightsomeness of truth and beauty. For these, the passing is an experience one might well dread, save that always even this is fraught with the infinite mercy of the Father.

No one however blackened his soul with the evil done in the body, but may ask for light from above and he will find it shining for him. It is a toilsome road back to goodness and truth, but ultimately that road will be travelled by every soul however corrupt at present it may be. For all the children of the Father who have sought to learn His laws and to live them in ways of rightness, the transition is nothing to dread.

I can not say this too often, I who so often said while I was of earth, that I hated death! With utmost ease, I learned how mistaken I was, for my transition was painless and with no anxious concern attached to it. Here where I now live, life is more radiant with beauty and joy and service than all the words of the world could express.

It is completely stimulating to drink at the Fountain of Pure Truth and learn the profound things of wisdom with never an error in our learning; to discover what a majestic experience it is to go on missions of helpfulness to the densest darkness of evil on earth, in the name of the Father and with the healing love of Christ.

Going thus, we are empowered to bless and cleanse and purify the understanding where ignorance had rooted and to plant the beautiful roses of love in the lives of them whose hearts had grown only the weeds of selfishness and appetite and craving for unholy power. Here, life at its best awaits all who come in simple eagerness of heart to worship and adore Him Whom they loved on earth. They will rejoice here in the raptures of freedom from all limitations, in the service and love that characterize life on these Inner Planes.

Never think death. It is nothing! Always think life. It is everything! And God the Father bless you in His Holy love, protecting you from all things untoward, leading you safely Home when your earth work is accomplished. Amen!

WHERE IT FINDS YOU

Service at its most vital may not be where you go looking for it. Perhaps you find it; perhaps not. The richest, most fruitful service finds you wherever you are! Be ready for it! The telephone bell may land it in your lap, or it may hold out appealing hands to you at the corner whither you go to post letters.

The point of sheer import is that you be alert to it and recognize it when you see it. You have had a long day of this unexpected sort of service. It has been mingled with good cheer but woven through the warp and woof of it, has run the gleaming golden strand of the spirit which shared the abiding certainties of faith that could only be helpfully imparted under such an aegis.

Give thanks for it, as for that early morning tinkle of the telephone bell. To surface thinking that was just a chat with a former friend. In reality, it was a field in a human heart where often the soil has seemed to be sterile. The morning evidences were clear that the sterile soil was showing the effect of careful cultivation, beginning to yield signs of harvest.

Give profound thanks for that! It is tremendously worth while. Every human heart offers rich soil for service in the name of the Father.

Be careful never to pass by any opportunity where you can serve for His sake and in His name. Through these open doors, life is developed that is rich in the power of faith and prayer and loyalty and love. Nothing on the heavenly planes is greater than these.

From our vantage points of clearer seeing, we watch as many of you go about the Father's business, sowing living seeds of God-love. These seeds are gifts from His store-house of unlimited good. But even these seeds will not germinate unless they are planted in the soil of the heart. You of earth are responsible for the planting!

We learn these lessons such as are put before you of earth. Often ours require us to go to farther-most parts of the universe. Your seeds usually are given to you for planting closer at hand. Either way, service in His name, proving the glory of sharing His wisdom and the bounty from His harvests, is the greatest joy life can give you.

Keep open mind to all such and never belittle any tiny seed for your sowing as of too small importance for your attention. Remember what I have often told you, that there is no great nor small to the Father. The motive is the deciding factor.

When you render even what you think is some tiny service, take heed to know that you offer it in consecration as upon His altar of worship in dedicated loyalty to Him, with not one single trace of selfish desire for personal glory.

When you do all as unto Him, an aura of such brilliance is imparted to your life as would amaze you, if you could see it. Some glad day, you will! Now turn to your rest, grateful for this great day of multiple service, crowned with the smile of His Holy approval. Amen in the spirit of radiance that pervades us on these High Planes!

TRUE LOVE

Since I came to this shining side of life, free from the limitations of the physical body, I have learned a thousand times more than in all the years I lived on earth. What have I learned? That question is as impossible to answer adequately as it is easy to ask. But I shall talk with you this evening about one which tops all others as a Treasure house of Wisdom and a Fountain of pure Truth, vast enough to occupy heart and soul for a millennium. This of which I speak to you is so overwhelmingly majestic that I lose myself in it, bathing my very soul in it as I seek to lose every vestige of earthiness, of denseness, of self-will, finding everything through losing everything!

This first of all is the creativity of love, the allness of love. Of this which definitely is a substance, the universes are made, the cohesive power of which holds together all things that it creates. This love is the very summit of life for every soul of every eon, however highly it evolves in God consciousness.

It relates man inseparably to his God and keeps him aspiring to greater nearness to the eternal Godhead. It transforms dense darkness of ignorance to the shiningness of galaxies of suns. It is the ideal after which all lesser loves are patterned.

I thought I knew something of the power of this love when I was of earth. But I learned then as a child who works only with the alphabet of the most tremendous power the universes know. Coming hither, I began to learn a little of what love, divine and infinite love, really is, its universality and its power beyond the brain of man to conceive.

When I have been here a million years, there will still be endless reaches of the might of God-love to learn and to experience. It is useless to try to compress it into earth words. For it can not be done! It is God and His majesty; His omnipotence; God and His Fatherhood and His tenderness; His understanding of the needs of the least of His creations! The three greatest words in language tell it as nearly as words can—God Is Love! Even they are but the preface of the great book of Eternal Love and Wisdom which is replete with the lovingness of God.

Really to know this in ways the human can, even when he has made the transition to realms of spirit, calls for experiencing this love which is worthy of archangels. But you should constantly reach out for more and always more of this love. It will make you over even while you live on your dense planet.

There are people living there who sometimes speak lightly of God-love as something they know about. Ask forgiveness if you have ever felt that light human way concerning this supreme influence that emanates from the Godhead.

Never let the word pass your lips save in atmosphere of worship and adoration, as if you were kneeling at the white shrine of the Holy of Holies within your heart, in His presence and by His grace. Seek to live the life in such beautiful humility as can prepare you for speaking the word which represents Him and His Holiness!

Another evening, I shall speak to you of a second mighty influence which is instrumental both on these High Planes and on earth, in transforming life. I bless you now with this Almighty love!

COSMIC UNIT

Men's thoughts are ranging wild, like frightened animals running, not knowing whither. Old bases of conduct and action are gone; old standards overturned and demolished; old dimensions wiped out of calculations. As yet mankind has found no secure snubbing post to which to fasten his thinking.

Logically he is frightened by this awe-full force which he has turned loose into the life of the world, so gigantic that the human cannot comprehend it. This atomic power unleashed in your world is one of the forces long known and studied here on our Planes of Knowledge. But the very fact of it is churning men's minds out of all semblance to quiet, orderly procedure. It is the most revolutionary physical factor ever projected into the world. No wonder man ponders what he has done!

When the human race really settles down to study how to harness this which is unleashed, for the good of the world and not for destruction of civilization, there will sweep over the minds of men a mighty consciousness of the sanctity of this cosmic force. It will be as the unveiling of the Father's face; as divine revealing of the illimitable radiations by which the world came into being at His Word, radiations that control the structure of this universe.

Never before has man come so close to handling the creative power of God! No wonder he is frightened and stands in awe. He begins to realize more fully that he is dealing with cosmic stuff. Heretofore, he dreamed and experimented limitedly. Now he has come to grips with creative God-power. He stands appalled. Civilization is involved. Man's destiny is at stake. The human will learn humility in the presence of this creative fact and realize that he stands on holy ground.

Get my point here! This inconceivable, imponderable force is a basic unit of creation. From it, man has just begun to get a glimpse of the omnipotence and the omniscience of the creation of the world out of the void!

Creative law is the foundation of this atomic force, law that has existed since God was! Dealing with God-stuff is no light thing. It behooves mankind to walk humbly. God is not a destroyer. He would that His laws bring life and peace to His children. But the law works! It plays no favorites!

The world is mightily shaken. It will be more so! The future poses grave problems in the realm of natural law which is God-law. This is a great and awful time in human affairs. But God lives and reigns. If man takes Him into the reckoning in the use of this cosmic unit, it will be well. Have peace in your soul. May the Infinite bless and enrich your life, the beauty of holiness resting upon you and abiding. Under the shadow of His wings, you dwell safely.

WHEN DAYS ARE DARK AND DIFFICULT

Courage to keep on when keeping on is a real test, is a radiant spiritual grace, especially so in this time of darkness that precedes the New Day. Courage does not weary if hours are long and the going rough. For it consists of large parts of faith that glows brightest when skies above you are black; of the pure essence of love which works always in glad harmony with faith and with the peace that enters in to the wonderful compound of spirit power.

Look where you will and you will find the grandest work being done, the most victorious lives being lived, the most potential influences projected out into the ethers, on this sure foundation of sheer courage. It never asks whether the work is easy or hard, the hazards many and difficult or the opposition severe enough to test one's very soul. Courage has played its wondrous role in all the mighty epochs of human history, sustaining men and women through days so black that they could not see an inch ahead. But courage abided and never let man or woman who went forth into the fray, armoured with this Divine grace of spirit, yield their cause though strain and stress were heavy.

Sometimes, with even the best of people, the spirit lags a bit. Often this is a matter of the fleshly body that takes a heavy toll and even tries to take proportionately a heavy toll of the spirit. But faith and love and peace and a dozen other rare spiritual essences which comprise this compound of courage, prevent the physical body from having its way to defeat the highest.

So take courage, sublime, glorious courage to your heart and let it lead you, comfort and strengthen you. Then you will never give up in the ignominy of defeat when the struggle is hard. Here is the crux of the matter. It is often easy to begin a task, not knowing what demands it will make upon you for courageous keeping on; knowing only that it is your task, your battle, your life, to win or lose.

Courage keeps the scales of living in balance when you stand firm. It helps you ride the high waves without shrinking. Through all human history, you fill any whose names are written large for achievement, had struggles unlimited when everything seemed against them.

But Divine, God-given courage, piloted them through dangerous waters that might easily have washed them overboard. And courage, in the name of the Lord of Hosts, let them ride out the ominous waves and reach the shores of grand achievement. Take this courage to your heart and see in it all that you need for safe conduct through dark and difficult days of earth. Hasta luega!

GREAT GLORY

To many of earth who sent special prayers for my spiritual growth in ways of wisdom and understanding, of power and love divine on this anniversary of my earth nativity, I send my warmest blessings of gratitude without measure. It has made this celebration of a recurring earth date, a time for me of unprecedented and devout dedication to the service of the Father and the Son.

There has surrounded me such a glow of holy light as I have not hitherto experienced and my soul seems to swell with more joy than I can well express. Such a celebration as friends from earth have given me by their loyal and loving prayers, for my growth in all things of the life of the Father and His spiritual kingdom, is something of which no thought had ever come to me.

But I could not fail to sense the power flowing into my soul in waves and billows of love and peace and eagerness to multiply myself in service to every single one to whom I may be sent on missions of mercy and kindness and inspiration.

My gratitude knows no bounds and I yearn to send back to each one whose prayers came like a great, billowing cloud of glory and joy enveloping me, the deepest gratitude and the love of my very soul.

While it all has blessed me, I know it has also blessed each one of earth who joined in this most rewarding spiritual service. Thank each one of you and may God's blessings of richest love divine rest upon your hearts and fill you with grace and peace and goodness supreme.

Such glory it was for me! It seems to me there is nothing I will not undertake with gladness and joy in the service of the Kingdom of God, in return for this mighty surge of power that has come upon me from the prayers of you of earth at this my anniversary. You know of course, that days and years are left behind when we lay aside the weight of the physical body and take on the life of the Spirit Planes. So I was not even remembering this date which was of significance while I was of earth.

It made this pure, white cloud as of rising incense of prayer and blessing which came and rested upon me and around me, such radiance of joy as eradicated completely all memory of everything that had been sorrowful and difficult while I was of earth and it has left me as if caught up in the rapture of God's glory.

This far surpasses everything earth could even conceive. Wait until you come Home and you will begin to sense something of what it really means and what it is of eternal rapture. Then you will understand what the prayers from loyal, remembering hearts of earth have done this day for me and my spiritual growth in ways of God the Father. I bless you, each of you! More than this I can not put into words. May His peace and love and power fill your hearts. Amen!

THE SIZE OF YOUR CUP

Strength comes for climbing whatever is the mountain in your path, when in loyal, loving earnest, you seek this strength. Never fail to seek! Whether your difficulty be small or large, it is a link in a chain of vitally important causes of which doubtless you do not know the significance. So ask for His strength, His guiding hand, His light upon your way, His love to purify and glorify life, as you face it daily.

Looking to Him is the secret of the victorious life. For it releases the influences that bring love into active participation and give love, His love, opportunity to serve as your active partner. The problem where love is concerned, is mankind's tendency to limit this love which is the mightiest power of the Unlimited God. Make sure that you never limit Him nor His power.

He can give you only as freely as you are willing and able to receive. Remember this! When you hold out your small cup to receive His Divine gifts of love and strength, you will receive in proportion to the size of your cup held forth. But if you hold out a vessel of great size and humbly ask Him to fill it to the brim of such spiritual graces as you need, He will honor your faith and you will receive abundantly, good measure, running over. Ask largely!

Let faith prove itself by holding out your largest concept of what you wish fulfilled. Never fear that you will be disappointed. God the

Father is the Fulfiller of your every need when you ask in accordance with His will. Never be content to ask in ways and degrees that reveal little faith and limited expectations.

Rather, honor Him and help yourself by asking abundantly, then set your faith actively at work to bring forth your good. Remember too, that your faith may not waver if you expect the results you seek. Realize that the Eternal God is the only power in all the universes. Let Him meet your needs completely and satisfyingly. Life will be transformed when you give Him full sway. These truths I have learned in full here on the Inner Planes. Amen!

THE ANSWER DEPENDS ON YOUR CHOOSING

Wonderful things come to pass in life when the right factors of any problem are used. You can not succeed if you substitute other than the correct ones. Suppose you try to use determination in place of faith in the Father. You will not get the answer you should have. If you try to use energy in place of His love, failure faces you. The way the Great God has planned for you of earth to find the solutions to your problems, is the gloriously right way.

Because He is Infinite and you are finite, it must be His way that you follow for the solutions that satisfy. When you are told that it is by faith that one finds God, it is this way and no other! When you are taught to love your neighbor as you love yourself, it is the love-way by which you find joy and peace, not by some way of your own. If only you of earth would learn that the sure way is always the God way, earth would speedily be freed of its darkness of evil. But most of you who are human still want it your way!

Then when you fail to get the answer you desire for your problems, you earth persons are inclined to lose what you call faith and say, "What's the use? There isn't any God!" It always works this way when you put your limited self ahead of and in place of the Limitless God, trying to make your small way work instead of the Divine way!

When you experiment and suffer and lose and prove that nothing less than the way the Lord God has prescribed, can correctly solve the perplexing problems which earth poses, then you turn to the unfailing God way, accepting it loyally and finding soon the solutions working out just as they should.

When the human comes hither to these Blessed Planes of Understanding and realizes how foolishly he has tried to substitute his frail human reasoning for God's wisdom, he begins to eat the bitter dust of true humility, willing to bow in worship and adoration before Him Who is All.

By this strange way it seems to be most often that the humans insist on going before they gratefully yield their small selves to the illimitable majesty of God the Father. He is the unfailing way to solve the problems of life. Learn, my friend, humbly, patiently, faithfully, lovingly, in the meekness of glad submission to His Holy Will. Stay strong in Him. Amen!

TAKING TIME

At this hour of communion, I wish to talk with you about taking time daily for quietness alone with God. It takes courage to sit alone with the Great God and open your soul to Him. For the wisdom of His all-embracing love sees to the very center of your being. If there is evil of any sort deep-hidden beneath the surface of your life, His eyes will discover it. There may be that which is out of harmony with His purity and patience and infinite goodness, concealed from men's eyes, but nevertheless present in your heart. Alone with Him, you become newly conscious of everything that should be put away from your life, if you and the Holy One are to be on close and intimate terms.

Alone with Him in the quietness of communion, plans for your life by which you set great store, may appear to you as falling short of His plans and purposes for you, that would lead you higher in understanding and closer to His heart of love. But isn't it often true that you do not wish your plans changed? So you shrink from being alone with Him in the silence of sweet communion.

Perhaps you prefer to pray in conformity with group prayers where ceremony and precedent prevent your feeling the searching gaze of His tender love penetrating deep within your consciousness and making you uncomfortable. It takes courage to open your inmost life to those Infinitely penetrating eyes and to hold still as He shows you how you need to be changed from negative thinking, jealous feelings, resentments and prejudices, unholy desires, even sometimes from worldly ambitions that are not geared to His holy service. But meeting alone with Him, thoughts of the world shut out, there will come such rapture of heavenly peace and power as nothing else can give; such understanding of the real meanings of life as is impossible when you are surrounded with swarming crowds of earth activities and duties.

Do not shrink from the daily quiet alone with Him or think to make it up in less personal contacts. For as I have learned beyond shadow of doubt since I came hither to live in the realms of spirit, the way to grow in greatness of true understanding, to rise steadily higher in spiritual consciousness, is to meet often with your Lord alone and let Him show you how to bring your life to His standards; let Him help you eradicate the worthless, earthy things you have cherished, then to take Him for all the goodness and glory that He can impart to your life. Never fear! Just trust Him and know Him and love Him. Amen!

WHEN THE BELL RINGS

What people call interruptions are really something else! There are no interruptions. Earth people call it interruption to answer the telephone or open the door to one who comes perchance with something to sell, both of which I remember vividly from my earth years. They annoyed me and were in the way of my schedule which did not lend itself to such breaks in my day's pattern. Sometimes I thought irritably that such calls wasted my time!

I see now how much I missed by sometimes turning away to what I told myself was more important, because I had made the pattern according to my own desires. Really it carried only such importance as my thinking gave it.

I used to say that the telephone was a tyrant. Perhaps so, if one allows that marvelous instrument of communication to irritate or annoy. But when one sees it as the medium of world commerce, of joy and interest, of fellowship and help and courage, it becomes magnificent influence for good.

When the telephone rings, whatever the circumstances, why not greet it with a silent blessing and know that it offers opportunity for poise and patience, often for helping some one. This over-tops any other things one could possibly do with those moments. Often some one calls whose heart is troubled, for whom a few words of faith and courage and cheer will give increased awareness of the presence of the Holy One.

You may not have wanted to stop hurrying around on your own affairs, to answer that call. If you were impatient at store or office or home, the likelihood is that you missed opportunity for helpfulness that now may never be rendered! You kept to your day's schedule but perhaps missed an eternally grand opportunity to help some one open his heart to faith or love or Omnipotent Good. I wonder which weighs more heavily. Was that call an interruption? Or opportunity?

Your door bell rings. You stop your work to open the door. "Just a salesman," you shrug. Suppose it is. Suppose you do not wish what he offers and you did not want to stop your work. It can not be bad to remember that whatever his color or race or manners, he is the child of the Father. And often they who ring door bells do it that they and their beloveds may eat and keep a roof over their heads.

Is it not better to breathe a silent blessing on him also, while with poise you say that you can or can not buy what he offers, but that you wish him success? Many a desperate heart is concealed behind the face of one who comes to your door, not knowing how else to live.

Close your door impatiently and you save a half dozen seconds. Also you send a child of the Father on his way, perhaps defeated in his spirit because you did not want to be interrupted, even for fulfilling your part in a divine plan for that moment of your day. Was it interruption? Or opportunity?

Is it not true that when the call breaks in to your pre-made plans, you can look back at the close of the day to see how much better it worked out than if you had had your way? Is it not reasonable that meeting with the grace of kindness even those unexpected demands that harass or perplex, will make your day more radiant with blessing and joy than the hasty word, the irritated voice, the impatient shrug of your shoulders or the hot slamming of the door?

The one reveals the inward grace of Our Lord and His way of meeting and helping people. I beseech you to forget the word "interruption" and remember instead, the privilege of service in His name to those of earth who need what you can so helpfully offer. Worth thinking through!

THE JOY OF THIS PURPOSE

The one purpose of these Messages from us who have passed beyond the Veil, is to help humankind learn the lessons which earth life intends for him to know. In this teaching and learning are the glory and greatness of overcoming littleness in living and of understanding beyond the bounds of the material and the physical.

The lessons reveal the power of love to take away the evil of all hatred, to cast out intolerance and substitute gentleness of spirit understanding when it is motivated by divine love. These glories are hidden away in earth lessons that are to be learned with the patience of which people sometimes grow weary of hearing.

But in all courtesy, until you of earth really learn that lesson of divine and infinite patience, in large and small matters, in homely ways, with people such as used to try my patience sorely until I realized that I often taxed their patience just as much, it is necessary to bring it to your attention.

The thrilling part of these lessons is learning them within the deep places of the heart, learning them so triumphantly that life is changed and never again is there need for relearning particular lessons.

Spirit lessons are the mountain tops of life. For the greatest things, the deepest experiences, the highest joys are in the unseen. It could not be otherwise. I beseech you to see clearly that at this time in the life of your world, the most important lesson for each one to learn is attunement with the Father and to learn to stay in tune with His love and peace and harmony and power.

This never comes easily. For every human has all the hurdles of earth to take and they often appear to head you for a fall. But these hurdles, whatever they are, must be cleared. When you are down, there is courage to learn, for rising and going on. If you feel defeated, you need to see the way that will lead you to your true success. If you are sick, it is for you to learn to tune into the vast reservoirs of healing power of the Almighty and claim His wholeness for your body and mind.

Irritated or peevish, impatient or shut-in, frustrated one way or another that tries you to the limit, all of you face learning your lessons; knowing that whatever your special lesson be, it will not let you pass higher until your report card of life shows your mastery of it. Never let yourself feel that life is unfair in giving you such constant discipline. In the midst of it, it is great to find that when joy and gratitude, praise and thanksgiving to the Great, Good God go into your learning earth lessons, you are speeded up tremendously and the hardness seems gone from the schooling which life gives all people on the earth plane.

Take it this way, my friend! Live it with radiant up-lift of spirit. Sing your way through the days. Sing and give thanks, and learn always to realize the blessed presence of the Father God within your heart.

This is worth more than any small rewards. It will fill life with keen satisfactions which come only when these lessons well-learned, become part of the very fiber of your being. God be with you!

MEETING A GLORIOUS CONDITION

"To them that love God!" You have heard that many a time; sometimes thoughtfully in its proper context; sometimes casually. It is one of the most potent words pertaining to man's life, fitting into many places and experiences and explaining many dark situations. It does not always explain in ways that man likes. But it brings man's thought to a focus and by those words, helps him to think more clearly.

People of earth sometimes twist those words into meaning what they want them to mean. In thus twisting these simple but potent words, they think they keep them from meaning what they do not want them to mean. "To them that love God!" This has the significance of a condition which man must meet or fail to meet. Right there is where many people dodge the implication because they are afraid to meet it, for it might go against their wishes or their convenience!

The other part of this verse is radiant. "All things work together for good to them that love God!" There you have it as countless of earth's people have lived by it. And found it trust-worthy. Just now it holds special sense of protection to all who will claim what earth seeks feverishly, futilely, looking everywhere for sense of security and finding none in the outer realms.

If only they would see that despite wars or pestilence or bombs, all things work together for good, provided you love God! That gives a protecting armour over you and your home, an ever-brooding good around and about you. But the first part of the verse may not be taken out of its context and made to stand alone. Without that conditional phrase, it promises much that should not come to pass, detrimental to man and to his civilization. "If you love God!" There is the mighty challenge, and it is part of the infinite condition, lest man pick up part of the promise and run away with it, in unconcern about living up to the whole wonderful assurance.

In its entirety, this verse puts a new aspect into living. Not that it is like a toy to a child to keep it on good behavior; nor like a bribe to hold one calm when life seethes around him. But it is worth everything to know that however severe the ordeal, however desperate the testing, it does work out for good, when you love God.

I beg you not to misinterpret that into meaning that He must be cajoled into bringing you through life's disciplines, to get you to love Him! It means that loving God, you look to Him for all necessary help, for guidance that will see you through, for strength and faith that will enable you to breast the waves and for patience to await the so-Wing of many complex problems, because you know that He dwells within you, His presence surrounds you, His love irradiates you, His joy holds a light for you through the dark and His power overshadows you.

It cannot ever be that His love could fall short of leading you to ways that are good and to life harmonious with Him. Not once are you promised that loving God, all things work together for what you want, in ways you want them and when you want them to come about! Just take this magnificent verse as a whole, reckon with the conditions that challenge you to your highest relationships with the Great God, then let joy and gratitude fill your heart that it is true for you, for every one of earth's children who meets that right and reasonable condition.

See the greatness of His love in the meshing of these two forces into one, all things working together for good for them who love God! His peace fill your heart as you acknowledge the rightness of the condition and live in glad harmony with it.

EARTH'S GREATEST GIFT

To live in His love, under the shelter of His protection, makes life gloriously wonderful. For His love knows no distinction between them called great and the humble; no distinction that welcomes certain favored ones to His presence and excludes those who have not had opportunities they have craved.

It is all as it should be. Favor or lack of it; opportunity and the absence of it; all shock up as tests that mankind faces on his way through earth life. For them who accept in deep reality, the love that is Divine, life is inspiring. For those who do not accept this gift of His love, life on earth and here on these Spirit Planes, is sure to be filled with remorse and agony of soul. They who come across from earth, having denied the offered love of the Father, find it indeed hell.

Even so, there never comes the time when there is no hope for the soul. Even after eons of refusal to learn and to love His way and His laws, every soul may turn and begin the difficult trek back again from ignorance and rebellion to this love which is the Father's most wondrous gift to His children.

Never forget this gift nor take it for granted. Rather accept it with complete dedication that with-holds nothing, living by it and testing every other interest by the purity and power of the Father's love. Whatever fails to measure up to this Divine standard, should be discarded as imperfect and undesirable. Let every interest of your life be measured by this standard.

It is worth living in this exacting way. It will reward you richly when you have come up over the limitations of earth to these Inner Planes where love is the very atmosphere. Each test of earth you have taken and passed successfully, gives you deeper understanding and wider ranges of service to those who need you.

How many such there are, you cannot even conjecture. Take my word for it. And know that the price one pays for rejecting the love of the Father, is too great to consider. The glory of accepting His Divine and Infinite love endures forever and never fails your highest longing!

And now I go to service far removed from your habitat where are those whose need is sore. To minister to them in His Holy Name is privilege beyond compare.

WHEN EARTH'S WAY IS HARD

Blessed are you for finding your way up from the depths where you allowed circumstances to submerge you and all but to doubt the validity of your faith! All because some people of unseeing vision had seemed to bait your very soul, seeking to take you down to their level!

The discipline is severe for you. But as you face it loyally, light will shine more and more brilliantly until you come into the clear. I beseech you not to yield to any down-pulling influences for your spirit. They have nothing good to offer. When temptation swings low to capture you, seek the protection of your soul's Fortress. Hide in His Pavilion under the shelter of His loving care and know for a surety that nothing can be your undoing except you, yourself.

These current experiences which prove so difficult to you are the door to goodness of which now you do not dream; nor will you until you walk bravely and with courage undaunted full into the face of it all and prove its nothingness. Grasp firmly the thorniness of the situation and prove that not one single thorn has power to sting you, save as you give it that power.

Then remember that God the Father has all power, that He literally is all power for every issue of life; for all forms of life in all the universes; for the circle of the firmaments; all power! How can you doubt His power for your personal needs? They are as a grain of sand, large though they seem to you who hold them so close to your eyes as to obscure all clear seeing.

Oh! learn to release them to His loving power; really release them; stop doubting; stop wondering whether! Just know! And your way will widen, your life will enlarge, your joy will overwhelm all former sense of humiliation. There is nothing to that. There is all goodness and glory to overcoming! Rise in the power of His might and accept your soul's rightful dominion. When depression swoops down on you, praise His Holy Name! When you think you are defeated, bless His infinite goodness to you and believe implicitly in His promises. Step out on them and prove their power to carry you through.

Saints of shining splendor have passed through the woes of the world and reached unspeakable radiance on these High Planes, having followed the rough and rugged ways of earth, more difficult far than yours. Let His peace and power, His love and His light be your strength and your guerdon. Amen!

MAGIC OF FORGIVENESS

One word grapples for attention. It is such an old word. Forgiveness! The aura surrounding it is brilliant and beautiful, wholly spiritual and of deep significance. Nothing earthy is in this aura because real forgiveness is of the deep places of the heart. It is as necessary to growth in spirit power as light and air for flowers and people. Forgiveness does not have any ulterior or selfish motive, when it is genuine. Rather it is quiet, sincere and profound in its effect on the life of him who forgives.

This forgiveness has nothing in common with resentment or avarice or bitterness, no matter what the cause. It is of the heart of God and is best illustrated by our Lord when He said, "Father, forgive them!"

Remember He was speaking of them who were taking His physical life in the most cruel way, for no reason save that He went about doing good, healing their diseases, opening their eyes, raising their dead and teaching the ways of God the Father. True, He did show them the ways of their sinning, where their lives were not fulfilling His instruction to "love one another."

They who were doing Him to death, hated Him Who was so good they could not understand Him; so pure they could not fathom His spirit; so royal they could not interpret His teachings. So when His life dazzled and dumfounded them, the thing to do was to put Him to death!

Even then, forgiveness! From the depths of His God-like heart. No drop of bitterness lingered in the cup He drank that day. He was above all hatred. He loved them even unto death, Forgiveness goes to the depths. When it is genuine and complete, all hate, even mild dislike, everything which is apart from love one to another, is rooted out. If it tears the heart, then it must tear, for any one in earnest to learn what it means to forgive.

Perhaps you thought you had left no one in all your circle, unforgiven. But up pops another memory. And you know instantly that forgiveness has not done its work there. Resentment stirs. Jealousy rears its ugly head. Self-pity tries to make you feel you have done your part, gone more than halfway and if the other person doesn't do his part, you can't help it.

Right there is the place to begin, to be willing to go the second mile toward understanding and harmony. Stop at nothing that will free you of the poison that has not been disposed of by the magic of forgiveness. When that settles in your heart, it will be like a sweet breeze and the perfume of Arcady!

Is there a letter you ought to write to some one to whom you do not wish to write? Or another approach of unselfish friendliness, when you are not certain how it will be received? How it will be received, is not the point. Doing it with desire to have every thing in your heart right and God-like, is what counts. If you meet rebuff, what of it? Your part is to let the spirit of forgiveness bear its fruit sweet to the taste and leaving no bitterness in the heart.

This goes to the quick many a time. It did with me when I was on the earth plane. But whatever the cost, it is supremely worth doing. For forgiveness is part of the basic law of love. Always it costs. Paying brings contentment and peace and joy. I beseech you to pay the price with all your heart and go free of any poison of unforgiveness festering within your heart.

Always He met His enemies with this unassailable weapon of forgiveness, its arrows tipped with the supremest love this world has ever known. His way works. I commend it to you always!

THE WAY OF THE FLOWER

Learning is always an unfolding. Real learning is never an external experience in which knowledge in the form of facts, is poured into the mind.

True learning rather, is the unfolding of understanding from deep within. This unfoldment is assisted and speeded up with the help of knowledge gained from the outside world. But the real learning, for any man or woman, comes in the interior nature of mankind where facts and all such are received into the deep places of the being, assimilated into the fabric of life and there left to develop and mature in understanding.

This is the way every flower comes to its beauty of blossom, always by opening from its heart where the life manifests. A great and mighty lesson is here for every human, a lesson that is to be lived before it can truly be said to be learned.

Thus in very truth as revealed in the blooming of every flower of earth, where the beauty of form and fragrance is unfolded from the center where the power of life lies concealed, all learning that is genuine unfolds those factors of spirit power of which mankind is possessed.

I beseech you to make the most of this interpretation of the origin and the process that constitute true learning. In pitifully many instances, learning consists of having facts poured in, often helter skelter and unrelated, good enough of themselves but not united by forces which combine to bring about what really deserves to be accepted as learning, in the right and high sense of this experience.

It is worth your while to heed the resistless force of even the tiny blossom which can teach you how always the coming to bloom is an interior process, designed and developed by the power of spiritual attraction and in your life can become a mighty value at the center of your being.

THE COMPASSION OF CHRIST

Christ made radiant use of holy compassion, reflecting it in every earth situation. Greater than pity, though pity is part of it; greater than sympathy, though sympathy enters into it; greater than unselfishness, though unselfishness is essential to it! Compassion is all of these to which must be added that vital quality of understanding which carries with it the divine spirit of love.

No weakness manifests in this essence of compassion. It is strength and power and tenderness and vast understanding of the mighty forces of the cosmic. Compassion makes any man greater, stronger, finer, because it makes him more like the Christ.

See Him with the sick, the troubled, the mentally unbalanced, the poor and hungry, them who did not follow where in love He led the way. See Him when His followers ripped off a roof to lower a sick man to His feet for healing. See Him when the Transition brought sorrow to Mary and Martha; and in the home of the girl upon whom He breathed so gently, so powerfully, that she opened her eyes and was restored.

See Him at the wedding when the wine was exhausted and His Mother Mary turned in utter confidence to Him for help. See Him when the cripple beside the pool could not get into the waters when they were troubled. See Him when His disciples were cold and hungry and discouraged and when the lad was torn by evil spirits that were rending body and mind. See Him when He Himself was on the cross, through those hours of ignominy which were hours of tremendous spiritual conquest. See Him that early Easter morning in the garden with Mary when with infinite compassion for her suffering, He spoke her name in tones that echo around the world these centuries since His lips framed, "Mary!"

See Him when He walked with His unseeing disciples who saw only their loss of His physical presence, not realizing His spiritual presence walking with them along the familiar paths. See Him giving His disciples His last earth blessing that they might be girded with patience and understanding and sympathy and strength and love and compassion when He no longer would be with them in the physical. See Him when the cloud was enveloping His body and He spoke His message to them—"Lo, I am with you alway, even unto the end of the world."

No thought of self, neither of worldly place nor power; no impatience when earth people thronged Him asking transient blessings; never a curt nor hasty word but always the Bread of Life to their souls which were sicker than their bodies. Compassion flowed out through His heart of love and was as water to their thirsting spirits.

He embodied the love of the Father Whom He came to earth to represent. With it were blended all the qualities of the love that sacrifices and calls it joy; of the power which rejoices in however humble the service; of the understanding that knows through having experienced the glory that abides when sorrow is turned into gladness and mourning into joy. To you I commend this majestic quality of compassion. And Him as the perfect Exemplar of this compassion that makes like unto God Himself!

THE KETTLE BOILS OVER

I want you to take this, however personal, for the values it will have for you and for others who experience the same sort of negative thing. You have been disturbed inwardly of late. Feelings of irritation rise within you at little things, irritability over small and unimportant matters. You know better. Of course. Not worth a breath nor a moment of time. Sometimes you express displeasure at sundry small matters which plague you when they do not function as they should.

It is not good. There should always be even balance in your spirit. Always you should see everything in its correct relation and proportion. You will come to that level of discipline some day if you keep on accepting the Divine grace that enables one to surmount these earth difficulties.

How well I remember them! With what heart burnings those memories come surging back upon me, times when I did my Lord no credit with quick flaring of hot displeasure, when I misjudged motives of others and brought upon them and me the same sort of muddled spiritual disconcertment of which you have been thinking to yourself lately. It is the human rising to the surface when you give it a chance. The trouble lies deeper than the surface. If the heart were as it should be, pure and clean and spiritual to the depths, there would be none of this sediment to rise to the top, on slight provocation, to boil over and stir up trouble.

Here is the crux. The human puts the lid on and thinks all is well. Yes, while there is no heat under and things are quiescent. But let the heat of criticism or difficulty or any of the human snags show themselves, the kettle begins to boil, the sediment comes to the top, overflows, and there is the mischief to pay!

How easily that used to happen to me when I was in the flesh, under the grill of vexations and disappointments and the disciplines of living!

Wrong thoughts, selfish thoughts, uneasy thoughts are allowed to settle to the bottom of your heart and stay there. On an instant, they surge up and overflow. It will always be so until Divine love clears out the inside of the heart, purifies it and leaves nothing that can form a scum of unspiritual composition or that muddies the waters of your spirit.

They should flow in crystal clarity through whatever channels life provides. The weariness of the flesh often is weighed down beyond all reason.

GOD-POWER

In this day of earth, everything seems gauged by terms of power. Issues are terrific. Competition is intense where power is involved. From our Inner Planes, we watch the growth of these tensions and marvel at them. If we did not know the outcome in ways of which earth does not yet know in detail, our alarm would be considerable. But joy overtops our anxious concern, for we do know as you can not know yet, that no earth power which man devises or implements, can even approximate that of the Almighty.

He is Supreme in the realm of mechanics, science, government and of man's every effort. It would seem futile to say these things, except that many living on earth today are distraught and overwhelmed by man's mad race for the greatest and the most, the deadliest and the fastest, everything that is superlative in terms of his transient power.

This mad race is in the human dimension, limited to the material, in which man thinks to enhance his grasp of power over civilizations and nations and mankind. Place all of this on one side of the scales of the cosmic; God-Power on the other side of the scales, and man's side weighs lightly. For he is dealing with that which endures for a relatively brief span of existence. God-Power was from before time began and endures beyond the end of eternity.

His Almightiness gives man all the elements and the laws that govern the functioning of life on the earth. God is not involved in any race for more and greater power. Only man is so tense in his ambitions to out-strip all others in the use of temporal power that he forgets the Almighty source of all power with which he deals.

It is strange that man seems to think he makes and can control power too awesome to consider with equanimity. And man will need to learn that Almightiness is above all else, Himself the Source of power, Himself the power! If only man would slow down his wild race for such power as abides briefly, then is gone, and would contemplate the

Source Who is. All Power and come under the spell of His eternal sway as Creator of this power that endures forever, the present human craze for speed and size and might, would be submerged in worship and adoration of the Creator!

The world would then lose its tautness, its tensions and frictions, its strivings after the biggest, the highest, the most appalling and destructive. Then man would merge his petty desires in amazing wonder at the vastness of the All-Power that formed the world, and man would come to clearer heights of spiritual understanding than are possible while he seeks to out-strip all others' human skills.

It is an intricately involved problem. But light shines on it. And God-Power will prevail on every front of human civilization and life!

HARVEST

I was present at your noon time when you were discussing the coming of these Messages, explaining the validity of them through evidences, and seeking to share something of the inspiration which has come to your life from them.

You will remember, my friend, that time must come to the aid of credulity with any to whom this vast experience and range of knowledge are wholly new and strange. To the uninitiated, a shade suspicious, they think.

So just let the truth grow in its own way and give the seeds of truth time to take their own root for safe growing.

More of them do take root than perhaps you think. Remember too, that you took your own time when first this line of knowledge began to open to you, before you showed more than slight interest or concern.

It is difficult for the human to realize that he doesn't have to "grow" his seed but only to plant it and give it fair opportunity to do its own growing.

The one with whom you were talking today went away with more to think about in the secret place of her own spirit, than you realize. And she will think about it too! Never doubt.

Don't you remember how I talked with you some months ago about your being a seed-sower? And that it has its own definite rewards for your spirit? Keep on sowing the seed that comes to you from these Spirit Planes. And never doubt that much of it will fall on good ground and bear its harvests of increased concern with things of life after the Great Transition.

New concepts will come about the growth of the soul and right knowledge of what the Transition really is and means. So do not weary in doing your task. It is your great opportunity!

PIN-PRICKS

Grace be with you and the mercy of the Most High that you may be conscious of His presence and His love. This is the one way of peace within your soul as you walk the tortuous path of earth on your spiritual climb to altitudes of understanding and wisdom.

The issues which are troubling you are merely pin-pricks. I remember how annoying these can be and fairly painful while one lives the earth life. But believe me, since I have been here on these Planes of Glory, I have learned beyond what earth taught me, how tiny such pin-pricks of annoyance really are. Usually they come from people who do not know better. So why let yourself be tormented when things said and done, are caused by ignorance? Drop them from your mind, the while you go climbing higher, learning the standards of eternity, refusing to be disturbed by pin-pricks, in whatever form they come to you.

Let this year be a time when you give faith its right of way and see it accomplish its marvels. Most people make faith so formal, hedge it about with efforts to believe until it can not do its real work.

Set faith free! Don't try to believe! Just believe! Then trust the rest to the marvels that faith, freed from bonds, will bring to pass. My coming to this Blessed Land was the severest trial of all for you who seemed completely bereft by it.

But as often is, the hardest ordeals are the opening doors to God's miracles of opportunity and wonder. My coming hither was the first signal that for you the way was opening to this world-wide service, greater far than anything you could have done, had I remained in the physical body.

Even as the Master said to His disciples that it was expedient for them that He go away, so for you it was necessary that I leave the body of flesh with its many limitations, to take up residence on these Inner Planes, so the great series of communications from here to there, could begin to flow word for word, to you and now are known and lived world-wide!

You see this wonderful way of the Father's working, don't you? In all future experiences see it the same way, that trials and doubts and things humanly difficult, precede the coming of miracles of divine good. Give thanks unceasingly for it. For so it is, miracles and marvels of the Father's wisdom. Blessings abound unto you and unto all. Amen and Amen!

LIGHT

I yearn to show you what Light really is; His Light; ineffable, more glorious than you dream Light can be; the Light that emanates from the Holy One Who spoke the universes into being, saying, "Let there be Light!" What follows was tremendous—"And there was Light!"

The power of creativeness is revealed to humans by these four simple words, power vaster than all the minds of the universes could conceive; His Light, evanescent, penetrating, permeating and utterly radiant, shattering whatever darkness exists and dissipating it. The exception to this is the human realm where man has free will, gift of the Father and never rescinded. And sadly, man often has loved darkness rather than light!

If man wishes to live in the darkness of evil, to stunt and dwarf his soul, he may. Not even creative Light can force man to accept it when he prefers darkness. There are many who do. It is the saddest thing in all the universes to know that man still loves darkness rather than Light. Millions of earth hug their dense blackness of sin, wrap themselves round with the awfulness that thrives in darkness and will not open their hearts to the bright shining of His Light.

Ultimately, as often I have said to you, each soul however darkened in its love of sin and depravity, does choose to return to the Father's house. It is always a remorseful journey, with struggles that must be experienced and suffering that must be accepted, once a soul has turned from God and His Light and chosen to immerse himself in the debaucheries of darkness!

But even from such a one, help that is asked is never withheld and the one returning is offered all the Light and the Love he is willing and able to receive. It is the acme of mercy divine!

I began this visit with you by expressing my yearning to show you something of the glory of Light here in the Heavenly Kingdom, inconceivable while you are in the denseness of earth. Joy inexpressible awaits you when you come Home and I may prove to you some of the rapturous beauty of which I have tried to tell you across the distance from your realm to ours—and it is no distance at all. The Father God and His Holy Angels bless and love you and keep you consciously in the knowledge of their presence and their help in every time of need. Amen!

SCHOOL

When we were children at school, whether it was the little country school to which I went or the city school where you attended, millions of children found that when once they had really learned this principle and that rule so as to use them when they were needed, it was not necessary to go back to relearn them.

It is as simple as this interpreted in terms of human life. Lessons are given by the Great Teacher and His helpers, lessons in life and how to live it, so as not to have to relive it and relearn these lessons. When the lessons are hard and the answers do not come quickly nor easily, when it seems to you that they are beyond your efforts and you want to be excused from further trying to master them, just remember that they are eternal lessons and are to be learned before you can pass on to the next higher level of understanding.

Remember too, that simple lessons are given only to children, them in the kindergarten of life, but the hard lessons that tear the soul and seem to rend life in twain, are absolutely essential for learning by those whose way winds high toward the gleaming goals of spiritual supremacy. When you are inclined to resent the disciplines of difficult lessons and want to turn from them, want some that are quick and easy to learn, ask yourself whether you are yet a toddling child who can master only the A B C's of the book of the world, whether that is the limit of your ability and whether you are content to remain the kindergarten grade of the school of life, going over and over those first simple rules that the beginner can learn.

Or are you steadily moving higher to problems that call for mature mind and powers of reasoning? In other words, are you content to stay a child or do you aspire to the responsibilities of maturity? It is a far-reaching question and opens the door to many lessons whose techniques are hard to master, essential though they be, before passing to higher grades. For so it is. Interpret all of this into conditions of your daily life. Can you take hard things and master them in poise, asking for still more difficult lessons, equal to whatever life puts before you, just so it will give you greater command over the powers with which the Great Master of Life endowed you? And will you learn these and still harder ones, so that some day you may stand unashamed in His Glorious Presence and hear Him say, "Well done, my child"?

Take each lesson as it comes; learn it thoroughly; move confidently up to the higher; asking the Teacher for help when you need it; accepting the problems and disciplines and lessons in the spirit of growth toward His divine stature, giving thanks always however hard it be because it all leads you nearer to His standards and His atmosphere of Holy Love. Amen!

THE WORKABLE WAY

When you have come up against stone walls that have appeared to have no way through or over or around, the way has always opened! For God is God. And He is Omnipotent! With Him all things are possible, if—! There comes the rub, as you earth people say.

The "if" is where you stumble. Sometimes you fall flat, thrown by that big, little "if." What is this "if?" Just this—that all things are possible, if you believe! The belief that works miracles, is not an intellectual belief. The mind can not achieve faith's results, however many try to use it for such purposes. They fail. Then they feel they are defeated.

The mind is impotent on these grounds. The believing that lets all things needful become possible with God, is purely spiritual, a perception and an action of the spirit. Man finds it difficult to understand this sort of believing. Blessedly you need not understand it. For again I say the human mind is unequal to it.

So drop it as an issue. Let the believing come through spiritual channels where it belongs, where it functions effortlessly and beautifully. The greatest achievements in the world of mankind have been brought to pass because man has believed with his heart and soul, staking everything on his faith, not trying intellectually to see how or why it works.

There again you are up against the difficulty which the mind can not surmount. Instead of trying, just let God show you how His Omnipotence works when you let yourself go, believing in Him, knowing with all your might that He is equal. For He is the Great God.

Countless times such things have been said, one way or another, about faith. But until you accept them and live them, the Inner Planes must say them over again. For man continues to stumble, without seeing why. The sole trouble is that he is going at the hurdle the wrong way. The electrician would not get desired results if he tried to make electricity work the way he thinks it should. He must follow nature's laws. Then the flash comes that is exactly right. As simple and as true as that!

Similarly you get satisfying results with faith only when you let go and trust yourself to God and His way of working. Then you will see such things come about as will thrill your very soul. Remember this faith that achieves is a spiritual perception, a spiritual process. It is better to work His way and achieve, than to hold out for your own way and fail!

My blessings of great joy be unto you.

TRYING TO LOOK BEYOND TODAY

Most people of earth, as I learned when I lived there, are inclined to try to do this which can not be done. Even so, we greet you from the Inner Planes with our loving blessings and want you to know that you are under our continuing watchcare.

Even though you do not see us when we drop in to visit a brief time with you, you are usually acutely conscious of our coming, because of the marked increase of the vibratory frequence which surrounds you.

When we find you with higher hope in your heart and better courage in your spirit, it helps us who come, as much as it helps you to have us come. Gratefully, we join in praise and thanksgiving to the Father and the Healing Christ.

Recently, you have been trying to look ahead of today that you might see what you think tomorrow and the days following, hold for you. This you can not do. No one who yet wears the physical garment can.

Trying it, only torments your whole being and depletes your courage for facing what comes when it comes. It is better far on every count, for you to rest assured that today is enough for you; today's steps are all you need to take; today's problems are all you must face. Let tomorrow strictly alone, to take care of itself.

And surely tomorrow will take care of its own opportunities and perplexities, when your entire trust is in the Father and the Son and you are knowing momentarily that Divine love and power are supreme.

When dark days come as they do for every one, it is the best of good times to prove that with God, not one thing is impossible. Just make sure that what you ask for from Him, is always asked in His Holy Name. Then the days coming in steady succession, will each bring you its fulness of joy and gladness, of opportunity to serve Him, often through serving some of His little ones, there on the tortured earth.

From here, we send you assurance of our loving care and our eager desire to be of all help which you may need, any day or in the darkness of night. Just ask us. And trust! But do not fear!

HIS PROTECTING PRESENCE

The protection for which you have just breathed your prayer and which I heard as I stood beside you, is more potent than you can dream. Because it is invisible to your physical eyes, you and most humans tend to the usual impression that probably it does not exist.

Or if there is such protection, likely it is more or less nebulous in its practical power value. Let me make very clear from these High Planes of Spirit that such is not the case, in any particular nor in any degree.

Surely you remember that mountain of old when Elisha's servant was frightened at the size of the enemy's army and Elisha told his servant to look to the mountain behind him. There were horsemen and chariots of fire, so awesome and majestic in their impressiveness that the enemy already drawn up in battle array, with-drew without joining battle.

Powerful as this illustration is, it is relatively a slight manifestation of the protection which the Almighty places round about His children who ask in faith and who never let their faith weaken.

This protecting presence is like a garment of God with which you can enwrap yourself and be impervious against harm or danger of any kind that may be directed against you. Remember always that this is not of yourself. It is of the Great God Whose children may have in proportion as they ask and believe.

If you of earth could know how it is over here, it would be very difficult for you to be content to remain within your small surroundings, shut in with density and tensions that are hard to experience. Therefore only a hint now and then is given, for keeping your anticipation strong and your faith firm, the while you work loyally to complete the tasks that are yours on the earth plane. Whatever they involve, you may always be armoured with the protecting mantle of His grace. This I told you shortly after I came from earth. But I repeat because earth's residents are in need of this consciousness. It is indeed a blessed knowing for each of you to experience. Amen!

WHY PRAY?

Signs increase. And he is indeed blind who fails to see the early dawning of the New Day. They who are of the light that endures, welcome its coming. For it foretells a greatness of growth not hitherto realized and responsibilities commensurate. To this end, I wish to talk with you of the second of two forces which are power supreme, both for you of earth and for us of the Inner Planes.

It is of prayer that I speak. The aspect which I wish most to emphasize is the potency of prayer and its life-changing qualities. Remember that prayer which the Master used as He taught His students. In its simplicity, it is utterly great. He was speaking to His Father with Whom He was in perfect harmony. Even so may you be; even so may you speak! His prayer began in adoration and glory which the Son ascribed to the Father. I urge you to pray this all-comprehending prayer many times daily in deep attitude of humble worship, pouring your very soul into it. Forget yourself and any material needs; remember only Him and His Omnipotence. Seeking ever closer fellowship with Him, open wide ajar the doors of your soul that He may flood your life with His understanding and wisdom, with mercy and humility and patience and faith and all qualities that characterize His perfect life.

Always remember that real prayer is deep communion when you ask nothing material, yearning rather to share His grace, to live His life and to rest in His love, conscious meanwhile only of Him and the pure peace that abides in fellowship with Him.

As we learn on these High Planes, we know to the depths of our souls that prayer is the infinite Fountain-head of power for every need of every soul. To sit in quietness with Him, pouring forth the love and adoration of your heart, listening for what He may say without words, is the acme of prayer.

The sublimity of its power is more than the human can ever understand. But every one, however untutored, may use this power of prayer and have his life changed by it; every one may bring his daily living above the littleness of earth routine into the radiance of His conscious presence, through using this majestic prayer power.

Learn to live in this prayer atmosphere and meet every moment of the day with this joyous worship powerful within you. When He speaks, be sure to listen, asking Him to make clear to you His meaning, if you do not understand His will for you. Come thus through using prayer at every issue of your life, to know that it is the very life-blood of your spirit, without which you could not live after His way and His will.

Let prayer be to you the very essence of power by which you may live triumphantly. If confusion stalks around you, be quiet within, undisturbed, because you know His presence with you, loving you, leading you, giving you grace and glory to manifest Him in the outer realm. Then nothing else matters much!

On our Inner Planes, prayer is our mainstay. It is our supply-line, even as it may be yours. It is our power for service which we are to render, and for growth in all ways God-like which is our chiefest desire. Prayer at its utmost of potency is in the silence when no barriers intrude themselves between Him and you, when He will fill your channel to the brim, of His limitless good and send you forth to conquer every obstacle in His Holy Name! And now, my blessing and protection!

YOUR THOUGHT

Blessings be upon you all! This very day, you are sending uncounted thoughts out among the humans who are of your world. Often they are fleeting and not well formulated, related to your reactions, your problems, toward others and your acceptance of them or your unfriendliness to them.

In the course of any single day, these reactions slip through your consciousness out into the ethers, to do according to their content. Nothing can prevent that. You sent some of them on negative errands when you may not have realized it. The negative thought must do negative work. The critical thought works its will and can do no other. People whom you hold in bondage to your thoughts of criticism, receive them and are further undone by them. Like winged birds, thoughts fly to their own destinations.

Your thoughts have power, for good or for harm. Don't forget that. And don't minimize the power!

From a heart filled with pessimism and doubt and fear, joy thoughts do not fly. As surely as you send out these depressing thought waves, they cast down those who receive them. Guard that well in your life and see to it that you give passage only to thoughts of helpfulness and gentle goodness.

Untapped reserves of energy are within each of you, waiting to be opened by the power of thought, about which men have pondered too lightly. Freight your thought daily with faith that God will direct it where it will have the mightiest values of helpfulness. Issues of life are determined in these ways.

Sow bitterness in your thoughts. And you reap bitterness ten times compounded. Sow love and justice and honor and truth and gentleness and peace. And you reap more joy than you may think the world holds. Thought is a very potential force for good or evil, according to its nature begotten in your heart. Use it rightly and it will transform your life! The sun shines. And all is well. God bless you and hold you by His Almighty arms. Amen!

TWO HALVES

Blessings always bring their responsibilities and they are commensurate with the blessings. This is in the order of keeping the balance true, one weighing equally with the other. The human of earth needs to keep this always in his consciousness. It is part of the Divine order and may never be set aside; part of the holy rhythm in which giving and receiving are halves of the same whole.

Mankind is responsible for one as for the other, counting either equal in blessing. Millions upon your planet seek always to get, letting the other side of the scales sag. They have not learned the blessedness of giving in the spirit of God's love and they look upon it as foreign to spiritual growth. They are mistaken. Giving is in no wise limited to material exchanges. This is the least form of the grace of giving.

Full-orbed giving covers every aspect of life and can be, indeed it must be, a sacrament of unselfishness if it is acceptable and true in the scales of life where things are weighed with relation to their motives. It means giving self, time, talents, resources, service as unto the Lord, if it is to bring its richest blessing.

Many love to receive, thinking they are getting something for nothing. Not so! Everything has its price. In its full-rounded significance, learning to receive is one of the deep lessons that life teaches which every one must learn, if he keeps his scales of life in complete balance.

Often pride is a factor in this matter of receiving and much is involved that is neither simple nor easy to perform. Frequently it amounts to major surgery in the life of the soul, where depths of the law of living are concerned. No matter! Both sides of this vast human, divine lesson must be learned, where one both gives and receives in selfless and sacrificial spirit of joyous service to God and to life.

Let erring human pride be gone, the while the great blessing be remembered and observed of keeping the balances of life in true equality. It means accepting and living the responsibility of giving whatever is in one's power to give, be it little or much—courtesy and tolerance and patience and justice and love above all, regardless of convenience.

This lesson is interlocked with the ofttimes more difficult one of learning to receive graciously and joyously, even when it cuts to the quick. Often it does! But it is part of the soul discipline that earth is set to teach and every man and woman, to learn. This comes from the Inner Planes through me, to earth and you, for sharing with the many who have this dual lesson yet to master and have not sensed the deep significance of it. Do not try to dodge this; rather, take it gallantly and be grateful for the blessings that are inherent in it, for the endless sweep of eternity.

WITHOUT HASTE OR HURRY

How greatly you will rejoice when you come Home, to realize that divisions of your sidereal time are done away with. They were necessary for you down there where all things had to be ordered by schedules. But it is part of the glorious freedom that you will experience to have no more any need of day time or night, to cease reckoning sun rise and the going down of the sun.

Here the day always shines and we are enveloped in the expansiveness of God's creation. Some wonderful things are coming through to completion on our Planes, that sooner than you might think, will give earth better ease and comfort in living. Never does any one here weary with work nor cease to be immersed in the glory of learning from the Source of all wisdom.

The more we work, the stronger we appear to be. The more we learn, the vaster fields we see of knowledge to be gleaned. But we have no sense of hurry or of fear lest we may not compass all that we should. It is great comfort to be freed from that unreasoning haste that possesses so many earth people and keeps them at feverish pitch. It is not conducive to calmness of spirit in which the Father would have His children spend the days on earth.

For in that feverish pitch, one cannot do his best work nor accept the lessons which earth discipline has to offer. So, my friend, the one who hurries fastest, is generally not doing the most efficient living nor preparing in best ways to present his credentials for appraisal up here.

Remember that your strength shall be as your days. Draw constantly upon the unfailing Source for all that you need. The Fountain will never run dry and you need never turn away unsatisfied. Take that into your heart. Learn from it. Live and grow and serve and rejoice in all good that comes to you!

But I must away now, my friend. It has been great joy to visit tonight with you on this night of memory which does not grow dim and for which I give thanks to the Father. All faith be yours in the successful outworking of each problem in your life-orbit at this time.

Have faith, my friend! I've told you that a thousand times, haven't I? Again I say it, for it is the lesson of all lessons richest in rewards for you. And now the Father endue you with His love, His vision, His peace and His conscious presence. Amen!

TAILSPINS

Little things that the human says are "just chance," have a great way of throwing one of earth into spiritual tailspins. I saw it happen with you today when I had stopped a moment to visit you on my return to Invisible Realms. Your afternoon caller had made a casual statement about some friend of hers living across the continent.

Immediately you interpreted it into terms of your personal situation and presto, down you went into a dismal discouragement of fear. Just plain fear that what had developed for this person whom you never saw, might be headed straight to you! You dyed the situation with all manner of blues which did not belong there.

Then of course, you had to work your way back again up to your rightful level and begin the struggle to rid yourself of the ogre of fear. When you had it out one door, suddenly you found it coming in by another entrance to your consciousness. Then that door had to be closed and bolted. Altogether it was waste which you should not have allowed yourself to experience. Forgive me for speaking plainly. But such things are not good and I want you to avoid them.

You lost several precious hours of time and strength and courage because you dived down below sea level and found nothing but darkness of gloom. It was a losing investment and the poise of your faith should be so completely centered in God the Father that nothing could throw you thus off-balance.

Please take this seriously. It is an aspect of many lives but far too costly for you to tolerate. It exacts payment in the coin of good cheer and joy and right interpretations of the way life should be lived on altitudes of trust in the Father's goodness.

There was no reason for you to catapult into doubt and fear as you did today, throwing away the peace and quietness of heart that have carried you safely through many an hour of perplexity. Guard yourself against ever letting this sort of thing take possession of your consciousness again. Remember you have the protectiveness of His mantle of grace to see you through and that it does wrap you round as long as faith holds.

It was good for you today to become aware of the weakness in your dykes of faith where some trickles of defeat grew into larger volumes that threatened possible disaster. But you plugged the leak and faith began to hold very firm. You can not afford lost power. No one can. God is in command. Go His way. Trust His Word. Walk where His light is shining and His hand is guiding in safety and Almighty blessing. Off now, having had this out with you.

FOG

The reason so many prayers, so many deep desires, are not brought to spiritual fruition, is that the quality of essential faith is not present when the request is made, as I have told you before.

When one asks God for the thing which appears to be needed and asks in faith, one must leave the request with Him, not carry it around in the heart, hoping for its fulfillment but doubting all the while. Leave it with Him! Forget about it! When thought returns to it, thank the dear Father that you have placed that issue with Him and that you leave it there, nothing doubting nor wavering. Then leave it! Go off about your business and never doubt the Father nor His power over that which you have committed to Him.

It is a difficult technique to acquire in the human heart which is so prone to wonder and worry and doubt and despair. But learn that lesson and its technique! It will repay you better than any other investment you could make. It is part of the process of growth in the ways of spirit.

Growth always brings its pains which the human does not enjoy. But without them, growth does not come. So you face one of the serious choices each time you meet a situation where it is trust or doubt. Trust is to win! Doubt is to lose! And there you have it! One is so vast, the other so tiny. One is of the eternal, the other as ephemeral as fog that hangs low over the landscape of your mind, shuts you in and never gives the opening ahead through which you may see far.

When that fog settles, it is all you can see, dingy, dark shut-in-ness that closes off all lines of helpfulness that would bring new courage for the struggle.

Steer clear of the fog of the spirit, my friend. It is so easy to lose your way! Instead, take the Trust Way where the radiance of God's love and power shines, where you can see clearly where the path leads, step by step. It is not necessary ever to lose the way under the guiding Hand which He holds out! Good night now.

SMUG

Is there ever a reason why man or woman should be smug? You know what I mean by "smug." You have met it. Everyone has met smugness who has been about with people. It is not a cardinal sin, not a sin at all, but an eruption on the surface of one's character like pimples on some people's skin that show something within which needs attention. Often one comes across a person who has all the symptoms that characterize these breakings-out. The one who has them sometimes wonders what is wrong but does not know where the trouble lies.

More often, he does not know that there is any trouble. This is one symptom of smugness, that the one who has it doesn't dream that anything is wrong with him. For smugness is a mark of undevelopment, of littleness; never of greatness. Smugness is harder on other people than on the one who has it. It is a case where the others need to ask for grace to be patient with it and for protection against contracting the first symptom of it themselves.

When a symptom does hint its coming, one should rid himself of the condition which is the cause at whatever price and come clean of the childish qualities of smugness in the ego. Why do I mention what might seem to be a light matter? Because nothing is light from the spirit view-point which concerns development of character.

Our Lord instructed His disciples to be perfect, even as the Father is perfect. The breaking out of inner imperfections, as in smugness, does not comport with that perfection toward which every person ought to strive. So this is not a light matter. When you come face to face with manifested smugness, always ask inwardly for patience and meekness and quietness of spirit that do not savor of the ego but of the character values which Our Lord stressed when He spoke from The Mount.

As an opposite to smugness, I caution you against the common error of worry about what can be handled and what cannot. It is as different from smugness as day is from night. Worry eats inward, gnaws at the core, destroys peace and poise which give life its grace. Smugness is likewise an inner imperfection but it preens and prides itself like a child that stands and primps in front of its looking-glass.

Of the two, worry, not showing on the surface as smugness does, is more insidious. It is a termite which unseen, eats away the props of life until faith is endangered and life itself shrinks below par.

Worry never brought any one through to triumphant living. God has never failed to do so, given His opportunity with the life that is involved with these spiritual termites. Smugness is not greatly concerned with much of anything except its own fancied self-importance.

Will the human learn? I beseech you to prove God in these two imperfections of character. For neither is trifling as part of the experience one meets on the testing grounds of earth; nor too serious for trusting Him with the entire issue!

As you meet and fence with both of these conditions, I commend you always to the Father. He is the most wonderful Foil for every difficulty and the most powerful Friend upon Whom to depend, when you find yourself facing either smugness or worry as they try to get a toehold in your life. Each one is bad for you.

May the lessons of life be increasing joy and challenge to you, as you learn them by the power of His grace!

REINCARNATION

You are thinking deeply these days on great themes related to cosmic realms and find yourself interested beyond what would have been possible a short time ago. Thus it is with growth. Little things are outgrown. By the same token, one moves into the larger as one leaves the smaller.

It is grand evidence of unfolding of mind and soul, than which nothing else is as important, by values of the Eternal. These values are stable through the ages. In a world such as yours where everything changes, where nothing is as it was, there is vast comfort in knowing that in Spirit values there is no variation.

This is another majestic provision with which the Great God blessed His spirit universe. And now I would talk with you again about that teaching of which I knew little while I was in the flesh, teaching which I rather flouted as a pagan doctrine unrelated to truths of God.

This is another case wherein I found how mistaken I had been while I followed the orthodox teachings of the church. You will find it so too, when you are finished with the turmoil and littlenesses of the earth plane.

I refer to re-incarnation. I took it for granted when I was in the flesh, that with the passing of the soul from its material habitat, it was the end of mortal existence, and that never again could that soul return to earth for further cycle of experience and growth. I thought also at that time, that a soul's entire future in the spirit world was determined wholly by what it was at the moment of the Transition. Again, I was in error.

I am not at liberty to delve into the deep places of the philosophy of reincarnation with you. Neither you nor any earth mind could comprehend it and no good would be accomplished. But I want to say that the soul which has completed one earth cycle and lays aside its physical frame for the brighter garb of Heavenly Spheres, may when the time is ripe, again be incarnated in a human body and come back to the narrower limitations of the flesh, beginning anew with its lessons for which there was not sufficient time in the former residence upon earth.

Thus is explained the many times when earth people have sudden flashes of acute remembrance of persons or events with which in their present incarnation they have had no relation whatever. The flash of remembrance is very keen and very genuine.

By the doctrine of reincarnation there come back to earth, those of many experiences with the Transition called death, each time learning more and moving higher in the scale of knowledge. Taking each time the physical form of a babe, the growing soul begins in the human housing just where it left off in the quest for knowledge and service.

Finally comes the time when so much has been acquired of mind and spirit, materiality so largely sloughed off, that for the last time the Great Transition is experienced and the spirit goes to the Ether Planes and higher, always higher in Realms of the Spiritual, until at glorious last, such illumination develops, such sublimation with the All-Good, the very God-head, that personality is merged into the cosmic and serves in that exalted way through the ages of eternity.

Endless questions surge to the surface of your thinking as I say these few things about so vast a doctrine with which earth is only at slight understanding or agreement. But you will believe me when I tell you that this is one of the mightiest provisions of the Creator God for the endless growth of His children. Minds of the most highly illuminated comprehend only little of all this. It is not strange that persons of the earth plane understand it so slightly.

But take it for truth. Read all you can about it. Believe it and grow into as high an understanding of it as is possible.

All these things enter into your sum total of achievement on spirit lines which will stand you in good stead when you come Home to this side of life and will understand more and serve more and reach higher toward your loftiest spirit stature.

God bless and keep you. Your horizon is extending for your advantage. The Inner Planes are in constant presence with you, guiding and supporting you. The peace of the Infinite rest upon you and abide!

READYING

All that really matters for men and women today is to be so attuned with the purity of spirit life that they be ready for imminent changes that will come shortly and that will make drastic changes in the order of living.

I may not give you details. No one of us on these Planes of Life is permitted to send those forth. It is well. But you must know that the day of the New Era will come suddenly. It will reveal so clearly that none may doubt how shallow and worthless are those material values which people of earth have struggled so hard to get and to hold.

They will show for the rubbish they are. The spirit, the will to love and to serve the Father and His children of earth, the will to sacrifice everything for the joy of helping those however humble, who are affrighted or dismayed or alone,—this is truly important and spiritually significant.

All possible time which you can devote to prayer of communion with the Father, to growing in the things of His grace and to lifting your consciousness high above the mundane world in which physically you function, will most reward you on spiritual levels. More and more, let ephemeral, unimportant issues go unresolved, while you devote yourself to acquiring deeper understanding of His Holy Will and the beauty of His love and peace. Sacrifice anything which may be necessary for the joy of coming into closer consciousness with Him and realizing His presence within and about you.

One of the best ways to accomplish this is to hold yourself ready to help any who seek you for light and help in whatever ways appear to be their greatest needs. Give yourself lavishly, gladly, as unto your Lord. And you will feel His power pour into your life in overwhelming volume.

Do not concentrate too intensely upon physical phenomena that almost from day to day, seem to bring new aspects of this change in the life of the world. Watch them, of course, yet do not lay too great stress upon them, until you know their spiritual meanings. All of this will be revelation to earth people such as they have never imagined. Let it find you spiritually ready.

Rejoice and be glad that you have opportunity to be prepared for your part in the change, other things slipping gradually from you as you see greater values in this which is to be. Good night, now!

ROUGH GOING

Squally times come to everybody of earth, when waves of disappointment dash high with the current seeming to run against you while you wonder what to do about it and most of all, why such times come.

The "why" often is not answerable, concealed among many misty causes and effects that are part of life. Any way, "why" is not as immediately important as weathering the emotional storm and finding yourself again in calmer waters. Causes that brought the high waves and dangerous tides with feeling too strong for safety on the spiritual basis, may be discernible, though probably not. Frequently these are concealed in the obscurity of a former life.

So look for the best way to handle the conditions in which now you find yourself and keep watch against repetition of any causes that easily could bring you again into stormy seas. The one sure way is to turn to the secret shrine within where your Lord dwells. Tell Him all about it, ask His directives for the next steps and His loving forgiveness where you have been in error, then release the emotional stresses that come flying in like thick concealing fog.

With His presence to protect and comfort you, you are safe as long as you rely wholly on Him and His infinite guidance. Then even if stormy waters dash against your personal citadel, they can not bear you down, for you are safe in His sheltering love.

Today's high tides that seemed ominous to you, in reality are not. As so often earth people do, you overemphasize them. I know the situation well. And it will clear. Go carefully with absolute faith in the One to Whom dangerous seas present no difficulty. Billows will not dash too high nor overcome you.

Spend more time than usual alone with Him in prayer and there, let the load roll off of your consciousness. When it has rolled, do not stoop to pick it up again. Mortals are prone to do that, you know. When you have released whatever the load is at any time, let it stay released, and you go free of its weight. Soon you will realize that it did not weigh as heavily as you thought.

Earth seas are running rough these times. But He is in complete command over winds and waves. As you look at all this in retrospect, you will know how truly I speak and what I say to you, I say to all who brave stormy seas of life today. Find comfort in Him. He is your protection, and your assurance of safe landing when your voyage on earth is complete. Meanwhile I send you blessings from the Inner Planes toward which you move. Blessings of cheer to each of you.

RELEASED POWER

Why does mankind, why do you, doubt that the way will be clearly shown when light has been sought and faith put actively to work? No one of you of earth knows a fraction of the power abiding in you if only you would recognize it, honor it, glorify it, live by it as your compass and expect it to produce results.

Acceptance of all this on the part of earth people is so lukewarm, so half-hearted, so uncertain, that no one can wonder at the halfway measures of success which come within man's heart. Great, abounding, overwhelming victories are possible to each of you and should be won. For that which is the essential, is within your reach for your claiming; just at your hand for your using!

If this sounds like preaching, it is! Just one glimpse of what the power of spirit is, and you would never again wonder whether your way will open, never again doubt the successful outcome of your prayers for guidance, for inspiration and substance. There is at your hand the same elemental stuff, the same creative material which is so confounding the whole world today because of fear of what it may bring in the world man has developed to its present civilizations.

I do not say that you have this power in things material, because you have not developed sufficiently to be able to command it. But potentially it is there within you, within every man who understands and accepts the releasing power of spirit over things of the material world.

Jesus Christ in His earth ministry used the releasing power of spirit over atomic structure and multiplied material substance by the power of His spirit.

Down intervening ages these have been called miracles when in reality, they were but His using the power of creative law and putting it into practice to gain results He needed to help humanity and to teach His lessons.

Release this power within you and you will be amazed at what will come. Mankind keeps himself locked up within the narrow scope of his own knowledge and understanding, instead of capitalizing on this Infinite resource which is offered freely by the Creator.

THE JOURNEY ACROSS

Gladly I greet you and bring again to your remembrance the happy fact that on this side of life, we need no rest. For we live in the world of spirit and are free of the limitations with which you of earth contend a while longer. Don't dread coming hither! Nor let any anxiety becloud your thought of that day when the Silver Cord will be loosed and you too, will make the Great Transition.

Generally, it is not a time of pain, though pain may have preceded it. Rather, it is a time of blessed release from discomforts of the flesh, lack of material resources, conflicts and littlenesses with which one must contend. All these and many more!

When you no longer need to wear the garment of flesh, your joy will be great. Rewards will surpass the trials and temptations and hazards of earth. You will see for yourself that life over here has such satisfaction, such growth and incentives to serve, such fellowships and such joy in worship, that you will know how understated my words to you have been.

The time seems long to you. But in reality, sidereal time passes quickly. There is much for you to do. Each day will help to teach you lessons of deep value which will stand you in good stead against the time of your slipping the ties of earth and coming on Home to the many who here await your coming.

Even though I have many times said it to you, it needs emphasizing for them who may not have learned it. So again I say it:—There Is No Death.—. Do not weary in making clear to others how not even the body dies. It undergoes complete change, takes on other forms, other qualities, does other work, but it does not die! Life is without beginning and without end. This stupendous thought stretches to the utmost any mind that tries to think it through. To comprehend it even in part does away with the indifferent attitudes of the many who hold that life is brief, soon over and done with!

It is not so! Life is part of God Himself, immortal, untouchable by death. It comes from God and returns to God, cycle after cycle. But it never ends! This makes it so vastly important to live with clear understanding of values, of what is right and true or of little significance.

We here who are responsible for these Messages, know that it is time to repeat this so-weighty truth that is interwoven with earth's deep fears and dreads. The journey across from the earth side of life to our Planes of Infinite Joy, is infinitesimally brief, in point of your reckoned time. There are no dark valleys, no ominous waves, no inhospitable shores. Would any of these be like the Great, Good God? No! Nothing in His universe, except what man has despoiled, is a thing to dread.

The brief journey from the earth phase of life to this one which is higher, is good and is not to be approached with fear or dread. I beseech you to use every opportunity to lighten this load which many carry heavily in their hearts.

Let the Transition be foreseen with joy, anticipated with faith and calm assurance of good. The half of all which it means, cannot be told you of earth. I am glad I could come on ahead to help assure you and the many others of the welcomes which await you. This is one of our ways of great service.

In this spirit, I give you His blessing which is beyond earthly computing.

FURTHER GLIMPSES

I wish to tell you more of certain aspects of life here, because it is highly desirable for you all to have deeper understanding. Please let me talk a bit more about vision, that being so close to my heart. It is hard now to remember that I had to struggle to see even a little, because of the glory that sweeps before our eyes, so clear, so ravishing, so beyond anything earth offers. You will remember that I was never given to exaggeration. Here as usual, I speak with restraint.

The trees on these Inner Planes sing the glory of God! So marvelous is their beauty that it seems as if we never saw trees before! Many varieties bear blossoms so gorgeous in colors and shapes, that they are utterly indescribable. And many trees yield perfume sweeter than any earth knows.

The shade of these heavenly trees is rich with a depth of beauty that you cannot imagine until you come Home to live and get acquainted with what I am trying to say. There is variety and aliveness to their beauty that baffles all effort at description. Here there is neither heat nor cold—just sheer perfection! All of this shakes my emotional nature even yet, though now I have been here for years.

The companionship on these Planes of Power is very wonderful, never marred by jealousy nor discord; with never a negative note, but harmony and understanding and mutual respect and appreciation of what each one is striving to accomplish spiritually. It is all in the spirit of service and for the love of God.

It took me a long time to veer my mind from the qualities in which earth is rife, where envy and avarice and greed and other ills of the spirit frequently manifested and wrought deep unhappiness in human hearts. Here we are blessedly free from all of this, surrounded with a glowing quality of divine love and the spirit of infinite peace.

Every moment is as if it were experience fresh from the bounty of the Father. The more you of earth free yourselves of every least taint of these earthy qualities that mean strife and bitterness, the better off you are. From them you have to be freed before you can progress spiritually. So cut away the least hint of them and never let them return to hinder your growth.

While I was of earth, I did not think often of the high quality of humility, good though I knew it was. Here we see such glittering spirits who came to their radiance in the realms of spirit by virtue of the mellowing, the gracious, Golden-Rule quality of humility. It has no vestige of cringing but it does have the great quality of recognizing relations of greatness and of learning to place high those who have earned it. The spirit of humility centers in love. And no service is lowly. For it is always as unto Him. This sanctifies it and makes glorious both the service and him who renders it. Cultivate this rare humility, my friend, for it has everything to commend itself.

In the organized activity which prevails here, there is no confusion, no overlapping, no idleness. Everyone is absorbed in some special task. The more I studied this, the more I learned how intently the great of earth from other ages, devote their vast abilities here to bringing to completion, such skills and services as will contribute to making earth a better place to live.

They are making ready for earth use that which will revolutionize the civilization of the future. And it will all be in the order of peaceful pursuits—not of war! Here life is the acme of peaceful activity, where accomplishment prevails and frustration is left behind. Everyone is motivated by the all-glorious love of the Father Who Himself is heaven! Amen!

THE NEW AGE

Conditions are rapidly changing in the world despite lack of knowledge on the part of millions of people who know nothing of what is impending. Not one person living on earth today but will be affected, many of them drastically.

The New Age is making rapid changes that will bring about vast differences in the format of the world and in civilizations that now exist but will not long continue to exist. When the Lord of all the Universes knows that the time is at hand for a great New Age to be born, rest assured all plans are perfect and all provisions made. The hosts of High Heaven are ready and equipped for meeting the changes that are beginning to appear. It will be a time of fear, especially for those who are not attuned to the will of the Highest, who have loved neither His laws nor His ways of life. Their day is all but done, however impossible that seems to those of materialistic vision which sees only with physical eyes and in whose understanding the true Light does not shine.

You are not to fear; but you are to be ready to serve in whatever ways you can be most valuable. The Great Ones will be in and out among you, with their lives of utter purity that make them like great towers of strength, guiding, protecting, advising, giving confidence and directions for service.

Earth people will come to see that there is but one God; only one Law and that is the universal Law of Love. When this concept is fully arrived in the hearts of the human, life will begin its greatest era of spiritual progress and beauty of living and understanding.

Each earth resident is judged by his own credentials, to see whether he is worthy of participating in the life of the New Age. If he is, such person will have immediately new and difficult lessons for learning. But they will be learned more easily than ever before, with joy and gladness and with eagerness to learn that has not hitherto prevailed.

Oh, make the most of this short remaining time to draw closer to the Lord in Love and in desire to conform completely to His will and to be as like unto Him as human can come to be. Seek only the spiritual! Let the old materiality slip by and live in Him in Whom is your whole life. All else is mist and fog. Remember I shall be close to you to guide and help you and as many others as I may.

Rejoice!

UNEXPECTEDS

They are always coming to the human; the good and that which looks bad; what you think you want and what, from your limited earth viewpoint, you are sure you do not want. Both of these are frequently in error.

You marvel that you did not control the projection of your desires into the ethers in which all things are formed. You thought you wanted this. You loosed your power of creative thought to forming it. Soon or late, here it came in unmistakable terms. When you saw it for what it was, you knew you did not want it.

Life lays certain gifts at your feet which mistakenly, you think you do not want. They are invaluable for your growth in spiritual development, than which nothing else in life is as important. And you grow by learning the lessons which life expects you to learn.

By "learning," I mean mastering them. This is to make each experience your own in the deep places of consciousness, to the extent that you will never again need to learn its particular lessons again. Snap judgment is undesirable when it comes to unexpecteds of experience that stay with you until they have done their work, and you are released from them.

An experience from a former embodiment may rise suddenly before you, as often good as bad, to be recognized and accepted and adjustments made. If it reveals injustice at a previous time in the life of your soul and the injustice manifests now in some unpleasant effect through which you must work your way, it will have important lessons to teach you. Do not seek to avoid these lessons. Be willing to learn from them. Let them draw you closer to the heart of the Father, as you adjust to them. Give thanks for them and seek to gain from them every lesson of love and service which they can yield to your soul. You will rise higher in consciousness as you are willing to accept whatever comes for your realization in the evolution of your soul.

Does this sound ponderous? Do you wish I would talk with you on easier phases of life? You should never wish for the exclusion of anything that is vital for the growth of the soul and I urge you who study these lessons coming through the ethers, to keep a learning heart toward any experience which comes into your life. See whether it be for good. When you are satisfied on that point, inner wisdom from the Father will guide you and you will know what to do concerning it.

Never rest upon your own understanding which is frail and undependable. His wisdom has the power of Infinity and when you seek it, you are always led aright, and taught the essence of value in each experience. From it, you will gain all the power it holds for you, all the love it can teach you, all the tolerance it can give you, all the wisdom in it which is related to your need.

When some unexpected comes from undesirable sources and you do not desire to face it, just know that any questionable quality can be transmuted into a great lesson that will lift you nearer your ideal for life. Study to make its inner teachings your strength and your good. Let nothing veer you aside from earnestly applying every lesson which life sets for you.

From our Higher Planes where our own lessons are more advanced, we bless you all and surround you with such power to keep on with your learning, that you never lose heart!

A SPIRITUAL SYNTHETIC

The gratitude of my soul goes in overflowing measure to the many whom it is my joy to serve. Though we do not fulfill our commissions of service from the Inner Planes for the sake of gaining gratitude, it does enrich our consciousness and double our joy in serving them who need us and ask for our help.

If people who temporarily call earth their home, realized the riches that gratitude gives to every situation in life and how it refines the very textures of their souls, they would be deeply determined to cultivate this divine grace until their living was impregnated with its power and beautified by its unselfishness.

Gratitude is what your today's scientists call a "synthetic," consisting of a variety of constituent elements. Inevitably and by its very nature, love is its major factor, imparting to gratitude the glory that only divine and infinite love can give and the shiningness of beauty that comes only with love.

With love, understanding comes as a part of gratitude and finds that joy and freely-given appreciation are amazing mixers, welding together the many vital factors in the development of the soul. Gratitude to others has a way all its own of shining up every situation which it touches and every one with whom it has contact. For always there is something, whatever the issue, for which to manifest gratitude; not stingily but graciously, ringingly expressing gratitude, though sometimes you think your heart is about to break. It won't! And the power of true gratitude even in toughest times and places, helps tremendously in the growth of the soul to its full-orbed stature.

Ponder the lives of any of the truly great of the roster of earth whose lives have blossomed even amid hardships and distresses and you will find strong evidence of the matchlessness of gratitude as part of the synthesis of that soul.

Unostentatiously gratitude has unsuspected power in removing rough places and touching up spots that are stained and dis-colored by the thoughtlessness of self-centered living. Thus are the plans and purposes of God speeded toward their fulfillment in your life, in the lives of all who are willing to practice the power of gratitude in the midst of daily strife and its struggles. There is where gratitude works best as a lubricant when the human machinery creaks and things look set for a crack-up. I had many such times on earth. I know of what I am telling you!

Some people are inclined to yield the gratitude of their hearts to those who are listed on their approved social lists—if from these Spirit Planes I may recall such follies as social lists. Don't restrict it thus, I beseech you. It will do you and everyone who tries it, more harm than can be expressed, seriously restricting the free-flowing richness of good that gratitude can yield to any life.

Let it flow without hindrance to every level of conscious existence, for you know that every created thing has its definite degree of divine intelligence, part of the lavish endowment which the Creator has bestowed upon His every created entity. Transforming thought, that! It will enlarge every life that accepts its truth.

Each tiniest living thing should receive your spiritually significant gratitude, not just once but continuingly as you are in contact with them. If you inhibit gratitude and shut it up behind barriers, the soil of your soul will become barren like rock.

Take gratitude into full partnership and give it free rein in every aspect of your life. Don't be afraid! Pour it forth to every one you meet, on all forms of created life, in understanding, sympathetic sharing. Then see life blossom like a rose, giving forth the rare fragrance that is part of the enduement of gratitude.

In all the earnestness of my soul, I send you this vital word from the High Planes of Spirit life, for cultivating all the factors of soul growth, against the day of full harvest.

GOD'S TRUTH

It was refreshing for me to drop in on you recently when you were asking for inspiration directed at a writing assignment you faced against time, then for me to be able to send you almost immediately all that you needed. Here is the vast power of thought transference which spans the universe in less than an instant of your time and by which I have talked with you these many years since I was promoted to these High Planes. It was wonderful to see your face brighten and to catch the lilt of gratitude in your heart as you expressed appreciation!

It did me as much good as it did you. Such experiences are necessarily a two-way channel along which thought flows unimpeded if the channel is kept free of clogging interference. Where there is rapport between those who commune together this way, great good comes through for mutual help that flows out far beyond the originating two.

You are heading now into the better time of the New Day when experiences expand and growth takes on new dimensions and service enlarges which you are to render in the name of the Holy One. Rejoice and be consumingly grateful for all of this. Hold nothing back! Give all to Him and His way of life intended for you.

Let the glittering, glowing aura of the at-hand New Age shed its light brilliantly into your heart, lifting and teaching you in ways that comport with the new sense of power inherent in the new civilization that will be established upon your earth. Ere long the whole world will know it for what it is, though many of earth are not ready to experience its satisfactions nor its expansiveness of understanding and wisdom and truth and good. The issue for you is clear, and for all who would share this world made new.

Supreme responsibility for all such is for complete dedication to spiritual living and learning, leaving out of your desires things worldly and transient. This I have told you previously. But in earth life, other interests sometimes interpose themselves above what is of primary importance. So it is essential to refresh your minds.

You will sense all of this joyously when finally you and I together talk it all through and you realize life as it is here on these Planes of Spiritual Splendor. I had to unlearn much that men of earth had taught as what they supposed was true. Here there is no man-made interpretation of truth. For all is God! His wisdom; His light; His power; His love! It is glorious beyond words to express.

When the barriers of earth are down, together we shall drink from the Eternal Fountain and know that all we learn is Truth forevermore, even as God the Father is Truth. And there is none other!

My blessings of patience and peace and His presence to envelop your heart with infinite love and give you exceeding joy.

THE SPLENDOR OF SERVICE

This is a great and wonderful shibboleth here on these Inner Planes and through it, we express our love and gratitude and worship to Him Who is the Giver of all. Nothing gives us greater joy than to serve one who has come hither or one yet in residence on the planet of earth. When I was in the flesh I used to think that the word service was overworked and worn rather thin. The word may be. But the fact is blessedly alive and every opportunity to exemplify it gives us deep joy.

We here suggest that you see service as your way to represent Him, to be His ambassador to any whom in any way you may help. Never belittle service! Remember that it is a high and priceless privilege to serve any one of His children, then however humble your commission, fulfill it in adoration to Him.

The humble heart is in His royal tradition Who always said that of Himself He could do nothing; it was the Father Who worked in Him. So it is with you. Any service should be in His name and for His sake, possible through His indwelling power. Think this through very carefully. Take it as eternal truth that can make-over the living of your earth span and yield you a sheaf of trophies when you reach Home!

However constantly you draw upon His resources of love and power, you can never over-draw nor deplete the resource. Always there is more than enough here. This is an amazing aspect of the spirit realms that there is lavishly more than enough of everything; of beauty and color; of glory and power and wisdom; more than enough of love and companionship with each other and with the Shining Ones who teach us in the simplicity of humility. Here all is as unending as God.

It will help you to remember that however many years your coming hither may be postponed, there will be no less of His unspeakable beauty and power and love than now. For there is no exhausting God! But one may appropriate God and His goodness and make life more richly serviceable by His grace.

Open your heart to profound understanding of these facets of infinite power which have been revealed to you and live by the lessons they teach you. They are given in the spirit of humility and with burning desire for you to make your living experience rich in serving and worshipping God the Father. My blessings be with you as by steady stages you come higher until you are ready to slip the inhibiting bonds of your earth body and accept the glittering garments of spirit radiance. More I cannot say. Higher I cannot go!

HIGHEST AND MOST HOLY

I bid you look deeply beneath the surface of Easter time for the majestic truth which raises it above every other earth season and surrounds it with a scintillating glory more wonderful than any other.

The Blessed Lord Christ came into earth incarnation at Bethlehem to bring His Father's love to the hearts of the world and to teach them His Way of Life. In His thirty-three years, He suffered and loved; He taught and healed and bore eternal witness of His Father's transforming love to the hearts of all mankind.

He surrendered completely His own will and was tempted on every score like unto mortal men. He ran the gamut of human experience, yet without sin. In the last galling hours of agony on Calvary, He asked His Father to forgive those who were doing Him to death because "they know not what they do."

He had left nothing undone that was His to do and had completed the commission which His Father had given Him before He came to earth. Then quietly, He told His Father, "It is finished." His tortured physical body needed no longer sustain Him and it was laid in the tomb, as the custom of man is.

Having finished His course and kept the faith, there remained the inexpressible and transcendent glory of demonstrating to all ages the truth He had taught, that there is no death. His tomb became irradiated with Light that never can be dimmed, even to the end of time. This was the climax of His earthly mission. Begun in mystery and wonder as encircling choirs of angels sang the story of His birth, it ended with such majesty of spiritual overcoming, such complete attunement with the will of His Father and such tremendous power for the lives of all men down the ages, that Easter stands the towering climax of all glory and power through Divine love, revealing the wondrous truth of life which death can not touch. This is the great lesson of Easter, surmounting all other! Amen!

THE SCORE BOARD

The fact that each of you of earth is charged with definite responsibility for service that none but you can render, is part of the great challenge that life poses the children of men. Each of you has some definite place in the economy of the world and of spirit realms that no one else can fill as you can. This is a true and solemn obligation for each one of earth to accept and to seek to fulfill.

If any one falls short through indifference or from feelings of inferiority and the notion that some one else can do it better, he is merely using alibis that do not alter the challenge. The Father has given each one of earth this vast responsibility for specific relationships to life and they are not transferable.

Failure to measure up to the challenge means that the one who fails will ultimately face a score-board that shows a dark spot where no accomplishment is registered; where the human fell short on what was given him to do. There can be no progress for that soul until the empty place on the score board of life has been filled, perhaps in some other chapter of human expression.

It is serious business to tamper with the plans and purposes of the Infinite God Whose laws are immutable, loving Father though He is. Sometimes men and women think the parts assigned to them in the great human drama are so small as to be not quite worth bothering about. Reasoning thus and wishing to be freed of them, many a one shrugs his shoulders and prefers to follow his own plans.

In the inner place of his being, he knows he has avoided an obligation which he should have met with loyalty and continuing devotion. This inner knowing is the Holy Spirit seeking to convince that one where his work is and the positive character of his relation to it. And joy comes only when each one loyally does the work that is his to do, that he came into his present embodiment to do. Size is no part of its value. The Father is judge of that.

Rejoice in your role; play it with your whole heart; develop it to its best; then lay it before Him Who gave it to you and hear Him say, "Well done, my loyal, loving child!"

CLEARER CONCEPTS

From here we watch the tides of earth turn from ebb to flow and tides of life within the hearts of men that clearly indicate rising influences of spirituality in the life of the world. This is in dramatic contrast to the materialistic goals toward which men have long striven desperately.

They have given up everything else for money and position and power, finding them gall and worm-wood, once they were attained. Neither joy nor security nor peace of mind come with these, but emptiness and hollow mockery. When joy and peace of mind are accepted with love and humility and tolerance and justice, to keep life in balance, they yield mankind comfort and pleasure and opportunity for loving service to others.

Finding how undependable things of earth are for true satisfaction and how quickly they take wings and are gone, men are eagerly seeing signs of great changes ahead. For the most part they cannot interpret these nor how long they will endure nor how they will give life the zest which it has lacked.

From these Inner Planes we realize increasingly how unsatisfactory men have found life because they have lived as if God were somewhere off on a cosmic shelf instead of being the Source of everything that is. This distorted thinking has caused wars to rage, lives to be maladjusted, values 0f living out of joint and filled with trouble and sorrow.

Never fail to realize that it is only as men keep God as their Center and their only Assurance, can life be the radiant experience it should be. It is on these lines that tides are flowing rapidly. Alarmingly the church turned from preaching God to discussing literary themes and scientific approaches to living, with occasional mentions of God, paying much heed to what is called the social gospel and trying to exemplify it. This is quite all right.

Our Blessed Lord stood clearly for the social gospel that reached out to heal men of their diseases, to raise their dead, to solve their problems and to make them men of spiritual power, witnesses to the God within them. But to try to implement this social gospel which does not center everything in God with power that is God-power, is to court failure.

This is an issue which your world faces and does not know how to solve. Only as men root their faith firmly in Him, can solutions come. Then streams of helpfulness will pour from the Perennial Fountain into hearts that do not know where to turn. This is tragedy. Men have searched far afield. Now with the rising tide of conviction that God is their solution, the picture of humankind is changing. Men of position are daring to stand forth to talk of God and His way of life, offering Him as the answer to the painful riddles of earth that have racked mankind down the long centuries.

Thus the muddy waters that have been roiled with things earthy and ineffectual, begin to show signs, as we see them from these Blessed Planes, of becoming purer. The rising tide of spirituality will sweep men away from the shallows where they have tried to live, out into the deeps where they will learn that only in God can living come to its fruition. Life changes when men begin to see this and actually to realize it. For nothing is beyond this God-power. Do not be satisfied with less than the best He wishes you to have. This "best" is without money and without price and with it you may transform life.

As you really prove God, life takes on new luster and men know that the Light is shining in what had been their darkness. This is the hope of your world and it is shining more brightly even through what seems unprecedented darkness of evil. Launch out into the deeps of His love and follow Him through every hour of your life. He is everything you can desire!

GOD!

Never before in all the annals of your world has there been such desperate need for realizing the conscious presence of the Most High God in all the councils of government and the affairs of personal living, as there is now.

In this time of crisis, it is God or nothing for the nations and the civilizations of earth. Nothing else will avail; only God and His way of life; only God and the peace which He alone can give when the hearts of the people of the world ask beseechingly for it. Otherwise peace will be another treaty and wars will continue.

Only God is the healing solace of hearts that bleed and of lives that are broken. Only God! How I yearn to say it so the whole world might see it as we here on the Inner Planes see it! His glory is so great that no archangel, highest though he be, can ever fail to bow in humble worship; so mighty that He holds the universes of His creation as in the hollow of His hands.

God is the completeness of perfection and no flaw has ever entered into anything He has made. All the errors and the swelling tides of evil have come from man's insistence on running according to his finite knowledge, the world God made by the power of His Infinite love; He, the Un-begotten, from before time began and to the everlastingness of eternity!

Very close at hand for you of earth comes the day when He shall rule the world and all of its nations with His creative love, and when the ghastly evil man has wrought will vanish from its place of imagined power.

The only safe place for you is at the Center of your being where always the Almighty God dwells. Let His love and His grace manifest in your life, withholding nothing from Him or His service. Then you will consciously experience Him and His presence as an Infinite garment of protection enfolding you. Amen!

A GRACE DIVINE

One of the most Christ-like graces—deep humility! Nothing servile is in it, nor any quality that is menial, no false modesty, no make-believe. True humility serves others without personal ambition intermingled. It reaches out eagerly to any one in need, offering every value available, with no vaunting of personal prowess. Though its powers be limited, they are truly, gladly, unselfishly offered to any who will be helped by them, without money or price.

True humility earned its crown of perfection in the magnificent stature of the Christ Who came not to be ministered unto but always to minister. There you have the crux of it—to do unassumingly, unostentatiously, unexpecting of rewards, looking only for opportunities to help some one higher, never for personal aggrandizement.

This is a tremendous commission for a human to undertake. Humility is one of the rarest graces of spirit that any human may acquire. It never comes easily nor quickly. It goes too deep and mounts too high to spring quickly into full growth in any heart. Like the oak tree of slow growth, it spreads its roots deep and far and wide into nourishing soil that never fails of yielding what the growing tree needs.

Thus does humility. It makes no pretensions among men nor has it any "show-off." Its deep roots are sturdy against storm of criticism or dismay or defeat. In exact proportion as its roots are deep do its branches spread far up and out. This balancing of roots and branches is necessary both for the giant oak and for genuine humility.

Only one whose roots of understanding and love and self-forgetfulness have plunged far below surface soil, can manifest these graces of humility. Otherwise a sudden flash of worldly interest or some passing parade of humankind, intent upon show for show's sake, might wash away its sturdiness and strength.

The rich quality of this humility should not be confused with sham arrays of modesty. It is the pure gold of the mine. In human form, it prefers to stand on the side lines, watching to help quietly and without notice of men. Never is it out in front, waving the banners nor cheering with the crowd. Its greatness is partly its unobtrusiveness, united to readiness to step effectively into any breach and carry through with poise and power.

Jesus Christ ministering in person upon earth, possessed this superlative grace of spirit, knowing the grandeur of soul which gladly bent to serve, then rose unto heights of ministry to others. Vast dignity characterizes true humility, likewise goodness and gentleness and kindness and patience which come to flower under the spell of divine and conquering love, which unifies them in perfection of spirit.

When Jesus rebuked them who did evil or sought to trip Him in controversy, when they accused Him of breaking the Sabbath with works of mercy, He manifested always the divine grace of humility which was reaching out to serve where there was need. All this was in utter forgetfulness of His radiant personality. He is true humility at its climax, example for all men everywhere to emulate.

Under the lash of materialistic greed for power through money and place and prestige on the planet of earth, humility is sorely needed but little appreciated. They who qualify are relatively few. Its disciplines are many and its lessons difficult. But take heart! The day is at hand when humility again comes into its own as men begin to realize that powers of spirit are coming to leadership.

The humble of heart will justify in un-selfed service, increasing the vibrations of power as they forget all save stooping to lift bewildered ones who need the outreached hand which humility offers. What glory will crown them whose hearts are filled with this grace! How surprised at the values which the modest and self-effacing grace of their humility has acquired! I beg you cultivate it with close attention and intelligent devotion. Then never lose opportunity to manifest it. The more difficult the situation, the greater the glory that will surround the truly humble of heart. Watch what I say in this Message and see it come to pass ere long!

SOUL

The soul is the very essence of the human; it is the "you" of every human; it is the part of "you" which endures from incarnation to incarnation. During intervals here on the Ether Planes, the soul is busily assimilating into its very fiber all the experiences which it had in the body in its most recent incarnation.

You will see that from a long and active life on earth, it is not a quick process for this assimilation to be made in completeness, so that the soul may be ready again for re-embodiment, if that be necessary for learning additional lessons. If the most recent incarnation was brief, a relatively lesser time is required for this assimilation.

For the soul is the essence of the entity. It never is born; it never dies; it registers all experience, all growth; it retains all knowledge that has ever entered the life of the human whose it is and it carries this wondrous record of knowledge, of good or ill from life to life and knows when the time is at hand in the passing of the cycles, when it need not return to earth again.

The soul is that which grows with its discipline or does not grow; which becomes more God-like or chooses to remain yet longer to feed upon the husks of the pleasures of earth life.

Essentially individualistic to each entity of the human, soul is invisible, though there be some who claim with a measure of validity, to have captured its likeness with the magic of the earth camera, as it was passing from its physical abode to the ethers, at the time of its Transition.

Its everlastingness, its assimilative powers, its memory in the subjective, its relation to spirit but with fine discrimination between soul and spirit, make mystery so vast, so overwhelming, that the mortal who attempts to interpret such mystery, needs to bow the head in wonder and awe.

In its recording of readiness or unreadiness for higher levels of living, the soul is the active agent beyond which none may go. The soul experiences, thrills, learns, is tempered like finest steel or refuses that tempering, according to what its human entity chooses. It is the identity of each human entity and with it, each one lives through the long cycles of his earth life.

Keep company with it, therefore, in all loyalty. Realize that nothing else in your earth life is as important as your attitude to your soul. For it is the God-ness within you, the gift of the Father, the part of you which never leaves you.

When ultimately after eons, you are merged into the God-head, having learned every lesson which earth life was designed to teach you, the soul yet retains its identity as "you," freed from every vestige of the flesh and alive with the glory of the Father.

Learn all you can about the nature of the soul while you are on the earth plane, always referring to the soul in terms of profound reverence to which it is entitled, by its Divine origin. Never refer to it in any other way, I beseech you.

CONCERNING RESULTS

Learning to wait is hard for almost everybody of earth. It was desperately hard for me when I was there in the flesh. I thought that what seemed important, was indeed important and that delays worked against results for which I aimed. So I struggled for results, not realizing that I was working against values which I thought I was advancing.

One should not work primarily for results. They come when work is rightly done, in dedication of self and service. This too, is difficult for the earth person to realize fully. So let me repeat: One's life is effective only when it is dedicated to some goal, expressed through life and service. Results should not be the concern. Leave them to the Higher Powers to integrate for the best good on the largest terms.

What should concern every human is so to live and work as to accomplish all for which his life was given him; to fail of nothing that is in the divine pattern for his life; to yield completely to the work that is his; accomplishing it with joy and gladness; anxious for nothing; impatient at nothing; neither restless nor ill-at-ease when results come slowly or do not appear to come at all.

Again I repeat: Results are not the evidences of value. What is evidence of value is the completeness with which one gives himself to what is his to do. When one learns this lesson as we used to say when I was a lad in country school, "by heart," he works from a different motive, sees the design clearly and is neither fretted nor disturbed by frequent waiting for results.

Once you lose this anxious concern about results and put that power into doing your work and following the pattern which is yours to weave, life will be devoid of the friction which often is apparent when the eyes are searching for results. The lesson is learned only when you can forget them, letting them take care of themselves. For this they will do any way!

All of this weaves into the business of learning to wait, without tension or fretting or thinking that everything is going to smash, unless! Relax to the degree where you can do and be your best in easy, peaceful flow of patience and faith, knowing that you are in the care of your Father.

This "knowing" is one of the greatest achievements the human can acquire. It is like the great human nerve center, controlling many bodily functions effortlessly, keeping the whole in perfect alignment.

When you have this "knowing," you will realize what great living is and you will experience joy in both living and working.

How deeply I wish I had learned these lessons when I was resident on earth! It would have done much for me then and have made my progress swifter when I reached these Shores of Marvelous Life. But I was not taught thus. I used to feel the stirrings of truth similar to this when I was trying to do my work in the world. But I learned haltingly. Now I know the vast influences that flow from such learning and how important it is for every human to work intelligently, with understanding rooted in divine truth!

Were it not so, there would be no point to putting these Messages into your care for sending out into life that needs this leavening. For these are truly spiritual yeast. They who work with me in preparing them realize that every idea discussed is valuable purely for its spiritual import, for furthering the work and the life which are gifts of the Father. We beg you all to remember and realize this.

Everything in your earth life you will find in its right place in your life record and you will face it unavoidably, after you have made the Great Transition. What has been done in error, must be set right before you may progress. What has not been done and should have been, must also be accomplished before your way higher will clear.

It is all just as important as this and I beg you to take it so. All of it is intended to be liberating to your spirit. Take it so. And grow. And learn. And rejoice that you may weave to the perfect pattern which is for eternal years. Amen!

GOD'S WAY OF WORKING

The goodness of Our God is beyond understanding! This I thought I knew while I was resident on earth. But since I came hither and have witnessed triumphs of the soul such as I never knew before and have seen what the love of the Divine may mean to those of earth whose struggle is difficult, I know with clarity and humility more than I ever dreamed, of the goodness of Our God.

It is poured out into human lives as rains descend upon barren and parched ground. Blessedly, however much He gives of supply and love and peace and power, there is always as much left as there was at the beginning. Mankind needs to learn this, for there is no diminishing of the bounty of the Father! Always there is as much as there was, however lavishly He has poured out His treasures into needy lives. Give ringing thanks to Him for this rich blessedness. And take this lesson to yourself.

When you give to others in selflessness, good returns to you in like degree. It works thus throughout the whole range of living and is one of the gracious manifestations of the goodness of Our God. He never permits them who are attuned to His laws of love, to suffer lack.

Throughout the universes His love and supply of every needed good come in overflowing bounty to any who asks in faith and with open heart, to accept His good gifts. In the working of this law, there is nothing of what we used to say when I was a boy, "You give me and I give you."

Instead it is the Infinite yearning of the Father to share His universal good with His children. He functions by laws which He has made and which control the universes that swing in the firmaments. Even so, He is not stern or austere. On the contrary, He is love in the most wonderful sense. And His Love is His Law! This calls for clear thinking and by it you should pattern your life.

Live His way; praise His way; love His way! And your joy will be full. Amen!

THE CUP OF LIFE

Do you not sense it? Do you not see it full circle round on every hand, throughout every day? Changes that are coming in your world are miracles of God's grace, marvels for which to praise His Holy Name! Many there be who see only the blackness of evil and darkness of sin filling the world. For appalling they are.

But their day does wane and the day of God draws close, so close that vibrations on every side tell the wondrous story of His plans coming to completion for the cleansing of the world, the making anew what man has despoiled with his greed for money and power, his evil thinking, lusting and desiring for things of the flesh.

There needs be drastic cleansing of the inside of the cup of life; the outside washed clean of the sin and shame and all things unworthy, the whole made again pure and holy. The turmoil and upheavals that earth now is experiencing point clearly to this which comes surely and soon, that the will of the Holy One may be regnant on earth and His laws become the code for man's governing. To see, you have but to look!

They who have been busy only with material interests begin to see more clearly that no satisfaction is to be found in these things which pass quickly and have no righteous relation to the soul of man. When the cleansing fires of the Holy One have done their purifying work in men's lives, they will see with the opening eyes of spiritual vision, that the confusions and turmoil and evil doings of the ages past have brought man nothing but disillusionment and sorrow and the futile worship of the Golden Calf.

None of this enables man to find his way higher to spiritual levels where he can the better understand God's ways and His purity that are to characterize the day beginning to arrive in the life of the planet of earth.

It will be a more drastic shake-up in the world of mankind than now you can quite picture. Old ways will be blacked out; old standards will be broken down; old amusements will be seen in their true and fallacious light. Liquor and drugs and all other dissipations which have afflicted man, will disappear from his possession. Cravings will be severe. But that which might temporarily quiet the cravings, will be gone, not to return.

Man will find that in God alone may peace be found, once his heart has been cleansed and his desires made clean and holy. In God alone does joy abide and only in Him can the life of the New Age come to its flowering.

It is a long way to go. But remember, He is with you! And all will be well with each one in whose heart the love of the Father abides. Pray for this day to come speedily that blessings may more richly abound and you of earth may truly know the peace of Him Who maketh the storm a calm. Amen!

* * *

G<small>OD IS GREATER THAN CIRCUMSTANCE</small>

THE LORD CHRIST DRAWS NEAR

Since I came to these Inner Planes of great glory, the mightiest and most majestic of the many learnings I have achieved within my soul, centers in the unspeakable, the almost unbearable glory of the Lord Christ as here we learn more of Him and His Infinity than earth could ever teach us.

Not that we see His face for He is so completely pure spirit, so Divinely sublime and of the nature of the Godhead, that eyes of lesser levels of spiritual seeing do not visualize Him in earth ways. Nevertheless His glory is manifested to us as we move upward toward loftier spiritual heights of understanding.

The surrounding ethers reveal His presence in ways of such mighty vibratory power as I could by no possible reach of inadequate words impart to you, vibratory power which earth can not conceive. This is particularly true when He reveals His great glory to us.

Here we learn, when we are receptive, that all of this means the drawing near of the Christ of God for some incredibly wonderful spiritual feast of worship. By colors that earth does not know; by unnumbered hosts of heaven singing in choral formation music that swells through the high courts of heaven with ineffable celestial harmony; by the shading and mingling and glowing of lights that are His Divine, breathtaking illumination unlike aught which earthians can even imagine; magnificence of spirit glory bows us low in utter adoration, as our souls flood with billows of Almighty love.

By these and countless indescribable ways, we know of the drawing close of the Lord Christ Who is One with the Father. The awe and wonder, the adoring worship that fills our souls, lift us beyond heights we have hitherto reached. On such occasions when the Christ comes closer, His presence of Holy Spirit fills all the vast reaches and mighty spheres of the invisible realms with greater glory than my soul can comprehend. The surrounding ethers are of such marvelous, mystic quality that the clumsy earth words at my command, fall short of describing them save as the rarest essence of distilled perfume. But this is far too physical a statement to stand the test of careful comparison.

Not until you experience all of this which I seek to share with you of earth, can you even imagine how such as these are, so ethereal, so pure, so God-like, filling the vault of the heavens and vibrating with unthinkable power above even the highest earth has ever achieved with all of its delvings into the imponderable mysteries of creative processes, or has even dared to dream.

By all of this we are utterly humbled; cleansed of whatever remains of earth's grossness; filled with such worshipful love for Him and His Father, as overwhelms us. His illumination which is beyond all description, permeates and penetrates the thronging souls of us who bow before Him, the Holy One, worshipping in adoration, learning by the raptness of His radiance to understand a little more of His infinite nature, like unto God, and becoming more worthy to serve Him through helping His needy ones, wherever they be.

While you abide in your earthly body, I beseech you to grow ever closer in love to Him, realizing with increasing clarity of conviction His dwelling within you, at the very center of your being. Thus you will acquire a more profound feeling of devotion to Him as your Lord of Light and Love and Life; a more penetrating understanding of what it will mean to each of you when, earth's work done and its lessons learned, you come hither to dwell in the house of the Lord forever! Amen!

* * *

> Prayer is the dynamic for every need of life,
> For every moment of time;
> Prayer for yourself and for all others
> Who are in any need.
> Remember always to pray in the spirit of love,
> And thanksgiving and praise and self-forgetfulness.
> Pray always when a sudden storm starts in your soul,
> Or when it is a quiet time.
> Pray for all who have injured you,
> Or whom you have injured.
> Pray that all stains of earthiness be washed away,
> And in their place, come heavenly graces.

www.ingramcontent.com/pod-product-compliance
Lightning Source LLC
Chambersburg PA
CBHW031312160426
43196CB00007B/494